Leisure Studies

Leisure Studies

Themes and Perspectives

Shaun Best

Los Angeles | London | New Delhi
Singapore | Washington DC

First published 2010

SAGE Publications Ltd
1 Oliver's Yard
55 City Road
London EC1Y 1SP

SAGE Publications Inc.
2455 Teller Road
Thousand Oaks, California 91320

SAGE Publications India Pvt Ltd
B 1/I 1 Mohan Cooperative Industrial Area
Mathura Road
New Delhi 110 044

SAGE Publications Asia-Pacific Pte Ltd
33 Pekin Street #02-01
Far East Square
Singapore 048763

Library of Congress Control Number: 2008939388

British Library Cataloguing in Publication data

A catalogue record for this book is available from the
British Library

ISBN 978-1-4129-0385-1
ISBN 978-1-4129-0386-8 (pbk)

Typeset by C&M Digitals (P) Ltd, Chennai, India
Printed in India at Replika Press Pvt Ltd
Printed on paper from sustainable resources

CONTENTS

CONTENTS

INTRODUCTION

What is the leisure experience? In the nineteenth century, paid work became a much more systematic and controlled activity – for the vast majority of people, paid work took place in factories, shops and offices that were physically separate from people's homes. Work also took place at specified times of the day and on specified days of the week. Importantly, the state came to recognise that in the often overcrowded urban environment, leisure was a potential threat to the public order and needed to be closely controlled. Most definitions of leisure take their starting point from this historical change in the nature of the working day. But what is the meaning of the leisure experience? Is it more than a period of time free from work and other obligations? We shall see in the first two chapters that leisure is about the attempt to fulfil pleasure and desire and about the construction of an identity that we feel comfortable with. The search for identity and the ways we choose to fulfil our pleasures and desires can often take on the form of addictions, deviant or criminal behaviour, adopting ways of behaving that may be morally questionable or cause harm to ourselves or others. It is against this 'dark' side of leisure motivation that the institutional framework for leisure emerged in the nineteenth century. The concept of rational recreation was used to control pleasure and desire and provide the working class people with a leisure experience that was morally uplifting. How this institutional framework for leisure emerged in the nineteenth century is explained in the early part of the book.

Debates about the need to control drinking and gambling that began in the nineteenth century have continued up to the present century. In addition, debates about access to open space and countryside also began in the nineteenth century and have also continued into the present century. State involvement in leisure can be local, national and international. At all levels, the state attempts to regulate pleasure and desire, whilst at the same time encouraging forms of leisure activity that benefit the community. There are a wide range of social theories and research on regulation, control, participation and constraint. In the early chapters of the book, we place the arguments about leisure participation and constraint into the context of these wider debates about the role of the state in the moral regulation of the population.

The book also addresses the changing nature of work. If we assume that there is a link between the type of work that we do and the type of leisure activities we choose to engage in, then we should expect that if the nature of the work we do changes, then the nature of the leisure we choose to engage with should also change. We trace the shift from Fordism to Post-Fordism and explain the significance this has had for leisure.

Many of the leisure activities we engage in are highly personal and we engage in them alone. However, much leisure participation is organised and participation takes place within bureaucratic organisations. The leisure sector covers the public, private and voluntary sectors and has to be managed by people who are qualified leisure managers. It is commonly assumed in leisure management texts that a good leisure manager is a person who has a sound grasp of generic but relevant management theory and applies this to the leisure sector. In this book, we evaluate a range of commonly used management theories, not simply in terms of what is the most effective way of applying a given theory to the leisure sector, but also we look at the validity and reliability of each theory, looking at the processes of data collection, data analysis, assumptions about employees and customer motivation. A number of management theories have their origin in the nineteenth century and it is possible to see how they relate to the state's desire to regulate the leisure experience, but we examine the suitability of traditional management theories for the management of the leisure experience. A case in point is Scientific Management, which we explore in some detail and show how this theory and body of research developed into a form of McDonaldised emotional or performative labour in the latter years of the twentieth century.

The latter two chapters are concerned with the impact of globalisation on the leisure sector. We explore the nature of globalisation by reference to a range of social, economic and cultural theories. The chapters trace the emergence of the information/network society, and examine the nature of the War on Terror and the motivations that terrorists have for selecting leisure targets. One of the central challenges facing the leisure manager today is how to manage the leisure experience under the threat of terrorism. The book looks at and evaluates the activities of some of the largest global companies and the products and services they offer for sale. We find that by the end of the first decade of the twenty-first century, global leisure provision is closely linked to new and more effective forms of consumption.

1

WHAT IS THE LEISURE EXPERIENCE?

By the end of this chapter, you should have a critical understanding of:

- what researchers have said about the nature of the leisure experience
- a range of theories and research in the area, including:

  o Joffre Dumazedier and Josef Pieper: leisure as a contemplative 'celebration' of human values
  o Robert Stebbins: 'serious' leisure and 'casual' leisure
  o Mihaly Csikszentmihalyi: flow as an element of the leisure experience

- what constitutes deviant leisure and how the motivation to engage in such activities relates to theory and research in the area
- the role of play within the leisure experience, including the notion of Homo Ludens and the play element within the wider culture of society
- the possibilities for a therapeutic leisure
- the role and status of 'Pleasure' and 'Desire' in the leisure experience
- leisure and the construction of a neo-tribal identity.

This chapter looks at the nature of the leisure experience. There is no agreement about what constitutes the leisure experience; there is no agreement about the role of leisure for the individual or for the wider society. For Parr and Lashua (2004), the word 'leisure' suggests a variety of thoughts, images and concepts from time free from work and other obligations to activities that promote greater self-understanding. For Kelly and Kelly (1994), much of the effort put into defining leisure has been in an attempt to establish a field of inquiry for Leisure Studies.

Whatever definition of leisure we choose to use, the leisure experience is commonly assumed to be different from the work experience; leisure experiences often take place in specific places or leisure venues and the leisure experience is something we look forward to participating in with positive expectations.

What is Leisure?

> ### *Activity*
>
> Kaplan (1975) attempts to answer the question, 'what is leisure?' Reflect upon your own view of leisure before reading on. At the end of the book, you might want to reflect on how your view of leisure has changed.
>
> Leisure:
>
> - is a relatively self-determined activity or experience that falls into one's economically free time
> - is psychologically pleasant in anticipation and recollection
> - contains a range of commitment and intensity
> - provides opportunities for recreation, personal growth and service to others
> - has positive expectations
> - has a friendly quality
> - is self-determined but this does not mean that leisure is a product of free will; we have to take into account constraining factors, such as:
>
>   o the availability of resources/facilities
>   o individuals' limited knowledge of the opportunities
>   o constraints of time and money
>   o opinions of spouses, parents, neighbours and friends
>   o social and moral obligations, for example:
>   - individuals feeling that they have to visit ageing relatives
>   - taking children on family holidays
>   - tending gardens.

Some definitions, such as that of Joffre Dumazedier (1974), define leisure as a residual time free from work and other obligations, characterised by a feeling of (comparative) freedom. In contrast, Pieper (1952) argues that leisure is one of the foundations of Western culture; leisure is central to the philosophical and theological conception of self. Aristotle in both the *Politics* (1981) and *Metaphysics* (2002) suggests that leisure is the centre point around which social life revolves. Leisure is a contemplative 'celebration' of human values and is only possible if people are 'at one with themselves' and with the world. Leisure provides people with the opportunity to renew the self and allows us to do better in performing our everyday activities.

> ### *Activity*
>
> Compare and contrast the definitions of leisure below. Which account do you find the most convincing – that of Csikszentmihalyi or Stebbins?

> Serious leisure is:
> 'the systematic pursuit of an amateur, a hobbyist, or a volunteer activity sufficiently substantial and interesting for the participant to find a career there in the acquisition and expression of a combination of its special skills, knowledge, and experience' (Stebbins, 1997: 17).
> For Csikszentmihalyi the foundation of any leisure experience is the individual subjective experiences of an activity that is freely chosen and completed for its own sake, such as enjoyment.

In addition, we have to take into account that definitions of leisure are often politicised. Coalter (1998) argues that a great deal of the theorising and research into leisure is conducted within a 'normative citizenship paradigm' that assumes publicly funded leisure provision is an essential part of 'social citizenship' and the commercial nature of modern leisure is largely ignored.

Serious Leisure

One of the most influential conceptions of leisure is found in the work of Robert Stebbins (1982, 1997) who made a distinction between 'serious' leisure and 'casual' leisure. For many people, paid employment is becoming less meaningful and, according to Stebbins, serious leisure allows an individual to develop a feeling of 'career' within their free time. This means that serious leisure is concerned with participants who pursue the leisure activities with an unusual passion and commitment.

For Stebbins, continued participation in serious leisure activities is explained by the 'profit hypothesis', in which the participant views the benefits of continued participation as outweighing the costs. Stebbins identifies six characteristics of serious leisure:

- perseverance
- following a 'career'
- personal effort
- benefits to the individual
- identification with the activity
- ethos of the activity.

These characteristics of serious leisure are central to a person's sense of self. A number of researchers have explored serious leisure: bass fishing (Yoder, 1997), barbershop singing (Stebbins, 1996), mushroom collecting (Fine, 1998), football fandom (Gibson et al., 2003), golf (Siegenthaler and O'Dell, 2003) and marathon running (Baldwin et al., 1999; Goff et al., 1997).

In their study of social identity and sports tourism, for example, Green and Jones (2005) found that sports tourism can provide participants with opportunities to engage in serious leisure. Participants used their leisure activities to construct a sense of identity by sharing an ethos with others. Similarly, Noreen Orr (2006) draws upon Stebbins to understand the motivations of heritage volunteers, and again found that serious leisure activities were central in the process of identity construction. The heritage volunteers became socialised into a subculture of knowledgeable individuals with whom they felt comfortable.

In his case study of a group of people in the United Kingdom who re-enact events from the American Civil War, Hunt (2004) concludes by suggesting that the re-enactment of historical events is from male-dominated 'living history' and not primarily an educational activity. The re-enactment is meaningful for the individuals involved, because it reinforces lifestyle interests through camaraderie, collective involvement and a subjective understanding of authenticity.

Gillespie et al., (2002) draw upon Tomlinson's 'culture of commitment' to understand why people participate in dog sports as a form of serious leisure. This commitment can generate conflict within families, notably about the amount of money some participants spend on their dogs.

When Gillespie et al. (2002) asked the participants where the time and money came from for their hobby, they found that many of the respondents got extra jobs or worked overtime to subsidise their dog expenses. In some cases, people re-mortgaged their houses. Most of the participants set new priorities in the family budgeting to accommodate dog-related expenses. Many said that their job came second to their dogs, at least psychologically, but also in some cases in terms of time. A number of the respondents informed new employers that they would be taking time off to attend dog events. Some people chose jobs (or job locations) that allowed them the maximum amount of free time for their dogs, and it was common to schedule work around dog training schedules. It is this 'counter-culture of commitment' that makes dog sports participants different from non-participants.

Stebbins' conception of the 'profit hypothesis' is also examined by Jones (2000) who investigated a group of Luton Town football fans in the late 1990s – the fans were willing to engage in an unrewarding activity, in that the benefits did not appear to outweigh costs, yet participation continued. Jones adapts Stebbins' model to suggest that in such circumstances, participants would draw upon one or more of four 'compensatory behaviours':

- in-group favouritism – a strong sense of belonging amongst others who share the same level of support for the team
- out-group derogation – fans of rival teams, notably the local rival Watford, were believed to have a range of undesirable traits, thus enhancing the benefits of being a Luton Town fan
- unrealistic optimism, anticipating exaggerated future rewards
- voice, stressing the positive aspects of identification with Luton Town.

In the case of the Luton Town fans, there is a strong element of Tomlinson's (1993) concept of a 'culture of commitment' in that 'fandom' is a form of leisure activity that stresses the collective and intense nature of serious leisure participation. Carroll Brown (2007) found that for many participants shag dancing is a form of serious leisure in which participants developed a distinct shag ethos. The casual shaggers are as committed as serious shaggers but approach the dance in different ways, whereas serious shaggers are first and foremost interested in improving their technical dance skills for competitive dancing.

According to Jayne Raisborough (2007), one of the strengths of Stebbins' concept of serious leisure is that it contests the conception of leisure rooted solely in hedonism. For Stebbins, leisure does not have to be a fun activity, or based upon enjoyment, freedom or choice. However, Raisborough argues that serious leisure remains for the most part apolitical in nature. Stebbins does not view serious leisure as a site where individuals can resist or reproduce societal power relations.

The concept of serious leisure is used by Raisborough (2007) to explore the dynamics of women's long-term leisure commitment in the Sea Cadet Corps. As we saw in the case of the shag dancers, one of the central features of serious leisure is the notion of a participant's progression via a serious leisure career. However, within the serious leisure career, as in the more traditionally understood occupational career, power relations and the impact of 'other social worlds' can impact upon career trajectories. Within leisure spaces, gender relations are both reproduced and contested and a woman's career progression can be restricted by gender power. Hunt's (2004) research into the world of battle re-enacting noted that women participants were restricted to the roles of nurses and soldier's wives – in other words, traditional female caring roles that were rejected by men; as such, these women were not regarded as authentic re-enactors.

Raisborough found a similar gendered division of labour operating with careers within the Sea Cadet Corps. Women's leisure careers were restricted by organising principles such as the female cover rule, a regulation that required that a female member of staff must be present when female sea cadets were involved in any SCC activity, especially if the activity was led by male staff. This rule reinforced the gendered assumptions that men are predatory by nature and that the women there are by nature carers who are responsible for the physical and emotional well-being of the cadets and are also the tea makers. These 'emotional labour' roles were assumed to be based upon skills that were naturally female and as such were not acquired skills; this made it difficult for women to present themselves as authentic and committed members of staff.

For Stebbins (1996), although most people assume that having a hobby is a good thing, there is a culturally dominant belief that all leisure is casual leisure and as such there is a cost for all people pursuing a serious leisure career. This is particularly true for women. As we shall discuss in later chapters, unmarried, young, heterosexual women are under great pressure to alter their leisure choices to accommodate romantic relationships (Herridge et al., 2003), and as Green et al. (1990) found, women's independent leisure pursuits, unlike men's independent leisure pursuits, are often considered to be incompatible with traditional romantic love. Married women have to negotiate with family members over time and space constraints, such as having a room to participate in their chosen activity, and have to overcome feelings of guilt when they are made to feel that they are putting housework, childcare and their other family responsibilities second. This includes a wide range of leisure activities from women who enjoy reading romance novels (Brackett, 2000; Radway, 1991), watch soap operas (Harrington and Bielby, 1995) and do quilting (Stalp, 2006).

Stalp (2006) found that quilting is a serious leisure activity that women turn to for the most part for reasons of escape, relaxation and creativity. On the one hand, quilting appears to embody a wide range of feminine characteristics in that quilts are often given as gifts to friends and family members helping to cement emotional ties. However, the activity involves a woman taking time for herself. For Stalp, family negotiations over serious leisure quilting contain hidden gendered components about the power dynamics within families, where women's activities are not directly related to paid employment outside of the home or to their roles as mother or spouse.

Casual Leisure

In contrast to serious leisure, in 1997, Robert Stebbins turned his attention to the relatively neglected concept of 'casual leisure' or 'unserious' leisure. Casual leisure was seen primarily as a marginal 'personal diversion' rooted in a highly personal perspective. For Stebbins (1997), 'casual leisure' can be understood under six headings: play, relaxation, passive entertainment, active entertainment, sociable conversation and sensory stimulation. However, what all forms of 'casual leisure' have in common is that they are all hedonic in nature; people participate in these activities because they bring pleasure in the form of 'self-gratification'. In his discussion of play, Stebbins draws upon the work of Kelly (1990) who views play in terms of activities that have a 'childlike lightness', activities that are intrinsic in terms of their motivation and involve participants in a 'non-serious suspension of consequences' in relation to their participation. Various forms of 'casual leisure' are said by Stebbins to be deviant in nature – such activities include cross-dressing, passively watching sex-related activities such as striptease or pornographic films, and also a number of more active sexual activities such as swinging, social nudism or group sex. Heavy drinking, gambling and drug use are also identified. However, even though 'casual leisure' may fail to 'generate flow' or allow a person to achieve 'optimal experience', more people are involved in casual leisure than in serious leisure. However, with the exception of Chris Rojek's (1995) discussion of postmodern leisure, the area of 'casual leisure' is largely ignored by leisure researchers.

Postmodern Leisure

Over the course of the twentieth and twenty-first centuries, many social commentators have suggested that Modernity gave way to Postmodernity. One of the central themes of the book is that social change has had a significant impact upon the provision and enjoyment of leisure. For Rojek (1995), postmodernity is characterised by a feeling of 'disembeddedness' where the world is becoming a universal, cultural space – in other words, on the far side of modernity, leisure spaces such as shopping malls, leisure centres and amusement arcades are losing their sense of the *local* and becoming universal, cultural spaces that mix fantasy and fiction with real events to construct the meaning of the leisure experience.

Stebbins' discussion of 'casual leisure' raises a whole series of issues about the nature and purpose of leisure participation and the nature of pleasure, deviance and desire as motivating factors. Richard Byrne (2006) has investigated a form of sexual adventurism known in the United Kingdom as 'dogging'. This is an activity in which consenting adults, who are not known to each other personally, meet at a given location for the purpose of exhibition, voyeurism and sexual adventure. Locations are posted via the internet to virtual communities. For Byrne, 'dogging' represents a distinct shift away from the traditional conception of 'lovers' lane' as a place of individual sexual exploration to an arena for organised, impersonal sex in public places. For Byrne, 'dogging' highlights a number of the disturbing trends in relation to consensual sexual activity within a leisure setting, including the development of new forms of deviant leisure in relation to new pornography and prostitution.

More generally, according to Reible (2006), popular culture, such as film, television, music, electronic and print media, draw upon a range of deviant behaviours as amusement for casual consumption. Soaps and popular police series make use of fictional cases of serious crime for our entertainment. Grand Theft Auto is a video game that provides the player with opportunities to be a character in virtual car theft, random killing and other deviant behaviours as a form of 'fun'.

This is in sharp contrast to Dumazedier (1974), Huizinga (1949) and Pieper (1952), who all assume that leisure is essentially 'good' in nature and benefits both the participants and humanity. In contrast, for Reible (2006), deviant leisure can become the background for the formation of an identity to resist the social pressure to conform that is common within the modern industrial society. Deviant leisure can provide people with a sense of being and belonging, helping to create alternative cultural values in a new community by the open rejection of those social controls that many people find dehumanising.

For Mihaly Csikszentmihalyi (1982), a central element of a good life is to have a focused and organised consciousness. However, in order to achieve this, the information we receive must be ordered in a predictable way – without this structuring of information, we are likely to experience unhappiness. Csikszentmihalyi has found in research from around the world that irrespective of structural constraints such as age, class and gender and irrespective of cultural differences, people understand optimal experiences in the same way. When a person has sufficient skills and information to deal with the situation without feeling overwhelmed, the person experiences what Csikszentmihalyi refers to as 'flow' – a balance between concentration and involvement that we experience as valuable and enjoyable. A 'good life' is achieved when our skills and abilities are just sufficient to meet the challenges we face – in other words, when we find a balance within our challenge–skills ratio. If we do not find this balance, we may experience anxiety. Interestingly, Csikszentmihalyi (1997) argues that many people find their non-work time to be more difficult to enjoy than their work time because many of our leisure activities are passive, such as watching television, and do not demand that we operationalise or engage our critical skills and abilities. Passive leisure experiences often induce a feeling of boredom where our skills are not fully required to participate within the experience. The characteristics of the optimal experience are:

- high concentration on the task
- deep but effortless involvement
- loss of track of time
- clear objectives of the task
- clear means to achieve the objectives
- sufficient understanding of the action taking place to make adjustments to our behaviour
- a decreased concern for self during the activity
- an enhanced sense of self on completion of the task.

However, there have been a number of criticisms of Csikszentmihalyi's work. Vitterso (2000) argues that what is measured by the challenge–skills ratio is unclear; Csikszentmihalyi gives insufficient attention to transforming the concept of 'flow' into indicators that can be measured at an empirical level. Secondly, it is unclear whether 'flow' refers to a short intense experience or to a longer period of overall life satisfaction. At times, 'flow' is synonymous with 'happiness', while at other times it is not. At times, 'flow' is understood in terms of doing things as an end in itself, while at other times, actions have to have a wider significance for a person's life.

In addition, there is also the possibility that 'flow' can function to satisfy a 'criminogenic need' – in other words, as a motivating factor in causing either crime or deviance. So-called 'healthy' leisure experiences may not have positive benefits for all participants. Taking his starting point from Csikszentmihalyi's conception of *flow*, Williams (2005) examined the role of recreation within sex crimes. Williams notes, for example, that the meaning of jogging and the cardiovascular and psychological pleasure jogging brings are very different for a paedophile who goes jogging in a park. Williams used a clinical case study of one sex offender's 'sexual assault cycle' – a repetitive process of the thought–feeling–behavioural chain in response to specific events, to trace the link between 'flow' and deviance. Early in the cycle, the subject explained that there was a need for 'recreation' in which both the victim and the subject could feel both comfortable and happy. Victims were often invited to participate in leisure activities when the subject was reported to feel bored and frustrated with his work. The leisure activities of the subject moved from hiking and exercising to drinking and drug use, but the purpose of the leisure activities was to 'maintain a cycle of secrecy' within which the assaults could take place.

Recreation and play

Recreation is a narrower concept than leisure and is best approached through the notion of *Play. Play* is a psychological concept that draws attention to the individual's orientation and experiences. In contrast, *Recreation* is the *social parallel* – defining activities that are socially recognised as playful – divorced from the serious business of living. According to Huizinga (1949), play is a voluntary activity performed at specific times and in specific places according to freely accepted, but absolutely binding, sets of rules. The aim of the activity is the performance of the activity in itself and the enjoyment of feeling tension and happiness that accompany the activity. Such activities and feelings that are generated are experienced as 'different' from 'ordinary life'.

Caillois and Halperin (1955) classified the games people play and argued that 'organisation' can be a way of introducing difficulty – which is incompatible with *fun* – the positive feedback given by the brain when suspending oneself from reality, but at the same time enjoying being faced with challenges that allow us to successfully exercise our skills.

Activity

Csikszentmihalyi (1975) explains that popular dance provides people with many flow-producing opportunities from the movement of the dancer's bodies, the emotional communication and the social aspects of the dance.

- Is there a link between flow and serious leisure?
- Can you think of any other recreational or leisure activities that might lead to involvement in crime or deviance? Think of an example and suggest a possible chain of events from leisure activity to crime.

Rojek (2000) suggests that Stebbins' conception of serious leisure is built upon a functionalist conception of community and solidarity, in that serious leisure helps to provide a degree of integration for the social system. In contrast, Rojek's argument takes its point of departure from Durkheim's conception of abnormal forms that Durkheim (1893) developed in the latter part of his book on the division of labour. Leisure can be viewed as 'normal' or 'abnormal' in nature. Abnormal leisure is regarded as deviant leisure because it often involves engaging in activities that are regarded as morally wrong. Rojek identifies three forms of abnormal leisure practice:

- Invasive – this is where individuals withdraw from social networks and engage in leisure activities associated with self-loathing and self-pity in which people push themselves beyond the limit to turn their back on reality.
- Mephitic – these are morally questionable leisure activities that involve gaining pleasure and satisfaction at the expense of others, such as engaging in prostitution or, in more extreme cases, engaging in acts of terrorism or serial killing as sources of pleasure.
- Wild – this form of leisure also involves going beyond the limit of what is commonly understood as acceptable behaviour, but it often involves engaging in the activity with similar-minded leisure partners in a carnivalesque spirit. Wild leisure activities include such things as football hooliganism and rioting. With the emergence of the network society, opportunities to seek out similar-minded leisure partners are significantly enhanced.

All three abnormal forms contain a degree of *liminality* which is understood as going beyond the threshold of normal behaviour. Liminality involves solitariness, in which the individual becomes unattached from the widely accepted moral codes that underpin society. In Durkheim's terms, the individual experiences a form of anomie, a sense of normlessness. This form of leisure is then on the edge of morality and society and a number of researchers, such as Lyng (1990), have referred to this form of leisure as on the edge of everyday life, as *edgework*, where a person chooses to engage in risky behaviours for fun. Examples include leisure activities such as sky diving and extreme sports. This edgework allows a person to experience a feeling of self-actualisation and self-determination similar to what Csikszentmihalyi refers to as 'flow'. Predee (2000) explains that such motivation can lead to leisure activities that become sadomasochistic in nature. He suggests that one of the consequences of greater commodification of everyday life and increasing levels of consumption is that hurting and humiliating others, engaging in damage to property and joy riding become increasingly pleasurable activities because they involve pushing oneself to the limit.

Therapeutic Leisure

Linda Caldwell (2005) has attempted to answer the question of why leisure is believed to be therapeutic by evaluating the empirical research in the area. She organises the research into three broad groupings: firstly, the research that suggests that leisure can prevent negative life events; secondly, that leisure can be used as part of a coping strategy for negative life events; and thirdly, that leisure can be therapeutic.

Wong et al. (2003) found that amongst older adults, regular walking improves fitness and cardio-respiratory function and can help prevent mobility problems in later life.

Kleiber (2004) has suggested that because leisure activities are often distracting, they can act as a buffer to negative life events. Some leisure activities can also generate optimism in that they allow people to reflect on the past and reconstruct the meaning of events that have affected them; hence leisure can become an instrument for personal change. This is particularly true in relation to work-related stress. Coleman (1993), Coleman and Iso Ahola (1993), Iso Ahola (1989), Iwasaki (2001), Iwasaki and Mannell (2000), Iwasaki and Schneider (2003), Iwasaki et al. (2005), Kleiber et al. (2002) Neulinger (1982), and Trenberth and Dewe (2005) have all investigated the role of leisure in the reduction of work-related stress and all found that leisure has a positive role to play in health promotion, particularly as a coping strategy for dealing with stressful work environments. Similarly, Iwasaki and Schneider (2003) found that the most common motives for leisure, such as relaxation, compensation, escapism and independence, all have stress-reducing properties. Iwasaki and Mannell (2000) have identified three leisure-based coping strategies:

- palliative coping – when a leisure-based activity gives an individual temporary respite from an issue that is of concern to them
- mood enhancement – such as watching a comedy
- companionship – spending time with friends in a commonly enjoyed activity.

In addition, Coleman and Iso Ahola (1993) talk about the role that leisure partners can play in the reduction of stress, because leisure activities provide people with opportunities to develop companionship and friendship.

Iwasaki and Bartlett (2006) investigated the role of leisure in the stress-coping processes of Aboriginal people with diabetes, living in Canada. The meaning and role of leisure is integral to Aboriginal culture in Canada and cannot be separated from the spiritual, cultural and social aspects of Aboriginal life. Iwasaki and Bartlett (2006) suggest that the social world is made meaningful for Aboriginal people through leisure.

On the other hand, some leisure activities are seen as potentially bad for health. Passmore and French (2000) found that 'uninvolved leisure activities', such as watching television alone, were related to negative mental health issues.

In the last analysis, however we define leisure and whatever its benefits for health or well-being, one would expect that the leisure experience should be a pleasurable one.

What is Pleasure and What Role Does it Play in the Leisure Experience?

Why would we want to define pleasure? Pleasure is pleasure and most people would find it impossible to define. However, for most people, pleasure is the coming together of desire and enjoyment, a state of consciousness and happiness. It is possible to talk about the 'pleasure' of reading a good book, eating, drinking, sexual experience or considering a work of art, for example. The problem here is that all of these things are *sources* of pleasure, and cannot be used to define pleasure in itself. We appear to be 'psychologically wired' to forms of desires that give us pleasure, and to avoid the things that might cause us pain. Whatever their origin, desires are great motivating factors because they allow us to make a judgement about which activities to perform and in what order – without desires, we would have no likes or dislikes.

What is pleasure?

In everyday life, most people assume that *pleasure* is the feeling we experience as a consequence of satisfying some physical, emotional or intellectual need and as such is appealing to whoever experiences it. *Pleasure* is about feeling good and happy and is often contrasted with feeling states such as *pain* or suffering that make us feel bad. There are at least three types of pleasure:

- sensory pleasure – gratification experienced in relation to food and sex
- aesthetic pleasure – gratification that is more abstract in nature, such as that derived from music and the arts
- pleasure achieved through personal value – such as performing well at a difficult task.

Pleasure is associated with hedonism, and Veenhoven (2003) explores the relationship between hedonism and happiness. Veenhoven drew upon the research findings contained within the World Database of Happiness, a data set containing findings from 705 studies from 107 countries, to establish the link, if any, between hedonism and happiness. Even in relation to stimulants such as alcohol, tobacco and drugs, the data suggested that hedonism did not lead to unhappiness. In relation to smoking, none of the heavy smokers were happier than moderate smokers, however, in later life heavy smokers did tend to become unhappy. In relation to drug use, psychotropic drug users were unhappy compared to non drug users.

Activity: Why it is generally pleasant to do what one desires to do?

When we have a sense of intrinsic value about an activity, that activity is believed to be of value in itself without reference to any other factors – this enhances our desire to participate. Elery Hamilton-Smith (1985) explains that in relation to the arts, the leisure experience is a subjective human experience that is characterised by intrinsic motivation and satisfaction, and the activity is defined as leisure if our reference group defines the activity as 'leisure'. However, Brewer (2003) argues that pleasure is different. With pleasure, a person must have an *occurrent* desire to engage in the activities in order to derive pleasure from them. In other words, the person must have a desire to engage in that activity for its own sake.

Gunn and Caissie (2006) explored the relationship between deviant leisure and serial murder. They examined acts of deviant leisure and serial murderers for 28 male and female serial killers between 1947 and 1992, and found that both male and female serial killers spent an excessive amount of time preparing, committing (trolling, kidnap, rape and torture) and reliving (via photographs, videotape, audiotape, trophies and souvenirs) the events during their free time. Gunn and Caissie concluded that serial killers used murder as a deviant and non-traditional form of leisure activity.

Is all pleasure intrinsically good? Would you accept or reject the idea that *only* pleasure is intrinsically good? A murderer may get pleasure from killing a victim; does this make the activity *intrinsically* good? In other words, we can only consider pleasure to be *intrinsically* good if the source of pleasure is considered separately from its consequences.

Should leisure be rooted in utilitarianism – where we should act so as to bring about the greatest good to the greatest number?

Outline the reasons for your answer.

Leisure activities provide individuals with the opportunities to fulfil their desires, and as such, these activities are seen as potentially dangerous for both the individual and for the wider society. Since the nineteenth century, many countries have seen state involvement in the regulation and control of leisure experiences. Foucault (1977) explained this 'social management of pleasure' in terms of the 'repressive hypothesis' – the Victorians were concerned with defining, regulating and locating pleasure in appropriate places. The Victorians did not want to ban leisure, or prevent people from enjoying pleasurable experiences, however activities had to be performed within appropriate leisure spaces.

This forms the basis of the concept of 'rational recreation', the idea that leisure activities should be morally uplifting for the participants and have positive benefits for the wider society.

Rational recreation

Rational recreation was a regimen that attempted to make leisure activities 'morally uplifting' and prevent national disorder. The idea was to provide the population with opportunities to maintain physical fitness, counter-balance the debilities of city life, maintain readiness for armed service, and provide self-discipline, self-control, public spirit, physical fitness and opportunities for teamwork.

What is Desire?

According to Brewer (2003), in Aristotelian philosophy, there is an idea that taking pleasure in an activity is sometimes simply a matter of engaging in the activity wholeheartedly. However, as Brewer goes on to explain, the proponents of this idea have not made it clear what type of wholehearted engagement is needed to transform indifferent activities into pleasurable ones.

Brewer builds upon Gilbert Ryle's argument that taking pleasure in an activity is the same as engaging in the desiring to do the activity. However, we still need to ask what makes an activity *pleasurable*. Pleasure is not always the reason to perform the activities that give rise to the pleasurable sensation. The motivation for desire is found in an independent set of values – in other words, a pre-reflective outlook. If we examine many desires, we find that people have a tendency to view their thoughts about the desire *as* reasons to act on the desire. Scanlon called this class of desires 'desires in the directed-attention sense' (1998: 37). Such desires comprise a persistent tendency to direct our attention towards particular circumstances or considerations, and to *see* them *as reasons for* our action.

Scanlon's argument allows us to identify common features between such unrelated desires as sexual desire, the desire to be successful in our job, the desire for world peace, and the desire to wear stylish shoes: they all involve a tendency to dwell on certain things as counting in favour of some action or outcome. It is important to note, explains Brewer, that even primitive desires such as hunger or the desire to have children are pruned and shaped by moral education and reflection, for example most of us would not consider stealing a child because we desire to be a parent. What is important for the leisure researchers is the argument that pleasure and desire are formed and constrained within a given culture.

According to Jonathan Dollimore (1998), Christians have associated desire and pleasure in general to be associated with sex, sin and death; for Christians, uncertainty is closely associated with sin, in that it is found *inside* desire and can cause death. Saint Augustine in the 'City of God' argued that death and sexual desire are inseparable. Even though many societies have experienced greater secularisation and a relaxation of morality in many areas of social life, the English speaking world has never totally rejected the Christian idea of sin. There is a psychology of sin that has an effect on our understanding of appropriate pleasure and desire.

The concept of desire is associated with an element of *loss* or *lack* in relation to self that is reflected in the metaphors for desire. Desire is often seen as an external force such as water: 'With a force that left her breathless, a wave of pleasure washed over her' (Patthey-Chavez, 1996: 89). Other metaphors associated with desire include:

- Desire is falling – 'fall in love'.
- Desire is insanity.
- Desire is loss of rationality.
- Desire is pain.
- Desire is illness.
- Desire is madness.
- Desire is appetite/hunger.
- Desire is animal.
- Desire is fire.

One of the central issues that needs to be addressed in relation to pleasure and desire is the paradox that people are very often aware that certain forms of consumption or behaviour are 'risky' and can cause illness and disease, yet people continue to participate. Lupton (1996) argues that people have personal health belief systems and that fulfilment of desire is central to our sense of self, including the ways we live in and through our bodies.

In 1999, the United Kingdom Prison Service and National Health Service announced a programme for developing closer links between prison health services and community health services. A central element of this programme was an increased focus on health assessment and the health promotion of prisoners. The people who find themselves in prison are not a randomly distributed group from within the whole population; lower socio-economic and other marginalised groups are much more likely to be represented. In addition, the 1999 government initiative found that the prison population has a much lower standard of physical and mental health than that of the rest of the population (Smith, 2002). However, many of the female prisoners that Smith (2002) interviewed rejected the dominant meaning constructed within the Prison Service health promotional discourse. The government assumes that the unhealthy condition of the prison population is associated with unhealthy or 'risky' lifestyles (illegal drug use, excessive alcohol consumption, diet, sexual promiscuity, cigarette smoking, etc.). Smith explains the Prison Service attempts to control the diet of women in an effort to make them 'conform' to the rules of the prison; 'good health' is demanded from the inmates. Health promotion through the banning of 'unhealthy' food and dietary behaviour is seen as an effective strategy for enhancing the health of women prisoners and bringing about a personal lifestyle change on release.

Desire is often associated with sex. Pinkerton et al. (2003) argue that the desire for pleasure is one of the most important reasons why people engage in sexual activities. However, the desire for pleasure is not the only reason why people have sex. Whatever the reason, people have sex because it feels good. Pinkerton et al. (2003) argue that studies in the area conceptualise pleasure as a non-specific underlying motive for engaging in sexual activities. These studies are not specific in terms of what particular activities or behaviours people engage in and how much pleasure is derived from each activity. Hill and Preston (1996) and Whitley (1988) viewed the search for sexual pleasure in terms of a general characteristic of sexual hedonism. Based upon a sample of undergraduates (145 women and 78 men) at a Californian university, Pinkerton et al. (2003) devised a 'pleasure index' to measure the degree of pleasure derived from: vaginal intercourse, anal intercourse, giving and receiving oral sex, masturbation alone and being masturbated by a partner, and asked the respondents to comment on their experiences of these activities. Their conclusion was that pleasure motivates sexual activity. Some people scored much higher on the 'pleasure index' than others, and Pinkerton et al. (2003) argue that people who find these acts more pleasurable are more likely to engage in them.

> ### *Activity*
>
> In many respects, leisure management is the 'social management of pleasure' but what is the optimal level of pleasure? And how is that optimal level of pleasure managed?

Stebbins and Csikszentmihalyi have made important contributions to our understanding of the leisure experience. Personal beliefs, motivations and choices are important in terms of understanding leisure, however; leisure is more than a state of mind. The leisure experience exists within a range of cultural, ideological and structural constraints. In the late twentieth century, the nature of the leisure experience significantly changed. According to Rojek (2005), much of our non-work or free-time activity had become commercialised.

Neo-tribes and Leisure Identity

Leisure participation can also be motivated by the desire to construct an identity around the leisure activity. According to Best (2003), there are two key elements to identity:

1. To be like the other within a group and
2. A common categorising of outward phenomena, such as the clothes that people wear or the music they listen to.

For many people, 'self' consists of two components: firstly, an apprehension we may feel about other people's evaluation of us, for example in terms of our physical appearance in relation to other people in our social groups and secondly, our self-evaluation, for example how we come to judge what we have done as part of a group in relation to our personal standards. The argument here is that self-image is linked to leisure preference and participation through a series of emotional–symbolic meanings. The research into leisure in relation to the construction and maintenance of identity has looked at a wide range of leisure groupings: football fans, rave culture, outdoor pursuits and modern primitives (people who engage in 'body modifications') to name but a few. For such people, discontinuing a leisure activity may be costly in personal terms because of the loss of friendships developed through their leisure participation.

In the latter years of the twentieth century, society moved from a rationalised social to an 'empathetic sociality' that manifested itself in terms of new ways of interacting with each other in public places. Taking his starting point from Durkheim's conception of solidarity, Maffescoli (1996) is concerned with understanding these new forms of 'interaction in public' by drawing upon the concept of *tribus* or the metaphor of neo- or metropolitan tribe. These groups are made up of people who share the same *habitus* and the same politics of everyday life. They are described as 'elective affinity groups' – such groups help to bring together and segment people's patterns of consumption, the neo-tribes have no longevity and are not fixed but they are distinguished by their members' distinct lifestyle and taste. As such, the neo-tribes provide a temporary source of identification for people who choose to belong. There is free movement between tribes, but tribes often generate strict forms of conformity whilst a person is affiliated. Maffescoli's argument is based upon the assumption that people contain a 'quasi animal like' need for sociality – to form and reinforce common bonds, we have a need to connect, link or band together into unstable forms of 'groupism' or 'emotional community'. We are pushed towards each other by a social configuration or inherent energy for communal being-together that Maffescoli terms *puissance*, and it is this *glischomorphic* tendency in all human relationships that underpins our processes of identification. *Glischomorphic* is a term that describes a tendency for communal being-together that Maffescoli believes all people to have. For Maffescoli, there is a natural sociality or reciprocity connecting individuals, and the habitus we share 'determine[s] the mores and customs that constitute us … and we should not be afraid to say it – we lead what is quite an animalistic life' (Maffescoli, 1996: 89–90).

Puissance is described by Maffescoli as 'the will to live' and is found wherever people can speak to each other freely in an open space such as nightclubs, cafes etc. Such spaces allow people to explore issues of difference and commonality.

For Maffescoli, the habitus is made up of three elements:

- the *aesthetic* – or shared sentiment
- the *ethic* – or collective bond
- the *custom* – common aspects of everyday life.

Close friendship networks have no fixed purpose other than giving people the opportunity to congregate for its own sake, with others around an informal culture. People become attached to networks through a device that Maffescoli terms 'proxemics' – a process of correspondence through which one person introduces one person to another who knows another person and so it continues. However, desire is no longer a matter of simple individual choice in relation to fandom, hairstyle, style of dress or choice of music, argues Maffescoli – rather, desire should be viewed as a form of conformity that is a consequence of global processes of massification.

Traditional class-based research on football fandom was based upon the assumption that individuals were locked into particular class-determined 'ways of being'; in contrast, Sandvoss (2005), drawing upon Maffescoli, views fandom as an active consumer choice that is central to a notion of self-constructed identity.

Traditional theories of fandom were concerned with the degree to which support for a team could be correlated with other key variables, such as class, gender, age and ethnicity. The focus on the shared 'authentic origins' of the individual fan made the modern fan-base appear to be internally homogeneous, with a set of shared social experiences that were rooted in a shared class location. Fan identity was read as something that was tightly bound, non-contradictory and 'pure'. A good example of such a modernist conception of fandom is found in the work of the Leicester School (Dunning et al., 1988) – most of the Leicester City fans they investigated were from a non-incorporated, rough, working-class council estate in Leicester and these fans shared a very strong 'place identity'. Place identity has an emotional meaning and it refers to 'the symbolic importance of a place as a repository for emotions and relationships that give meanings and purpose to life' (Williams and Vaske, 2003: 831). It has been linked with the concept of self-identity (Williams et al., 1992), and is seen as a part of one's self that results in developing emotional attachment to a specific place (Williams et al., 1992). Place identity can enhance an individual's self-esteem and supporting the local team can increase feelings of belonging to the community. Such forms of fandom are a simple reflection of class culture within tight-knit communities and are not the product of the actions of individual choice or human agency. Such approaches have the tendency of reifying fandom around the concept of class and say nothing about the real enjoyment that people experience at a game. However, there are now new ways of doing fandom involving many different ways of engaging with the accelerated commodification of European soccer economies. These 'customer' sports fan identities involve subscription to satellite television sports channels and the use of the internet. Such fans are said to lack the deep-rootedness and personal commitment of fans in the past.

Activity: What is a fan?

John Fiske (1992) suggests that a fan is an 'excessive reader' and therefore not opposed to non-fan or ordinary people, except in that fans collect a great deal of information about the thing they are fans of. For Fiske, fans accumulate a high degree of cultural capital in relation to the thing they are fans of – this cultural capital often takes the form of textual or semiotic productivity as, for example, found in fanzines. In other words, fans collect a great deal of information about the thing they are fans of and reconstruct that information in a supportive manner that allows them to communicate with other fans with a degree of authority.

Reflect for one moment on your own fandom. Are you a fan of a football team, a band or some other form of activity? What makes you different from non-fans? Traditional theories of fandom were concerned with the degree to which support for a team could be correlated with other key variables, such as class, gender, age and ethnicity. Is your own fandom related to your class, gender, age and/or ethnicity?

Gary Crawford (2004) rejects what he claims to be the false opposition between 'authentic' supporters and 'inauthentic' fan consumers. As the more 'traditional' sources of community identity – family, work, the church, neighbourhood networks – decline in relative importance in the late modern era, the sense of community and 'primary group' belonging offered by contemporary sport becomes increasingly important and is increasingly commodified. Liquid modern football becomes both a product to be sold to eager consumers and a way for people to 're-invent' or to 're-imagine' a sense of locality through their sporting ties. Crawford draws upon Maffescoli's (1996) concept of 'neo-tribes' to account for today's more fluid and more dynamic sports fan cultures. Crawford concludes that being a football fan is first and foremost a consumer act and, hence, fans should be seen, first and foremost, as consumers. Large European clubs have attempted to market themselves without reference to 'place' or 'location'. English Premier League clubs provide potential fans from across Europe and beyond with signification value and opportunities for self-projection through acts of consumption. In a similar fashion, Sandvoss' (2003, 2005) focus is on fandom in relation to the construction of self-identity via narratives. Fans draw upon texts in a narcissistic manner and mirror or refashion their conception of self through interpretations of texts. In this case, a text is not simply a written document such as a match-day programme or fanzine, but can include hairstyles and products endorsed by celebrity players. Sandvoss develops the concept of 'neutrosemy' to explain how fans take bits of meaning from a wide range of texts to define the boundaries of self.

Rave Culture and Identity

McRobbie argues that the act of dancing 'carries enormously pleasurable qualities for girls and women which frequently seem to suggest a displaced, shared and nebulous eroticism rather than a straightforwardly romantic, heavily heterosexual "goal-oriented drive"' (1984: 134). In a similar fashion, rave culture can be central to the construction of an identity. Green (1998) argues that when ravers are banned from public leisure spaces, many 'choose individually or collectively to create their own private space for leisure' (Green, 1998: 178). According to Glover (2003), Hilker (1996), Linder (2001), Stiens (1997) and Weber (1999), in the early years of the 1990s, rave culture provided many young people with an opportunity to rebel against their parents' norms of behaviour, escape their conventional identity and feel a sense of belonging with other ravers. The unsupervised and hedonistic nature of the rave scene made rave a form of resistance. Rave culture provided middle class youths, in particular, with the opportunity to adopt a deviant identity and an opportunity to play with other 'members of a community by actively sharing and partaking in the rave' (Linder, 2001: 4). The use of recreational drugs such as Ecstasy enhanced feelings of harmony and well-being. Weber (1999) suggests that the choice of music is central to understanding why people were attracted to a rave. Dance music was used to change people's assessment of the situation and mood, and became central to the construction of the raver's identity. The music was said to encourage ravers to hold people close and touch in a way that was affectionate, not explicitly sexual. Tomlinson found that: 'rave is something you immerse yourself in with other people. There is no guitar hero or rock star or corresponding musical-structural figures to identify with ... You are just one of many other individuals who constitute the musical whole' (1998: 203).

Glover (2003) draws on research by Martin (1999) to argue that Ecstasy disrupts the Freudian concepts of the self and creates 'a unity between the Id and the Ego, and a unification of these with the sensuality of the body and the intensity of the moment of the dance' (Martin, 1999: 92).

Bennett (1999) draws upon Maffescoli's conception of neo-tribes to explain the engagement of young people in dance music. Unlike the class-based conceptions of subculture popularised by the Birmingham University Centre for Contemporary Cultural Studies in the 1970s, the notion of neo-tribe rejects the traditional class-based assumption that individuals were locked into particular class-determined 'ways of being'. In contrast, engagement with dance music is viewed as an active consumer choice that is central to a notion of self-constructed identity.

However, it should be noted that Maffescoli's theoretical and conceptual framework remains unsupported. He assumes that giving a new name to an old problem or issue is sufficient. It is not. If Maffescoli wants to argue that people are herd animals, or have an instinctual need to form groups, he needs to do much more than simply name this as *puissance*. Not all fandom is a form of consumer-based, unstable and shifting cultural affiliation. We need to know how fandom is constituted, and why there has been a change in relation to the way people engage with commodities. Is there more to identity than the creative use of commodities?

Emotional involvement is a significant component of leisure experiences and much research suggests that strong emotions are evoked by wilderness experiences, experiences that would appear to be far removed from the world of commodities. Scherl (1989, 1990) asked a sample of adult participants on an Outward Bound programme in the Australian wilderness to keep a diary of their perceptions, feeling states and emotions over a nine-day period. Their personal narratives had a focus on self-awareness, especially in relation to coping when other group members were not available for support. These findings are reinforced by McIntyre and Roggenbuck (1998) in a study of a black-water rafting trip in a cave in New Zealand, and by Arnould and Price (1993) in their study of a lengthy raft trip on the Colorado River through the Grand Canyon.

Leisure is a significant factor in the construction of an identity that people feel comfortable with, but it is important to recognise that leisure constraints, those factors that may prevent or restrict leisure participation, are also factors that limit the person's ability to construct their preferred identity. It is important to note that a number of researchers have identified 'structural' barriers to leisure participation and these constraints can impact upon our identity. Shores et al. (2007), for example, found from their study of outdoor recreation amongst Texans that individuals' socio-demographic characteristics, notably the respondents who were elderly, female or ethnic minorities with lower socio-economic status (SES), experienced more constraints to their participation in outdoor recreation. This is a finding reinforced by Martin (2004) who conducted a simple content analysis of racial representation in over 4000 magazine advertisements for outdoor recreation pursuits placed in *Time*, *Outside* and *Ebony* between 1984 and 2000. Martin argues that his research provides evidence of a racialised outdoor leisure identity represented in the advertisements. Black models were much more likely to be found in urban and suburban settings, whilst absent from wilderness leisure activities.

Floyd and Gramman (1993) argued on the basis of their own findings that the under-representation of people of a Mexican-American heritage in outdoor recreation was a product of socialisation of children into activities other than those associated with outdoor recreation.

However, as we shall discuss in later chapters, many African-Americans point to safety concerns, the fear of crime and perception of discrimination as factors constraining their participation in outdoor recreation activities.

Conclusion

In this chapter, we have looked at the nature of the leisure experience. The idea that leisure is a relatively self-determined activity or experience that falls into one's economically free time is widely accepted. Leisure can be a period for self-reflection and personal growth. Whatever definition of leisure we choose to use, the leisure experience is commonly assumed to be different from the work experience; leisure experiences often take place in specific places or leisure venues, and the leisure experience is something we look forward to participating in with positive expectations.

Leisure can be therapeutic leisure, it can provide people with coping strategies and the social world is often made meaningful for people through leisure.

So-called 'healthy' leisure experiences may not have positive benefits for all participants.

A number of social science perspectives have emerged to make sense of the socio-economic and cultural arrangements within which the leisure experience is to be found. It is to these perspectives on leisure that we now turn.

References

Aristotle (1981) *The Politics* (Revised edn), edited by T.J. Saunders and translated by T.A. Sinclair. London: Penguin Classics.

Aristotle (2002) *Metaphysics* (2nd edn), translated by Joe Sachs. Santa Fe, New Mexico: Green Lion Press.

Arnould, E.J. and Price, L.L. (1993) 'River magic: extraordinary experience and the extended service encounter', *Journal of Consumer Research*, 20: 24–45.

Baldwin, J.H., Ellis, G.D. and Baldwin, B.M. (1999) 'Marital satisfaction: an examination of its relationship to spouse support and congruence of commitment among runners', *Leisure Studies*, 21: 117–31.

Bennett, A. (1999) 'Subcultures or neo-tribes? Rethinking the relationship between youth, style and musical taste', *Sociology*, 33: 599–629.

Best, S. (2003) *Beginner's Guide to Social Theory*. London: Sage.

Brackett, K.P. (2000) 'Facework strategies among romance fiction readers', *The Social Science Journal*, 37: 347–60.

Brewer, T. (2003) 'Savoring time: desire. pleasure and wholehearted activity', *Ethical Theory and Moral Practice*, 6: 143–60.

Brown, C. (2007) 'The Carolina Shaggers: dance as serious leisure', *Journal of Leisure Research*, 39 (4): 623–47.

Byrne, R. (2006) 'Beyond lovers' lane: the rise of illicit sexual leisure in countryside recreational space', *Leisure/Loisir*, 30 (1): 15–28.

Caldwell, L.L. (2005) 'Leisure and health: why is leisure therapeutic?', *British Journal of Counselling and Psychology*, 1: 7–26.

Caillois, R. and Halperin, E.P. (1955) 'The structure and classification of games', *Diogenes*, 12: 62–75.

Coalter, F. (1998) 'Leisure studies, leisure policy and social citizenship: the failure of welfare or the limits of welfare?', *Leisure Studies*, 17: 21–36.

Coleman, D. (1993) 'Leisure based social support, leisure dispositions and health', *Journal of Leisure Research*, 25: 35–43.

Coleman, D. and Iso Ahola, S. (1993) 'Leisure and health: the role of social support and self determination', *Journal of Leisure Research*, 25: 11–28.

Crawford, G. (2004) 'The career of the sport supporter: the case of the Manchester storm', *Sociology*, 37 (2): 219–37.

Csikszentmihalyi, M. (1975) *Beyond Boredom and Anxiety: The Experience of Play in Work and Games*. San Francisco, CA: Jossey-Bass.

Csikszentmihalyi, M. (1982) 'Towards a psychology of optimal experience', in L. Wheeler (ed.) *Review of Personality and Social Psychology*, Vol. 2. Beverly Hills, CA: Sage.

Csikszentmihalyi , M. (1997) *Finding Flow: The Psychology of Engagement with Everyday Life*. New York: Basic Books.

Dollimore, J. (1998) *Death, Desire and Loss in Western Culture*. London: Routledge.

Dumazedier, J. (1974) 'Leisure and the social system', in J.F. Murphy (ed.), *Concepts of Leisure*. Englewood Cliffs, NJ: Prentice-Hall.

Dunning, E., Murphy, P. and Williams, J. (1988) *The Roots of Football Hooliganism*. London: Routledge.

Durkheim, E. (1893) *The Division of Labour*, translated by George Simpson. Basingstoke: Macmillan.

Fine, G.A. (1998) *Moral Tales: The Culture of Mushrooming*. Cambridge, MA: Harvard University Press.

Fiske, J. (1992) 'The cultural economy of fandom', in L.A. Lewis (ed.), *The Adoring Audience*. London: Routledge.

Floyd, M.F. and Gramman, J.H. (1993) 'Effects of acculturation and structural assimilation in resource based recreation: the case of Mexican Americans', *Journal of Leisure Research*, 25 (1): 6–21.

Foucault, M. (1977) *Discipline and Punish*. London: Tavistock.

Franklin-Reible, H. (2006) 'Deviant leisure: uncovering the 'goods' in transgressive behaviour', *Leisure/Loisir*, 30 (1): 10–35.

Gibson, H., Willming, C. and Holdnak, A. (2003) '"We're gators ... not just gator fans": serious leisure and University of Florida football', *Journal of Leisure Research*, 34: 397–425.

Gillespie, D. Leffler, A. and Lerner, E. (2002) 'If it weren't for my hobby, I'd have a life: dog sports, serious leisure, and boundary negotiations', *Leisure Studies*, 21: 285–304.

Glover, T. (2003) 'Regulating the rave scene: exploring the policy alternatives of government', *Leisure Sciences*, 25 (4): 307–25.

Goff, S., Fick, D. and Oppliger, R. (1997) 'The moderating effect of spouse support on the relation between serious leisure and spouses' perceived leisure-family conflict', *Journal of Leisure Research*, 29 (1): 47–60.

Green, C.B. and Jones, I. (2005) 'Serious leisure, social identity and sports tourism', *Sport in Society*, 8 (2): 302–20.

Green, E. (1998) 'Women doing friendship: an analysis of women's leisure as a site of identity construction, empowerment and resistance', *Leisure Studies*, 17: 171–85.

Green, E., Hebron, S. and Woodward, D. (1990) *Women's Leisure, What Leisure?* Basingstoke: Macmillan.

Gunn, L. and Caissie, L.T. (2006) 'Serial murder as an act of deviant leisure', *Leisure/Loisir,* 30 (1): 27–53.

Hamilton-Smith, E. (1985) 'Can the arts be leisure?', *World Leisure and Recreation*, 27 (3): 15–19.

Harrington, C.L. and Bielby, D.D. (1995) *Soap Fans: Pursuing Pleasure and Making Meaning in Everyday Life*. Philadelphia: Temple University Press.

Herridge, K.L., Shaw, S.M. and Mannell, R.C. (2003) 'An exploration of women's leisure within heterosexual romantic relationships', *Journal of Leisure Research*, 35: 274–91.

Hilker, C. (1996) 'Rave FAQ', *Youth Studies*, 15 (2): 20.

Hill, C.A. and Preston, L.K. (1996) 'Individual differences in the experience of sexual motivation: theory and measurement of dispositional sexual motives', *Journal of Sex Research*, 33: 27–45.

Huizinga, J. (1949) *Homo Ludens: A Study of the Play Element in Culture*. London: Routledge.

Hunt, S. (2004) 'Acting the part: "living history" as a serious leisure pursuit', *Leisure Studies*, 23 (4): 387–403.

Iso Ahola, S. (1989) 'Motivation for leisure', in E.L. Jackson and T.L. Burton (eds), *Understanding Leisure and Recreation: Mapping the Past, Charting the Future*. State College, PA: Venture.

Iwasaki, Y. (2001) 'Contributions of leisure to coping with daily hassles in university students' lives', *Canadian Journal of Behavioural Science*, 33 (2): 128–41.

Iwasaki, J. and Bartlett, J.D. (2006) 'Culturally meaningful leisure as a way of coping with stress among Aboriginal individuals with diabetes', *Journal of Leisure Research,* 38 (3): 321–38.

Iwasaki, Y. and Mannell, R.C. (2000) 'Hierarchical dimensions of leisure stress coping', *Leisure Sciences,* 22: 163–81.

Iwasaki, Y., and Schneider, I.E. (2003) 'Leisure, stress and coping: an evolving area of inquiry', *Leisure Sciences*, 25: 107–13.

Iwasaki, Y., MacKay, K. and Mactavish, J. (2005) 'Gender-based analyses of coping with stress among professional managers: leisure coping and non-leisure coping', *Journal of Leisure Research*, 37: 1–28.

Jones, I. (2000) 'A model of serious leisure identification: the case of football fandom', *Leisure Studies*, 19: 283–98.

Kaplan, M. (1975) *Leisure: Theory and Policy*. New York: Wiley.

Kelly, J.R. (1990) *Leisure* (2nd edn). Englewood Cliffs, NJ: Prentice-Hall.

Kelly, J.R. and Kelly, J.R. (1994) 'Multiple dimensions of meaning in the domains of work, family, and leisure', *Journal of Leisure Research*, 26 (3): 250–74.

Kleiber, D.A., Hutchinson, S.L. and Williams, R. (2002) 'Leisure as a resource in transcending negative life events: self-protection, self-restoration, and personal transformation', *Leisure Sciences*, 24: 219–35.

Kleiber, P. (2004) 'Focus groups: More than a method of qualitative inquiry', in K. deMarrais and S. Lapan (eds), *Foundations for Research Methods of Inquiry in Education and the Social Sciences*. London: Lawrence Erlbaum Publishers. pp. 87–102.

Linder, M.J. (2001) 'The agony of the Ecstasy: raving youth', *Red Feather Journal of Graduate Sociology*, 4. Retrieved 1 January, 2001 from http://www.tryoung.com/journal-grad.html/4Shon/linder.html.

Lupton, D. (1996) *Food, the Body and the Self*. London: Sage.

Lyng, S. (1990) 'Edgework: a social psychological analysis of voluntary risk taking', *American Journal of Sociology*, 95: 887–921.

McIntyre, N. and Roggenbuck, J.W. (1998) 'Nature/person transactions during an outdoor adventure experience: a multiphasic analysis', *Journal of Leisure Research*, 30: 401–22.

McRobbie, A. (1984) 'Dance and social fantasy', in A. McRobbie and M. Nava (eds), *Gender and Generation*. London: Macmillan.

Maffescoli, M. (1996) *The Time of the Tribes: The Decline of Individualism in Mass Society*. Trans. Don Smith. London: Sage.

Martin, D. (1999) 'Power play and party politics: the significance of raving', *Journal of Popular Culture*, 32 (4): 77–99.

Martin, D.C. (2004) 'Apartheid in the great outdoors: American advertising and the reproduction of a racialized outdoor leisure identity', *Journal of Leisure Research*, 36 (4): 513–35.

Neulinger, J. (1982) 'Leisure lack and the quality of life: the broadening scope of the leisure profession', *Leisure Studies*, 1: 53–63.

Orr, N. (2006) 'Museum volunteering: heritage as serious leisure?', *International Journal of Heritage Studies*, 12 (2): 194–210.

Parr, M.G. and Lashua, B.D. (2004) 'What is leisure? The perceptions of recreation practioners and others', *Leisure Sciences*, 26: 1–17.

Passmore, A. and French, D. (2000) 'A model of leisure and mental health in Australian adolescents', *Behaviour Change*, 17: 208–21.

Patthey-Chavez, G.G. (1996) 'Using moral dilemmas in children's literature as a vehicle for moral education and teaching reading comprehension', *Journal of Moral Education*, 25 (3): 325–41.

Pieper, J. (1952) *Leisure: The Basis of Culture*. London: Fontana.

Pinkerton, S.D., Cecil, H., Bogart, L.M. and Abramson, P.R. (2003) 'The pleasures of sex: an empirical investigation', *Cognition and Emotion*, 17 (2): 341–53.

Predee, M. (2000) *Cultural Criminology and the Carnival of Crime*. London: Routledge.

Radway, J. (1991) *Reading the Romance: Women, Patriarchy, and Popular Literature*. Chapel Hill, NC: University of North Carolina Press.

Raisborough, J. (2007) 'Research note: the concept of serious leisure and women's experiences of the Sea Cadet Corps', *Leisure Studies*, 18: 67–71.

Rojek, C. (1995) *Decentring Leisure: Rethinking Leisure Theory*. London: Sage.

Rojek, C. (2000) *Leisure and Culture*. Basingstoke: Palgrave.

Rojek, C. (2005) *Leisure Theory: Principles and Practice*. Basingstoke: Palgrave.

Sandvoss, C. (2003) *A Game of Two Halves: Football Fandom, Television and Globalization*. London: Routledge.

Sandvoss, C. (2005) *Fans: The Mirror of Consumption*. Cambridge: Polity Press.

Scanlon, T.M. (1998) *What We Owe to Each Other*. Cambridge, MA: Harvard University Press.

Scherl, L.M. (1989) 'Self in wilderness: understanding the psychological benefits of individual wilderness interaction through self-control', *Leisure Sciences*, 11: 123–35.

Scherl, L.M. (1990) 'The wilderness experience: a psychological evaluation of its components and dynamics', in A.T. Easley, J.F. Passineau and B.L. Driver (compilers), USDA Forest Service General Report RM-193. Fort Collins, CO: Rocky Mountain Forest Experiment Station. pp. 11–26.

Shores, K.A., Scott, D. and Floyd, M.F. (2007) 'Constraints to outdoor recreation: a multiple hierarchy stratification perspective', *Leisure Sciences*, 29 (3): 227–46.

Siegenthaler, K.L. and O'Dell, I. (2003) 'Older golfers: serious leisure and successful aging', *World Leisure Journal*, 1: 47–54.

Smith, E. (2002) Leisure education prevention program for junior high. Pennsylvania State University. At http://www.pop.psu.edu/admin~core/grants/grant_listing/leisure.html

Smith, C. (2002) 'Punishment and pleasure: women, food and the imprisoned body', *The Sociological Review*, 50(2): 197–214.

Stalp, M.C. (2006) 'Negotiating time and space for serious leisure: quilting in the modern US home', *Journal of Leisure Research*, 38 (1): 104–32.

Stebbins, R.A. (1982) 'Serious leisure: a conceptual statement', *Pacific Sociological Review*, 25 (2): 251–72.

Stebbins, R.A. (1996) *The Barbershop Singer: Inside the Social World of a Musical Hobby*. Toronto, ON: University of Toronto Press.

Stebbins, R.A. (1997) 'Casual leisure: a conceptual statement', *Leisure Studies*, 16 (1): 17–25.

Stiens, E. (1997) On peace, love, dancing, and drugs: a sociological analysis of rave culture. At http://www.phantasmagoria.f2s.com/writings/raveindex.html

Tomlinson, A. (1993) 'Culture of commitment in leisure: notes towards the understanding of a serious legacy', *World Leisure and Recreation*, 35: 6–9.

Tomlinson, L. (1998) '"This ain't no disco" … or is it? Youth culture and the rave phenomenon', in E.S. Epstein (ed.), *Youth Culture: Identity in a Post-modern World*. Malden, MA: Blackwell. pp. 195–211.

Trenberth, L. and Dewe, P. (2005) 'An exploration of the role of leisure in coping with work related stress using sequential tree analysis', *British Journal of Guidance and Counselling*, 33 (1): 101–15.

Veenhoven, R. (2003) 'Hedonism and happiness', *Journal of Happiness Studies*, 4: 437–57.

Vitterso, J. (2000) 'Review of Csikszentmihalyi (1997) *Finding Flow: The Psychology of Engagement with Everyday Life*', *Journal of Happiness Studies*, 1: 121–3.

Weber, T.R. (1999) 'Raving in Toronto: peace, love, unity and respect in transition', *Journal of Youth Studies*, 2 (3): 317–36.

Whitley, B.E. Jr (1988) 'The relation of gender role orientation to sexual experience among college students', *Sex Roles*, 19: 619–83.

Williams, D.J. (2005) 'Functions of leisure and recreational activities within a sexual assault cycle: a case study', *Sexual Addition and Compulsivity*, 12: 295–309.

Williams, D. and Vaske, J. (2003) 'The measurement of place attachment: validity and generalizability of a psychometric approach', *Forest Science*, 49: 831–40.

Williams, D., Patterson, M., Roggenbuck, J. and Watson, A. (1992) 'Beyond the commodity metaphor: examining emotional and symbolic attachment to place', *Leisure Sciences*, 14: 29–46.

Wong, N., Rindfleisch, A. and Burroughs, J.E. (2003) 'Do reverse-worded items confound measures in cross-cultural consumer research? The case of the material values scale', *Journal of Consumer Research*, 30 (1): 72–91.

Yoder, D.C. (1997) 'A model for commodity intensive serious leisure', *Journal of Leisure Research*, 29: 407–29.

2

SOCIO-ECONOMIC AND CULTURAL APPROACHES TO LEISURE

By the end of this chapter, you should:

- be familiar with a number of social theories and how they have been applied within a leisure context
- have an understanding of the nature of leisure constraint developed within these social theories
- have a critical understanding of the barriers to leisure participation
- understand the nature of social division
- comprehend and question the role of social class and gender, as potential barriers to leisure participation
- have a critical understanding of the theory and research in the area.

Introduction

A wide range of social theories have been used to develop our understanding of the leisure experience and of the role of leisure in the wider society. In this chapter, we will examine those perspectives that have been most commonly used to aid our understanding. Firstly, the Functionalist perspective argues that individual people perform roles within a social system and that these social roles interact with each other to form social systems. Leisure institutions have a role to play both for individual people and for maintaining the social system as a whole. We shall contrast this view with the Marxian and neo-Marxian perspectives that suggest capitalism shapes the nature of work and leisure and developed leisure as a form of consumption. Leisure choices are restricted by our income and working-class people exercise little control over the social allocation of those resources. The chapter will also address the Feminist approaches to leisure, including an evaluation of why many leisure activities were assumed to be inappropriate for women. The suggestion of both the Marxian perspectives and the Feminist perspectives is that leisure reflects social divisions that are ultimately rooted outside the leisure experience itself.

The Interactionist perspective will also be explored. Kelly (1983) argues that the basis of social solidarity is found in social interaction around the leisure experience. Leisure contributes to social identification and cohesion. Leisure is the social space of friendship, parenting, community interaction and the family. In the late 1990s, it became fashionable to discuss the leisure experience in terms of its *plasticity* – leisure had become 'decentred'; it was no longer separated from our other experiences. Leisure is central to the way people choose to construct their identity and was central to an emerging life politics, a politics of individual self-realisation.

The Functionalist Approach

From a functionalist perspective, leisure has a number of roles or functions to perform for the wider social system, including helping to bridge the gap between the individual and the wider social system. National sporting events in particular have a role to play in bringing about greater social integration. The reader might reflect on the purpose of opening and closing ceremonies, uniforms, medal and award ceremonies, and shaking hands with opponents at the end of a game.

Functionalism

Functionalism is a perspective within the social sciences that argues that individual people perform roles within a social system. These social roles interact with each other to form social systems. Within social systems, there are institutions that perform functions for both individuals and for the social system as a whole. Finally, the social system is underpinned by a set of common values. Leisure institutions have a role to play both for individual people and for the social system as a whole.

Talcott Parsons: A Functionalist Approach to Social Systems

For Talcott Parsons (1951), there are two essential reference points for the analysis of social systems:

- the categorising of functional requirements of a social system
- the categorising of the cybernetic hierarchy within a social system – in other words, an analysis of the processes of control within the social system.

The starting point for Parson's functionalist analysis is the *action frame of reference* – the social actions and interactions of individual people that make up the social system. Individual people developed a strategy of responses based upon a range of possible expectations about a given situation.

As a functionalist, Parsons believed that the social system had to overcome four basic problems:

- adaptation – dealt with by the economy
- goal attainment – dealt with by the political system
- pattern maintenance/tension management – dealt with by the family
- integration – dealt with by a range of leisure and cultural organisations.

Underpinning the social system was a 'common value system'. In a *simple* society, Parsons describes the common value system as characterised by Pattern Variables A, whilst in a complex society the common value system is characterised by Pattern Variables B.

- Functionalism undervalues the human agent – in other words, it is assumed that individual people have very little free will or individual control over what happens in their lives – forces outside of their control push them about.
- Functionalism is often assumed to be a perspective that is politically conservative in nature.

Kenneth Roberts (1999) argues that the functions of leisure are to:

- consolidate the social system
- act as a safety valve for the wider social system by easing stresses and strains
- imprint values such as leadership, teamwork and fair play
- provide people with an opportunity to develop their skills
- help to compensate for the unrewarding and unsatisfying aspects of life.

For Roberts (1999) leisure choices are as free as can be expected. In contrast to the Marxian and Feminist approaches, the Pluralist approach rejects class as a significant factor in shaping leisure participation. Rather, pluralists accept the capitalist economic framework, especially the notion that the consumer is sovereign and should be free to pursue their own interests. Companies try to make money from leisure, but only if they provide what the public want to buy. Leisure pursuits come and go because of the changing nature of consumer demand.

If the state does intervene in leisure provision, this is only to police the leisure market and to increase choice rather than restrict it, by preserving areas of natural beauty or promoting public welfare via the provision of public parks, swimming pools and libraries and theatres, or through bodies such as the National Endowment for the Arts, the Arts Council or Sport England, all of which help to reduce exclusion from leisure spaces.

For Roberts (1999), if publicly funded leisure and sports provision were not available, then many economically disadvantaged people, including children, would have very limited recreational opportunities.

A Functionalist Approach to Work and Leisure – Stanley Parker

Taking his point of departure from Harold Wilensky's concepts of 'spillover' (where leisure time activities are a continuation of work-related activities) and 'compensation' (where leisure is used to make up for the dissatisfaction experienced during work time), Stanley Parker provides a functionalist account of the link between work and leisure. However, Parker is critical of earlier functionalist accounts in the area, such as that of Edward Gross (1961). For Gross, work is defined in terms of 'free' time; moreover, work gives a person the *right* to leisure. Work is instrumental and compulsory; leisure is expressive and voluntary; both work and leisure have a role to play in the maintenance of culture and socialisation into cultural traditions – learning rules of behaviour, what is acceptable what is not, fair play, etc. A range of skills are also acquired through work and leisure that are important for the maintenance of the social system.

Gross emphasised that leisure has important *tension management* functions to perform, allowing individuals to restore their sense of self after the stressful experience of work. The social system's *adaptation* functions are also serviced by leisure, in that leisure provides people with opportunities for joining voluntary associations in their non-work time that help to maintain 'instrumental values'.

Leisure has in the past provided examples of national symbols and has been used to identify skills and abilities that people have. Gross argues that this gives leisure an important role to play in the area of *goal attainment*. Leisure also provides opportunities for individuals to involve themselves in group activities that help to maintain group solidarity – an important integration function for any social system.

Parker (1976) argues that Gross' analysis is little more than an artificial attempt to put leisure behaviour into four boxed categories that add little to our understanding of the link between work and leisure.

Stanley Parker (1976) looked at the relationship between work and leisure in terms of two concepts:

- *Fusion* – where we refuse to view work and leisure as distinct parts of our lives.
- *Polarity* – where we insist on work and leisure as distinct parts of our lives.

The nature of employment may directly affect what people choose to do in their non-work time or leisure time. Stanley Parker outlined three distinct patterns of leisure that have developed as a reaction to the experiences people have at work. These three patterns are based upon the assumption that the activities people engage in during their work time may directly affect their non-work time or leisure time:

- Firstly, there is a group of people who continue their working life into their leisure hours – the *extension* pattern. Parker describes such people as 'stretched' by their work and he gives the examples of successful business people, doctors, teachers and social workers.
- Secondly, there is a group of people who develop leisure patterns that are clearly in opposition to their work – the *opposition* pattern. Parker gives the examples of miners and oilrig workers. Parker describes such people as 'damaged' by their work.
- Thirdly, there is a group of people who display neutrality about the type of leisure activity they are involved in – leisure may be separate from work but this may not be planned to be so – the *neutrality* pattern. Parker gives the examples of occupations that are neither fulfilling nor oppressive and he describes such people as 'passive', 'uninvolved' and often 'bored' by their work.

By way of criticism, we could argue that Parker provides little or no justification or evidence for the occupations that he cites as belonging to each category. In addition, he assumes that people's leisure time activities are determined by their work activities, irrespective of the level of personal choice or personal involvement. In other words, assuming that all miners and oilrig workers have leisure patterns that stand in opposition to their work, Parker falls into the functionalist trap described above, of undervaluing the role of the human agent in making personal leisure choices. In addition, Parker does not take into account that our individual choices may be rooted in individual pleasure and desire and not determined by the type of paid work we do.

The Marxian Approach

From the Marxian perspective, if a group of people own the means of production, they not only have economic power, they also have political power. The state is viewed as an institution that helps to organise capitalist society in the best interests of the bourgeoisie (the ruling class). Many working-class people maintain the legitimacy of the system because they are seen as victims of a false consciousness. In other words, working-class people are said to hold values, ideas and beliefs about the nature of inequality, which are not in their own economic interests to hold. Working-class people have their ideas manipulated by the media, schools and religion, for example, and regard economic inequality as fair and just.

What does Marx understand by the term class relations? For Marx, capitalist society is a form of society in which factories, shops and offices are privately owned, rather than owned by the government. Within capitalism, there are a number of economic classes, but Marx investigates two: the Bourgeoisie, who own the means of production and the Proletariat, who do not. These two groups have a structural conflict of interest. In order to make profits, the bourgeoisie must exploit the proletariat, whilst to improve their own living standards, the proletariat must reduce the profits of the bourgeoisie by transferring more profit to the workers as wages.

The theory that Marx develops to explain class exploitation is called 'the labour theory of value'. According to Marx, because the bourgeoisie buy the materials of production from other capitalists, who have a rational perception of their situation, these materials are bought at their true market value, hence the source of profit for Marx can only come from exploiting labour power. It is extracting surplus value from the labour force that provides the difference between the amount of money it takes to set up the production process and the amount of money made at the end of the production process. In addition, we should note that surplus value is not simply profit, it also includes the cost of setting up the production process again for the next production run.

For Marxists, the dominant ideas of any historical period are the ideas of the ruling class, the bourgeoisie. The notion of a 'dominant ideology' refers to a system of thought that is manipulated by the bourgeoisie and imposed upon the proletariat in support of capitalism. The Marxian conception of ideology is based upon a humanistic notion that consent should be based upon an authentic consciousness free from any distortion. For Marxists, the term ideology suggests that the bourgeoisie do something to the way in which working-class people think about the world. The bourgeoisie create a 'worldview' for the proletariat, which is shaped via the mass media, the education system and organised religion, together with other institutions that are concerned with ideas. Class interests shape ideas and the bourgeoisie distort the ideas of the proletariat by imposing 'false consciousnesses' upon them. Television manipulating the ideas of individual people is an often-considered example. Working-class people make use of their false consciousness to justify their own subordination within the capitalist system.

However, the Marxian analysis of ideology contains a very simplistic view of 'representation'. Representation is concerned with how something we see or hear reminds us of something else, for example a heart shape may remind a person of love and romance, or a smile may be a representation of happiness. These are issues of 'cognition', where something happens inside our brain – the process of cognition – which suggests that we think about a person, place or thing when a representation of it presents itself to us. In the Marxian analysis of ideology, this is because working-class people have their ideas manipulated. This means that the bourgeoisie are able to redefine how objects, ideas and beliefs have meaning for us. The bourgeoisie are said to be capable of taking any object, idea or belief and substituting a new representation within our consciousness, and this new representation is supportive of capitalism, against our own interests, and legitimises both the position of the bourgeoisie and the exploitation of the working class.

Marx never developed a research interest in relation to leisure and it was not until the 1980s that the Marxian perspective took a serious interest in the role of leisure in capitalist society.

The Neo-Marxian Approach to Leisure

In the mid 1980s, John Clarke and Chas Critcher (1985) developed an approach to the commercialisation of leisure that was strongly influenced by the work of Marx and later Marxian thinkers such as Antonio Gramsci. Clarke and Critcher argue that capitalism shapes the nature of work and leisure. Before the Industrial Revolution, there was no clear dividing line between these two areas of life. The Industrial Revolution and the development of capitalism had two main effects: firstly, capitalism removed opportunities for leisure, leading to a clear demarcation between work and leisure. Secondly, the state and capitalist enterprise became the key influences of leisure. Central to this was the role of the state in licensing certain leisure activities: pubs, casinos, betting shops; films and DVDs are also cleared for release. In addition, by the use of health and safety legislation, the state also regulated what can be consumed.

Antonio Gramsci and hegemony

Antonio Gramsci rejected the economic determinism contained within traditional Marxian approaches. Writing from his prison cell in the 1930s, Gramsci (1971) made a distinction between two parts of the state:

One part of the state he named political society, which contained all the repressive state institutions, such as the police and the army; the second part of the state he named civil society and this referred to the part of the state that contained the institutions, such as the mass media, that attempted to manipulate our ideas.

The state maintains order by generating consent amongst working-class people – although the state has the ability to use force if necessary to maintain the social order, it would always prefer to produce a compromise. The state attempts to form a historic bloc, which involves making compromises with different groups, in an effort to maintain solidarity. Consent is maintained by hegemony, a body of ideas, which becomes part of our consciousness and which we accept as right. For Gramsci, only by challenging and reformulating hegemony and establishing a new historic bloc can working-class people cause the downfall of capitalism.

Clarke and Critcher (1985) were also highly critical of the functionalist approach to leisure – they argue that for the functionalist, leisure is the site of desirable experiences: freedom, choice, the fulfilment of needs, self-actualisation and self-expression. Leisure is assumed to reflect the life of individuals who have satisfied their basic biological needs for food, clothing and shelter. However, the functionalist approach ignores the fact that leisure remains the compensation that has to be earned through paid work in capitalist enterprises.

Clarke and Critcher (1985) are critical of the link between work and leisure in Stanley Parker's work – they argue that his model:

- is suggestive and not based upon any systematic data collection
- relies upon a weak functionalist analysis
- assumes that any social pattern/activity can be explained by identifying the function it performs for the wider social system
- assumes that leisure is a function of the work experience
- gives little attention to human agency
- assumes that social behaviour is a cultural reflex
- is not comprehensive, and ignores the leisure of women with children.

There has been a long-running concern about the dangers of leisure and the creation of a leisure society. Free time is open to abuse. There are a number of concerns about the danger of leisure, mainly in relation to excess and misuse. Hence, the state has to license and regulate. Clarke and Critcher (1985) argue that under the guise of maintaining public order, the state attempts to impose a form of socially acceptable leisure activity. Solutions to the problem of working-class leisure take three forms:

- 'off the streets'
- 'under supervision'
- 'something constructive to do'.

One of the central institutions for the imposition of acceptable leisure is education. For Clarke and Critcher, traditional 'arts' education such as Fine Art or English Literature assists young people's understanding and appreciation of the country's rich cultural heritage and helps to develop young people's civilising faculties. They also develop the argument that the state encourages a form of rational domesticity among working-class women.

Leisure is becoming subjected to increasing *capitalisation*, losing its elements of freedom and choice and becoming more like paid work. The class structure determines the shape of both employment and leisure activities.

The market and state have constructed leisure; they control the supply and created leisure as a form of consumption. This creation of the leisure consumer was the product of social processes. The commercial sector was allowed to become dominant; even in the state sector, distribution of resources was always via a commercial model. Acceptance of the rhetoric of consumer sovereignty is also used to conceal power relationships.

For Clarke and Critcher, contemporary leisure can usefully be understood in terms of class, even though the class structure may be changing and the working class is diminishing in both size and influence. Clarke and Critcher argue that leisure choices are based upon access to resources that are unequally distributed and therefore our leisure is materially and culturally constrained by class divisions. Our leisure choices are restricted by our income and working-class people exercise little control over the social allocation of those resources.

With the rise of rational recreation in the nineteenth century, working-class people had their use of public space curtailed. Middle-class people viewed the street as a thoroughfare and put pressure on the state to discourage the informal use of public space for working-class social interaction: doorstep banter and other types of gossip may be fine but children playing, teenagers hanging about, the maintenance of cars and skateboarding are all potentially disruptive to public space. Even today, shopping centres are patrolled to control working-class behaviour in such public spaces.

Clarke and Critcher argue that there are three possible relations between the individual citizen and a cultural institution:

- a *member* with an active commitment to the institution
- a *customer* who has a relationship based upon a service contract
- a *consumer* who is a person with neither a commitment nor a formal contract.

For Clarke and Critcher, large corporations have the power to influence consumers' needs. The leisure industry creates new products and then tries to persuade consumers that they should purchase them. As such, patterns of leisure participation are not the outcome of individual choice, as suggested by Roberts' pluralist/consumer model. In addition, leisure is also organised around a number of subcultures rooted within social divisions in relation to class, race, age and gender – leisure opportunities are always unequally structured in both a material and a cultural sense:

- Material resources include time and money.
- Cultural resources include the perception of what is appropriate leisure behaviour for a member of a particular social group.

The class analysis within Clarke and Critcher's work is based upon a three-class model: upper class, middle class and working class.

The upper class is numerically small but powerful. Leisure style is central to who they perceive themselves to be. Gentlemen's clubs, West End theatres, royal garden parties, and places like Ascot, Henley and St Moritz are all important in defining the class boundary. This approach is fine but is a significant departure from the traditional Marxian approach. Clarke and Critcher depart significantly from the central concepts and ideas of the Classical Marxian tradition; in particular, they ignore the labour theory of value in their analysis and have a much greater emphasis on consumption within the process of class formation rather than production. Leisure style, class and social status become indistinguishable in Clarke and Critcher's analysis. Without the labour theory of value, class can become very difficult to define.

The middle class is also difficult to define because of the unclear class boundary. Compared to the working class, the greater income of middle-class people gives them more open access to the leisure market. The middle class is more likely to participate in 'private' leisure activities, such as gardening and DIY house maintenance, and more likely to frequent 'public' leisure venues such as theatres and restaurants. The middle-class leisure participation is seemingly more individualistic in nature and often involves participation in voluntary and charitable work.

Leisure participation is central to the maintenance of cultural inequalities. Going out for a meal may be common to all classes, but there are crucial differences in the sorts of food and choice of restaurants. For the working class, playing sport and club membership are as common as they are amongst middle class people, although again there are significant cultural differentials, for example membership of a private golf club is different from belonging to a pub football team.

Clarke and Critcher discuss social divisions other than class, for example age, that have an impact on the kinds of leisure activity people get involved in. They dismiss the role of personal interest, biological factors and physical ability as factors that restrict leisure participation. Rather, they argue that it is what activities are perceived as appropriate for older people to be seen participating in that is significant. Clarke and Critcher suggest that age is a social construction imposed upon individuals and as a consequence age becomes a socially imposed leisure constraint.

Clarke and Critcher conclude by arguing that leisure reflects social divisions that are ultimately rooted outside the leisure experience itself. Leisure 'realises' social divisions – becoming one of the powerful means by which social divisions receive expression and validation. Moreover, in contrast to the pluralist position that Roberts adopts, for Clarke and Critcher, leisure is far more a restricted activity. However, the Marxian assumptions that Clarke and Critcher's analysis rests on are not adequate to develop such an argument about the social construction of age, gender and sexuality as barriers to leisure participation.

Feminist Approaches to Leisure

Within Leisure Studies, there is a huge feminist literature that draws upon a range of different social, political and philosophical traditions: radical feminism, socialist feminism, post-feminism, post-modernist feminism. Although feminism is not a unified perspective or set of ideas, there are some shared meanings and assumptions, in relation to what we understand by the concepts of 'female' and 'male'. The concept of patriarchy is widely used amongst feminists and is both a description of and a theoretical explanation for the social position of women. The terms sex and sexuality are more problematic. 'Sex' is an activity, a classification of a person, a desire, a descriptor of anatomy, and a source of pleasure and fantasy. For most radical feminists, 'sex' is treated as a 'given' and the notion of patriarchy has the status of a universal truth. In recent years, the category of *woman* has become problematic. What is it that constitutes the category of *woman*? It is not something that we can simply assume; this criticism came initially from 'black' feminists who were unable to develop any form of sisterhood with 'white' feminists. If there is no foundation, then the category of *woman* is of little value to us. In Judith Butler's work, she argues that gender is 'performative' rather than fixed.

Activity

For the term "patriarchal" implies a model of power as interpersonal domination, a model where all men have forms of literal, legal and political power over all women. Yet many of the aspects of women's oppression are constructed diffusely, in representational practices, in forms of speech, in sexual practices. (Coward, 1983: 272)

What does it mean to be a *woman*? Share your answer with fellow students and identify any similarities and differences between the responses of males and females.

Many radical feminists argue that women have a distinct epistemology (theory of knowledge) and ontology (theory of what constitutes reality), as women have knowledge that men could not possess and women think in different ways from men.

For Walby (1998), patriarchy needs to be conceptualised at different levels of abstraction – we need to recognise that it can take different forms and that it need not be a universalistic notion which is true in one form at all times and in all places. Drawing upon the processes found in Giddens' theory of structuration, Walby attempts to construct a more flexible model of patriarchy which can either be in a 'public' or 'private' form, and constructed out of six partially interdependent structures which have different levels of importance for different women at different times and places, rather than a simple universal base-superstructure model.

At its most abstract level, patriarchy exists as a system of social relations, built upon the assumptions that whenever a man comes into contact with a woman he will attempt to oppress her. The second level of patriarchy is organised around six patriarchal structures: the patriarchal mode of production; patriarchal relations in paid work; patriarchal relations in the state; male violence; patriarchal relations in sexuality; patriarchal relations in cultural institutions, such as religion, the media and education.

Patriarchy is not universal – it can take different forms and is dependent upon a range of structures. If one structure of patriarchal relations is challenged and becomes ineffective, another can easily replace it. Patriarchal relations are not simply *given,* they are created by individual people as a *medium* and an *outcome* of the practices of their everyday lives. Men draw upon the structures of patriarchy in order to empower themselves and make their social actions more likely to be effective. By doing so, men reinforce these very patriarchal structures, hence Walby's argument that patriarchal relations are not simply *given* – they are created by individual people as an outcome of the practices that make up their everyday lives. The structures of patriarchy are in constant flux as they are drawn upon by men, reinvented, reinforced and recreated.

Walby's argument opens up the idea that all sociological notions of what constitutes 'femininity' and 'masculinity' are socially constructed. However, if our notions of 'femininity' and 'masculinity' are socially constructed, not only can they be constructed differently, but they can be deconstructed out of existence.

Many feminists see patriarchy as a significant barrier to female participation in a range of leisure activities. Many leisure activities are assumed to be inappropriate for women. Similarly, patriarchy prescribes many activities as suitable for men; leisure activities often provide a site in which men have to continually demonstrate their masculinity.

An Interactive Approach: John R. Kelly

For John R. Kelly, leisure roles are related to, but are not determined by, the economy, the family and the community. Traditional definitions of leisure insist that leisure is 'doing something', in the sense of being a chosen activity rather than a state of mind.

However, for Kelly, the economy, family and community are distinct dimensions of our lives, within which we perform a range of social roles that have a differing degree of obligation, fun and interest.

The Interactionist Approach

Interactionism has it origins in the work of a diverse group of theorists and researchers at the University of Chicago between 1890 and 1940. In essence, we understand social action because it is symbolic and reciprocal in nature. Social actions are human behaviours that have an intention behind them – we as members of a society can read and understand the meaning of behaviours that we observe.

For Herbert Blumer (1962), what is distinctive about human relationships is our ability to construct and share our social worlds. Blumer argues that the term 'symbolic interaction' refers to the unique character of interaction that takes place between humans. Human beings interpret or 'define' each other's actions and do not merely react to the actions of others, and our 'response' is based on the meaning that we assign to the actions we observe. Human interaction always involves an interpretation of symbols that carry meaning. Blumer assumes that:

- society is a framework within which interaction takes place, but society does not determine social action
- social change is a product of interpretation, not brought about by factors outside of the person.

From Blumer's perspective, no factors can influence social action, outside of this process of self-indication. Only interpretation precedes the act. This approach stands in sharp contrast to Marxism and functionalism – in these perspectives, claims Blumer, human behaviour is seen to be a product of stimulus–response variables such as social class. In both these approaches, the actions of the individuals who make up human society are simply the product of wider social forces, and the individual's personal motives and intentions in relation to leisure choices or any activity are ignored by the analysis.

The field of Leisure Studies is based upon the assumption that the leisure experience is qualifiedly different from other experiences in social life. For Kelly and Kelly (1994), the distinctiveness of leisure is to be found in the 'dimension or quality of action', rather than in terms of leisure as a 'separate domain'. Kelly and Kelly (1994) reject any form of 'artificial segregation' of leisure and instead develop a life-course framework for attempting to identify continuities and changes in roles associated with the leisure experience. They argue in favour of a *life-course framework*, an approach that provides a useful point of view because it combines the ways in which people choose to shape their own self-definition but within changing contexts of their other intersecting social roles and responsibilities.

This means that if an individual has a strong commitment to their paid employment, this does not mean there has to be less of a commitment to other dimensions of their life. People develop a form of reciprocity between paid work and their other roles and identities found in their leisure activities. We experience a constant shifting balance between the dimensions of our lives. Work can provide opportunities for play, deeper involvement in the wider culture and greater social interaction, but it is never without obligation. We have to maintain a balance between the different dimensions of our lives at a given stage of our life course. Social roles both add and subtract from leisure opportunities and constraints. In this approach, leisure is the representation of self by the use of a symbolic and pleasurable encounter with the environment. Leisure is much more than a feeling state, it is embedded in a wide range of activities in all areas of social life. In summary, Kelly is concerned with leisure interaction as a factor in the development of our identity through the life course, in which individual people come to construct an identity that they feel comfortable with.

Leisure is central to the maintenance of society and to the development of a social space for the development of intimacy. Kelly (1983) argues that the basis of social solidarity is found in social interaction around the leisure experience. Leisure contributes to social identification and cohesion. Leisure is the social space of friendship, parenting, community interaction and the family. Leisure is not unrelated to the social or environmental context – it is not totally idiosyncratic and esoteric. Kelly would agree with Roberts that leisure is pluralistic in nature and is never fully determined by factors external to the individual. Low income and poverty may restrict the range of leisure activities that are possible, but not all poor people engage in the same set of leisure activities.

Variation in style and content of leisure is related to regularities based upon the life course. Changes in roles are accompanied by shifts in leisure expectations. In contrast to Parker's view of leisure as a leftover period of time, Kelly defines leisure in relation to social networks and changing social roles and responsibilities over time. Periods of unemployment, parenthood, grandparenthood, etc. all impact on our leisure expectations, and leisure is seen as something that is complementary to our other social roles. We reconstruct our identity because of the perception of others and, at the same time, how a person chooses to act within their social roles is partly shaped by personal identity and how a person views themselves in the role. Kelly's argument is built on a dialectical relationship between several central concepts:

- *Personal identity* – one's self-definition in a role context.
- *Social identity* – the definition by others of our taking a role.
- *Presentation* – the mode of enacting a role in order to receive a social definition of an intended personal identity.
- *Role identity* – how a role is enacted, a style of behaviour.

Kelly (1981) explains that the philosophical origins of his interactive approach are rooted in the work of Berger and Luckmann (1966) who argue that *reality* – which they define as 'a quality appertaining to phenomena that we recognize as having a being independent of our own volition' (1966: 13) – is socially constructed. The world has its origins in our thoughts and ideas and is maintained by our thoughts and ideas. Kelly (1981) makes it clear that he rejects the deterministic mode of explanation contained within the Marxian and functionalist perspectives. The leisure experience is not isolated from issues of power or resource allocation, access, exclusion and reward – structural forces related to economic structures can restrict our leisure choices but we still have to take the personal motivation of the individual into account.

For Kelly (1981), almost any activity can be understood as leisure, because it is the *quality* of the pursuit rather than the activity in itself that makes a social action a leisure activity. Leisure is never clearly segmented from our other social roles nor from the ways in which individuals choose to perform their roles. Kelly uses the concept of 'role identity' to link self-conscious action with the social context in which the action takes place. This allows observers to place personal identity within an elated social category and therefore *personal* identity becomes *social* identity.

For Kelly, leisure research should be conducted within the naturalistic setting of 'ordinary life' – whether this is exploring the practices of a children's football team or gambling in a casino, both activities are part of the ongoing construction of everyday life. The everyday minutiae of the day, the insignificant activities that people engage in together, what Berger and Luckmann call the *life world* or the *world of lived experience,* are central to life. There is much more to life and leisure than theme parks and cruises. Everyday life and leisure are organised out of activities such as dinner table talk, family holidays, cleaning the house, messing about, caring for each other and daydreaming. For Kelly (1997), in our everyday lives, reality is simply taken for granted – we rarely question the construction of reality because it appears both 'normal' and 'self-evident'. This assumed acceptance of normality is what Berger and Luckmann call *the natural attitude*; reality has a quality of *compelling facticity.*

We experience everyday life as an ordered or factual reality. It appears to have a prearranged logical pattern that is independent of what we think and do, but it is not.

For Kelly (1981), the social forces in everyday life, whether we know them or not, help to shape our 'social stock of knowledge' and typifactory schemes that help to shape both our behaviour and the interpretation of our behaviour. The role context people find themselves in, together with the roles we choose to play, are central to our understanding of self. Leisure and the roles we perform within the leisure experience are central to the construction and negotiation of our identity.

We interpret the individuals and the situations we encounter in everyday life by reference to a 'social stock of knowledge' made up of typifactory schemes that provide detailed information about the areas of everyday life that we operate within. We use the typifactory schemes within the stock of knowledge to classify individuals into types, such as 'men', 'girls', 'Chinese', 'disabled', etc. Such typifications also inform us of the most appropriate way of dealing with these different types of people. In addition, we use language to place ourselves in what we consider to be an appropriate category, and we use the social stock of knowledge to define the situation we are in and the limits of our capabilities. The reason why humans involve themselves in these activities, claim Berger and Luckmann, is because in the last analysis, all social reality is uncertain and society is a construction to protect people from insecurity.

The Plasticity of the Leisure Experience

For Berger and Luckmann, people also have a link with the environment through their biology, but they are very clear in stressing that there is no human nature in the sense of a biologically fixed core determining the socio-cultural leisure formations. Berger and Luckmann argue that the human organism is primarily characterised by its ability to change the limits and parameters that are imposed upon it. People are characterised by their plasticity – our individual biography and what we understand to be our personal identity are not wholly individual – they are based upon our subjective meanings acquired through the processes of socialisation. The potentially subjectively meaningful has to be made objectively available to us in order to become meaningful. What is subjectively meaningful to us can only be meaningful if those subjective ideas are interpreted against the typifications that are contained within the social stock of knowledge. When an individual performs a role, such as the role of a disabled person, then that role and the person who performs it are defined by the use of typifications. The role of the disabled person is typified by personal tragedy and loss, and although such roles can be internalised by the people who perform them and can become subjectively real to them, it is important to note that for Berger and Luckmann, this is not an irreversible process. The stock of knowledge, the typifications, the perception of roles and our subjective reflections and internalisations can all be redefined. We can redefine the unity between history and biography. Taylor (2003) attempted to test the relationship between social identity and stereotype theories. Taylor identified twelve leisure activities and used them as a means to assess whether leisure stereotypes exist for women. Stereotypes consisting of between four and eleven words were obtained using the checklist method, with 40 participants contributing to each stereotype (120 participants contributed in total). The stereotypes were found to include characteristics that were both positively and negatively valued and, consequently, they had a range of favourableness ratings. All but one, golf, were positively evaluated images.

In summary, Symbolic Interactionism assumes that what is distinctive about human relationships is our ability to construct social worlds. The theoretical starting point is the autonomous self, defined by intentions, goals, attitudes, values, and beliefs formulated through social interaction. The primary task of the individual is self-definition, for example, 'Who am I?'. Symbolic interactionists argue that leisure stereotypes may exist and could have an impact on our identity. Kelly (1990), for example, assumes that central to leisure research is the notion that people's recreation is a medium for personal enhancement and self-development. The non-obligatory nature of leisure provides a distinctive life space in which people can cultivate their preferred self-definitions. People often buy products not for the functional benefits that they bring, bur rather for their symbolic value in terms of enhancing self-image. Products with a distinct brand image act as symbols of how we perceive ourselves. Products such as cars, clothing, fragrance, home furnishings and a range of leisure products have a high symbolic value to certain segments of society.

Activity

Below is a list of points that are drawn from John R. Kelly's (1987a) *Freedom to Be: A New Sociology of Leisure*. What do you feel would be the Marxist, functionalist and feminist views of these points?

The leisure experience has a variety of elements that can be identified and analysed, but at the same time every leisure experience is also a new creation with its own elements.

Consider the following:

- Leisure is the product of a free decision and action.
- Leisure is a process, not fixed but developing and created in its time and place.
- Leisure is situated and constructed in an ever-new context.
- Leisure is production in the sense that the meaning of the leisure is always reproduced in its situation rather than appropriated from some external source.

Postmodernity and Leisure

Postmodernists believe that the world is a risky and uncertain place because of the loss of trust and the loss of meaning in the world, both at the level of individual interactions and at a more global level. However, there is little empirical research into how people cope with this uncertainty, but it is commonly assumed that leisure is central to the strategies that people adopt to cope with uncertainty. The world of work is also very different within the postmodern condition. The postmodern organisation should contain de-demarcated and multi-skilled jobs – unlike the Prussian style bureaucracy as outlined by Weber (1922/1978), the postmodern organisation should be 'de-Prussianised', it should be free of formal rationality, loosely coupled and complexly interactive, it should be a 'collegial formation' with no vertical authority, but with forms of 'networking'. These networks should reflect the new 'cultural and social specialists' needs and cultural capital and allow the specialists to resist control by traditional bureaucracy.

The Weberian form of organisation has rules, structures and procedures that are clearly defined and fully understood. The postmodern organisation represents a shift from the 'punishment-based' hierarchy contained within the Weberian conception of bureaucracy to a 'consent-based' flattened hierarchy.

However we choose to define postmodernism, it is commonly recognised to be a collection of theories about what life is like beyond the far side of modernity. Friedrich Nietzsche (1844–1900) invented many of the central ideas of postmodernism. Nietzsche's work is described as anti-foundationalist in nature, in that he wanted to undermine what he considered to be the arbitrary nature of the foundation of knowledge, truth, morality and identity. This tendency often presented itself in slogans such as: 'God is dead'. Nietzsche's approach provides the foundation for the two central assumptions that underpin postmodernism:

- Epistemological uncertainty – epistemology is a theory of knowledge and it attempts to answer the question: how do we know what we know? When postmodernists use the phrase 'epistemological uncertainty', they are suggesting that in the last analysis, we do not know fully what we believe in or why we believe in it.
- Ontological plurality – this is the suggestion of uncertainty as to what reality consists of.

In *The Postmodern Condition*, Lyotard (1983) argues that modernity is built upon grand narratives. These are 'big stories' such as socialism or feminism that explain to followers what the world is like and how it works. In the postmodern condition, people have lost faith in such universal belief systems. In the postmodern condition, the meaning of 'leisure' is now unclear and postmodernists emphasise the:

- dissolving of boundaries between spheres of life
- de-differentiation of experience
- aestheticisation of everyday life
- anti-hierarchical character of postmodern experience
- opposition to normative value distinctions
- experience of the contingent and uncertain, exhibiting multiple trajectories
- aesthetic experience marked by a sense of intoxication, sensory overload, intensity and disorientation
- experience consumed as a form of distraction with a multiplicity of fragmented, frequently interrupted looks or in dream-like states.

Chris Rojek (1995) argues that 'traditional' theories of leisure were born out of, and thus reflect, the rigidities of the production/consumption divide, associated with the Fordist modernity of *homo faber*. Fordism is a form of social organisation based upon a centralised nation state that takes responsibility for the management of the economy and society. This form of society is industrial and the economy is dominated by the manufacture of mass-produced products.

While mass consumption established new leisure habits, the post-Fordist shift to greater diversity has enabled individuals to tailor leisure activities to their own requirements. The multiplication and diversification of television channels, radio stations and weekly magazines aimed at specific market niches rather than mass markets provide examples of this. Lash and Urry (1994) argue that the decline of the package holiday is another example, for the package holiday exemplified Fordist patterns of consumption. The Fordist holiday experience involved a complete package that combined holiday destination, travel, accommodation, catering and entertainment; a standard product, with limited variation in accommodation or resort; advertised through the mass media and sold through travel agent chains at high volume to keep prices low.

They point out that the Thomas Cook company, whose founder created the package holiday, has re-branded itself into a global operation that focuses on providing holiday *information,* so that customers can construct their own packages instead of buying one out of the brochure. They also suggest that travel could be replaced by what they call the 'post-tourist' experience of 'travel by television'.

Leisure under modernity was narrowly conceived as relating primarily to those interests and activities pertaining to recharging the energies of the individual for renewed effort in the workplace. Rojek recommends an alternative direction for leisure theory, associated with the *homo ludens* model in which 'leisure' and play are seen as informing and reflecting human needs and motivations. We need to reconceive leisure so that:

- leisure becomes 'decentred'
- leisure is no longer separated from our other experiences
- leisure is integral to human action, not peripheral and meaningless or 'inauthentic' experience
- in postmodern leisure, people are less likely to seek the authentic experience
- leisure becomes an end in itself – not an escape from work
- modern leisure is associated with the life cycle
- postmodernity breaks down barriers in social life
- leisure is central to identity and identity politics
- in modernity, leisure providers are experts, however today people are no longer content to let others organise their leisure for them.

There are a number of contradictions within postmodern writing. Firstly, postmodernists stress the irrational, however the instruments of reason are regularly used within postmodern writing. Secondly, postmodernists reject modern criteria for assessing theory – this raises issues about the criteria for judging the validity of research. Finally, postmodernists reject and abandon truth claims in their own writing.

Activity

Read the passage below and attempt to construct a pluralist, feminist or functionalist 'reading' of the film.

Peter Dean (2007) contrasts a Marxian with a postmodern reading of the film *Star Wars.* From a Marxian perspective, the film suggests that the rebel Alliance could be seen as a representation of an oppressed group within a capitalistic bourgeois-dominated political system and that the rebel Alliance, not the Empire, should hold legitimate power and authority in the galaxy. Through its structure and narrative, the film strengthens the class divisions

(Continued)

(Continued)

in society. The film celebrates the achievement of capitalism by stressing the importance of speed, technology and industrial power. *Star Wars* reinforces the capitalist hegemonic nature of society. However, at the same time, the film gives moral support to the working class in their battle to overcome the Empire.

In contrast, Dean suggests postmodernism is very good at understanding the media-dominated, technological and computerised content of the film. In addition, because the film draws heavily upon a range of conventions from film genres, such as the spaghetti western, epic adventure and a range of other popular cultural forms, Dean suggests that the film is a postmodern pastiche. In the last analysis, a postmodern reading of the film would suggest that *Star Wars* provides moral support to the oppressed, outnumbered and under-resourced rebel Alliance in their struggle against the capitalist hegemonic power of the Empire.

Leisure and Life Politics

Giddens (1994) discusses 'high modernity' under four headings: trust, risk, opaqueness and globalisation. All individuals strive for a 'pure' relationship in Giddens' analysis; this is a relationship based solely upon trust, and cannot be underpinned by any guarantee. In previous ages, it was possible to trust an individual in an intimate relationship, because of their family background or because of their professional background. This guarantee of trust can no longer be given in the 'new times' of 'high' modernity. In terms of politics, the significance of these developments is that within modernity we have moved from 'emancipatory politics' – which is itself a product of modernity – to 'life politics' which is the key factor pushing new social movements to campaign for a form of polity which is on the far side of modernity. Emancipatory politics has two main elements:

- an effort to break free from the shackles of the past
- the overcoming of illegitimate domination, which adversely affects the life chances of individuals.

For Giddens, life politics is a politics, not of life chances, but of lifestyle, and as such it is concerned with breaking down barriers that prevent people from living a life that they feel comfortable with. The disputes and struggles within this form of politics centre on the relationships between individuals and humanity. People should be free to live in a world where tradition and custom should not be used to prevent a person from living as they choose. In the past, life politics disputes would have included the decriminalisation of consenting, same-sex sexual relationships.

Beck (1992) develops the concept of individualisation to explain the problems associated with living a life in a risk society. The concept suggests that each person has a biography, but that biography is now in their own hands – it is much less likely to be determined by factors outside of their control. Our biographies have become *self-reflexive* or self-produced and our leisure choices are central to the construction of a self that we feel happy with.

For Giddens, the self is reflexive and this reflexive monitoring of self is primarily about the maintenance of a basic security system. In pre-modern times, the self had an 'environment of trust' which was built upon kinship, the local community, religious cosmologies and tradition. This pre-modern environment of trust allowed people to stabilise social ties within a familiar place according to familiar rules. The 'environment of trust' is much less secure and we attempt to stabilise our social ties by personal relationships, notably by attempting to find a pure relationship, a relationship based upon trust.

For Rojek (2001), traditional political economy assumed leisure to be a non-political aspect of our lives, an opportunity to choose a range of activities, to unwind and escape from the stresses and strains of the work process. The concepts of risk, individualisation and life politics, as developed by Giddens and Beck (1994), can be used to redefine the relationship between leisure and the new forms of identity in a world where leisure is no longer dependent upon work. However, as we shall see in the chapters on work and leisure, there is a problematic relationship between the concept of 'life politics' and the concept of 'a leisure society' in which people are liberated from paid employment altogether.

For Rojek (2001), life politics is a product of living in a 'risk society' – in such a society, modes of production and information are still at the centre of issues concerning social control but they cannot always be recognised as belonging to specific nation states, social classes or political elites. People in these societies have a much stronger perception of risk and a much weaker perception of the basic security of self than in pre-modern societies. Within late modernity, there is:

- universalisation of risk – particularly from the risk of nuclear accident and ecological destruction, which affect people irrespective of age, race, class or gender
- globalisation of risk – risks are stretched over time and space, decisions made in institutions on the other side of the globe, which we may well be unaware of or unable to influence, can directly affect us
- institutionalisation of risk – institutions have emerged which have 'risk' as their central organising principle, such as financial markets and insurance
- reflexiveness of risk – risk has an element of 'manufactured uncertainty' – the unforeseen consequences of individuals or institutions taking an action can have significant effects, as seen in the unforeseen link between animal feed and CJD.

A number of factors, related to the disappearance of local communities, make the occurrence of risk subjectively feel more severe. This leads to the notion of 'opaqueness', the feeling of uncertainty associated with the lack of any guidelines on how to behave in any given situation, making life have an unpredictable feel to it, and the lack of trust that we have in abstract systems because we know such systems have design faults and that the people who run the systems are likely to make errors.

Giddens does explain the typical reactions people develop to combat uncertainty and risk:

- Pragmatic acceptance – in which people repress their unease about risk and lack of trust, and adopt a business-as-usual standpoint.
- Sustained optimism – in which people have a belief that the situation will improve because of some factor outside of the control of the individual.
- Cynical pessimism – in which there is a belief that the person should enjoy the here and now.
- Radical opposition – in which the person joins a social movement and actively attempts to bring about a change to their situation.

People in risk societies make use of their leisure experiences to construct a sense of self that they feel content with and which offers them a degree of protection from the uncertainty that is found in other areas of their lives. For Giddens, to be reflexive is to have a *life narrative*; to choose a character, mould our personal identity and decide upon the moral and rational organising principles that we might use to make sense of the reservoir of subjective experience. This narrative is what we use to authenticate ourselves as a self. Individuals, then, have to create and constantly recreate themselves, choosing from lifestyle resources to develop and monitor their chosen life narrative.

In Giddens' analysis, however, individuals have become reflexive in order to compensate for the breaking down of the basic security system of customs and traditions within local communities, brought about by the advancement of late modernity. This is a situation which individuals may find personally troubling, because the protective framework of the local community gave psychological support to individuals and without it they may feel the ontological insecurity of personal meaninglessness and dread.

In summary, *risk* has become an increasingly pervasive concept of human existence in Western societies. According to Beck (1992):

- risk is a central aspect of human subjectivity
- risk is associated with notions of choice, responsibility and blame.

Beck argues that modernity is breaking free from the contours of classical industrial society and we are in the midst of a transition from an industrial society to a risk society. The risk society is not a class society, as both rich and poor are subject to ecological risks. The risk society is global and knows no national boundaries – for example, the effects of Chernobyl. Beck's analyses are based upon a three-stage historical progression from pre-industrial to industrial to risk societies. Each of these three types of society contains risk and hazards, but there are qualitative differences between them in terms of the types of risk encountered. In modern industrial societies, there are industrially produced hazards. The risk society, however, is a society in which 'risks' have become the central principle of social organisation.

In Giddens' analysis, risk society is not postmodernism, rather modernity is increasingly becoming an essentially post-traditional and post-nature form of social order, which brings with it the threat of personal meaninglessness. Moreover, an underlying element of modernity is that as a social form, modernity begins to reflect upon itself. According to Giddens, in traditional cultures, the risk environment was dominated by the hazards of the physical world. Individuals may find this situation *existentially troubling*. Giddens' discussion is similar in a number of important respects to the discussion of risk in Beck's work.

A key element in any fully developed modernity is the single person, cut loose from previously supportive social forms, for example social class or fixed gender roles. Individuals are reflexive for reasons of basic security, and individuals change in order to make themselves feel an enhanced sense of ontological security. In their leisure pursuits, people are reflexive in order to enhance their opportunities to fulfil their desires.

Conclusion

How are we to understand the leisure experience? The leisure experience is more than simply 'free' time. The leisure experience can be therapeutic in nature, involving self-reflection and personal growth. The leisure experience is different from the work experience, in that the leisure experience is a relatively self-determined experience within which we expect to find pleasure and fulfil desire, although in some cases this can be in the form of a deviant or criminal activity. The social science perspectives on leisure suggest that leisure can be functional for both the individual and for the wider society, that it can be pluralistic in nature, and that it can support capitalism and other mechanisms of oppression and exploitation. In the next chapter, we shall look in more detail at social class and gender, and further evaluate the theories and research into leisure participation and social class and gender as constraints to leisure participation.

References

Beck, U. (1992) *Risk Society*. Cambridge: Polity.

Berger, P.L. and Luckmann, T. (1966) *The Social Construction of Reality: A Treatise on the Sociology of Knowledge*. New York: Anchor Books.

Blumer, H. (1962) 'Society as a symbolic interaction', in J.G. Manis and B.N. Meltzer (eds), *Symbolic Interaction: A Reader in Social Psychology*. Boston: Allyn and Bacon.

Clarke, J. and Critcher, C. (1985) *The Devil Makes Work*. Basingstoke: Macmillan Houndmills.

Coward, R. (1983) *Patriarchal Precedents: Sexuality and Social Relations*. London: Routledge and Kegan Paul.

Dean, P. (2007) 'From one side of the galaxy to the other: the *Star Wars* trilogy from a Marxist and postmodernist perspective', published by the Society and Culture Association. Available at http://www.ptc.nsw.edu.au/scansw/starwars.html#anchor24027

Giddens, A. (1994) *Beyond Left and Right: The Future of Radical Politics*. Cambridge: Polity.

Giddens, A. and Beck, U. (1994) *Reflexive Modernisation*. Cambridge: Polity.

Gramsci, A. (1971) *Selections from the Prison Notebooks*, translated and edited by Q. Hoare and G. Nowell-Smith. London: Lawrence and Wishart.

Gross, E. (1961) 'A functional approach to leisure analysis', *Social Problems*, 9 (1): 2–8.

Kelly, J.R. (1981) 'Leisure interaction and the social dialectic', *Social Forces*, 60 (2): 304–22.

Kelly, J.R. (1983) *Leisure Identities and Interactions*. London: George Allen and Unwin.

Kelly, J.R. (1987a) *Freedom to Be: A New Sociology of Leisure*. London and New York: Macmillan.

Kelly, J.R. (1987b) *Peoria Winter: Styles and Resources in Later Life*. Lexington, MA: Lexington Books.

Kelly, J.R. (1990) *Leisure* (2nd edn). Englewood Cliffs, NJ: Prentice-Hall.

Kelly, J.R. (1997) 'Changing issues in leisure–family research – again', *Journal of Leisure Research*, 29 (1): 132–4.

Kelly, J.R. and Kelly, J.R. (1994) 'Multiple dimensions of meaning in the domains of work, family, and leisure', *Journal of Leisure Research*, 26 (3): 250–74.

Lash, S. and Urry, J. (1994) *Economies of Signs and Space*. London: Sage.

Lyotard, J. (1983) *The Postmodern Condition*. Manchester: University of Manchester Press.

Parker, S. (1976) *The Sociology of Leisure*. London: George Allen and Unwin.

Parsons, T. (1951) *The Social System*. London: Routledge & Kegan Paul.

Roberts, K. (1999) *Leisure in Contemporary Society*. Wallingford: CAB International.

Rojek, C. (1995) *Decentring Leisure: Rethinking Leisure Theory*. London: Sage.

Rojek, C. (2001) 'Leisure and life politics', *Leisure Sciences*, 23: 115–25.

Taylor, T.L. (2003) 'Issues of cultural diversity in women's sport', *Journal of the International Council for Health, Physical Education, Recreation, Sport and Dance*, 39 (3): 27–33.

Walby, S. (1998) *Gender Transformations*. London: Routledge.

Weber, M. (1922/1978) *Economy and Society: An Outline of Interpretive Sociology*, vols 1–3, eds G. Roth and C. Wittich. New York: Bedminster Press.

3

PARTICIPATION AND CONSTRAINT – CLASS AND GENDER

By the end of this chapter, you should:

- be familiar with the nature of constraint within a leisure context
- have an understanding of the 'structuration' of leisure constraint
- have a critical understanding of the barriers to leisure participation
- be in a position to evaluate the 'constraints model' in leisure research
- understand the nature of social division
- comprehend and question the role of social class, gender and sexuality as potential barriers to leisure participation
- have a critical understanding of the theory and research in the area.

Introduction

Participation is about interaction with others and involvement in the common activities of a group. Participation in leisure activities is not randomly distributed within the population. This chapter will explore the nature of some of the central social divisions within contemporary society and explore how social division impacts upon leisure participation. The divisions explored will include social class and gender.

The Constraints Model

The constraints model has dominated the research and discussion of leisure participation. Are individual people powerless to resist leisure constraint? We shall explore the *structuration* of constraint, the relationship between agency and structure and barriers to leisure participation.

In Leisure Studies, *constraint* is commonly understood in negative terms as something restricting or limiting leisure participation. According to Samdahl and Jekubovich (1997), the *constraints paradigm* has shaped leisure research.

Leisure Studies have always had concerns about the barriers to participation and lack of equality of leisure opportunity. The emphasis is upon the impact of demographic characteristics such as race, class, age and gender as structural constraints that designate an individual's place in the wider society and restrict opportunity for participation. In addition, many researchers assume that such constraints are central elements in the formation of our identity. Researchers often attempt to predict participation on the basis of these shared characteristics. Jackson (1990) argues that both leisure researchers and leisure participants have assumed that constraints restrict leisure preferences, participation and enjoyment of leisure. Gruneau (1984) argues that constraint should be seen in terms of parameters that:

- prescribe certain actions
- proscribe certain actions
- describe boundaries within which action takes place.

The constraints model is built upon the assumption that the need to participate is a central element in our *essential* human condition and that non-participation is a *problem* or *issue* to be overcome. Even personal preference or motivation, such as 'lack of interest', is treated as the problem of 'intrapersonal constraint' (Crawford et al., 1991) – in other words, people who do not want to participate are assumed to 'lack something'.

Such approaches significantly underestimate or undervalue the role of the human agent, or personal motivation, in the selection of leisure choices. The choice to conform and behave in a way that we are expected to behave is still an active choice – in this case, to avoid the consequences of breaking the expectations of others.

Leisure constraints model

Crawford et al.'s (1991) constraints model identifies three levels of constraint:

Intrapersonal – psychological states and attributes act together with personal inclination to shape our leisure choices.

Interpersonal – close, interpersonal relationships with others help to shape our leisure choices.

Structural – factors over and above the individual, such as age, race, class and gender, that obstruct participation.

The Crawford et al. (1991) model is described as hierarchical in nature:

Negotiation of constraints at the intrapersonal level must be accomplished before attempting to overcome constraints at the interpersonal level.

Negotiation of constraints at the interpersonal level must be accomplished before attempting to overcome structural constraints.

If negotiation at all three levels is successful, then participation should take place.

Based upon in-depth interviews with 88 adults, Samdahl and Jekubovich (1997) were concerned with identifying the factors that shape leisure within the everyday lives of people. They argued that the constraints model does not capture the vibrant set of circumstances within which people's leisure are actively shaped and developed. Towards this end, they outlined a critique of leisure constraints as a framework for understanding factors that influence people's leisure choices. In much leisure research (Buchanan and Allen, 1985; Jackson and Searle, 1985; Searle and Jackson, 1985a, 1985b), constraint is conceptualised as a 'mechanism for better understanding barriers to activity participation'. Participation often becomes the dependent variable to be explained within a framework of given constraints.

Jackson (1988), for example, suggested that leisure constraints should be seen as a subset of incentives for not engaging in a particular leisure activity.

In the 1990s, a number of researchers challenged the assumption that leisure constraints were the sole factors influencing leisure participation (Kay and Jackson, 1991; Shaw et al., 1991). Samdahl and Jekubovich (1997), for example, did not interpret their data by reference to a leisure constraints model or framework – rather, drawing upon a form of grounded theory, they placed individuals' responses into a number of categories that they subdivided over the course of the data collection as the categories became saturated. Using this approach, the nature of constraint emerged, as links between categories became more clearly established. In other words, rather than imposing ideas about the nature of constraint upon their respondents, Samdahl and Jekubovich allowed the nature of any constraints to emerge as they interpreted the responses given.

Samdahl and Jekubovich identified factors that traditional approaches would describe as structural constraints, the most common of which were time, money and health. Even people in full time work with an adequate income mentioned that the expense of certain activities kept them from participating in a number of them. However, these 'structural factors' did not exclude people from participating in leisure activities totally.

Interpersonal factors were also identified as a constraint by Samdahl and Jekubovich's respondents; notably, the quality of social relationships had an impact upon leisure participation, with examples including: the lack of a leisure partner, or having a mismatched leisure partner – an individual who did not share the respondent's interests – and family responsibilities that restricted a person's freedom to engage in their chosen leisure activities.

Respondents also revealed deeper troubles and uncertainties that were a source of dissatisfaction with their lives. This also impacted on their leisure participation. Samdahl and Jekubovich identified four themes that emerged from their research:

- Making time for self – individuals took an active role in restructuring the many demands on their time, and many of the respondents successfully altered their routines or changed their daily routine to incorporate leisure into their lives.
- Coordinating time with others – family responsibilities and work schedules were often described as a source of great dissatisfaction, making participation difficult to arrange. However, again, respondents often found creative solutions in order to find time for participation.
- Compromising on activity – people compromised with their leisure partners on the nature of leisure activities, in contrast to the traditional leisure constraints model that places a central importance on explaining a specific activity. Samdahl and Jekubovich found that 'doing things together' was often more important than the nature of the activity itself.
- The significance of sharing – leisure participation is important in maintaining relationships and, as such, sharing as an end in itself emerged from Samdahl and Jekubovich's respondents as a fundamental component of many leisure experiences.

In summary, the traditional constraints model is an artificial construct based upon the deterministic assertion that everyone experiences constraint with equal strength. Such assertions undervalue the role of the person or the human agent within the construction of their own leisure choices.

In a similar fashion, Raymore (2002) points out that one of the central problems with the constraints paradigm is that the absence of a constraint does not necessarily lead to participation. Negative body image is a well-researched constraint on young women participating in swimming. However, James (2000) found that young women who are pleased with their body may still choose not to swim. Leisure in relation to subjectification (the construction of a self) and leisure as an enabling concept is ignored by the constraints model.

What is the nature of our commitment to a leisure constraint?

A central element in these processes is the emotional attachment to leisure activities. We understand the constraint on participation by deducing it from forms of participation. Howard S. Becker (1960) argued that one of the central issues in social science was the attempt to explain consistent human behaviour. People engage in 'consistent lines of activity' or 'consistent behaviour' often over long periods of time. Possible reasons for the rejection of one form of activity could include moral reasons, fear of sanction, fear of risk or practical reasons.

As Kyle and Chick (2002) explain, personal involvement in any leisure activity reflects the degree to which a person devotes him- or herself to an activity or associated product – involvement reflects the strength or extent of a person's need to maintain a sense of self, including their values, attitudes and beliefs around the activity.

Towards this end, Burch (1969) developed the idea of a 'personal community hypothesis', in which leisure participation was based upon the degree of connectedness to a circle of friends, colleagues and family and their leisure interests. Such forms of connectedness give meaning to our lives. Our participation is related to the development of similar tastes to people we are friendly with. Johnson (1991) argued that commitment was a function of three processes:

- Personal commitment – the individual motivation to participate.
- Moral commitment – the feeling that you should participate.
- Structural commitment – the feeling that factors are helping to shape your leisure choices.

Class, Inequality and Exclusion from Leisure Participation

Inequality may be *real*, but class analysis is a set of concepts. Class analysis is a range of possible explanations for these persistent inequalities. The foundation of class analysis is found in the work of Marx and Weber.

In the nineteenth century, Marx singled out class divisions as the factor that pushed history forwards. Marx argued that ownership and non-ownership of the means of production was the central element in class division; this is the basis of Marx's *abstract model* of class – the model found in his most influential book *Capital* (1867). For Weber, a social class is a group of people who share the same class (market) position.

- Market situation – people in the same class earn a similar amount of money.
- Work situation – people in the same class have similar conditions of service at work.

However, for Weber, social class was only one aspect of a person's *stratification position;* other aspects included status – defined as the social estimation of honour – and party – the holding of political power. Weber argued that status was independent of both social class and party – in other words, a person could have a high social-class position but this does not guarantee that they will have a high status position. Similarly, a person may have a low social-class position but high status.

Pierre Bourdieu

Bourdieu had a significant impact upon how we understand class in relation to leisure participation. He was interested in identifying the social and political structures that underpin individuals' participation and tastes – what Bourdieu refers to as the 'practices of distinction'. Culture or good taste are based upon the possession of cultural capital – conceptual skills, confidence to participate, etc. – that people acquire in the course of their schooling and family life. Although the appreciation of various cultural products appears to be personal and based upon a natural inclination, cultural capital gives people the skills and inclination needed to enjoy a range of activities. Moreover, this self-exclusion was read as 'proof' that working-class people unsurprisingly lack 'taste'. Bourdieu (1998) has three key concepts that he uses to explain the nature of social life: *habitus, field* and *practice*. The objective social structures that we come across in everyday life are directly linked to the everyday activities of ordinary people through the practices that we perform. Bourdieu takes his starting point from the assumption that social life is essentially *practical*. Practices are formed within a habitus – a social context in which the individual is exposed to a range of wider institutional, social and cultural contexts and traditions, which are used by individuals to inform their own practices. It is through practice that individuals 'become themselves', however practices also act as signifiers of taste and people draw this element of practice in an effort to make a distinction between themselves and others. People invest in certain practices in an effort to gain a reward. In addition, there is a class affiliation to a given habitus that an individual is exposed to. The resources that we come across within the habitus are forms of cultural capital that we use to guide tastes and leisure preferences. Cultural capital allows us comfortable access to sites of cultural practice.

Bourdieu rejects dualisms such as agency and structure and views practice as both a medium and an outcome of people living in a structure. We use these practices, such as a taste for fine wine or classical music, to live out our everyday lives. Bourdieu argues that we experience practice as having a rule-like quality.

People who live in the same area and share the same class membership are more likely to share the same *social field*, to share the same habitus and engage in similar practices. In other words:

Habitus + Field = Practice

Habitus is a constructed system of structuring qualities that are found in the 'active aspect' of leisure participation, 'an acquired system of generative schemes'. Although habitus has no specific designer or rule that it has to follow in advance, by its nature, 'practice' has a structuring quality and generates regular and durable forms of leisure participation, including our ideas of what is 'reasonable' and what is 'common-sense'; we internalise the habitus as a second nature. Our perception of the world, including its economic relations, family relations and the division of labour, are shaped by the habitus. Habitus is constituted by practice and at the same time our future practice is shaped by the habitus. What Bourdieu is doing here is attempting to explain the paradox of attempting to explain the objective meaning of the leisure experience but without rejecting the subjective intention of the leisure participant. Simply stated, for Bourdieu, there is a link between taste and class habitus. The activity of people in the higher-class positions restricts the access of lower-class people to certain forms of less desirable lifestyle and taste choices.

Jukka Gronow (1997) discusses how in the nineteenth century a distinct class-based theatre culture developed in the United States. Until the latter years of the century, irrespective of class background, people watched performances of Shakespeare in the same tent or saloon. However, by the turn of the century, performances had transferred to separate theatres. The barrier to entry for working-class people was not simply the price of the ticket, but having to display the appropriate forms of behaviour and to satisfy the given dress code.

Bourdieu identifies three broad class/taste groupings:

- The legitimate – classical music, broadsheet newspapers, non-fiction books, Tuscany.
- Middlebrow – Inspector Morse, the *Daily Mail*, skiing.
- Popular – TV soaps, tabloid (red top) newspapers, commercial music, Lloret de Mar.

It is through taste that one classifies others and defines them in relation to one's self. For people to successfully engage in practice, they have to work within an identifiable habitus – people feel an obligation to share in the lifestyle, tastes and dispositions of a particular social group. However, at the same time, people have to improvise beyond the rules and conventions of the habitus because, claims Bourdieu, habitus structures but does not determine the choice of participation.

These ideas, in relation to working-class women, have been explored empirically by Beverley Skeggs (1997). The women in Skeggs' study spent a great deal of time generating, accumulating or displaying their cultural capital. Not only were the women's bodies markers of social class and respectability but also their homes, relationships and the clothes they wore. The women's bodies were seen as a setting upon which distinctions could be drawn, protecting the woman from any association of negative value. The way a person chose to dress and wear make-up was used to display their status and demonstrated the women's desire to pass as respectable. Heterosexuality was a central organising principal in this process, as to be seen to be without a man was undesirable and carried a social stigma that increased as the woman grew older.

Anthony Giddens: The Structuration of the Leisure Experience

In the last analysis, people create the structures of everyday life that they believe exercise a constraint upon various aspects of their everyday life. The structures that people create through the processes of structuration also include such durable and impersonal structures as the structure of social classes.

The implication for the constraints paradigm of Giddens' analysis is that individual people may be responsible for creating the very constraints that prevent leisure participation. Giddens (1978) outlined two forms of structuration that the individual human agent draws upon in the process of creating structures:

- Proximate structuration is concerned with the acceptance of authority, the respectability of our occupation and the status of the things we are seen to consume.
- Mediate structuration is concerned with the relationship between parents and children.

Mediate structuration has a significant impact upon leisure choice. Parents socialise their children into what constitutes appropriate leisure participation and introduce them to a range of leisure institutions, not always accessible by the wider society, from tennis clubs and polo clubs to rugby clubs.

There are some leisure activities that we admire; not only do we hold the activities in high regard but also the people who participate in them. Such people are granted a high status because of their choice of leisure activities. This is particularly the case when the leisure activities are ones that we aspire to but feel that we lack the experience, skills, abilities or money to participate in them, or feel that we are not worthy to engage with the other participants. The choice of leisure activities that we aspire to is highly personal, perhaps derived from the unconscious, but motivation for actual and appropriate participation, like all forms of taste that we act upon, may well be formed within parameters initially imposed by parents.

Similarly, there will be some leisure activities that we do not have a high regard for, and even though such activities are well within our financial means, we would never choose to participate in them.

The notions of 'people like us' and 'appropriate for people like us' are constructed by the use of our practical consciousness and are central elements in our notion of self – such notions allow us to differentiate between 'self' and 'other'. Without a conception of self and other, we would not be in a position to find appropriate leisure partners with whom to share activities. Simply stated, the constraints paradigm has no adequate theory of the selection of leisure partners. If leisure activities exist as active pursuits, there must be participants; the nature of the barriers preventing a potential participant from active involvement with 'the other' is not explored within the traditional constraints paradigm. It seems reasonable to assume that some activities are more likely to fulfil our desires than others; however, if we have been socialised into a social network that includes family, friends and leisure partners, then we have an existing set of rules and routines, including a pattern of leisure participation that allows a degree of ontological security. To break with the network of partnerships may generate feelings of insecurity. We choose to participate from a position of existing participation, not from a position of non-participation as the constraints paradigm would have us believe. To reject one form of participation in favour of another is to reject an existing social network and established leisure partners. This can place us in a position of potentially causing offence to people within our existing social network with whom we are close.

Participation does not involve a shift from non-participation to participation, but a re-ordering and re-definition of patterns of participation and choice of partners. Given that most of us have very full lives without great spaces of time empty of commitments, such as personal obligations to the maintenance of family relationships and of self, cleaning, cooking, working and leisure commitments, such re-ordering of time for leisure will involve judging the leisure activity in terms of its ability to satisfy our needs and desires. The rejection of a leisure activity that one is currently engaged in may involve severing the links with leisure partners, or explaining to them that the pattern of leisure that you share with them is no longer satisfying or fulfilling your needs.

In the traditional constraints paradigm, non-participation was assumed to be a condition brought about because the individual was engulfed by external determining factors. Such factors were outside of the control of the individual and prevented the exercise of a free choice over leisure participation. In contrast, it is possible to view non-participation as an active choice in which an individual draws upon their decision-making capabilities and decides that they are unwilling to disrupt an existing pattern of leisure participation and existing leisure partners. The inconvenience of reorganising our lives, or breaking commitments to others, may be seen to outweigh the possible benefits to be gained by changing our pattern of participation.

Leisure participation is both a medium and an outcome of social division. We are socialised into a given social network, which may for example be a social class grouping – we choose to maintain our existing patterns of behaviour and commitments, and by doing so, we reinforce the class-based nature of our leisure participation. At any point, we could choose not to participate, not to maintain our commitments, and to re-order or refocus our leisure activity, but we choose not to. Non-participation is not a reflection of our powerlessness, or our inability to overcome external constraint, but an active choice to maintain our leisure arrangements.

Structuration as a challenge to the traditional constraints paradigm

Giddens' theory of structuration and its application to leisure participation raises a number of serious issues for the traditional constraints paradigm. Firstly, the constraints paradigm assumes, without justification, that non-participation is in opposition to the essential human condition. Secondly, social divisions are under-theorised and assumed to be 'given'. Moreover, social divisions are assumed to determine the nature of leisure participation. This assumption seriously undervalues the role of the human agent in participation. Thirdly, there is an assumption that the absence of constraint will automatically lead to participation. Fourthly, the constraints paradigm has no adequate theory of the selection of leisure partners. If leisure activities exist as active pursuits, there must be participants; the nature of the barriers preventing a potential participant from active involvement with 'the other' is not explored within the traditional constraints paradigm. Fifthly, discussion of participation within the traditional constraints paradigm is from an assumption of non-participation and the role of existing participation as a barrier to future participation is ignored.

What does it mean to be a consumer?
The teenager as an unacceptable *flaneur*

For many young people, the shopping centre or mall is an important leisure space. It provides teenagers with a safe and comfortable space in which they can act in a similar fashion to the *flaneur* described by poet Charles Baudelaire in the 1840s – wandering around the streets, passages and glass-covered arcades, reflecting on the contents of the shop windows. The mall has a magic for teenagers, it is a less restricting space than home and it contains a constant flow of people (who may become new friends), music, noise and lively surroundings where they can mix socially. However, for Bauman (1998), teenagers are often seen as flawed consumers, as they do not have the spending power to legitimately be in the space. Many adults view the presence of groups of young people hanging around in a space for consumption as unacceptable and often menacing. Matthews (2000) has argued that this boundary dispute between teenagers and adults can be understood within a cultural politics of difference and identity. Adults attempt to impose a spatial hegemony on teenagers – the concepts of 'age-related space' and 'out of bounds' are based upon discourses of pollution of the space; asserting a right of presence when challenged by security guards to move on is seen by Matthews (2000) as a cultural politic that challenges the marginality of the teenager in an adult space.

Leisure Participation and Gender
Relations

Traditionally, women were assumed to have a natural inferiority to men. Differences in 'sex' were assumed to be the cause of a range of social inequalities. As a consequence, women had far fewer legal rights, political rights and career opportunities than men. Women appear to face barriers to participation that do not exist for men. There is a body of evidence that suggests that Physical Education in schools can help to reinforce rather than challenge gender stereotypes inside and outside sport. Kay and Jeanes (2008) argue that PE in schools is much less effective at acknowledging the needs of young women than the needs of young men. Kay and Jeanes (2008) are concerned with two issues:

- how gender relations are evident within present-day sport
- how sport influences present-day gender relations through the transmission of patriarchal values and beliefs.

Sport is a particularly powerful medium for the social construction of masculinity; sport is used by men to construct and maintain masculinities. Sport is still considered to be a man's territory. This is a product of the way in which the institutional framework for sport emerged in a way that suited men rather than women. Kay and Jeanes (2008) suggest that three rationales underpin opposition to women's participation:

- the medical rationale, that women are physiologically unsuited to sporting activity and may be damaged by it
- the aesthetic rationale, that women engaging in sport are an unattractive spectacle, and
- the social rationale, that the qualities and behaviours associated with sport are contrary to 'real' femininity.

Traditional ideals of romantic love encourage women to place their heterosexual romantic relationships at the centre of their lives. The impact of 'hegemonic masculinity' in producing the *ideal* version of an ideal woman means that there is great pressure on women to establish heterosexual partnerships and behave in a 'feminine' way. Female bodies are expected to be decorative and passive and therefore not involved in sport.

Leisure and masculinities: the resistance of young women to PE in schools

In her Chapter, '"Boys muscle in where angels fear to tread"' – girls' sub-cultures and physical activities', Sheila Scraton (1995) uses the notion of subculture to explain the resistance of young women to PE in schools.

The influence of biological changes during puberty was less significant than the expectations placed upon young women as to how they should be reacting to physical changes.

Young women's experiences in adolescence centre around the 'culture of femininity'.

Young women are not expected to run around, get dirty or sweat.

Peer group pressure intensifies the culture of femininity – encouraging 'dropping out'.

PE appears to be incompatible with their expected lifestyle.

Team games are associated with masculine values.

(Continued)

(Continued)

'Young, fit, virile men are expected to revel in group camaraderie and team spirit. It is less acceptable for their adolescent sisters.'

Resistance to school uniform by adolescent young women is intensified during PE.

'To many young women the wearing of a standard tee shirt, regulation navy shorts/skirt plus ankle socks is one of the greatest indignities and embarrassments placed on them . . . At a time when fashion, jewellery and make-up are central to their concern with appearance the uniform, asexual PE kit is an anathema.'

There is an expectation that young women should meet the desired body shape.

Those who deviate from the norm face acute embarrassment and often unkind comment.

'Adult women are not expected to expose their bodies and are encouraged to dislike their body shape unless it conforms to the "ideal" feminine stereotype. During adolescence the PE changing room or shower area is an exposed situation where young women's developing bodies are put "on view."'

PE fails to provide 'meaningful experiences' for many young women.

Resistance is related to:

- the development of muscle
- sweat
- communal shower/changing facilities
- the 'childish', asexual PE kit
- low-status activities.

Source: adapted from Scraton (1995)

Questions

- What do you understand by the phrase: the 'culture of femininity'?
- Are team games associated with masculine values?
- Does Sheila Scraton's argument reflect your own experiences of PE for girls?

Patriarchal domination is a political set of arrangements organised around the web of *compulsory* heterosexual relations for the non-economic oppression of women. In her early work, Sylvia Walby (1997) argues that much feminist theorising was seriously flawed because it was large scale and assumed one sole basis upon which patriarchal practice had its foundation or causal base. If one structure of patriarchal relations is challenged and becomes ineffective, another can easily replace it. Patriarchal relations are not simply *given,* they are created by individual people as a *medium* and an *outcome* of the practices that make up their everyday lives, and by doing so, men reinforce these very patriarchal structures. The structures of patriarchy are in constant flux as they are drawn upon by men, reinvented, reinforced and recreated.

Globalisation also directly addresses women as sexual beings, in that women's labour is being sexualised. Ursula Biemann (2002) argues that globalisation is a highly gendered process and that there has been a 'feminisation of migration', in that compared with migrants in previous decades, today a significant number of economic migrants in the world are women. Biemann argues that the processes of globalisation directly address women as sexual beings, in that women's labour is being sexualised. The migration politics of European states, including European Union member states, and North America, directly encourage migrant women into the sex industry. The Swiss government, argues Biemann, will only issue 'cabaret' visas to non-European female migrants that are dependent upon employment contracts with the cabaret sector. Each year, there are 500,000 migrant women recruited into the European entertainment industry, mainly from the former communist countries of Eastern Europe. Biemann argues that although the official policy of the European Union is to combat human trafficking, such migration policies in relation to non-European female migrants allow the sex industry to benefit from a continuing supply of marginalised and economically disadvantaged women.

Walby (2003) argues that civil rights and sexual governance within the European Union ignores marginalised and economically disadvantaged women, particularly if they are said to have chosen to go into sex work. The people who draw up the policies and protocols of the European Union cannot understand why a woman would want to be a sex worker and therefore cannot understand why such women may be in need of employment regulation. For those non-EU female migrants who do not go into the sex industry, the other main avenue of employment is domestic service.

Romantic love as a leisure constraint

When people come together in a romantic relationship as a couple, this will also have an impact upon their leisure participation. Conflict within couples over what are considered to be acceptable leisure activities for the individuals concerned, either as a couple or as individuals, is common. Green et al. (1985) were amongst the first researchers to explore this issue.

Woodward, Green et al.: Romantic love as a leisure constraint

Green, et al. (1985) conducted the first publicly funded survey of female leisure participation. Read the points below and answer the question.

(Continued)

(Continued)

Looking at women's leisure in Sheffield, Green et al. (1985) used a combination of research methods.

The Sheffield study looked at the effect of men on women's leisure at three points in their lives:

- courtship
- co-habitation
- splitting up.

A woman is obliged by the man to move in his social circles with his friends and also to give up seeing some of her old ones.

However, the 'lads night out' on Fridays remains sacrosanct. Men tend to remain in contact with their old friends much more than women do. Sometimes, women in the study responded by having a Friday night out with girlfriends.

Saturday night is for couples to spend time together.

Women see life as a couple as the ideal and expect their leisure to become more restricted as a consequence of coupling.

Co-habitation implies an unequal share of domestic work and childcare – whether married or living together.

Men and women share the view that men are entitled to some independent leisure, but not women.

With kids, joint leisure breaks down.

Women's leisure is more child-centred.

On splitting up, women have an initial loss of confidence, sense of identity and a change in status but overall there is a positive effect on leisure.

The Sheffield study claims to show that women's leisure is constrained by shared social expectations that favour men.

Question

Think about couples you know, or about yourself if you have a partner – how many of the criteria apply to yourself or others?

Does the fact of the first publicly funded survey of female leisure participation reinforce your view that women's leisure is constrained by shared social expectations that favour men?

The feminisation of love

The feminisation of love is significant for an understanding of women's leisure within heterosexual romantic relationships. Men and women have distinct *styles of love*, but it is how women are believed to experience love that has become widely accepted as 'real' love. Women become more skilled at talking about relationships, feelings and personal experiences, and love has become defined in these terms. Women's identity is based upon attachment while men's identity is based upon separation.

What is hegemonic masculinity?

Hegemonic masculinity is an ideal version of masculinity. It is a combination of structural, institutional and ideological power which generates a masculine culture that rewards physically aggressive, competitive, task-focused achievement and inferiorises all forms of femininity.

'Hegemonic masculinity can be defined as the configuration of gender practice which embodies the currently accepted answer to the problem of the legitimacy of patriarchy, which guarantees (or is taken to guarantee) the dominant position of men and the subordination of women' (Connell, 1995: 77).

Leisure is a space where men can reconstruct masculinities.

For Messner (1992), sport is part of boys' establishment of their masculinity by forming boundaries around their identity.

The emphasis changes from participation to winning as the man learns that in order to receive attention he must be successful.

Wearing (1998) argues that sport and leisure help to maintain hegemonic masculinity and play a role in male hegemony whilst at the same time disadvantaging many men.

Before you read on, you might want to reflect upon this point. What evidence can you point to that would support Wearing's argument?

Could *masculinism* be a male response to the success of the feminist movement?

A central concept in the constraint of women's leisure is the notion of the *ethics of care*, a term first used by Gilligan (1982) to describe the ways in which females are socialised into catering for the needs of others at the expense of their own self-fulfilment and happiness. Socialisation encourages women to put the needs of others before their own needs. The ethics of care has been identified as a constraint to women's leisure (Harrington et al., 1992; Henderson and Allen, 1991; Lamond, 1992). Married women, in particular, are made to feel guilty about engaging in leisure experiences of their own choosing. However, in contrast, there is research that points to the positive impact of the *ethics of care* on women's leisure (Henderson et al. 1996).

Leisure and masculinities

'The dominant structures and values of sport came to reflect the fears and needs of a threatened masculinity' (Dunning, 1986: 274).

Rugby was developed to bolster a threatened masculinity.

(Continued)

(Continued)

The institutional framework for sport provided men with a female free space.

In a patriarchal society, men lack the ability to be in touch with and express their emotions (except anger).

It is difficult for men to form strong and stable emotional relationships (Seidler, 1989).

In the twentieth century, work became increasingly less likely to support ideas of masculinity.

Men turned to leisure pursuits to shore up and prove their manhood.

For Kimmel (1996), this process had several elements:

- self-control in sport was seen as character building and against effeminacy
- there was the creation of men-only clubs or fraternities in US universities
- it allowed escape through new forms of literature such as the western
- it helped to maintain masculinity in an increasingly feminised culture.

Questions

- Would you accept or reject the view expressed above that 'in a patriarchal society, men lack the ability to be in touch with and express their emotions (except anger)'? State the reasons for your answer.
- Do men have an *ethics of care* in relation to their children?
- Why then is men's self-control in sport seen as character building and against effeminacy?

Drawing upon the work of Foucault, Connell (1995) attempts to deconstruct the categories of male and female, while in addition, the centralised state maintains a patriarchal society. For Connell, power is a set of social relations that act as a constraint on social practice, including leisure participation. At the core of the power structure of gender, there are four components:

- the hierarchies and workforces of institutionalised violence – military, police, prison
- the hierarchy and labour force of heavy industry – steel and oil companies – and the hierarchy of high technology
- the planning and control machinery of the central state
- the tendency of the traditional working-class environment to stress the importance of toughness and men's association with heavy machinery.

Before you read on, you might want to reflect on whether the categories of male and female are something that we can deconstruct in the way that Connell suggests or whether the categories of male and female are biologically given.

Leisure and the Beauty System

A woman's concern about her body image is often a key factor in her enjoyment of a leisure activity. There is a great deal of research to suggest that concern about a woman's body image can act as a constraint upon participation:

- Drewnoski and Yee (1987) found that the ideal body image for men is one of muscularity and strength.
- However, many researchers have argued that the ideal image for women is primarily one of thinness, for example Martz et al. (1995).
- Cash and Henry (1995) and Dattilo et al. (1994) found that if a woman's body image falls short of what she considers to be societal expectations, this will significantly reduce participation.
- Silverstein et al. (1986) argue that the internalization of thinness was promoted by female images in magazines, films and television, creating a social expectation of thinness.
- Cash et al. (1986) found that it was not simply a matter of overall body shape that affected participation – women were much more judgemental about individual aspects of their body: legs, chest, buttocks and face.

The argument that women are constrained by ideas of beauty was first suggested by Dean MacCannell and Juliet Flower MacCannell (1987) who developed their ideas into a systematic critique of what they termed *the beauty system*. The beauty system polices all aspects of a woman's appearance:

- body size and weight
- head and body hair texture, colour and visibility.

MacCannell and Flower MacCannell view one of the central themes of the beauty system as that every flaw in a woman's body detracts from the ideal of beauty, but can be corrected by painstaking observance of a beauty discipline.

Naomi Wolf (1990) argues that even though the women's movement has had significant victories in a range of areas of social life through the 1970s and 1980s, women do not feel as free as they should do given the victories they have had. The beauty system is used effectively to prevent full female liberation, preventing women from exercising their hard-won rights and generating low self-esteem. Women are made to feel concerns about such things as body shape, hair and other aspects of their physical appearance. Wolf argues that it is no accident that so many women, including many potentially powerful women, feel this way. The beauty myth is a key element in a powerful backlash against feminism. Ideas about what constitutes female beauty are used as political weapons to covertly control women, reinforcing the glass ceiling, excluding women from power. Women are made to feel a permanent sense of insecurity over becoming fat and ugly.

However, Wolf's argument about who controls the beauty myth is unclear. She seems to suggest that it is women who are to blame for the maintenance of the beauty myth.

Beauty therapy is linked to the wider social transformations that Beck, et al. (1994) have described as *reflexive modernisation*. For Black (2002), the salon is a space in which women gather the resources to present an 'appropriate' gendered performance as a woman. Pampering, grooming and corrective treatments are used by women who visit the salon to underpin their coping strategies in the workplace. Women in the workplace have to be feminine but not over-feminine, sexual but not over-sexual – there needs to be an appropriate level of feminisation and normality.

Drawing upon Erving Goffman's (1963) dramaturgical model, Tseelon (1995) argues that women have a lower body image than men; they are more likely to perceive themselves to be heavier than they are and are more concerned about their bodily attractiveness than men are about their bodies. In addition, women have a lower body satisfaction than men and are more dissatisfied with some aspect of their appearance – and this includes not only mature women but children as young as six years of age. For all people, irrespective of whether they are men or women, a low body image has a significant detrimental effect upon psychological health, romantic relationships and sexuality.

A number of feminist writers have argued that images of beauty directly link gender and sexuality with class. In Skeggs' (1997) study of female adult students returning to study, the women were unable or unwilling to identify themselves within a given class position or class category. Class was something imposed upon women, something *'they* work out', rather than something *she* as a woman lives through. In the study, Skeggs describes women being ascribed to a given class position or class category as the *emotional politics of class*. The label 'working class' was to be avoided by the women in Skeggs' study because the label damaged a woman's claim to be caring, respectable and responsible. When applied to women in Skeggs' study, the label of working class was used to signify a woman that is dirty, dangerous and without value. The women in Skeggs' study spent a great deal of time generating, accumulating or displaying their cultural capital. Not only were the women's bodies markers of social class and respectability but also their homes, relationships and the clothes they wore.

Also drawing upon Erving Goffman's dramaturgical model, James (2000) argues that a girl's decision to swim is dependent upon two factors:

- Her *situational body image* – her overall body image, influenced by media representations, peer pressure, etc.
- Her *desire to swim* – influenced by her perception of the potential for embarrassment or ridicule in front of the audience balanced by her desire to be included in the activity. James (2000) argues that potential embarrassment from the girl's presentation of self was the biggest constraint on participation. Girls were conscious of the 'critical gaze' of others when they were at the pool.

In her later study of girls' bedrooms as a leisure space, James expands upon these arguments – *situational body image* is a central element of a girl's overall body image defined in relation to a particular audience and place and perceived as having a high potential for ridicule. The bedroom provided shelter from potentially critical audiences, notably boys, and provided a space where girls could express emotions that they believe would be ridiculed in a public space. In addition, because girls also had control over access to their bedrooms, they could choose to be alone or to invite friends or family members into the space or the space could be used to evade demanding parents. James also found that other constraining factors over girls' leisure that made the bedroom an appealing leisure space included:

- physical factors, such as the need for security, the desire for exercise out of the gaze of others, the fear of injury
- control factors – girls had a need to control their own space and have an area in which they were free from verbal abuse.

The Cancer Experience and Women's Leisure

Shannon (1997) argues that cancer as an illness has serious physical and social psychological impacts for women that range from the disruption of family life and loss of friendships to the emergence of significant new constraints on leisure activities. Shannon (1997) examines the impact of cancer on two leisure constraints: body image and ethics of care. There is great pressure on both women and men to live up to a societal body image. The ideal for men is rooted in the values of muscularity and strength. In contrast, for women, the image is rooted in the values of youth and thinness. Both men and women internalise these ideals as central to their ideal body image. The frequent exposure to these images via the mass media reinforces this internalisation. However, the gap between fantasy and reality is often real and measurable. Most real bodies do not match the societal body ideal. Many leisure activities believed to be appropriate for women more often than not emphasise aesthetics and body shape. The female body becomes an object subject to the male gaze. In addition, further research by Cash et al. (1986) found that women are much more likely to focus on the aspects of their body which are objectified such as legs, buttocks, face and chest; this is unlike men who will focus on the dynamic aspects of the body as a functioning physical carrier of the self. In other words, for men, what is most important are the physical aspects of the body and whether it is seen to work more effectively than other men's bodies. Falling short of the ideal body image may constrain leisure participation (Shaw, 1994) and significantly reduce the enjoyment of participation if the barrier can be overcome (Frederick and Shaw, 1995). Cancer can lead directly to body image anxiety, and can threaten the body image of women who previously had a very positive body image. Chemotherapy can result in hair loss and swelling to the face and other parts of the body. Mastectomy, the loss of a breast, can significantly reduce positive body image.

As we saw above, Gilligan (1982) first introduced the concept of women possessing an *ethic of care* – this is the sense of responsibility and commitment to others, for example women are often cast in the role of primary caregiver within the family. Moreover, this role often forms a central element of the woman's identity as wife and mother. Gilligan argues that the ethic develops via the process of socialisation. Henderson et al. (1996) argue that the *ethic of care* is a constraint to leisure, particularly for married women.

Women with cancer often have difficulty placing the needs of their family over their own needs. Recovery may require a much greater focus on the needs of the self. In addition, the physically demanding nature of the bodily changes that women can experience during cancer often leaves women with no time or energy for leisure.

The Inverted Male Gaze

Patterson and Elliott (2002) argue that most research assumes that advertising involves a linear communication process in which audiences come to understand and accept messages uniformly and uncritically. Male bodies depicted in magazine advertising are more likely to be *hypermasculine;* that is, strong, muscular and hard. Such male bodies are not representative of the male population. As male bodies become objects for display, subject to the male gaze, how are men to consume such advertisements?

Most advertising campaigns invoke gender identity, the body and its visual representation, as such advertising often draws upon conceptions of masculinity and helps to reinforce masculinity. Traditionally, masculinity was understood as opposed to and in relation to femininity. Advertising impacts directly on the lived experience of men, and its discourse reflects and creates social norms, codifies consumer images and can be particularly useful as sites of identity formation. What will be seen as sexy, attractive and desired by others is related to advertising – the male gaze has opened up new possibilities for cultural conceptions of gender, being, desire and male identities.

Schroeder and Zwick (2004) analyse the cultural construction of masculinity by reference to the way in which the male body is visually represented in advertising. Fashionable images of the male body in advertising articulate a number of contradictory conceptions of masculine identity that are entangled with the conception of hegemonic masculinity.

Representations do not simply articulate masculinity, rather advertising produces and manipulates social signifiers that individuals use to find appropriate symbolic value.

Organised team sports are also a site for the construction of masculinity. Young and White (2000) investigate the role of hegemonic masculinity in the creation of sports injuries and other physical risks. In short, they argue that there is a clear connection between aggression and the processes of masculinisation. It is a key element in demonstrating one's masculinity that men exhibit physically risky and aggressive behaviours in a sporting context. Such shows of aggression are one element of the reflexivity that sport brings to men's lives.

Activity

'When the gaze is turned on itself, men are more likely to move through a range of responses such as rejection, identification and desire' (Patterson and Elliott, 2002: 241).

Questions

Has there been an increasing feminisation of masculinities, as Patterson and Elliott (2002) suggest, or does masculinity remain a fundamental social, psychological and cultural category? Outline the reasons for your answer.

Richard Dyer (1982) found that representations of men as sex objects, or celebrities, usually show men looking off to one side or up, but not directly into the camera lens. What do you think is the significance of this finding?

Sexuality, Leisure and Masculinities

Bodies are central to defining gender identities. The inversion of the male gaze presents problems for the feminist argument in that the gaze is essentially male and heterosexual.

The politics of the 'gay space'

The issue of who can use and consume within a recognised *gay space* has been taken up by Beverley Skeggs (Binnie and Skeggs, 2004; Moran et al., 2002). In 2002, straight people were seen to pose a threat to the gay space that constitutes the gay village in Manchester. Straight people are viewed as violent and restrict the free movement of gay individuals wishing to gain access to the space. A sexual politics of commodified space has developed, around the issues of entry policy and dress codes. The area, because it is marketed as a cosmopolitan spectacle, makes the space attractive to straight people whose presence dilutes the very thing that makes the space special. A central issue becomes a matter of access and knowledge: who should use the space, and who should be excluded from consumption.

Before reading on, reflect upon the role of space and the control of leisure space.

Sexual practices are regulated by nation states. The academic study of sexuality is concerned with understanding the major discourses surrounding sex, sexuality, sexual acts, identities and relationships. Scientific disciplines and state regulatory controls form a 'bio-politics of the population' (Foucault, 1990: 139).

Drawing upon Foucault's work into penal reform and sexuality, Pronger (2000) argues that homosexuality and sport are socially constructed regulatory systems that are used to police bodies and their engagement with desire. Although bodily interactions between players are prohibited from becoming openly homoerotic, there are homoerotic undercurrents in sport, argues Pronger, in that irrespective of the sexual identity of the participants, the culture of sport helps to reproduce ideas of orthodox heterosexual masculinity in mainstream men's and boy's sporting activities.

Rowe et al. (2000) ask: what does it mean to be a man? The answer is blunt: 'to be a man is "not to be gay"'. Homosexuality does not easily co-exist with sporting excellence in the minds of many men or women. The hegemonic masculinity that underpins this perception enhances the significance of gender in sports participation, subordinates women, subordinates non-aggressive forms of masculinity and helps to legitimise homophobia.

However, a critique of Foucault's work has revolved around the issue of whether Foucault had overstated the extent to which people could be 'subjected', leaving them little scope for resistance. With the opening of borders, especially within the European Union and to a significant degree globally, together with the internet allowing the cross-border transmission on explicit materials, there are fewer effective state restrictions on sexuality. Locations have become specific spaces for forms of sexual activity and are often marketed to the world in these terms – Amsterdam is known for its safer and regulated heterosexual scene and gay club scene; Hamburg has its sex shows and bar culture; Krakow contains the EU's only lesbian sauna; the Greek island of Mykonos has its gay resorts.

It is important not to assume that all lesbian and gay men experience the world in the same way. Understanding the notion of 'space' has a central role to play in the research on leisure and sexuality. Pritchard et al.'s (2002) research into Manchester's 'gay' village attempted to identify the socio-cultural processes that shape this particular homosexual leisure space, the tensions between gay men and lesbians, straight men and the way in which they draw upon a heterosexual stare when coming into contact with lesbians within a public space. All of these factors affect the socio-cultural construction of gay space and the powerful dynamics that underpin the emotional geography of the village, specifically in relation to the experiences of lesbians. Gay and lesbian spaces are assumed to be empowering places, providing a sense of both community and territory: 'sites of cultural resistance with enormous symbolic meaning' (Myslik, 1996: 167). However, such places are not only subject to heterosexual attack, either via violence or by intrusion from 'straights' that lead to a 'degaying' of the space, but also a reduction in the strength of the feelings of community as the space becomes another leisure venue for the general population. Pritchard et al. (2002) argue that a male gay presence, with its emphasis on power and control, dominates the gay space and threatens lesbian space.

Similar themes, such as escaping from the dominant heterosexual milieu, the need for safety, the need to feel comfortable with like-minded people, in specifically gay spaces, also underpin the tourism choices of lesbians and gay men. In a series of interviews with lesbians and gay men, Pritchard et al. (2000) argue that a number of nation states have attempted to exclude lesbians and gay men from leisure spaces. In 1998, a Norwegian cruise liner carrying 900 gay men was refused permission to dock in the Cayman Islands on the grounds that the men were unlikely to maintain standards of behaviour that the Cayman Islands government expected of its visitors.

There have also been instances of lesbians on cruise ships docking in the Bahamas, being harassed by protesters chanting and waving placards reading 'No gay ships'.

. Amongst those interviewed by Pritchard et al. (2000), issues in relation to sexuality did influence a number of choices in relation to holidays – destinations, packages, booking methods and accommodation. Motivations related to sexuality included the need to:

- seek safety in gay spaces
- be amongst like-minded individuals
- be oneself
- be accepted
- escape from heterosexism
- be openly affectionate with one's partner
- assert one's cultural power
- escape those forces which attempt to control and constrain behaviour and identity.

Pritchard et al. suggest that gay space reinforces the feeling of community and provides a sense of order and power.

The question then is why lesbian women and gay men want a leisure space free from the gaze of straights. According to Lofland (1985), people in the urban environment commonly attempt to colonise public space in an effort to maximise contact with individuals with whom they share known characteristics: social, cultural and physical. Such regular contact reduces the uncertainty of the urban environment by reducing contact with potentially hostile outsiders.

Lesbian leisure

Lesbian households with children, either via donor insemination, adoption or fostering, can be variously named: the reinvented family, dual-orientation households, lesbian-led families, planned lesbian mother families, etc. Patterson (1992) found that lesbian and gay parents and their children are a diverse group. However, they face the common prejudicial assumption about their parenting. The assumption by the wider straight community appears to be that development of the child's sexual identity may be impaired by having lesbian or gay parents, in that children themselves are more likely to become gay or lesbian, or may experience difficulties in social relationships, be stigmatised and teased.

Building upon her earlier research, Bialeschki (1999) investigated the leisure patterns of lesbian mothers with dependent children from a feminist cultural studies perspective; that challenges the traditional heterosexual family and essentialist notions of difference that accepted heterosexual hegemony of the dominant culture. Bialeschki argues that the research on family leisure was written from a traditional heterosexual view that ignored the leisure experiences of lesbian families and the diversity of family structures.

Using a range of in-depth, open-ended, semi-structured interviews, Bialeschki attempted to identify the ways that lesbian mothers attach meaning to their everyday lived experiences. The women in the study often experienced conflict between their chosen lifestyle and their choice to be parents. The women believed that people from the straight world refused to accept their household arrangements as a legitimate family, or that the women themselves had real parenting responsibilities. However, the women also experienced problems having social leisure experiences as a family with lesbian friends who did not have children:

- Lesbian families were 'outsiders' to both the lesbian and heterosexual communities – for example, the women described the difficulties they experienced attending family social events at work. In contrast, other lesbians often viewed the women as 'selling out' to heterosexual culture.
- Leisure was used by the women to provide entry into both the lesbian and straight communities.
- Leisure was also used to confirm the identity of the family as a *family*, helping to provide a sense of autonomy and identity.

In her earlier research, Bialeschki found that most of the research into patterns of family leisure had focused on a narrow range of traditional heterosexual family structures. A number of feminist researchers have argued that women neglect their own leisure preferences because of the duty of care that the wife–mother role imposes upon women within patriarchal societies. Bialeschki and Pearce (1997) investigated the meaning and importance of leisure within the non-traditional family structure of the lesbian couple with children. It would be reasonable to expect that lesbian couples would be free of 'hegemonic masculinity' and would have to negotiate all aspects of their partnered roles. Lesbian families with children provided the opportunity to investigate families that were not built upon heterosexual power relations.

Leisure is seen by Bialeschki as part of a strategy used by lesbian parents to establish a degree of independence from or resistance to hegemonic demands found in the wider culture. Leisure experiences were also used by lesbian parents to construct a context for the family that operated both inside and outside of both the heterosexual and lesbian cultures. Additionally, leisure activities became a form of cultural resistance, providing a space for social interaction that allowed the lesbian parents to construct their own sense of identity and autonomy as a family.

In addition to the traditional heterosexual family, lesbian and gay families have additional difficulties:

- Lesbian families face social rejection and social vulnerability.
- Their family relationships lack social status – they are not regarded as 'real' families, because of the absence of gender differences between the couple.
- The media only ever depict images of the normal heterosexual family, giving heterosexual families a degree of social validation and excluding lesbian families from the wider society.
- Lesbian families also face laws against homosexuality.

Drawing upon data gathered from qualitative interviews conducted with nine lesbian couples with dependent children, Bialeschki and Pearce (1997) asked the women to describe how they allocated household and childcare responsibilities. They found that the women negotiated their roles and responsibilities on the basis of their personal interests and in terms of meeting household and childcare responsibilities. The negotiation of responsibilities has a direct implication for leisure participation.

Partners did not have a clearly defined division of domestic labour or assigned task responsibility. Rather, completion of household tasks was based on likes and dislikes, with mutually disliked tasks often performed on a rota. Most couples worked out schedules that were agreed to be fair and balanced. The issue of 'who had time' underpinned the women's understanding that whoever had the time would take responsibility for completing the task. In a number of cases investigated, the women decided to purchase the services of someone to help with domestic work and the reasons given were for family members to have more opportunities for leisure.

When asked about forms of leisure, the women marked out their leisure time into three separate contexts:

- Leisure for self – the need to have time and space, free from obligation, to do whatever the woman chose as her way to relax. Such personal leisure time was assumed to help maintain a woman's happiness.
- Leisure for the couple – the women placed a great deal of significance on making time to spend together as a couple, and on valuing their partner's desire for leisure.
- Leisure for the family – family interaction in and around leisure activities was very important to the lesbian mothers in the survey. These shared experiences often served as a way to bond family members, and helped to strengthen the lesbian couples' feeling of themselves as a family. The perception of the family group as a 'family' in the wider society was also enhanced by leisure participation as a family group.

Overall, leisure participation helped lesbian families in overcoming the invisibilities and prejudices that exist.

Feminist critique of leisure theory

When you have finished reading this book, you might want to return to this chapter and reflect upon the points below:

Sheila Scraton (1992) has observed that:

- For the future, it is important that critical work in physical education is maintained and extended to ensure that not only girls and young women, but also boys and young men, receive a physical education that is sensitive to, aware of and prepared to challenge gender inequalities.
- Leisure theory developed from a male perspective, thus feminism explains both the way the theory has developed and suggests its inadequacies.
- Leisure theory and research have largely ignored or underplayed the experience of women.
- Most leisure theory is written by men, and for women.
- Research on the connection of paid work to leisure is primarily interested in men's work and only takes into account women in the context of family.
- The male experience also dominates research into the relationship between unemployment and leisure.
- The definitions of leisure, common within textbooks, feature ideas of relaxation and recuperation from work that seem to have in mind paid male work.
- Most theoretical approaches within the field of Leisure Studies look at gender as just another variable, alongside age, class and ethnic background.

Question

Assess each of the above points in turn. Would you accept or reject each of the points made? State your reasons for the answers given.

Conclusion

In order to explain the ordered nature of people's leisure choices, a number of constraint models have been developed, all of which assume that *constraint* should be viewed in negative terms as something restricting or limiting leisure participation. The nature of constraint within these models is very varied from negative body image to issues about the status of social divisions as *determining factors* in leisure participation.

Drawing upon the work of Anthony Giddens (1975), it is possible to talk about the structuration of the leisure experience – parents socialise their children into appropriate forms of participation. Often, parental actions are an attempt to use leisure participation to enhance the child's social status. We have seen again in this chapter that women appear to face barriers to participation that do not exist for men and that even romantic love can be seen as a leisure constraint. The feminisation of love is significant for an understanding of women's leisure within heterosexual romantic relationships, especially as leisure is often used as a space for men to reconstruct masculinities. Sexuality can act as a constraint on social practice, including leisure participation, and we saw that lesbian families face social rejection and social vulnerability. However, there was evidence to suggest that leisure participation helped lesbian families in overcoming the invisibilities and prejudices that exist.

References

Bauman, Z. (1998) *Globalization: The Human Consequences*. Cambridge: Polity Press.

Beck, U., Giddens, A. and Lash, S. (1994) *Reflexive Modernization: Politics, Tradition and Aesthetics in the Modern Social Order*. Cambridge: Polity.

Becker, H.S. (1960) 'Notes on the concept of commitment', *The American Journal of Sociology*, 66 (1): 32–40.

Bialeschki, M.D. (1999) 'Physical activity for women. What park and recreation departments can do', *Journal of Physical Education, Recreation & Dance*, 70 (3): 36–9.

Bialeschki, M.D. and Pearce, K.D. (1997) '"I don't want a lifestyle – I want a life": the effect of ...', *Journal of Leisure Research*, 29 (1): 113–32.

Biemann, U. (2002) *Been There and Back to Nowhere: Gender in Transnational Space*. London: Routledge.

Binnie, J. and Skeggs, B. (2004) 'Cosmopolitan knowledge and the production and consumption of sexualized space: Manchester's gay village', *Sociological Review*, 52 (1): 39–62.

Black, P. (2002) 'Ordinary people come through here: locating the beauty salon in women's lives', *Feminist Review*, 71 (1): 2–17.

Bourdieu, P. (1998) *Practical Reason: On the Theory of Action*. Palo Alto, CA: Stanford University Press.

Buchanan, T. and Allen, R.L. (1985) 'Barriers to recreation participation in later life cycle stages', *Therapeutic Recreation Journal (TRJ)*, 19 (3): 39–50.

Burch, W. (1969) 'Social circles of leisure: competing explanations', *Journal of Leisure Research*, 1 (1): 125–47.

Cash, T.F. and Henry, P.E. (1995) 'Women's body images: the results of a national survey in the USA', *Sex Roles*, 33 (1/2): 19–28.

Cash, T.F., Winstead, B.A. and Janda, L.H. (1986) 'The great American shapeup: body image survey report', *Psychology Today*, April, 30–7.

Connell, R.W. (1995) *Masculinities*. London: Allen & Unwin.

Crawford, D., Jackson, E. and Godbey, G. (1991) 'A hierarchical model of leisure constraints', *Leisure Sciences*, 9: 119–27.

Dattilo, J., Dattilo, A.M., Samdahl, D.M. and Kleiber, D. (1994). 'Leisure outcomes and self-esteem in women with low incomes who are overweight,' *Journal of Leisure Research*, 26 (1): 23–38.

Drewnoski, A. and Yee, D.K. (1987) 'Men and body image: are males satisfied with their body weight?', *Psychosomatic Medicine*, 49: 626–34.

Dunning, E., (1986) 'Sport as a male preserve: Notes on the social sources of masculinity and its transformations', in N. Elias and E. Dunning (eds), *Quest for Excitement: Sport and Leisure in the Civilizing Process*. Oxford: Blackwell.

Dyer, R. (1982) 'Don't look now', *Screen*, 23: 61–73.

Foucault (1990) *The History of Sexuality vol 1. An Introduction*, translated by R. Hurley. Harmondsworth: Penguin.

Frederick, C.J. and Shaw, S.M. (1995) 'Body image as a leisure constraint: examining the experience of aerobic exercise classes for young women', *Leisure Sciences*, 17 (1): 57–73.

Giddens, A. (1975) *The Class Structure of the Advanced Societies*. New York: Harper & Row.

Giddens, A. (1978) *Studies in Social and Political Theory*. London: Hutchinson.

Gilligan, C. (1982) *In a Different Voice*. Cambridge, MA: Harvard University Press.

Goffman, E. (1963) *Stigma*. Englewood Cliffs, NJ: Prentice Hall.

Green, E., Hebron, S. and Woodward, D. (1985) 'A woman's work . . . is never done', *Sport and Leisure*, July/August: 36–8.

Gronow, J. (1997) *The Sociology of Taste*. London: Routledge.

Gruneau, R. (1984) 'Commercialism and the modern Olympics', in A. Tomlinson and G. Whannel (eds), *'Five-ring Circus: Money, Power and Politics at the Olympic Games'*. London: Pluto Press. pp. 1–15.

Harrington, M., Dawson, D. and Bolla, P. (1992) 'Objective and subjective constraints on women's enjoyment of leisure', *Society and Leisure*, 15 (1): 203–22.

Henderson, K.A. and Allen, K.R. (1991) 'The ethic of care: leisure possibilities and constraints for women', *Society and Leisure*, 14 (1): 97–113.

Henderson, K.A., Bialeschki, M.D., Shaw, S.M. and Freysinger, V.J. (1996) *Both Gains and Gaps: Feminist Perspectives on Women's Leisure*. University Park, PA: Venture Publishing.

Jackson, E.L. (1988) 'Leisure constraints: a survey of past research', *Leisure Sciences*, 10: 203–15.

Jackson, E. (1990) 'Recent developments in leisure constraints research', in B. Smale (ed.), *Leisure Challenges: Bringing People Resources and Policy into Play*. Proceedings of the Sixth Canadian Congress on Leisure Research. Toronto: Ontario Research Council on Leisure. pp. 341–4.

Jackson, E.L., and Searle, M.S. (1985) 'Recreation non-participation and barriers to participation: concepts and models', *Loisir et Societé*, 8: 693–707.

James, K. (2000) '"You can feel them looking at you": The experiences of adolescent girls at swimming pools', *Journal of Leisure and Recreation,* 32 (2): 262–80.

Johnson, M. (1991) 'Commitment to personal relationships', *Advances in Personal Relationships,* 3: 117–43.

Kay, T., and Jackson, G. (1991) 'Leisure despite constraint: the impact of leisure constraints on leisure participation', *Journal of Leisure Research,* 23: 301–13.

Kay, T. and Jeanes, R. (2008) 'Women, sport and gender inequality', in B. Houlihan (ed.), *Sport and Society,* 2nd edition. London: Sage.

Kimmel, M. (1996) 'Masculinity as homophobia: fear, shame and silence in the construction of gender identity.' Conference paper presented at The Construction of Caribbean Masculinity: Towards a Research Agenda Conference, University of the West Indies, Trinidad, January.

Kyle, G. and Chick, G. (2002) 'The social nature of leisure involvement', *Journal of Leisure Research,* 34 (4): 426–48.

Lamond, C.C. (1992) 'Constrained by an ethic of care? An exploration of the interactions between work, family, and leisure in the everyday lives of female staff registered nurses'. Unpublished master's thesis, University of Waterloo, Waterloo, Ontario.

Lofland, L.H. (1985) *A World of Strangers*. Prospect Heights, IL: Waveland Press.

MacCannell, D. and Flower MacCannell, J. (1987) 'The beauty system', in N. Armstrong and L. Tennenhouse (eds), *The Ideology of Conduct: Essays on Literature and the History of Sexuality*. London: Methuen. pp. 206–38.

Martz, D.M., Handly, K.B. and Eisler, R.M. (1995) 'The relationship between feminine gender role stress, body image, and eating disorders', *Psychology of Women Quarterly*, 19 (10): 493–508.

Marx, K. (1867) *Capital: Critique of Political Economy*. Harmondsworth: Penguin.

Matthews, N. (2000) *Comic Politics: Gender in Hollywood Comedy after the New Right*. Manchester: Manchester University Press.

Messner, M. (1992) *Power at Play*. Boston, MA: Beacon Press.

Moran, L.J., Skeggs, B., Tyrer, P. and Corteen, K. (2002) *Sexuality and the Politics of Violence and Safety*. London: Routledge.

Myslik, W.D. (1996) 'Renegotiating the social/sexual identities of place: gay communities as safe havens or sites of resistance', in N. Duncan (ed.), *Bodyspace: Destabilizing Geographies of Gender and Sexuality*. London: Routledge. pp. 156–69.

Patterson, C.J. (1992) 'Children of lesbian and gay parents', *Child Development*, 63 (5): 1025–42.

Patterson, M. and Elliott, R. (2002) 'Negotiating masculinities: advertising and the inversion of the male gaze', *Consumption, Markets and Culture*, 5 (3): 231–46.

Pritchard, A., Morgan, N.J., Sedgley, D., Kahn, E. and Jenkins, A. (2000) 'Sexuality and holiday choices: conversations with gay and lesbian tourists', *Leisure Studies*, 19: 267–82.

Pritchard, A., Morgan, N. and Sedgley, D. (2002) 'In search of lesbian space? The experience of Manchester's gay village', *Leisure Studies*, 21: 105–23.

Pronger, B. (2000) 'Homosexuality and sport: who's winning?', in J. Mckay, M.A. Messner and D. Sabo (eds), *Masculinities, Gender Relations and Sport*. London: Sage.

Raymore, L.A. (2002) 'Facilitators to leisure', *Journal of Leisure Research*, 34 (1): 37–51.

Rowe, D., McKay, J. and Miller, T. (2000) 'Panic sport and the racialized masculine body' in J. McKay, M.A. Messner and D. Sabo (eds), *Masculinities, Gender Relations and Sport*. London: Sage.

Samdahl, D.M. and Jekubovich, N.J. (1997) 'A critique of leisure constraints: comparative analyses and understandings', *Journal of Leisure Research*, 29 (4): 430–52.

Schroeder, J.E. and Zwick, D. (2004) 'Mirrors of masculinity: representation and identity in advertising images', *Consumption, Markets and Culture*, 7 (1): 21–52.

Scraton, S. (1992) *Shaping up to Womanhood: Gender and Girls' Physical Education*. Milton Keynes: Open University Press.

Scraton, S. (1995) '"Boys muscle in where angels fear to tread" – girls' subcultures and physical activities' in C. Critcher, P. Bramham and A. Tomlinson (1995) *Sociology of Leisure: A Reader*. London: E. & F. N. Spon.

Searle, M.S. and Jackson, E.L. (1985a) 'Socioeconomic variations in perceived barriers to recreation participation among would-be participants', *Leisure Sciences*, 7: 227–49.

Searle, M.S. and Jackson, E.L. (1985b) 'Recreation non-participation and barriers to participation: considerations for the management of recreation delivery systems', *Journal of Park and Recreation Administration*, 3: 23–35.

Seidler, V. (1989) *Rediscovering Masculinity: Reason, Language and Sexuality*. London: Routledge.

Shannon, C. (1997) 'The impact of a cancer experience on women's leisure: an examination of body image and ethic of care as constraints to leisure', *Journal of Leisurability*, 24 (2): 1–19.

Shaw, S.M. (1994) 'Gender, leisure, and constraint: towards a framework for the analysis of women's leisure', *Journal of Leisure Research*, 26 (1): 8–22.

Shaw, S., Bonen, A. and McCabe, J. (1991) 'Do more constraints mean less leisure? Examining the relationship between constraints and participation', *Journal of Leisure Research*, 23: 286–300.

Silverstein, B., Perdue, L., Peterson, B. and Kelly, E. (1986) 'The role of mass media in promoting a thin standard of bodily attractiveness for women', *Sex Roles*, 14 (9/10): 519–32.

Skeggs, B. (1997) *Formations of Class and Gender*. London: Sage.

Tseelon, E. (1995) *The Masque of Femininity*. Thousand Oaks, CA: Sage.

Walby, S. (1997) *Gender Transformations*. London: Routledge.

Walby, S. (2003) 'Gender and the new economy: regulation or deregulation?'. Paper presented to ESRC seminar 'Work, life and time in the new economy', LSE, October 2002.

Wearing, B. (1997) *Leisure and Feminist Theory*. London: Sage.

Wolf, N. (1990) *The Beauty Myth*. London: Chatto & Windus.

Young, K. and White, P. (2000) 'Researching sports injury: reconstructing dangerous masculinities', in J. McKay M.A. Messner and D. Sabo (eds), *Masculinities, Gender Relations and Sport*. London: Sage.

4

PARTICIPATION AND CONSTRAINT – ETHNICITY, DISABILITY AND AGE

By the end of this chapter, you should:

- be familiar with a number of social theories and how they have been applied within a leisure context
- have an understanding of the nature of leisure constraint developed within these social theories
- have a critical understanding of the barriers to leisure participation
- understand the nature of social division
- comprehend and question the role of race, age and disability as barriers to leisure participation
- have a critical understanding of the theory and research in the area.

Introduction

In this chapter, we shall look at the nature of race, ethnicity, disability and age in relation to leisure constraint. We shall explore the idea that the perception of these social divisions has shaped the opportunities for leisure – in other words, that society generates forms of discrimination and exclusion that children, old people and disabled people have to cope with; all of these groups are in a position where other people are attempting to control their leisure activities on the grounds that they are incapable and dependent. People's leisure motivations are not always rational, and this has been used to exclude disabled people from a wide range of leisure settings and activities that people who are not seen to be disabled do not face.

The central concept in research in the leisure activities of ethnic minorities, children, older people and people with disabilities is *essentiality*. There are leisure activities that are believed to be appropriate, by nature, for 'those kinds of people'. A range of activist groups have pointed to these imposed forms of differential leisure participation and, as such, access to leisure has become a highly politicised area, based upon discourses of what constitutes reasonable and acceptable behaviour for identified groups of people: ethnic minorities, lesbians, gay men, people with learning difficulties, disabled people and children.

Racial identity is the degree to which a person identifies with a racial group. In other words, a central element of a racial identity is feelings of commonality and affinity that one has with other people within the same racial group. Racial identity can be shaped by both positive and/or negative factors. Writing from a Marxian perspective, Cox (1945) suggested that racial prejudice was generated by the bourgeoisie, although Cox has difficulty explaining racism amongst working-class people. In contrast, Weberian approaches to the study of race and ethnicity attempt to locate race and ethnicity within the context of Weber's theory of stratification.

Cruz-Janzen (2003) argues that it is commonly assumed that *race* is a biologically determined factor, based upon the physically determined differences between people and based on factors that are outside of their control, such as genetics and heredity. However, before the colonial expansion by European powers, informed opinion within Europe was that all humans were of one race and species. The ranking of people by skin colour, mental ability and moral qualities was simply a justification for their harsh treatment.

As St Louis (2002) makes clear, we have been aware for a long time that *race* has no real biological foundation and is socially constructed through discourse, which acts to *racialise* different groups.

Although race may no longer be regarded as a biological fact, it is still a social fact. People are still very keen to identify differences between themselves and the Other. According to Alexander and Alleyne (2002), race is still a primary signifier for exclusionary practices. Racial and ethnic difference and ethnicity are conceptual devices concerned with defining individuals as types and drawing borders to exclude, legislate and police citizens on grounds of their Otherness.

For Charlie Husband (1974), racism is built into the culture of Western societies. Communication between people is only possible if they share common frameworks of interpretation, if they share the same meanings for the same symbols. For Husband, this framework of interpretation is a structure of shared mental categories that allow us to make sense of the world. When we think about 'coloured' people, the common framework is built upon the colonial past that makes all white people have a predisposition to accept unfavourable images and beliefs of black people. In simple terms, all white people are racist because they are born and brought up within a racist culture. White people have to make a conscious effort to break away from the common culture to be non-racist.

Racialisation is a concept that attempts to decentre the idea of an essential notion of race, the idea that people have a given and identifiable biological component that defines the *nature* of the person. Miles separates the concept of 'race' from the 'ideas' of 'race' which form a cultural resource that people can draw upon to maintain social divisions. Bolaffi et al. (2003) explain that racialisation assumes that 'race' is socially constructed and is used to refer to any situation to which racial meanings are attached. If individuals are looking at events from the perspective of race, assuming that race is a significant factor in a situation, then they are involved in a process of racialisation. The arbitrary nature of the processes of signification can be seen by the fact that only certain physical characteristics, notably skin colour, are used to signify or define race, and skin colour is treated as a given and natural division of the world's population. Skin colour is only a fraction of the totality of human physiological variation. For Miles (1980), 'races' are socially imagined or socially constructed rather than biological realities.

Despite its arbitrary nature, the term 'race' is widely used in everyday life – newspapers run features about institutionalised racism, organisations have policies to combat racism and promote equality of opportunity, and the term is well established within legislation.

Postmodernism and its theoretical aversion to essentialism, brings with it a change in how we view the Other. Stuart Hall (1992) developed the concept of 'new ethnicities' to challenge the essentialist reductionism of race. He argues that we should move away from the conceptual autonomy of race, end the essential black subject and dismantle the simple distinction of white oppressor/ black oppressed. Race becomes a linguistic categorisation, constituted outside of a pre-social biologically determined 'nature'.

Fanon argues that *blackness* and *whiteness* are mutually reinforcing cultural categories; when we construct the Other, we also construct ourselves. 'The negro' is a socially constructed identity that the white colonisers – the dominant strangers – managed to successfully essentialise as a dominant form of 'corporeal malediction,' reinforced by images of tom-toms, cannibalism, intellectual deficiency, fetishism, racial defects, slave ships and 'sho'good eatin' (Fanon, 1952).

Activity – What is an 'ethnic group'?

Ethnic groups are said to have the following characteristics:

- a common culture
- a belief in a common origin
- a sense of group identity
- social ties and interaction within the group.

Do you belong to an ethnic group? Give your reasons and review them after reading the next section.

The Social Construction of *Whiteness*

It was stated earlier that racial classification detaches the body from the self – irrespective of who the person is or what characteristics, skills or abilities they may have, we view them through the category. However, 'whiteness' is not seen as a category – if anything, it is the absence of a category, it is constructed as a person without ethnicity – normal, a non-label. As Martin (1999) explains: 'Whites just "are"' (p. 31). Fanon's (1967) contextualist argument has also played a central role in the social construction of whiteness because, as we have seen, Fanon argues that blackness and whiteness are mutually reinforcing cultural categories; when we construct the Other, we also construct ourselves. Long and Hylton (2002) argue that there is little analysis of 'race' and cultural difference in the study of leisure and sport, and the concept of 'whiteness' is something of a 'silent other' as it has largely escaped examination in the leisure and sport literature.

White people have more control over the definition of themselves and are highly unlikely to be classed as Other on racial grounds, even when in a tiny minority. In the United States, a number of groups whom we would now consider to be 'white', such as the Irish, Italians and Jews, had to struggle and campaign to be recognised as 'white', which reinforces the argument that 'whiteness' may appear to be a 'natural' and neutral category, but in the last analysis the concept is historically constructed through discourse.

Dyson (1999) develops the following arguments:

- Whiteness is regarded as the positive universal whereas blackness is the negative particular.
- Whiteness represents ethnic cohesion and is the instrument of nation building.
- Whiteness limits and distorts our conceptions of blackness.

Dyson explains that it is through this dominant but invisible meaning of whiteness that white people were able to label other races, particularly black people, for their inability to behave in a way that is fully human.

Frankenberg (1993) suggests that 'whiteness' implies dominance and privilege and, according to Long and Hylton (2002), this is particularly true in the field of sport. This is surprising, given that sporting competitions usually raise issues about location and identity – in some cases, in terms of nation states with national teams competing in competitions or local teams that represent towns or cities. Both identifiers and the people who are identified as 'white' have tended not to engage in any dialogue about what it means to be 'white' in a 'white society'. Media reports would be unlikely to refer to David Beckham as 'the white footballer, David Beckham'. However, Long and Hylton found that 'whiteness' was continuously reproduced in football, cricket and rugby league, and white dominance in sport can take a number of forms. Long and Hylton (2002) found from their study of rugby league crowds in northern England that of the 31,000 people who were spectators at the grounds in one match, only 24 were recognised ethnic minorities. One area of particular concern for Long and Hylton was that of governance – the Rugby Football League had no black employees, and less than 20 per cent of cricket clubs had a black committee member. There was also significant under-representation of black match officials.

On the field of play, Long and Spracklen (1996) found evidence of stacking in rugby league. Loy and McElvogue (1970) first developed the concept of stacking – it was they who first pointed out that racial segregation in professional team sports is positively related to a position of centrality on the field of play. Black players were much more likely to be allocated to non-central positions on the field of play. Spatial location on the field of play directly affects the nature of the tasks to be performed during the game and the frequency of interaction with other players – the more central a person's spatial location, the greater the likelihood that coordinative tasks will be performed and the greater the rate of interaction with the occupants of other positions. In American Football, central positions are defined as:

- quarterback
- centre
- offensive guards
- linebacks.

In Baseball, the central positions are defined as:

- catcher
- infielders.

Coaches assume that black players lack the ability, skills and attitudes to meet the demands of the central positions in terms of fulfilling the responsibilities and leadership requirements that are directly related to the success of the team.

Participation and Race

Overt discrimination, such as the racial segregation of swimming pools, playgrounds and other leisure facilities, was once common in a number of countries. However, even after the legal restrictions on participation have been lifted, race is still believed to have a significant impact upon leisure participation. Dovido (1997) argues that 'aversive' racism, a form of racism in which individuals generate feelings of anxiety or discomfort about others on the basis of their perceived race, is common. Moreover, the aversive racist exhibits no explicit racism and is often unaware of the offensive nature of their behaviour toward others. Phillip (1995) investigated the relationship between race and what he considered to be two basic measures of leisure constraint: appeal and comfort. He argued that the model of leisure constraint developed by Crawford and Godbey in the 1980s was not used to directly address the impact of race on leisure participation. This was surprising because it was widely accepted that race was a significant constraining factor in areas such as housing, employment and education. However, there were flaws with the Crawford and Godbey model; politicians and researchers alike have misused intrapersonal factors ('psychological states and attributes' – Crawford and Godbey, 1987: 122) to justify black Americans' lack of participation in a range of areas of social life. Phillip explains that a range of personality disorders and dysfunctions have been used for over 100 years to explain 'problematic' aspects of black people's behaviour.

In other words, personality dysfunctions and disorders were used as an excuse or justification for inequality, segregation and discrimination. Fernando (1988) goes so far as to argue that the black American 'personality' cannot be theorised independently from the effects of institutionalised racism.

Phillip (1995) found that leisure activities that were located outside of the neighbourhood were unpopular with black Americans – in contrast, leisure activities that had the highest appeal and comfort were located in the immediate neighbourhood.

Later, Phillip (1999) investigated the different perceptions of black Americans and European Americans as to how 'welcome' black Americans were made to feel when participating in 20 leisure activities. Phillip (1999) found that both middle-class black Americans and middle-class European Americans had a high level of agreement on places where black Americans were likely to be welcome. Leisure activities appear to be coded with information about what is suitable and appropriate for a black American to participate in. In contrast to the perception of many white Americans, many black Americans do not feel welcome at a range of leisure venues. Phillip considers this form of discrimination to be a barrier to participation. All parents, irrespective of race, placed a high value on similar leisure activities for children, however black Americans felt much less welcome in going to the beach, camping, boating and going to a classical concert. Interestingly, from the position of a constraints model, going to a museum was rated as one of the highest activities for black children. However, museums were one of the few places that were believed to have a low level of racial acceptance. Overall, black Americans rated leisure as less important for their children, but Phillip argues, this may be because a feeling of not being welcome leads black parents to devalue a range of leisure activities.

This is important because lack of participation has a significant impact on health:

- Amesty and Juniu (2002) found a high incidence of diabetes amongst Latinos. They investigated the barriers to leisure-time physical activity in the Latino immigrant population and found that poverty, poor literacy, social networks and place of residence were barriers to physical activity.
- Crespo et al. (2000) and McGinnis and Foege (1992) found that Latinos have lower levels of leisure-time physical activity than white Americans, and that this together with poor diet is a major cause of death.
- Droomers et al. (1998) found that physical activity is important for a person's psychological well-being and for a reduced chance of being depressed, and that it can prevent premature death.

Marginality thesis

The early research on black Americans' leisure participation assumed that factors related to economic class were the most significant barriers to participation. Examples of such research include the following:

- Washburne (1978) found that black Americans were less likely to participate in outdoor pursuits such as camping than the rest of the population.
- Schuman and Hatchett (1974) argued that even in integrated areas, black Americans participated in different forms of leisure activities than other Americans.

The marginality thesis argues that resource allocation is the most important factor in determining the constraints on participation. Washburne (1978), for example, argues that the history of inequality in resource allocation is an important factor constraining the leisure activities of black Americans and other ethnic minorities – factors such as the cost of activities and transport problems were greater barriers to participation than they were for white Americans. In a similar fashion, Edwards (1981) found that transport problems, inadequate information, the unequal distribution of recreational services, a lack of interesting programmes and differential allocation of recreational opportunities were significant factors limiting black Americans' leisure participation.

Stodolska (1998) also argues that most of the constraints research has largely focused on problems of the general population without much attention to ethnic/racial minorities or immigrants. As Karla Henderson (2006) explains, leisure researchers must be careful not to compel people to fit in to a theory that is appropriate as an explanation for their behaviours. Making use of Jackson's (1997) definition of constraint as factors that are assumed by researchers and perceived or experienced by individuals to limit the formation of leisure preferences and to inhibit or prohibit participation and enjoyment in leisure, Stodolska (1998) investigated the leisure activities of Polish nationals who had emigrated to Canada. Stodolska (1998) argues that in addition to being subjected to the leisure constraints that the general population commonly encountered, immigrants may experience a number of additional barriers that she describes as *dynamic characteristics* that are related both to their minority status and to problems with adaptation to the new cultural and economic environment. Assimilation in itself was a dynamic characteristic in that it involved both an initial stress associated with the shock of the new environment and the socialisation into what were assumed to be the dominant cultural patterns of the host society. Stodolska found that the Polish immigrants were generally less likely to hold professional or management positions, and more likely to be unemployed, have below average incomes, and live in poverty, than the rest of the population.

Ethnicity thesis

The ethnicity thesis argues that cultural differences within minority groups shape leisure styles and forms of participation, and that resource constraints have little impact upon participation. Woodard (1988) found that pressure from family members and peers often limited the choice of leisure activities available to black people and restricted their leisure space to local areas. Researchers in the United Kingdom looking into the leisure patterns of girls of South Asian heritage in the 1980s found that religious beliefs, the strict dress code, the limited availability of single-sex facilities and the lack of parental approval for sports and a range of other activities outside of the home were all barriers to participation (see Carrington et al., 1987; Glyptis, 1985; Taylor and Hegarty, 1985).

In the 1980s, cultural factors in relation to the concept of ethnicity were seen to shape leisure choices and it became recognised that racial discrimination was a factor in shaping participation. Parks are widely recognised as spaces in which a range of often highly ritualised activities take place that help to establish or maintain bonds within a community. One of the earliest research projects in this tradition was by Lee (1972) who found that Americans could identify public parks as either 'white' parks or 'black' parks. In addition, black Americans said that they were made to feel uncomfortable using parks outside of the area that they lived. Hutchinson (1988) and West (1989) came to similar conclusions in their research into participation in Chicago's parks. In the United Kingdom, Wolley and Amin (1999) found that less than half of teenagers of Pakistani heritage made use of public parks. Ravenscroft and Markwell (2000) examine the role of the park with reference to Foucault's concept of *heterotropia*, a concept that suggests that people have the ability to engage in the construction of a 'compensatory world' in which they experience a form of 'freedom' or subversion, but within the closely drawn code of behaviour – in other words, young people construct the open space of the park as a legitimised 'deviant' space.

Ideas about what constitutes a legitimate leisure activity are often acquired through the processes of socialisation. Broman et al. (1988) found that highly educated black Americans have a strong sense of racial group identity which impacts upon the leisure choices of their children. Parents are role models but, in addition, parents often monitor their children's leisure activities before allowing them to participate.

In an effort to test the hypothesis that the more interracial contact, the greater the similarity of leisure preferences, Floyd and Shinew (1999) conducted a survey of Chicago park users. Drawing upon the work of Blau (1977) who suggests that higher racial contact should increase opportunities for social interaction and Bourdieu's (1977) argument that increased social interaction provides greater opportunities for cultural exchange, their research found that Chicago was a divided city – especially in terms of participation in the city parks. However, they did find that for those white people who did have a degree of interracial contact, there was similarity in terms of participation. In addition, the survey also raised issues about the level of intraracial leisure preferences within the black American community. However, all people viewed leisure and recreation in terms of exclusion and social justice, and leisure opportunities can be a major source of interracial conflict.

Phillip (2000) found that basketball was one of the favourite sports amongst male and female black adolescents. Ogden and Hilt (2003) have explored the links between basketball and a collective black identity in the United States. They were interested in why there has been a significant decline in the number of black Americans participating in baseball (both in the audience and on the field of play), whilst the numbers participating in basketball have increased. In 2001, only five per cent of the audience at Major League baseball games were black. This was the lowest figure since 1968. In contrast, basketball has become central to the individual self-image of many black males in urban areas and the game is used to create a comfortable social space. In the first half of the twentieth century, it was baseball that captured the imagination of black urban youth. However, the migration of the best black players from the Negro American Leagues to the Major Leagues led to a decline in its level of skill and eventually by 1961 to its financial demise. The end of the Negro American Leagues created a situation where black Americans were unable to pass on to their children a tradition of baseball as a game over which they had any sense of ownership. At the same time, basketball became much more evident in urban areas. Like jazz or hip-hop, the game of basketball was used by black urban youth to communicate a sense of blackness to others. Ogden and Hilt (2003) explain that because of the predominance of black role models in basketball, many black youths choose to draw upon basketball as a resource for self-expression and empowerment, and many black Americans view basketball as a sport that provides people with opportunities for upward social mobility.

In a United Kingdom sporting context, Carrington and McDonald (2003) argue that the Sports Council's 'Sport for All' campaign identified participation as a citizenship right within a liberal democracy. However, after the riots in the summer of 1981, the British government had a distinct racialisation of its sports policy, with a movement away from enhancing equality of opportunity towards greater social control – targeting groups within the population who were likely to be a threat to public order, such as urban black youth and working-class males. From 1982 to 1985, 15 Action Sport projects were launched in response to the riots.

Also at this time there was a shift away from assimilationist models of race relations and a greater emphasis upon multiculturism, in which there was an acceptance of difference and diversity. The Sports Council (1994) started to place a great deal of emphasis upon identifying the perpetrators of racism and the effect that racism has upon sport.

In 'Black and ethnic minorities and sport' (1994), the Sports Council asked sports organisations to be proactive in identifying and dealing with forms of discrimination.

In their 'Racial Equality Policy Statement', the Sports Council stated the central elements of their approach.

- Britain is a multiracial society and black and ethnic minority communities have specific sports needs and aspirations.
- Racial disadvantage and discrimination are still present in sport and are key factors which influence the nature and the extent of involvement in sport by black and ethnic minority communities and individuals.
- Eliminating racial discrimination and disadvantage from sport is an ongoing task and we are committed to working towards the elimination of racism from sport, both as a council and with our various partners.
- Positive action is needed to meet the sporting needs and aspirations of black and ethnic minorities and we will also encourage our partners in pursuit of these objectives. *Source*: Sports Council (1994: 6)

In his book *Black Sportsmen*, Ernest Cashmore (1982) suggests that many black children approach the school leaving age with a great deal of pessimism. Sport provides black children with an opportunity to compensate for unsatisfying relationships at work and in school. In addition, sport provides black children with an outlet for self-expression that does not exist in most other areas of everyday life. Sport is a resource that the black child can draw upon in the construction of their self-definition. Cashmore argues that teachers have a stereotype of the black child as physically more suited to sports and encourage black children to take up sport at the expense of their academic work.

Leisure and Disability

Traditionally, disability was defined in terms of pathology, which caused bodily impairments that predisposed people to functional limitations in their everyday lives. This view of disabled people as incapable and dependent also shaped the opportunities for leisure, with it being common practice to exclude disabled people from a wide range of leisure settings.

For much of the latter part of the twentieth century, severe disabilities were regarded as an important public health concern. However, for a long period up until the late nineteenth century, the 'abnormalities' of disabled people were a source of entertainment for the able-bodied. The able-bodied have a long history of using the disabled as a source of entertainment. In the Middle Ages, wealthy households would keep them as 'court jesters', 'fools' or in the role of pets – people with various degrees of impairment whose 'idiocy' was consumed as a form of entertainment. The poor could consume the performance of the disabled in village markets and fairs, and at festivals. Madhouses were open to the paying public to gaze upon the entertaining feeble-minded inmates. In the nineteenth century, the 'freak show' developed. According to Bogdan (1996) this was a: 'formally organized exhibition of people with alleged physical, mental or behavioural difference at circuses, fairs, carnivals or other amusement venues' (p. 25).

Rosemarie Garland Thomson (1996) examines the rise and fall of the freak show from the 1830s through to the 1940s; she argues that the term 'freak' in the nineteenth century meant a whimsical fancy. In the 'freak shows' of the nineteenth and early twentieth centuries, a wide range of 'freaks' were put on display for the amusement of the public: bottled foetuses with severe impairments, congenitally disabled newborns, commonly known as 'armless and legless wonders' or 'monstrous births', together with bearded ladies, fat ladies, albinos, living skeletons, Siamese twins, frog eaters and sword-swallowers. Such displays of freakishness and their presentation as entertainment facilitated the conditioned response of revulsion and amusement, and formed the basis of the modern-day beauty myth, especially as applied to women with visible impairments. For Thomson (1996), the freak show created the notion of *embodied deviance*, and 'simultaneously reinscribed gender, race, sexual aberrance, ethnicity, and disability as inextricable yet particular exclusionary systems legitimated by bodily variation – all represented by the single multivalent figure of the freak' (Thomson, 1996: 10).

Previous research concentrating wholly on disabled women and the beauty myth is limited. Some research has found that disabled women are seen as failing to measure up to the 'definition of femininity as pretty passivity' (Morris, 1991: 21). Disability in a woman has been used in the various cultural media in much the same way as it has been used with disabled men, that is, to signify evil or revulsion. However, research suggests that images of disabled women also conjure up associations of being passive, deprived and dependent. Due to the fact that women do not have to be portrayed as disabled to present the passive female image, disabled women tend not to be required for any role in mainstream advertising.

Biklen and Bogdan (1977) and later Colin Barnes (1992) identified the following dominant representations of disabled people in the media as:

- pitiable and pathetic
- an object of violence
- sinister or evil, with the disabled child as the reward for the evils of the parents
- atmosphere
- 'super cripple'
- laughable
- her/his own worst enemy
- non-sexual
- incapable of fully participating in everyday life
- normal.

Harlan Hahn (1997) argues that the emphasis on beauty and bodily perfection has led to the exclusion of disabled people from the media. Moreover, it is assumed that the non-disabled audience dislike viewing images of disability and that fear of becoming disabled has made advertisers wary of employing people as models who have any form of impairment. Bodily perfection has become advertising's ideal. Representation of the disabled in the mass media has focused on their participation in telethons, as tragic victims of circumstance or social problems in news presentations (Woodhill, 1996). The disabled are presented as 'pitiable victims of tragic negative stereotypes by presenting fate, as noteworthy only when they've done something extraordinary and incapable of a fulfilling life' (Christians, 1998: 6).

The BBC's annual 'Children in Need' campaign uses the image of a caricature bear with an eye patch as its mascot. The representation of disability in mainstream advertising is rooted in a medical/rehabilitation set of discourses and is never positive representation, restricted exclusively to fundraising campaigns (Brolley and Anderson, 1986). Haller and Ralph (2002) investigated the changing imagery of charity advertising in the 1980s and found that images of disabled people were presently reflecting the 'medical model' of disability. As Barnes (1996) explains, the proliferation of 'able-bodied' values and the misrepresentation of disabled people reflect a dominant able-bodied policy that discriminates against disabled people.

In the United States, the law was used to exclude disabled people from participation in the wider society – for example, a 1911 Chicago municipal ordinance (that became known as the Ugly Laws) stated that:

No person who is diseased, maimed, mutilated, or in any way deformed so as to be an unsightly or disgusting object or improper person to be allowed in or on the public ways or other public places in this city, shall expose himself to public view, under a penalty of not less than one dollar nor more than fifty dollars for each offense.

This ordinance remained on the Chicago Municipal Code until 1973. Imrie (1996) argues that similar ordinances are still on the statute books of cities such as Columbus in Ohio and Omaha in Nebraska.

Today, across Europe, North America, Australia and New Zealand, there is a legislative framework that provides disabled people with a degree of legal protection from discrimination. This legal protection covers barriers to participation in many areas of the leisure sector. Cinemas, theatres, restaurants and other similar places of leisure and entertainment have to provide ease of access for wheelchair users.

Much of the legislation that forms the legal framework of protection is rooted in a medical model of disability. However, as we shall see below, there are many leisure spaces (clubs, bars etc.) that appear to operate outside of the legislative framework. Such leisure spaces are sites for the reinforcement of stereotypes about the disabled.

The Medical Model of Disability

The medical model of disability has a long history, but as a sociological approach, it was Talcott Parsons (1951) who developed the model. The key assumption underpinning Parsons' medical model is that disability is a personal tragedy. The loss of a function that the rest of us take for granted or some other biological abnormality establishes the disabled person as having an inferior, stigmatised status. Disability rights campaigners have long campaigned against viewing disability from the perspective of biologically based personal tragedy, instead looking to a social constructionist view of disability, with the concept of disability rooted in discourses of prejudice and exclusion.

The Social Model of Disability

According to Barnes (1994), Parsons assumes that physical, sensory or intellectual impairment is the primary cause of a person's 'disability' and any economic, political or cultural difficulties encountered by people labelled 'disabled' is in the last analysis caused by the impairment.

Parsons argued that we should view disability in the same terms as *the sick role*: 'disablement [together with the sick role] ... constitute fundamental disturbances of the expectations by which men live' (Parsons, 1951: 442).

In contrast, the social model of disability places a greater emphasis on *needs* rather than *personal tragedy*. Wider social forces beyond the immediate control of the person with disability are responsible for the problems disabled people face. Society generates forms of discrimination and exclusion that disabled people have to cope with. The *problem* is to be found in the *social constructions* of prejudice that surround disability and not in the bodies of disabled people.

For Shakespeare and Watson (1997), the social model has a number of characteristics:

• The model advocates a social analysis of disability.
• The model advocates a social construction view of disability.
• The model *de-invidualises* the relationship between medicine and disability by placing the doctor–patient relationship into a social context.

The model recognises that people manage their physical issues in various ways, but all disabled people recognise that physical and social barriers are, in the last analysis, rooted in prejudice and discrimination.

From this perspective, disability is not a *thing* unconnected from the social context. Disability has meaning because of the interrelationship between the concept and social reality. The individual person as a disabled person and disability are socially constructed.

Taking their starting point from Foucault, Hughes and Patterson (1997) question what a *normal* body is – it is worth reflecting upon this for a moment before you read on.

However, Susan Wendell (2001) has argued that the social constructionist view of disability ignores the fact that not everything is discourse and social construction – people have bodies and bodies matter. Many healthy people with disabilities and many unhealthy people with disabilities experience physical or psychological problems that no amount of social justice can do away with.

In addition, the 'turn to impairment' within Disability Studies has tended to ignore the problems faced by people who are said to have 'learning difficulties'. The medical model remains the dominant perspective from which to view 'learning difficulties'. Within the medical model, Goodley (2001) identifies three commonly held criteria for identifying a person with learning difficulties:

- low intelligence
- social incompetence
- maladaptive functioning – or culturally abnormal behaviour.

It is assumed that factors indicate biological malfunctioning within an impaired individual.

Goodley's conclusion is that low intelligence, social incompetence and maladaptive functioning are not valid scientific categories. The definition of what constitutes *learning difficulties* is commonly assumed to be a value-free objective fact. However, the three categories are widely distributed amongst the population, amongst people who are not regarded as having learning difficulties. There is no compelling evidence that these categories are evidence of biological impairment; rather, such categories are behavioural in nature – in other words, *epistemes* of *assumed* impairment. We *read* bodies through hierarchical categories.

Sexuality: Epistemes of Impairment

It is in the area of disabled people's sexuality that the epistemes of impairment are most clearly visible, and this significantly impacts upon the leisure participation of the disabled. Brown (1994) argues that people with disabilities are perceived as either: asexual or oversexed, innocents or perverts.

Disabled people are often in a position where other people are attempting to control:

- the level of their sexual experience
- the level of their sexual knowledge
- their choices in relation to issues of consent
- their access to sexual education – which in contrast to that of the able-bodied person is often solely about informing the disabled person of how to control or eliminate their sexual interest.

This social construction of femininity is particularly harmful to women with disabilities. Moreover, as Ruth Butler (1999) points out, within the lesbian and gay community, there is the same 'ableist obsession with the perfect body' that we find in the straight society. The discourses that construct the female beauty myth define the body of a woman with disability as unfeminine, unappealing and asexual. Disabled women are not subjected to the male gaze that Naomi Wolf describes, but to what Rosemarie Garland Thomson (1997) defines as the *male stare*: 'If the male gaze informs the normative female self as a sexual spectacle, then the stare sculpts the disabled subject as a grotesque spectacle' (Thomson, 1997: 285).

In other words, the beauty myth is constructed via a series of ableist hetero-patriarchal discourses that separate the normal from the pathological body. Disabilities are signs of pathology and inferiority as well as an abnormal body. As Thomson goes on to explain, the stare is a material gesture that generates disability as an overwhelmingly oppressive social relationship in which some categories of bodies are not valued. It is the classification of some body types as superior and more desirable than others that is found at the centre of both disability and beauty oppression.

These issues are highlighted by Sarah Earle (1999, 2001) who found that many young people with disabilities, who are living at home with their parents, lack the opportunities to explore their sexuality. As Butler (1993) points out, there is a high degree of attempted suicide amongst young people who come to look at themselves as lesbian or gay but who lack knowledge and support. Going to university is for many people a time to explore their sexuality. However, some people with disabilities may require assistance – what Earle calls *facilitated sex*. The term *facilitated sex* can mean a number of different things: help in attending clubs, parties and other leisure venues where potential sexual partners can be met; assistance in having sexual intercourse; negotiating with prostitutes; assistance with masturbation. Personal assistants were reluctant to participate in facilitating sex for people with disabilities, especially when the disabled person was attracted to same-sex relationships. The assistants did accept that sexuality was a central element in a person's life, but were unwilling to acknowledge that people with disabilities should have a need to explore their sexuality.

Within any society, some people assume that power and control define and regulate the sexual practices and behaviours of others. The more powerless a group is, the more they lose the ability to define and regulate their own sexuality. Enjoying personal intimacy and sexuality is not seen as an important part of disabled people's lives. At several points in history and in various places, eugenics has been popular – it was expected that people who were labelled as disabled should neither reproduce nor be reproduced in an effort to prevent the incidence of disability.

In an effort to apply these ideas to the leisure sector, Shakespeare et al. (1996) conducted research on 'ableist' prejudice within the gay community and, from the interviews conducted, found the following examples:

- A man with a gay rights T-shirt who had a learning disability was asked at the door of a bar if he knew the bar was a gay bar.
- Wheelchair users were not allowed in gay clubs on grounds of 'safety'.
- There was a patronising attitude of staff and customers.
- Disabled people were used as the token disabled friend at parties.

Much of the literature on the sexual experiences of people with disabilities, and particularly people with learning disabilities, is placed firmly within the medical model. Sexuality is perceived as a problem in need of a cure. In the United Kingdom, according to the Sexual Offences Acts 1956 and 1967, a person with a severe learning disability is considered to be incapable of giving their consent to a sexual encounter. In addition, Cambridge and Mellan (2000) argue that men with learning disabilities are judged by different standards from other men who use pornography which, they argue, reinforces the pathological view of the sexuality of men with learning disabilities.

Cambridge and Mellan (2000) go on to argue that in the United Kingdom, men with learning disabilities who engage in same-sex relationships are unlikely to be given a safe-sex education which allows them to take into account HIV risk assessment, the need to wear condoms, and strategies and techniques for negotiating safer sex. In the recent past, positive images of homosexuality and safe sex were not made available to men with learning disabilities because sex educators feared that providing such information would break Section 28 of the Local Government Act 1988 which prevented local authorities from *promoting* homosexuality. Cambridge and Mellan also argue that most men with learning disabilities who desire same-sex relationships become isolated, have feelings of guilt, denial and a negative self-image because they are separated from the network of self-help groups and other forms of support and information to gay men who do not have learning disabilities.

There are examples of local authorities censoring images of sexual expression by disabled people. Butler (1999) gives the example of Westminster Council in London attempting to censor the film 'Crash' on the grounds that it contained an erotic scene involving a disabled woman.

When it comes to gaining entry into leisure spaces such as clubs and bars, culturally dominated people such as people who are seen to have a disability are often in a situation where they are both marked out by stereotypes and at the same time become invisible. The network of dominant meanings that disabled people experience in leisure spaces do not come from other disabled people, rather they come from able-bodied people who have little or no understanding of disability. However, if we accept the argument that both homosexuality and disability are socially constructed, then they can also be socially de-constructed and subjected to reconsideration and restructuring in the interests of disabled people.

Old Age and Childhood

Old age and childhood are commonly assumed to be different from adulthood for several reasons. Grant (2001) conducted interviews with 15 men and women over 70 years of age about their experiences of being physically active and playing sport. Being older and wanting to participate is not simply about overcoming physical barriers to participation, but having to negotiate socio-cultural expectations that contribute to a whole range of social barriers that can prevent older people from becoming physically active. Many of the respondents believed that for some unknown reason, many older people accepted the common assumption that physical activity 'wasn't for older people'.

In the latter half of the twentieth century, many countries experienced an increase in the number of *old people* within the population. The old are regarded as a distinct grouping within the population, and in a similar fashion to race, sex, sexuality and childhood, this distinction is believed to be biological in nature. Robert Butler coined the term *ageism* in 1969. Looking at data on labour market trends in the United Kingdom, Loretto et al. (2000) demonstrate the extent of ageism. From the early 1970s onwards, there has been an accelerating trend in 'early exit' from the labour market, especially during periods of recession. There are a number of different routes out of employment for the older person: early retirement, redundancy, dismissal and ill health. Moreover, very few of these individuals return to full-time employment. Loretto et al. argue that such discrimination is irrational and based upon negative stereotypes of older people rather than on sound commercial grounds. Older people are believed to be less productive, have fewer important skills, are opposed to change and new technology, are less willing to be trained in new skills, and are more likely to be absent from work through absenteeism or poor health.

Leisure and later life

The *old* are believed to be different because they are beyond maturity. Age-based categories are often assumed to be biological divisions rather than social divisions. However, is there a 'normal' childhood or a 'normal' old age? Old age is often seen as a period in a person's life where they can be seriously challenged physically, cognitively and mentally. Adaptation to life without paid employment could be considered as the most important stage in a process of successful ageing for the older person. The rationalities and technologies of governmentality underpin the social division and give rise to the discourses that support age identities. Is there a link between leisure and successful ageing?

During the 1960s and 1970s, the relationship between leisure and ageing was given a great deal of attention, in Britain from Long (1987) and Parker (1982) and in the United States and Canada from Havighurst (1961), Kelly (1987), Kelly et al. (1987), Ragheb and Griffith (1982), Riddick (1985), Romsa et al. (1985) and Russell (1987). Much of this work was based upon activity theory, disengagement theory or continuity theory.

The concept of successful ageing has been described by Torres (1999) under four headings:

- maximising self-potential and reaching a high level of physical, social and psychological well-being
- possessing the capability of adapting to changes that occur in later life
- possessing capabilities similar to those of younger people
- managing to remain productive.

One common approach to the measurement of psychological well-being is the Life Satisfaction Index (LSI). The LSI was developed by Neugarten et al. (1968), and was based upon a questionnaire designed to measure the subjective feeling of life satisfaction experienced by older people living in the community. The subjective life satisfaction was measured by responses to 20 statements in relation to: enjoyment of daily activities, perceiving life as meaningful, a sense of success in achieving principal life goals, positive self-image, optimism and general happiness.

The old experience bodily changes, but the changes are universally greeted with fear and repulsion. The beauty system applies to older women in no uncertain terms – advertisements for beauty products warn individuals to constantly be on the look out for signs of ageing and to deal with them quickly and efficiently. Carrigan and Szmigin (2000) argue that the advertising industry either ignores older people or presents them via a set of negative stereotypes or caricatures: decrepitude, imbecility and physical repugnance. Dementia, for example, is the name given to a behavioural syndrome that involves individuals exhibiting a range of unacceptable behaviours, such as:

- loss of intellectual capacity
- loss of memory
- difficulty in retaining information
- difficulty in decision making
- difficulty in thinking through complex ideas
- difficulty in carrying out practical tasks, notably in acquiring new skills and competencies.

Advertisers fail to reflect the 'real life' of older people. Even in advertisements for products that are aimed at older people, advertisers still make use of younger models. Growing old is a sign of increasing constraints upon the good life. Minichiello et al. (2000) found that words used to describe and explain aspects of the old person's life were not words used by older people to describe their own experiences. Older people are aware that they are seen as being 'old', and many old people attempt to distance themselves from the wider group of 'old' people.

Such ideas can be reinterpreted as forms of oppression against older people. Towards this end, Simon Biggs and Jason L. Powell (2001) draw upon Foucault's analysis of 'technologies of self' to argue that the identities of older people are maintained through the deployment of integrated systems of power and knowledge and a routine operation of surveillance and assessment.

A number of authors have explored the argument that old age should be examined by use of the social model of disability to understand the position of old people in society. Discourses of later life form the basis for forms of discrimination and allow professional carers to control key aspects of the older person's life. Oldham (2002) argues that the social model of disability can apply to later life in terms of:

- the political argument, notably the emphasis on self-advocacy
- the distinction between impairment and disability – individuals are prevented from participating because of discourses of disability. Old age is seen in medical terms, as a personal tragedy, a form of chronic illness and as dysfunctional, irrespective of the abilities of the individual.

Activity Theory

Activity theory is based upon the assumption that in order to protect psychological well-being in old age, it is essential to sustain a high level of involvement in a range of outdoor and indoor activities (Havighurst, 1963). Activity theory suggests that *successful ageing* means the maintenance, as far and as long as possible, of activities and attitudes of middle age and that people should find substitutes for their paid work. Kart and Manard (1981) argue that activities in old age provide social roles that have a positive impact on a person's conception of self and on their life satisfaction. Doing well as an old person takes place when people maintain active lifestyles and replace their former social roles, lost because of the ageing process, with new roles.

A significant number of studies have supported this approach: Chiriboga and Pierce (1993), Fernandez-Ballesteros et al. (2001), Hall and Havens (2002), Kelly (1987), Mishra (1992), Riddick and Stewart (1994) and Shmanske (1997).

Activity theory is broadly a functionalist approach that assumes old people have a need to maintain their middle-age lifestyle for as long as possible, so as to avoid a drop in life satisfaction. Activity theory makes the assumption that old age has a sharp division from other age groups and that ongoing social activity, within recognised social roles, is important for the maintenance of a person's self-concept. Havighurst (1963) argues that old people need to address the following issues if they are to maintain activity – they need to adjust to:

- declining health and physical strength
- retirement and reduced income
- the death of a spouse or family members
- living arrangements different from what they are accustomed
- the pleasures of ageing such as increased leisure and time to play with grandchildren (Havighurst, 1963).

A number of researchers have found that health problems are reported much less frequently amongst people who regularly engage in leisure activities. There was also a link between life satisfaction and leisure participation. Participation in hobbies, crafts, visiting friends and swimming was also found to be strongly related to psychological well-being (Brown et al., 1991; Dupuis and Smale, 1995).

Arthritis is the most common chronic illness amongst people aged between 65 and 75 years of age in Europe and North America. In addition, arthritis is a major cause of depression amongst this age group. In a study of the role of leisure in maintaining the health of older people with arthritis, Payne et al. (2006) argue that leisure activities can help to optimise the health and well-being of older people with arthritis, playing a positive role in maintaining their physical, mental, social and spiritual health.

However, research findings on activity theory have been varied. Howe (1988) suggests that, by itself, activity theory cannot explain the fullness and sense of involvedness. The breadth of the leisure activities engaged in was more important for enhancing well-being in old age than the frequency of the activity (Bevil et al. 1993; Ragheb and Griffith, 1982; Romsa et al., 1985). Neugarten et al. (1968) initially developed continuity theory as a more flexible alternative to Activity theory, believing it to be a theory that acknowledged the many different trajectories within ageing.

Continuity theory

Continuity theory is a variation of activity theory – this approach suggests that if older people make use of strategies that are well-known to them, they will find it easier to adapt to changes associated with ageing and maintain their well-being and outward social behaviour (Godbey, 1999; Mannell and Kleiber, 1997). Atchley (1989, 1993) tried to explain old people's fondness for continuity in their lives. The theory suggests that individuals attempt to maintain stability in the same roles they had occupied during their working lives, even though their age may impose some obstacles in gaining access to those roles.

According to Sarah Burnett-Wolle and Geoffrey Godbey (2007), continuity theory assumes that the psychological well-being of older people is to be found in three areas:

- the maintenance of inner psychological states
- the maintenance of outward social behaviour
- the methods people use to negotiate change.

However, Atchley (1989) argues that continuity theory only applies to people who go through 'normal ageing', and are not subjected to a process of 'pathological ageing'. People who experience normal ageing are older people who maintain an independent self-concept and identity. They have sufficient resources to meet their housing, health care, nutrition, clothing, transportation and recreational needs. These people are not disabled or poor and, in that sense, continuity theory does not fully take into account the external material reality that many older people have to manage to maintain their inner psychological states and outward social behaviour.

Selection, Optimisation and Compensation Theory

An approach that does attempt to take into account the external material reality that older people find themselves in is selection, optimisation and compensation theory (Baltes and Baltes, 1990; Baltes and Carstensen, 1996, 2003). This approach attempts to understand the methods that older people with limited resources use to achieve their goals. Baltes and Carstensen (1996, 2003) argue that older people who age successfully make use of three basic strategies to sustain themselves and grow:

- Selection – the prioritisation of limited resources and the identification of goals that will give the greatest satisfaction and the rejection of unattainable goals.
- Optimisation – maximising performance by looking at how others achieve the same goal, and deciding on how much time and effort should be given to a specific goal.
- Compensation – adapting to limitations by developing new skills or making use of technology. If an older person has declining eyesight, they can still enjoy reading but may have to read larger-print books. If a person has mobility problems, they can make use of social networking websites.

This approach assumes that the older person is a rational utility maximiser in relation to their leisure activities. However, people's leisure motivations are not always rational. Many older people may have impaired abilities and fewer opportunities to make selections.

The central concept in Nimrod's (2007) research in the leisure activities of older people is *essentiality*. The concept of essentiality is built upon Kelly et al.'s (1987) notions of 'meeting role expectations' and 'competence and skill development', but it also includes a sense of gratification through helping others, and a sense of belonging. Nimrod's findings indirectly support continuity theory (Atchley, 1989, 1993). Leaving paid employment involves a shift in our identity from 'producer' to 'non-producer' – for many people this transition can be seen as a threat to the 'essentiality' of their sense of self. However, leisure activities that have a career or vocational feel can help to maintain the retired person's sense of 'essentiality'. The leisure activities do not need to be activities that are similar to the person's previous career to contribute to life satisfaction or well-being. Nimrod's findings also provide an important clarification to activity theory. For Nimrod, it is important for the retired person to maintain a high level of involvement in activities that are positively correlated to the benefit of essentiality, as this will enhance their life satisfaction. However, only activities that contributed to a person's sense of 'essentiality' made a contribution to life satisfaction. Therefore, Nimrod suggests that we should narrow off the activity theory to specific activity areas. Positive leisure experiences can counter the negative impact of factors such as: low income, poor health or absence of spouse, on one's psychological well-being; a finding that is consistent with Kelly et al. (1987) and Fernandez-Ballesteros et al. (2001).

Sociological theories of the social position of old people within the wider society

Theorising about old age is diverse.

Disengagement theory: this approach was first suggested by Cummings and Henry (1961) and is described as broadly functionalist in nature. Disengagement theory is primarily concerned with the role of old age within the social system – its focus is on the functioning of the social system rather than on individual adjustment or attitudes. All individuals are conscious of their own death and functionalists assume that there should be a mutual severing of ties in society. This is an inevitable process in which the most important social roles are abandoned by the old order to maintain social order. The process might be initiated by the ageing person or by other elements within the social system, and the withdrawal may be partial or total. Old people are phased out of the most important social roles as their competence diminishes, and replaced by younger people. The assumption here is that this replacement will reduce potential disruption to the social system.

Subculture theory: old people have a set of shared values and beliefs that are not widely shared within the population; an 'age consciousness'. In addition, the old are separate from the wider society because of retirement.

Personality theory: old people can be one of two personality types: *reorganisers* who replace work and the middle-age lifestyle with an alternative set of arrangements and *the disengaged* who withdraw from a whole range of activities.

Labelling theory: this approach is derived from the work of Erving Goffman (1959) and suggests that individuals who are perceived as *old* are likely to have a range of stereotypical constructions imposed upon them, such as being 'senile'.

Marxian theory: Chris Phillipson (1982) presents 'a critical account of the position of older people in a capitalist society' (p. 1). Phillipson argues that the logic of capitalism as a system of accumulation and exploitation is incompatible with the needs of older people. Capitalism puts profits before the needs of individuals – and old people have more needs than most and less ability to pay. Hence, older people are more likely to be in poverty and poor health.

Childhood

In contrast, many parents are concerned that their children should not 'play' outside of the house without adult supervision. Adults see the urban environment as a dangerous place for children. There are discourses of appropriate leisure for various age groups within the population that have a significant impact upon levels of participation. Playgrounds are designed by adults to provide a safe space for children to play. However, as Lia Karsten (2003) points out, children in urban areas find it difficult to meet playmates face to face, outside of the gaze of adults. Therefore, children find it difficult to maintain and develop social networks. Karsten (2003) also found from her study of playgrounds in Amsterdam that social class, gender, age and ethnicity were all central factors in determining levels of participation; playgrounds do not serve girls, ethnic minorities and younger children equally.

Children are different from adults because:

- children are in full-time compulsory education
- children are not allowed to do full-time paid adult work
- children are the economic and moral responsibility of their parents
- a state-sponsored protective framework of regulation protects children.

Question: Do you agree with the list presented above? Are there any points you would add? Are there any you would take away from the list?

However, as Phillip Aries (1962) points out, childhood has a history. Childhood is a distinctly 'modernist' conception that has its origins in the manifesto of childhood, *Emile* (Rousseau, 1762/1993). Aries (1962) argues that childhood did not exist in medieval society. The notion of childhood is also a gendered conception; it did not apply to women. The female child went from swaddling clothes right into adult female dress. She did not go to school.

It was not until the late seventeenth century that we find the introduction of special childhood games. For Jenks, a 'forced commonality of an ideological discourse of childhood' developed (1996: 122):

- Childhood is a social construction, distinct from biological immaturity.
- Childhood is not a natural or a universal aspect of the human life cycle.
- Childhood is a socio-political concept, in a similar fashion to race, gender and sexuality; it is a variable of social analysis.
- Children do not passively accept the imposition of childhood definitions upon their behaviour; they actively interact with and rebel against adults' conceptions.

Similarly, Stuart Hanson (2000) identifies the following themes within the dominant construction of childhood:

- The notion of the child is rooted in nature.
- The child is en route to adulthood – the 'incomplete adult'.
- The child is vulnerable and in need of the protection of adults.

Neil Postman (1983) argues that leisure had a central role to play in the social construction of childhood. He argues that the conception of childhood was disseminated by print literacy. Children's books distributed a clear set of ideas about appropriate ideas and ways of behaving for children.

Devine (2002) draws upon Anthony Giddens' (1984) work on 'agency' and 'structure', to discuss the experience of childhood in Ireland. Devine argues that Irish children do not passively accept the dominant discourse or adult social construction of 'childhood'. There is a continued active process of negotiation between adults and children on what constitutes appropriate behaviour for a child. Children continually evaluate and monitor their own behaviour (by use of both their practical and discursive consciousness), in light of their interactions with others' expectations and evaluations in a process of reflection, critical engagement and negotiation. In summary, Jenks (1996) has argued that childhood is constructed as 'different' from adulthood – dominant discourses of childhood are based upon assumptions of innocence and vulnerability that constrain the capability of the child to construct or define themselves as capable or independent human agents. What children do and say is not interpreted in relation to the child's understanding of the world, but in relation to the discourses of childhood that the state uses to manage its citizens effectively. In the United Kingdom, the 1989 Children's Act was based upon the *paramountcy principle* – that the needs of the child came first.

McNamee (2000), drawing upon Foucault's notion of the heterotopia, argues that the boundaries of childhood are constructed in such a way that childhood is subject to increasing boundaries, and that for children, 'other' spaces are created through everyday leisure. James (1993) notes the restriction on children's space and activities in private space – 'to teachers and school class-mates, family and close friends, to children's TV, children's games, children's books, children's films … the culture of childhood is quite literally poised on the "edge"' (James, 1993: 107). In other words, children's leisure has become so tightly controlled in domestic space that activities, notably video games, play an increasingly important role in children's lives. The boundaries around childhood and the 'real' outside are so closely policed and controlled that such forms of children's leisure have become a form of escape from the control that parents impose upon children in their everyday lives.

One of the areas in which barriers between adults and children are believed to be breaking down is in the area of television. Postman (1983) has argued that childhood is disappearing, and that the dividing line between childhood and adulthood is being eroded because of the accessibility of television – a total disclosure medium – and other leisure technologies. He takes the pessimistic view that childhood is on a 'journey to oblivion', mainly because there is nothing left to conceal from children, no 'mysteries' for adults to reveal. The adult world is available to them through television at any time. In particular, via the medium of television, children are given too much information at too early a point in their lives about sexuality. Many countries have adopted an evening watershed that states that programmes deemed unsuitable for children should not be aired before that time.

Kelley (1999) argues that for 'conservatives', such access encourages permissiveness in a variety of forms: crime, drug use, teenage pregnancy, etc. In summary, too much sexual knowledge at too young an age is dangerous for children. However, from the position of children's rights, all children should have the right to view information that deals with interests that is of concern to them.

Kelley (1999) is concerned with the ways in which children understand the content of programmes designed for adults. How children make sense of the portrayal of sexual encounters is difficult because of the different contexts in which sex is presented: in the context of marital relations, outside of such relations, associated with pleasure, violence, often illicit, often not. It was found that younger children had more controls over their viewing habits than teenagers. Moreover, younger boys attempted to distance themselves from romance, and would often generate banter and teasing, if boys were seen to enjoy such programmes. Sexuality, when it was at a distance, for example within the context of a sit-com, could be enjoyed, as in the case of *Friends* or *Frasier*. However, when sex is discussed in a context of 'talking dirty', as in the case of the post-watershed version of the British TV soap 'Hollyoaks', this is of major concern to conservatives. Access to images and discourses of sexuality on television is seen by Kelley (1999) as a resource drawn upon by children to construct a strategy in the formation of a heterosexual identity and as an index of maturity.

Conclusion

This chapter, in a similar fashion to the last chapter, has explored the nature of some of the central social divisions within contemporary society and of how those social divisions impact upon leisure participation. The exclusion of people from leisure activities on the grounds of race, age and disability status has become a politicised area, based upon discourses of what constitutes reasonable and acceptable behaviour for identified groups of people: ethnic minorities, people with learning difficulties, the disabled, children, etc. The previous chapter concluded that the traditional constraints model is an artificial construct based upon the deterministic assertion that everyone experiences constraint with equal strength.

References

Alexander, C. and Alleyne, B. (2002) 'Introduction – framing difference: racial and ethnic studies in twenty-first century Britain', *Ethnic and Racial Studies*, 25 (4): 541–51.

Amesty, S. and Juniu, S. (2002) 'Structural barriers to leisure-time physical activity in the Latino immigrant community in the US'. Paper presented at the 7th World Congress on Leisure, Kuala Lumpur, Malaysia, October 21–5.

Aries, P. (1962) *Centuries of Childhood: A Social History of Family Life*. London: Vintage Books.

Atchley, R.C. (1989) 'A continuity theory of normal aging', *The Gerontologist*, 29: 183–90.

Atchley, R.C. (1993) 'Continuity theory and the evolution of activity in later adulthood', in J.R. Kelly (ed.), *Activity and Aging*. Thousand Oaks, CA: Sage.

Baltes, M.M. and Carstensen, L.L. (1996) 'The process of successful ageing', *Ageing and Society*, 16: 397–422.

Baltes, M.M. and Carstensen, L.L. (2003) 'Social psychological theories and their applications to aging: From individual to collective', in V. Bengtson and K.W. Schaie (eds), *Handbook of Theories of Aging*. New York: Springer.

Baltes, P.B. and Baltes, M.M. (1990) 'Selective optimization with compensation', in P.B. Baltes and M.M. Baltes (eds), *Successful Aging: Perspectives from the Behavioral Sciences*. Cambridge: Cambridge University Press. pp. 1–34.

Barnes, C. (1992) 'Qualitative research: valuable or irrelevant', *Disability, Handicap and Society*, 7 (2): 115–24.

Barnes, C. (1994) *Disabled People in Britain and Discrimination: A Case for Anti-discrimination Legislation*. London: C. Hurst and Co Ltd.

Barnes, C. (1996) 'Disability and the myth of the independent researcher', *Disability and Society*, 11 (2): 107–10.

Bevil, C.A., O'Connor, P.C. and Mattoon, P.M. (1993) 'Leisure activity, life satisfaction, and perceived health status in older adults', *Gerontology & Geriatrics Education*, 14 (2): 3–19.

Biggs, S. and Powell, J. (2001) 'A Foucauldian analysis of old age and the power of social welfare', *Journal of Aging & Social Policy*, 12 (2): 93–112.

Biklen, D. and Bogdan, R. (1977) 'Media portrayals of disabled people: a study in stereotypes', *Interracial Books for Children Bulletin*, 8 (6–7): 4–9.

Blau, P.M. (1977) *Inequality and Heterogeneity: A Primitive Theory of Social Structure*. New York: Free Press.

Bogdan, R. (1996) 'The social construction of freaks', in R. Garland Thomson (ed.), *Freakery: Cultural Spectacles of the Extraordinary Body*. New York: New York University Press. pp. 23–37.

Bolaffi, P., Braham, S., Gindro, T.T. and Bracalenti, R. (2003) *Dictionary of Race, Ethnicity and Culture*. Thousand Oaks, CA: Sage Publications.

Bourdieu, P. (1977) *Outline of a Theory of Practice*. Cambridge: Cambridge University Press.

Brolley, D. and Anderson, S. (1986) 'Advertising and attitudes', in M. Nagler (ed.), *Perspectives on Disability*. Palo Alto, CA: Health Markets Research. pp. 147–50.

Broman, C.L., Neighbors, H.W. and Jackson, J.S. (1988) 'Racial group identification among black adults', *Social Forces*, 67: 146–58.

Brown, H. (1994) 'An ordinary sexual life? A review of the normalisation principle as it applies to the sexual options of people with learning disabilities', *Disability & Society*, 9 (2): 123–44.

Brown, R. M. (1991) *No Duty to Retreat*. New York: Oxford University Press.

Burnett-Wolle, S. and Godbey, G. (2007) 'Re-thinking research on older adults' leisure: implications of selection, optimization, and compensation and socioemotional selectivity theories', *Journal of Leisure Research*, 39: 498–513.

Butler, J. (1993) *Bodies That Matter. On the Discursive Limits od Sex*. New York: Routledge.

Butler, R. (1999) 'Double the trouble or twice the fun? Disabled bodies in the gay community', in R. Butler and H. Parr (eds), *Mind and Body Space: Geographies of Illness, Impairment and Disability*. London: Routledge.

Cambridge, P. and Mellan, B. (2000) 'Reconstructing the sexuality of men with learning disabilities: Empirical evidence and theoretical interpretations of need', *Disability and Society*, 15 (2): 293–311.

Carrigan, M. and Szmigin, I. (2000) 'Advertising and older consumers: image and ageism', *Business Ethics: A European Review*, 9 (1): 42–50.

Carrington, B. and McDonald, I. (2003) 'The politics of "race" and sports policy', in B. Houlihan (ed.), *Sport and Society: A Student Introduction*. London: Sage.

Carrington, B., Chilvers, T. and Williams, T. (1987) 'Gender, leisure and sport: a case-study of young people of South Asian descent', *Leisure Studies*, 6 (3): 265–79.

Cashmore, E. (1982) *Black Sportsmen*. London: Routledge.

Chiriboga, D.A. and Pierce, R. (1993) 'Changing contexts of activity', in J.R. Kelly (ed.), *Activity and Ageing: Staying Involved in Later Life*. Thousand Oaks, CA: Sage.

Christians, C. (1998) 'The sacredness of life', *Media Development*, 45: 3–7.

Cox, O.C. (1945) 'Race and caste: a distinction', *American Journal of Sociology*, 50(5): 360–8.

Crawford, D.W. and Godbey, G. (1987) 'Reconceptualizing barriers to family leisure', *Leisure Sciences*, 9: 119–27.

Crespo, C.J., Smit, E., Andersen, R.E., Carter-Pokras, O. and Ainsworth, B.E. (2000) 'Race/ethnicity, social class and their relationship to physical inactivity during leisure time', *American Journal of Preventive Medicine*, 18 (1): 46–53.

Cruz-Janzen, M.I. (2003) 'Out of the closet: racial amnesia, avoidance, and denial – racism among Puerto Ricans', *Race, Gender and Class*, 1(3): 64.

Cummings, E. and Henry, W. E. (1961) *Growing Old and the Process of Disengagement*. New York: Basic Books.

Devine, D. (2002) 'Children's citizenship and the structuring of adult–child relations in the primary school', *Childhood*, 9: 303–20.

Dovido, J. (1997) 'Aversive racism and the need for affirmative action', *Chronical of Higher Education*, 43: A60, 25 July.

Droomers, M., Schrijvers, D.T.M., van de Mheen, H. and Machenbach, J.P. (1998) 'Educational differences in leisure-time physical inactivity: a descriptive and explanatory study', *Social Science and Medicine*, 47 (11): 1665.

Dyson, A. (1999) 'Inclusion and inclusions: theories and discourses in inclusive education', in H. Daniels and P. Garner (eds), *World Yearbook of Education 1999: Inclusive Education*. London: Kogan Page. pp. 36–53.

Earle, S. (1999) 'Facilitated sex and the concept of sexual need: Disabled students and their personal assistants', *Disability and Society*, 14 (3): 309–23.

Earle, S. (2001) 'Disability, facilitated sex and the role of the nurse', *Journal of Advanced Nursing*, 36 (3): 433–40.

Edwards, P.K. (1981) 'Race, residence, and leisure style: some policy implications', *Leisure Sciences*, 4: 95–112.

Fanon, F. (1952) 'Le syndrome d'Afric nord', *L'Esprit*, February, Paris.

Fanon, F. (1967) *Black Skin, White Mask*. Trans. Chales Lam Markmann. New York: Grove.

Fernandez-Ballesteros, R., Bruyn, E.E.J. de, Godoy, A., Hornke, L.F., Laak, J. ter, Vizcarro, C., Westhoff, K., Westmeyer, H. and Zaccagnini, J.L. (2001) 'Guidelines for the assessment process (GAP): A proposal for discussion', *European Journal of Psychological Assessment*, 17: 187–200.

Fernando, S. (1988) *Race and Culture in Psychiatry*. Philadelphia: Temple University Press.

Floyd, M.F. and Shinew, K.J. (1999) 'Convergence and divergence in leisure style among whites and African Americans: toward an interracial contact hypothesis', *Journal of Leisure Research*, 31 (4): 359–84.

Frankenberg, R. (1993) *The Social Construction of Whiteness: White Women, Race Matters*. London: Routledge.

Giddens, A. (1984) *The Constitution of Society. Outline of the Theory of Structuration*. Cambridge: Polity.

Glyptis, S. (1985) 'Women as a target group: the views of the staff of Action Sport West Midlands', *Leisure Studies*, 4: 347–62.

Godbey, G. (1999) *Leisure in your Life: An Exploration* (5th edn). State College, PA: Venture.

Goffman, E. (1959) *The Presentation of Self in Everyday Life*. Edinburgh: University of Edinburgh Social Sciences Research Centre.

Goodley, D. (2001) '"Learning difficulties", the social model of disability and impairment: Challenging epistemologies', *Disability and Society*, 16 (2): 207–31.

Grant, G. (2001) 'Older people with learning disabilities: Health, community inclusion and family caregiving', in M. Nolan, S. Davies and G. Grant (eds), *Working with Older People and their Families*. Buckingham: Open University Press.

Hahn, H. (1997) 'New trends in disability studies: implications for educational policy', in D.K. Lipsky and A. Gartner (eds), *Inclusion and School Reform: Transforming America's Classrooms*. Baltimore: Brookes. pp. 315–28.

Hall, M. and Havens, B. (2002) 'Social isolation and loneliness', *NACA Writings in Gerontology on Mental Health and Aging*, pp. 31–42. (Available at: http://www.ccnta.ca/writings_gerontology/writ18/pdf/writ18_e.pdf)

Hall, S. (1992) *Formations of Modernity*. Cambridge: Polity Press/Basil Blackwell/OU.

Haller, B.A. and Ralph, S. (2002) 'Current perspectives on advertising images of disability', in G. Dines and J. Humez (eds), *Gender, Race and Class in Media*. Thousand Oaks, CA: Sage.

Hanson, S. (2000) 'Children in film', in J. Mills and R. Mills (eds), *Childhood Studies: A Reader in Perspectives of Childhood*. London: Routledge.

Havighurst, R.J. (1963) 'The nature and values of meaningful free-time activity', in R. W. Kleemeier (ed.), *Aging and Leisure*. New York: Oxford University Press. pp. 309–44.

Henderson, K.A. (2006) 'Urban parks and trail, and physical activity', *Annals of Leisure Research (Australia-New Zealand)*, 9 (4): 201–11.

Howe, C. Z. (1998) 'Using qualitative structured interviews in leisure research: illustrations from one case study', *Journal of Leisure Research*, 20 (4): 305–23.

Hughes, B. and Patterson, K. (1997) 'The social model of disability and the disappearing body: Towards a sociology of impairment', *Disability and Society*, 12 (3): 325–40.

Husband, C. (1974) *Race*. London: Routledge.

Hutchinson, R. (1988) 'A critique of race, ethnicity, and social class in recent leisure–recreation research', *Journal of Leisure Research*, 20: 10–30.

Imrie, R. (1996) *Disability and the City: International Perspectives*. New York: St. Martin's Press.

Jackson, E.L. (1997) 'In the eye of the beholder: A comment on Samdahl and Jekubovich (1997), "A critique on leisure constraints: Comparative analysis and understandings"', *Journal of Leisure Research*, 29: 458–68.

James, A. (1993) *Childhood Identities: Self and Social Relationships in the Experience of the Child*. Edinburgh: Edinburgh University Press.

Jenks, C. (1996) *Childhood*. London: Routledge.

Karsten, L. (2003) 'Family gentrifiers: challenging the city as a place simultaneously to build a career and to raise children', *Urban Studies*, 40: 2573–85.

Kart, C. S. and Manard, M. (1981) *Aging in America*. Sherman Oaks, CA: Alfred Publishing.

Kelley, P. (1999) 'Case studies', in M. Bullis and C. Davis (eds), *Functional Assessment in Transition and Rehabilitation for Adolescents and Adults with Learning Disabilities*. Austin, TX: Pro-Ed. pp. 79–88.

Kelly, J.R. (1987) *Freedom to Be: A New Sociology of Leisure*. New York: MacMillan.

Kelly, J.R., Steinkamp, M.W. and Kelly, J.R. (1987) 'Later-life satisfaction: Does leisure contribute?', *Leisure Sciences*, 9: 189–200.

Lee, R.G. (1972) 'The social definition of outdoor recreation places', in W.R. Burch, N. Cheek and L. Taylor (eds), *Social Behavior, Natural Resources, and Environment*. New York: Harper & Row. pp. 68–84.

Long, J. (1987) 'Continuity as a basis for change: leisure and male retirement', *Leisure Studies*, 6 (1): 55–70.

Long, J. and Hylton, K. (2002) 'Shades of white: an examination of whiteness in sport', *Leisure Studies*, 21 (2): 87–103.

Long, J. and Spracklen, K. (1996) 'Positional play: racial stereotyping in rugby league', *The Bulletin of Physical Education*, 32: 18–22.

Loretto, W., Duncan, C. and White, P. (2000) 'Ageism and employment: Controversies, ambiguities and younger people's perceptions', *Ageing and Society*, 20: 279–302.

Loy, J.W. and McElvogue, J.F. (1970) 'Racial segregation in American sport', *International Review of Sport Sociology*, 5: 5–23.

McGinnis, J.M. and Foege, W.H. (1992) 'Actual causes of death in the United States', *JAMA*, 268: 2207–12.

McNamee, S. (2000) 'Foucault's heterotopia and children's everyday lives', *Childhood*, 7 (4): 479–92.

Mannell, R.C. and Kleiber, D.A. (1997) *A Social Psychology of Leisure*. State College, PA: Venture.

Martin, G. (1999) *Why Americans Hate Welfare: Race, Media, and the Politics of Anti-Poverty Policy*. Chicago: University of Chicago Press.

Miles, R. (1980) 'Class, race, and ethnicity: a critique of Cox's theory', *Ethnic and Racial Studies*, 3: 130–43.

Minichiello, V., Browne, J. and Kendig, H. (2000) 'Perceptions and consequences of ageism: views of older people', *Ageing and Society*, 20 (3): 253–78.

Mishra, S. (1992) 'Leisure activities and life satisfaction in old age', *Activities, Adaptation, & Aging*, 16: 7–26.

Morris, J. (1991) *Pride against Prejudice*. London: The Women's Press.

Neugarten, B.L., Havighurst, R.J. and Tobin, S.S. (1968) 'Personality and patterns of aging', in B.L. Neugarten (ed.), *Middle Age and Aging*. Chicago: University of Chicago Press.

Nimrod, G. (2007) 'Expanding, reducing, concentrating and diffusing: post retirement leisure behavior and life satisfaction', *Leisure Sciences*, 29 (1): 91–111.

Ogden, D.C. and Hilt, M.L. (2003) 'Collective identity and basketball: an explanation for the decreasing number of African-Americans on America's baseball diamonds', *Journal of Leisure Research*, 35 (2): 213–27.

Oldham, A.L. (2002) *2Stoned*. London: Secker & Warburg.

Parker, S. (1982) *Work and Retirement*. London: George Allen and Unwin.

Parsons, T. (1951) *The Social System*. London: Routledge & Kegan Paul.

Payne, L.L., Mowen, A. J. and Montoro-Rodriguez, J. (2006) 'The role of leisure style in maintaining the health of older adults with arthritis', *Journal of Leisure Research*, 38 (1): 20–45.

Phillip, S.F. (1995) 'Race and leisure constraints', *Leisure Sciences*, 17: 109–20.

Phillip, S.F. (1999) 'Are we welcome? African American racial acceptance in leisure activities and the importance given to children's leisure', *Journal of Leisure Research*, 31 (4): 385–403.

Phillip, S.F. (2000) 'Race and the pursuit of happiness', *Journal of Leisure Research*, 32 (1): 121–4.

Phillipson, C. (1982) *Capitalism and the Construction of Old Age*. London: Macmillan.

Postman, N. (1983) *The Disappearance of Childhood*. London: W.H. Allen.

Ravenscroft, N. and Markwell, S. (2000) 'Ethnicity and the integration and exclusion of young people through urban park and recreation provision', *Managing Leisure*, 5: 135–50.

Ragheb, M. and Griffith, C. (1982) 'The contribution of leisure participation and leisure satisfaction to life satisfaction of older persons', *Journal of Leisure Research*, 14: 295–306.

Riddick, C. (1985) 'The relative contribution of leisure activities and other factors in the mental health of older women', *Journal of Leisure Research*, 16: 136–48.

Riddick, C.C. and Stewart, D.G. (1994) 'An examination of the life satisfaction and importance of leisure in the lives of older female retirees: a comparison of blacks to whites', *Journal of Leisure Research*, 26 (1): 75–87.

Romsa, G., Bondy, P. and Blenman, M. (1985) 'Modeling retirees' life satisfaction levels. The role of recreational, life cycle and socio-environmental elements', *Journal of Leisure Research*, 17: 29–39.

Rousseau, J.J. ([1762]1993) *Émile*, translated by B. Foxley. London: Dent.

Russell, R. (1987) 'The importance of recreation satisfaction and activity participation to the life satisfaction of age segregated retirees', *Journal of Leisure Research*, 19: 273–84.

Schuman, H. and Hatchett, S. (1974) *Black Racial Attitudes: Trends and Complexities*. Ann Arbor, MI: Survey Research Centre.

Shakespeare, T. and Watson, M. (1997) 'Defending the social model', *Disability and Society*, 12: 293–300.

Shakespeare, T., Gillespie-Sells, K. and Davies, D. (1996) *The Sexual Politics of Disability*. London: Cassell.

Shmanske, S. (1997) 'Life-cycle happiness in a discounted utility model', *Kyklos*, 50 (3): 383–407.

Sports Council (1994) *Developing Sport Through CCT* (ISBN 1872158885).

St Louis, R. (2002) 'Sex as a discriminating variable in organizational reward decisions', *Academy of Management Journal*, 19: 469–76.

Stodolska, M. (1998) 'Assimilation and leisure constraints: dynamics of constraints on leisure in immigrant populations', *Journal of Leisure Research*, 30 (4): 521–51.

Taylor, M.J. and Hegarty, S. (1985) *The Best of Both Worlds … ? A Review of Research into the Education of Pupils of South Asian Origin*. Windsor: NFER-Nelson.

Thomson, R.G. (1996) *Freakery – Cultural Representations of the Extraordinary Body*. New York: New York University Press.

Thomson, R.G. (1997) *Extraordinary Bodies: Figuring Physical Disability in American Culture and Literature*. New York: Columbia University Press.

Torres, S. (1999) 'A culturally-relevant theoretical framework for the study of successful ageing', *Ageing and Society*, 19: 33–51.

Washburne, R.E. (1978) 'Black under participation in wildland recreation: alternative explanations', *Leisure Sciences*, 1: 175–89.

Wendell, S. (2001) 'Unhealthy disabled: treating chronic illnesses as disabilities', *Hypatia*, 16 (4): 17–33.

West, P.C. (1989) 'Urban region parks and black minorities: subculture, marginality and inter racial relations in park use in the Detroit metropolitan area', *Leisure Sciences*, 11: 11–28.

Wolley, H. and Amin, N. (1999) 'Pakistani teenagers' use of public open space in Sheffield', *Managing Leisure*, 4: 156–67.

Woodard, M.D. (1988) 'Class, regionality, and leisure among urban black Americans: the post Civil Rights era', *Journal of Leisure Research*, 20: 87–105.

Woodhill, J. (1996) 'Natural resources decision making beyond the Landcare paradox', *The Australasian Journal of Natural Resources Law and Policy*, 3 (1): 91–114.

5

THE EMERGENCE OF AN INSTITUTIONAL FRAMEWORK FOR LEISURE

By the end of this chapter, you should have a critical understanding of:

- the concept of rational recreation, which will be explained and then followed by a discussion of why it became significant in nineteenth-century leisure in relation to:
  - o the development of mass tourism and the rise of the British seaside resort
  - o the control of gambling and the public house
  - o the role of Physical Education and schools in the processes of rational recreation
- constraints on women's leisure participation in the nineteenth century
- employer-sponsored rational recreation
- the functionalist account of leisure and social change
- figurational sociology with specific reference to The Leicester School of Football Hooliganism
- relevant theories and research in all of the areas above.

Introduction

The second half of the nineteenth century was a period of rapid social and economic change that saw the emergence of 'modernity': the modern industrial society. Modernity brought with it serious issues in relation to public health, sanitation and unplanned urbanisation. The State had serious concerns about the changing nature of class, class conflict, public order and work. Unlike in the pre-industrial rural economy, under the new industrial factory system, people worked in more rational and formalised settings with regulated hours. Time spent earning a living dictated time left over for leisure. The separation of 'work time' from 'leisure time' that was central to modernity emerged during this period, although the leisure activities of some sections of the working class raised serious concerns in the minds of Victorian opinion formers. In particular, there were concerns that working-class leisure was often accompanied by alcohol. There was movement for greater State intervention to regulate working-class leisure in public places and concerns about moral content and public order implications of working-class leisure. In this chapter, the emergence of the 'rational recreation' movement will be explained. Rational recreation was one of the key factors in the emergence of a national framework for leisure.

Rational recreation was based upon a basic humanitarian sympathy with the plight of the urban working class. According to the historian Bailey (1978), in the 1830s and 1840s, there were serious problems of public health and poverty. Within middle-class circles, there was a serious debate on the 'Condition of England' and in particular the problem of the 'dangerous classes'. In particular, Chartism was perceived to be a threat to social stability and public order. Recreation was seen as an instrument for educating the working classes in the social values of middle-class orthodoxy. Regulated amusement was seen as a safety valve for 'eager energies'. There was a need for 'regulated amusement'; Victorian opinion formers wanted to cut back on the working-class excesses of drunkenness, feasting, brawling, fornication and other 'regrettable indulgences'. There was a need to provide alternative recreations that stimulated and restored the mind. After Chartist agitation in 1842, for example, Benjamin Heywood, a Manchester banker, reformed the Manchester Lyceum to create a 'community of enjoyment' that would engender 'reciprocal feelings' between employer and employee.

Reformers agreed that there was a need for more recreational amenities in the manufacturing towns. In the United Kingdom, the Select Committee on Drunkenness (1834) recommended the provision of: public walks, public gardens, open spaces, libraries, museums and reading rooms. In 1845, for example, Sir Robert Peel made a gift of £1000 towards the establishment of Peel Park in Manchester. Again in the United Kingdom, the Libraries Act (1850) allowed town councils to levy a small rate to pay for the housing and servicing of libraries, but as Bailey points out, not to buy books. Reformers recognised the need for example-setting by the *superior classes*.

Bailey (1978) suggests that within the community, moral constraints on the worst excesses of working-class leisure activities were imposed in the hope that such moral obligation would become stamped on the minds of working-class people and become self-acting imperatives.

The aim was to stimulate working-class self-help. The general strategy of rational recreation was to provide new amenities that would divert working-class men from the pub and provide an environment in which working-class men would be exposed to middle-class values. Those values would ultimately be internalised. As Bailey argues, it was these assumptions that underpinned such things as the tea party and the soiree, where the good manners of the middle class would rub off on the working-class guests.

Rational recreation

... social policy concerns not only related to public health and fitness of the workforce but also to the moral welfare of the working class, with the content of their leisure. These concerns – which are evidenced in such legislation as the Museums Act 1845 and the Libraries Act 1850 – are usually referred to as the 'rational recreation movement' ...The concern of this movement was to provide alternatives to the perceived degeneracy of working class social life, to provide a cultural content for leisure time. (Henry, 1990: 6)

Rational recreation was a regimen that attempted to make leisure activities 'morally uplifting' and prevent national disorder. It was important to provide the population with opportunities to maintain physical fitness, counter-balance the debilities of city life, maintain readiness for armed service, and provide self-discipline, self-control, public spirit, physical fitness and opportunities for teamwork.

Mass Tourism and Seaside Holidays

Lowerson and Myerscough (1977), in their study of leisure in Sussex, argue that during the course of the nineteenth century 'leisure revolution', the lives of most people became polarised into distinct work and non-work time and that many of today's leisure habits still have a distinctly Victorian feel to them. Rapid urbanisation reduced the opportunities for working-class people to engage in regular exercise. In addition, there were few opportunities for working-class people to improve intellectually. Although Lowerson and Myerscough (1977) do not explore the process of class formation, they do explain how 'social imitation' had a role to play in the changing quantity and quality of leisure time. Seaside resorts developed during this period by providing seaside holidays for the middle classes and day excursions for the working classes.

Nineteenth-century seaside resorts became characterised as 'rough' or 'respectable'. *Black's Guide* goes on to compare Brighton unfavourably with Eastbourne on the grounds that Eastbourne is 'more select than Brighton' (cited in Lowerson and Myerscough, 1977: 37).

John Urry: Mass tourism and the seaside resort

Why did the industrial working class come to think that going away for short periods was an appropriate form of social activity? John Urry (1990) asks the question: why did the tourist gaze develop amongst the industrial working class in the north of England?

The seaside resort represented a new mode by which pleasure was organised. Urry (1990) argues that the seaside holiday was one of a number of invented nineteenth-century leisure pursuits, as indeed were:

- the Royal Tournament (1888)
- the Varsity Match (1872)
- the Highland Games (1852).

The growth of such tourism represents a 'democratisation of travel' (Urry, 1990: 16). Mass tourism was a feature of nineteenth-century industrialisation. As travel became more democratic, distinctions of taste were established between different places. Where one travelled also became socially significant: a major difference of 'social tone' was established, a resort 'hierarchy' developed, and some places became symbols of mass tourism and viewed by the dominant groups as tasteless, common and vulgar.

Urry (1990) argues that in the eighteenth century, there was an increase in sea bathing. However, the beach was a place of 'medicine' rather than 'pleasure', and 'treatment' was regulated by 'dippers' – women were responsible for immersion into the sea water. It was not until the nineteenth century that the Victorians replaced the *medicalised* beach with a *pleasure* beach.

The development of costal resorts was spectacular, as Urry (1990) argues:

- there was a population growth of 2.56 per cent per annum, compared with 2.38 for manufacturing towns
- Brighton increased its population from 7000 to 65,000 in less than 50 years
- the population of 48 leading seaside towns increased by 100,000 between 1861 and 1871
- by 1911, 55 per cent of people in England and Wales took at least one trip to the seaside, and 20 per cent stayed for a longer period each year.

This rapid growth was a product of several factors – Urry (1990) identifies the following:

- an increase in the economic welfare of the industrial population
- a quadrupling of national income per head over the nineteenth century
- an increase in working-class savings
- rapid urbanisation: in 1801, 20 per cent lived in towns, but by 1901, this was 80 per cent
- high levels of poverty and overcrowding in urban areas
- self-regulating working-class communities
- few areas with public spaces such as parks and gardens
- the growth of a more organised and routinised pattern of work leading to attempts to develop a corresponding rationalisation of leisure
- campaigns against drinking, idleness, blood sports, bad language and fairs

(Continued)

(Continued)

- the reduction of working hours as work became more rational
- factory owners beginning to acknowledge 'wakes weeks': periods of regular holiday
- total closure of the mill, which was seen as contributing to efficiency
- improved transportation: in the 1830s, the railway companies concentrated on goods traffic
- Gladstone's Railway Act 1844 which obligated companies to make provision for the 'labouring classes'. The Railway companies attempted to create their own resort: Silloth.

In 1848, Urry estimated that 100,000 day trippers travelled from Manchester to Blackpool in Whit week, while in 1850 over 200,000 made the journey in the same week. Blackpool had no scenic attractions – the aim of the resort was to provide fun for working-class people. The social tone of Blackpool became downmarket. Blackpool invested large sums of money in fun attractions; private investment in hotels; £1.5 million on the promenade and gardens; £400,000 on swimming pools; £1.25 million on a park; and £1.25 million on the Winter Gardens. Seaside resorts normally had one pier; Blackpool had three, and a tower. Blackpool Pleasure Beach opened in 1906 – architect Joseph Emberton had attempted to create an 'Architecture of Pleasure', with light, sun, fresh air and fun. Jack Radcliffe gave it a new look in 1950. The Pleasure Beach still attracts more than 6.5 million visitors per year.

Wealthier holidaymakers went elsewhere: 'Holiday-making is a form of conspicuous consumption in which status attributions are made on the basis of *where* one has stayed and depends in part upon what the *other* people are like who also stay there' (Urry, 1990: 23).

Activity: Mass tourism and the seaside resort

By the early nineteenth century pressure was put on the government by many social reformers and philanthropists to improve living conditions, and by the end of the 1880s most urban areas were providing sewers, running water, public baths, public parks and open spaces. The concept of government responsibility for the health and quality of life of the people was born. (Doggett and Mahoney, 1999: 12)

Question: In the nineteenth century, reformers were campaigning for more open space, fresh air and exercise to improve general health and fitness of the working class and to improve their productivity. To what extent did Blackpool fulfil the reformers' expectations?

Gambling and the Public House

For Huizinga (1949), gambling is the dark side of play, an entirely negative activity. The control of gambling and drinking were central to the movement for rational recreation. However, in the nineteenth century, both the gambling and drinking businesses were commercially successful and both were morally condemned. In the case of gambling, Flavin (2003) argues that there was a conflict between the desire to control working-class leisure and the desire by capitalist entrepreneurs to make a profit from their leisure. For Flavin, the argument was won by the entrepreneurs over the moralists.

From the Middle Ages onwards, primarily because of the influence of the Puritans, gambling was regarded as a moral issue in the United Kingdom. Acts of Parliament in 1823 and 1826 made lotteries illegal and ended state-sponsored lotteries. The 1845 Gaming Act made all gambling debts, such as a wager between two individuals, unenforceable by law. The Betting Houses Act (1853) was primarily concerned with the suppression of cash betting between working-class people and betting-shop owners. Betting was believed to encourage idleness and crime, particularly theft from employers to fund the increasingly popular habit of cash betting. There was a significant increase in the number of betting shops in the early years of the nineteenth century and the 1853 Act attempted to place cash betting within the same context as other morally contemptible activities such as drunkenness and violence. Gambling was not morally uplifting, often encouraged people to take risks with their family income, encouraged people to behave in ways that were irrational and did not help people to prepare for a healthy work or family life. The Betting Houses Act (1853) was to stay in force until 1960 when betting shops were made legal but under strict regulation.

Activity: Gambling

Gambling was one of the most popular leisure activities in the early nineteenth century. Mark Clapson (1992) argues that the long tours of duty during the Napoleonic Wars together with lax systems of credit allowed men to defer payment of gambling debts until they had returned from a period of fighting. However, from the eighteenth century, there were restrictions imposed on gambling in coffee houses and public houses. Also, restrictions were placed on the games that could be played elsewhere and the amount of money that could be played for. In 1822, individuals found playing unlawful games, or keeping a house for gambling, could be charged under the Vagrancy Act and be classed as vagabonds.

Rendell (1999) argues:

Concerns with the immorality of gambling were voiced by both the upper classes who feared losing their money to working class entrepreneurs, and the rising middle classes who saw gambling as an upper class vice, opposing values of stability, property, domesticity, family life and religion. For capitalists, on the one hand, gambling was favourable, since it involved speculation – a process central to the accumulation of capital; on the other,

(Continued)

(Continued)

it provided the opportunity for working classes to earn money without labouring, a concept entirely opposed to the work ethic of capitalism and described as lazy and extravagant ... The potential instability of class hierarchy indicated by gambling resulted in its representation as an immoral and dangerous pastime. (Rendell, 1999: 180–81)

Questions: Would you accept or reject Rendell's argument that gambling was seen as immoral and dangerous because it demonstrated the 'potential instability of class hierarchy'? Are there other reasons why people might consider gambling 'immoral and/or dangerous'?

More recently, in the United Kingdom before 1960, off-course cash betting was illegal and bookmakers would employ 'runners' to gather bets from 'punters' in pubs and working men's clubs. In the Thatcher years, the betting industry was deregulated, and a number of pieces of legislation were introduced, notably the Betting Act (1986) which allowed bookmakers to open on Sundays and in the evenings. A number of authors have pointed to the benefits gained by the exchequer because of the decriminalisation of betting and its subsequent deregulation (Cornish, 1977; Munting, 1996; Paton et al., 2002; Reid, 1995; Smith et al., 2006). Paton et al. (2002) suggest that excise duties, such as that on gambling, constitute 10 per cent of total UK government revenue. However, because of factors such as Person-to-Person (P2P) betting over the internet and offshore betting over the internet and telephone and the establishment of the National Lottery, the level of revenue collected by the government started to decline in the later 1990s. Paton et al. (2002) argue that as a consequence of people changing their betting habits and playing the National Lottery, the amount of money placed on football pools declined by 60 per cent between 1993 and 1999; similarly, the number of bingo clubs also declined by a similar level over the same period. In 2001, the Chancellor of the Exchequer outlined plans for a major rethink of betting tax, with the introduction of a 'gross profits tax' on the net profits of bookmakers. There have been similar debates on betting tax and the impact of the internet in Australia and the United States.

In the United States, gambling policy and taxation of gambling is at state level. In addition, because Native American tribes have the status of sovereign nations, this has also provided the opportunity for Indian casinos and riverboat casinos to emerge. Paton et al. (2002) explain that in 1978, only Nevada allowed casinos to operate legally, but by 1999, 27 states had legalised casino gambling. Much of the debate in the United States, argues Paton, is focused on the potential social costs and moral problems that can arise with gambling. In an analysis of gambling in Australia, Smith (2000) also found that taxes from gambling make up a significant amount of tax revenue, and much of the debate is about how to maintain the competitiveness of businesses against overseas competition.

In the United Kingdom, the Gambling Act (2005) established the Gambling Commission, a non-departmental public body, sponsored by the Department for Culture, Media and Sport, but funded by licence fees from the gambling industry. The Commission regulates all commercial gambling, including betting on horse racing, football and other sporting events, bingo, casinos, lotteries, pool betting, amusements with prizes (gaming machines) and UK-based remote betting (for example, betting over the internet, by mobile phone or interactive TV). The only areas of gambling not regulated by the Commission are the National Lottery and spread betting. Spread betting is regulated by the Financial Services Authority and there are currently four companies that dominate the market: Cantor Index, Spreadex, Sporting Index and IG Index.

The Commission's objectives are:

- to prevent gambling from having any connection with crime
- to make sure that gambling is managed fairly and openly
- to protect children and others in potential danger from being harmed or exploited.

Local Authorities issue operating licences on behalf of the Commission to people who want to run gambling businesses. The Commission has a strict code of practice for the management of gambling facilities and powers to monitor licence holders, impose fines or withdraw licences. The Commission can also investigate and prosecute illegal gambling under the Gambling Act. In addition, the Commission is the British government's main advisory body on gambling.

Since the nineteenth century, the British government has taken the position that regulation of gambling is in the public interest. However, with the establishment of the Gambling Commission, there has been a definite shift in emphasis – under the Commission's own regulations, the stance currently taken is that gambling activities must always be seen as *risk-based*. As long ago as the mid-1960s, Rosett (1965) and Weitzman (1965) described gamblers as 'risk loving'.

Edgework: Voluntary Risk Taking

Stephen Lyng (1990, 2005) argues that while there has been movement to reduce the threats to our general well-being in the workplace and elsewhere, there is a group of people that actively seek out activities that may cause personal injury or death in their leisure activities. Hand-gliders, sky-divers and rock-climbers appear to find risk taking necessary to the maintenance of their well-being. It is commonly assumed that such people have a personality type that pushes them toward such risky activities. Stress is needed to fulfil arousal. Lyng attempts to put this risk taking into a broader social and historical context by drawing upon the work of Marx and Mead. From Marx, Lyng takes the idea that people are by their nature creative beings that enjoy the exercise of their skills and from Mead, Lyng takes the idea that people can gain pleasure by enhancing their conception of 'I'.

The common features of edgework are that the activities are on the border between order and disorder and involve a serious threat to a participant's physical or mental well-being or a threat to a participant's ordered existence. With gambling, in particular, there is a strong reliance on the participant's individual context-specific skill and capacity to maintain personal safety.

Getting as close to the edge without going over often involves alterations in the participant's perception and consciousness – a feeling of *oneness* with the environment. In many respects, the self-determination and self-actualisation, heightened perception and consciousness is similar to Csikszentmihalyi's (1990) conception of flow.

Lyng (1990) argues that men rather than women are more likely to engage in edgework. However, Rajah (2007) uses the concept of edgework to explain the strategies that women can use to negotiate their relationship with intimate partners who have a tendency towards violence.

This is not to suggest that women do not gamble. Emma Casey (2003, 2004, 2006) has explored the interconnection between women's gambling and their sense of self, social roles and family responsibilities. Playing the National Lottery is one of the most popular forms of gambling amongst women in the UK. As a leisure activity, playing the National Lottery requires very little time or space and does not require separation from the family or any abandonment of women's duty of care responsibilities. Playing the lottery allows women to gain pleasure without ever leaving behind their caring selves. Drawing on Skeggs' (1997) conception of 'respectability', women who play the lottery carefully and 'responsibly' never let playing the lottery interfere with their role as careful family budgeters. Women can negotiate the right to play the lottery if they can demonstrate to others that their caring lives were never disrupted. The women lottery players who Casey interviewed always carefully distinguished themselves from the irresponsible and wasteful gambling of 'other' women who spent the family budget on scratch cards and lottery games. Reference to these 'irresponsible women' was used to reinforce a self-image of responsible gambling behaviour.

Activity: Gambling and risk

Kingma and Boersma (2004) investigate the liberalisation of gambling in the Netherlands by drawing upon Ulrich Beck's (1992) conception of *risk society*. Gambling liberalisation in the Netherlands included: the decriminalisation of amusements with prizes (slot machines) in 1986; the expansion in the number of casinos in 1989; the introduction of a postcode lottery in 1989; and the privatisation of the state lottery in 1992. There was concern that these moves would put people at greater risk of becoming addicted to gambling. However, there were disagreements between the political parties as to the potential risks involved in each of these areas. Kingma and Boersma state that with liberalisation, there was a shift from an *alibi model* of gambling, in which people looked for reasons as to why a person became addicted, to a *risk model* in which it was accepted that high stakes could bring high levels of enjoyment. Addiction may be psychological in nature – in many cases, the symptoms are not visible until well established. However, addiction needs to be seen within the context of a social construction of moderate and acceptable risk. Gamblers Anonymous, political parties and the media all have a role to play in this social construction. What constitutes an acceptable and enjoyable level of risk and if and when this level becomes unacceptable is not clearly stated by organisations who are involved in commentating on gambling.

Questions: What constitutes an acceptable level of risk in terms of gambling? Could you argue that gambling is a form of *edgework*? What behaviours would a person have to engage in for you to label a person a gambling addict? Who do you believe is responsible for a person's gambling addiction?

Activity

P2P betting is a form of 'bet brokerage' over the internet in which a company acts as an intermediary allowing people to come together online and lay and accept bets. The companies who run the websites do not offer odds but simply provide a service for a small commission. The market leader in internet gambling is currently Betfair. Smith et al. (2006) explain that online betting exchanges provide customers with a list of the best odds that other customers are currently offering. Alternatively, customers can state the odds and the stake they are willing to wager on a given event so that other customers can accept the bet if they so choose. These prices are often much better than high street bookmakers are willing to offer.

Question: What potential problems do you think might emerge from such transactions?

Why do people gamble?
The functionalist account

Devereux (1949, 1968) develops a functionalist account of the role of gambling within the social system of the United States. Devereux (1968) suggests that gambling serves a number of important psychological functions and even the disapproval of gambling is functional for the wider social system. Within any social system, people face a range of difficult psychological problems generated by the conflicts within the economic system, strains and ambivalences. Gambling can provide an 'institutionalised solution' for many of these embedded stresses and strains generated by the economic system. Gambling provides a channel for 'disruptive speculative tendencies' and also has important 'value reinforcing' and 'scapegoating' social functions. Bloch (1951) suggests that gambling has wider social functions for the social system, notably that gambling helps to reinforce stability and routine within the social system in that it gives people an opportunity to explore and predict uncertainty.

Gambling: the interactionist account

In contrast to Devereux, Downes and Bloch, Erving Goffman developed an interactionist conception of gambling. In Goffman's analysis of gambling, people have expectations at two levels: firstly, maintaining the emotional solidarity with others' *expressive order* by informal behavioural or psychological expectations and, secondly, more rigid decision making that draws upon a layer of reflexivity that is *outside of the interaction itself*. In his essay, 'Where the action is', Goffman (1967) discusses these two levels of expectation in relation to the motivation of gamblers and other similar risk takers. All decisions take place within one of three 'action spaces':

- 'Killing time' – when people are killing time they are not involved in any activity that has consequences for other areas of their lives.
- 'Routine activity' – activities that are described as 'routine' in nature consist of the regular business of everyday life.
- 'Action' which is behaviour focused on 'an occasion generated by the exercise of self-determination, an occasion for *taking* risk and *grasping opportunity*' (Goffman, 1967: 161) – in other words, on taking chances, such as gambling. As Goffman explains: 'by the term *action* I mean activities that are consequential, problematic, and undertaken for what is felt to be their own sake' (Goffman, 1967: 185).

For Goffman, breaking with routine allows a person to exercise their creative capacity, and when they successfully overcome risk, this transforms routine activity and brings about social change.

Neal (1999), in an ethnographic account of betting shops in the United Kingdom, found that there were distinct categories of 'core punters' in the betting shops he visited: 'morning punters' who bet higher stakes and placed more combination bets (round robins and yankees) rather than single bets. Other categories included 'weekday lunchtime punters', 'weekday afternoon punters' and 'people who only bet on Saturday'.

Developments in the role of the public house

Outside of the home, there was a range of drinking establishments and inns which provided their customers with a range of services including food and accommodation as well as a wide range of alcoholic drinks. Alehouses and public houses also provided food but not accommodation. The number of beer houses increased significantly after the 1830 Beer Act that allowed anybody who paid poor rates to use their home as a beer house if they paid two guineas in excise. With the expansion of the railways in the 1840s and 1850s, many traditional inns suffered a loss of revenue to the newly established railway inns. In Brighton, where there was one drinking establishment per 210 residents, Lowerson and Myerscough (1977) found there were a number of specialist pubs, catering for the needs of specific client groups such as 'the superior class of servants' (Lowerson and Myerscough, 1977: 66). In addition, they found that Brighton's drinking establishments had many female clients – the pubs in Church Road, for example, they argue, were used by prostitutes. However, drinking during the day, especially on Mondays, was common amongst married women, and couples would go out drinking on Saturday nights in pubs that ran a 'free and easy'. Towards the end of the nineteenth century, new theatrical entertainments emerged, notably the music hall. Whereas pubs provided opportunities for local amateur acts, the music hall made use of professional acts.

According to John Greenaway (1998), the temperance movement in the nineteenth century was prohibitionist in nature and its stated aim was to completely abolish public houses. However, because of the limited success of the movement, especially amongst working-class people, between 1870 and 1950, there was a 'lively debate' about the role of the public house. There was a distinct shift in the strategy of many temperance supporters towards promoting an 'improved public house' that would promote alternative interests to drink and promote temperance and sobriety. The Mayor of Birmingham, Joseph Chamberlain, believed that the way forward was to eliminate the vested interest of the publican to increase sales. For Greenaway, local authority control was a mechanism for reducing the demand for intoxicants and at the same time for promoting civic improvements and social reform.

Chamberlain adopted the 'Gothenburg system' from Sweden that allowed local authorities to transfer all the spirit licences in their area to a single company. The managers of the pubs were given no financial reward from the sale of alcohol – the shareholders were to receive a 6 per cent return on capital, and any surplus would go to the rate payers. Other similar attempts at local authority control were attempted elsewhere in the United Kingdom, notably in Carlisle after 1915.

However, with the outbreak of war in 1914, the state became increasingly concerned about the drunkenness and absenteeism of shipyard and munitions workers. In 1915, the Central Control Board was established and imposed restrictions on the alcoholic content of drinks and limited the opening hours of public houses. In Britain, it was only with the election of the Thatcher government in 1979 that limited deregulation of opening hours took place.

Physical Education and Schools

A key institution for socialising children away from the evils of gambling and drink was the school. In addition to providing moral and religious guidance, schools also catered for the physical well-being of the child.

The notion of Physical Education is a contested concept and has been the centre of bitter debate for over 150 years in the United Kingdom. Currently, Physical Education is a National Curriculum subject and all children in the

United Kingdom have Physical Education classes at school. With initiatives such as 'Learning through PE and Sport' (April 2003), the United Kingdom government is investing heavily to transform Physical Education and improve school sport facilities. The Blair government believed that school sports has a role to play in averting social exclusion. The National Curriculum for Physical Education requires schools to use six categories of activities: games, gymnastics, athletics, dance, outdoor and adventurous activities, and swimming and water safety to facilitate learning in the following areas:

- acquiring and developing skills
- selecting and applying skills
- tactics and compositional ideas
- evaluating and improving performance
- knowledge and understanding of fitness and health.

In the 1850s, Physical Education in the United Kingdom took the form of drill and was rooted in the assumption that marching and other military manoeuvres and exercise were morally uplifting. As Kirk (2003) explains, military forms of drilling and exercise for young primary school children in the 1880s were based upon the assumption that children had to be controlled and disciplined. In fee paying schools, boys and girls had played games as a central element of their Physical Education since the 1850s. The first official government syllabus for Physical Education in schools was published in 1909 and was based upon the Ling system of physical education, or as it was sometimes known, the Swedish Movement System – a system of freestanding exercises devised by Per Henrick Ling, based upon the assumption that good health could be achieved by improving blood circulation through exercise. At this time, Physical Education in schools was known as Physical Training, and the Ling system was viewed as progressive and based upon a 'therapeutic rationale'. The Ling system greatly influenced the later development of Physical Education in British schools because of its association with rational recreation, notably the assumption that exercise aided moral and character development.

However, by the 1930s, many teachers believed that the Ling system was too regimented and an alternative system, based upon the ideas of Rudolf Laban, called Kinetographic Laban or Labanotation, became popular. Laban believed it was possible to identify general laws of movement to form a looser and more creative form of gymnastics based upon a system derived from dance notation in which all bodily movement was recorded.

By 1946, the term 'Physical Education' became widely adopted in the United Kingdom, with some teachers, mainly women trained in private, single-sex Physical Education colleges, favouring dance and gymnastics, whilst another group of mainly male teachers returning from wartime service believed that Physical Education should be based upon team sports and games.

Team Sports

The nineteenth century also saw developments in the field of sports built upon the Puritan ideals. So called 'disorderly pursuits', usually involving cruelty to animals, were replaced by a range of 'orderly and healthy games' that stressed 'human athletic endeavour' as a form of self-improvement. The Football Association was formed in 1863 and the Rugby Football Union in 1872.

According to Cherry and Munting (2005), organised team sports, especially a well contested game of cricket, were believed to be morally uplifting and important to both physical and mental health. Such activities were believed to encourage the natural healing powers of the body. It was for these reasons that team sports became integrated into the school curriculum. Well contested, organised team sports were central to the concept of 'muscular Christianity'. During this period, mental health problems were believed to be caused by a 'hereditary taint' and Cherry and Munting (2005) argue that team sports and games were believed by medical opinion to have therapeutic benefits. From 1850 to 1950, around three people per 1000 of the population were diagnosed as being of 'unsound mind' and found themselves in county asylums or work-houses. The causes of mental illness at this time were assumed to be physical in nature, caused by a range of 'toxins' in alcohol and sexually transmitted diseases. Men risked their sanity by associating with prostitutes or by self-abuse that was a central cause of 'spermatorrhoea' – the diminution of vital power and bodily function. In addition, because the number of patients was so large, individual care was not possible and medical opinion turned to the benefits of team sports. Cherry and Munting (2005) explain that the games ethic was immersed into the culture and values of Victorian England. Cricket and other team sports helped to maintain the mental well-being of boys' public schools and inmates in mental hospitals.

From the 1890s, when association football had secured its reputation as a less violent, contested, well-organised team sport, it too was included as a form of therapy.

Women and Leisure Participation in the Nineteenth Century

In the nineteenth century, the emerging institutional framework for leisure had a distinct patriarchal and fraternal structure. Women were often excluded from participation by patriarchal structures. However, fraternal affiliations, based upon class, politics and nationalism were used to exclude certain categories of men. Women were often excluded from shops, clubs – including the Jockey Club and the Marylebone Cricket club – coffee houses and taverns. The establishment and control of clubs by men gave men control over the shaping of the legislative framework for leisure and sport. Jane Rendell (1999) explains that in the early nineteenth century, there was a shift from private patriarchy, with a focus on the control of women in the home, to more public displays of patriarchy with a focus on the control of women in public leisure spaces.

Catriona Parratt (2001), striking a balance between structural forces and choices made by human agency in shaping leisure choices, argues that rational recreation was a central strategy in the creation of a set of social arrangements that gave nineteenth century industrial capitalism a patriarchal feel. In particular, Parratt (2001) argues that gender was an important constraint on women's leisure and that leisure institutions built and reinforced gender hierarchies, inequities and identities. However, many women did resist the constraint and used leisure spaces as an arena in which to confront and even resist patriarchy. One example of resistance that did enhance the leisure of middle-class women in the Victorian period was the development of the Assembly Rooms. In her study of Almack's Assembly Rooms, Rendell (2002) argues that the Assembly Rooms were organised and run by women as a private club, but acted as a 'matrimonial market'. Women controlled entry to the space by strict dress codes for both men and women and by charging a subscription. Although the layout of the rooms did vary, the purpose was always to provide women with a space to enjoy concerts, balls and masquerades with the intention of meeting suitable men outside of the control of the home environment.

There was a rise in disposable income during the nineteenth century and Victorian men experienced a range of developments in relation to their leisure activities, although Victorian women, of all social classes, were largely restricted to home-based leisure. Women were expected to be chaperoned when they were outside of the home. Women's leisure participation was within the context of the family – shopping and visits to fairs, the music hall and the theatre, etc. would almost certainly be with other family members. For a woman to be seen without her chaperone was socially unacceptable and unescorted women were assumed to be prostitutes. With the constraints that nineteenth century women experienced in areas such as age, marital status, parental status, employment status, income and deeply entrenched patriarchal ideas about the appropriateness of any given leisure activity, it was only a minority of women who were in a position to exercise their skill and ability to overcome patriarchal assumptions about appropriate leisure pursuits for women.

In contrast to this view of female participation, in his account of the 're-gendering of consumer agency' in the United States during the nineteenth century, Terrence Witkowski (2004) draws upon research from Gordon and McArthur (1988), Perkins (1991) and Slater (1997) to show that before the mid-nineteenth century, it was men rather than women who were the active consumer agents for their households. This is a point reinforced by Rendell who argues, in the case of England, that distinct styles of dressing, talking and walking emerged in the early nineteenth century that reflected middle-class men's newly formed pre-occupation with self-presentation and public display. Within the fashionable streets of central London, newly established tailors, hatters, cravat makers, hairdressers, perfumers, jewellers, gun shops, booksellers, theatre ticket agents and sporting prints exhibitions were supplying the male consumer.

Witkowski defines consumer agency as: 'actively seeking, learning about and wanting new things; initiating and influencing household decision-making; and dealing with merchants, bringing things home, and then managing their consumption' (2004: 262–3).

Drawing upon concepts and approaches from art history, visual culture and postmodernism, Witkowski provides a 'visual account' of the changing gender ideology to trace the increasing feminisation of consumer agency and the making of market consumerism. Witkowski uses the art of Francis W. Edmonds (1806–1863), Lilly Martin Spencer (1822–1902) and others as a guide to understanding social attitudes and cultural conventions in the mid-nineteenth century United States. The work of these artists contains four ideological positions: female initiative and competence; male passivity and consumer ineptitude; the association of women with rising standards of living; and the sensualising and eroticising of household consumption. Not only were more women represented in art alone or in the company of other women in public spaces, but there was an increase in the representations of women performing household consumption-related activities. For Witkowski, women in the nineteenth century played a significant role in shaping consumerism.

Employer-sponsored Rational Recreation

Many nineteenth century employers believed their workforce needed to be more efficient, but they left the task of managing citizens in the hands of the state. This regulation took the form of measures such as the regulation of gambling, drink and prostitution. However, large-scale public organisations such as the post office, prison service, railway companies and police force took it upon themselves to organise after-work culture, including recreational activities for their employees. In her study of police leisure, Haia Shpayer-Makov (2002) argues that leisure was used by the police employers as an instrument of control, partly because it made officers more appreciative of management but also because of the nineteenth-century belief that regular physical exercise produced greater discipline and order in the force.

The strategies used by the employers to control officers outside of their work hours took a number of forms. In addition to helping enhance the physical capability of the men, police leisure was also expected to build character, enhance discipline and commitment and reinforce behaviour and attitudes believed by police leadership to be appropriate to the police officer. Police officers worked long hours and were often called back to duty during the day or night without additional pay. Police officers were geographically segregated from the wider community because of the residential policies of the police. Married officers had to live near the station in police housing and single officers in the police section house. Officers were expected to be moral exemplars in terms of their good character and exemplary conduct. Without their reputation, the employers assumed that officers would be unable to maintain the moral authority needed to do their job effectively. Senior officers assumed that policemen should have morally sound family relationships and regularly intervened in the policemen's choice of a bride, as wives were also expected to behave in a moral, respectable manner.

Police regulations discouraged officers from having any meaningful contact with people from outside the force, hence activities such as visiting pubs, gambling and associating with prostitutes were all contrary to police regulations. Such restrictions on leisure participation were not always popular with the officers concerned and *The Police Review* received many letters from resentful officers.

The railway companies also imposed similar controls over leisure activities of their employees. This was investigated by Redfern (1988) in his case study 'Crewe: Leisure in a Railway Town'.

What explanations have been suggested as to why leisure went through a period of social change during the nineteenth century? In the remainder of the chapter, there will be an investigation of two possible explanations: the Functionalist account of social change and the Figurational account of social change.

The Functionalist Account of Leisure and Social Change: Malcolmson

Malcolmson (1973) argues that in 1700, the status of popular recreation was still not secure, partly because leisure activities were organised within an 'oral tradition', not within an institutional framework. Drawing upon a range of historical sources and making use of a number of Functionalist assumptions about the nature of the nineteenth-century social system, Malcolmson describes the emergence of the institutional framework for leisure between 1700 and 1850. The institutional framework for leisure placed barriers to participation on the grounds of gender, age and class. Malcolmson, for example, quotes from John Strype writing about leisure in London in 1720. Strype explains that: 'the more common sort divert themselves at Football, Wrestling, Cudgels, Ninepins, Shovelboard, Cricket, Stow-ball, Ringing of Bells, Quoits, pitching the Bar, Bull and Bear bating, throwing at Cocks, and lying at Alehouses' (Malcolmson, 1973: 34). Social class was clearly a significant factor in the choice of leisure activities at the beginning of the eighteenth century and remains so up to the present day.

The Puritan tradition was still strong in England in 1700 and any 'recreational indulgence', such as drinking and dancing, could damage our conscientious application to work. Drinking was widely believed to add to a culture of licentious and loosening of sexual inhibitions at festive events such as May Day. However, in rural areas, the 'conservative tradition' of involvement in a range of festive events, such as the annual parish feast or *wake* and recreations associated with the changing nature of the seasons, notably the completion of the harvest, was strong enough to resist the largely urban and authoritarian Puritan values. In addition, key events in the life cycle – birth, death and marriages – were also seen as occasions for festive events. Commercial fairs for the sale of horses, cattle, sheep, cheese, etc. were also seen as opportunities for recreation. Winter holidays included 'Plough Monday' that fell on the first Monday after the twelfth day of Christmas. Malcolmson (1973) describes the 'Plough Monday' events in Messingham, Lincolnshire in the late eighteenth century as a situation in which the public house was the main venue for cock fights in the morning, whilst in the afternoon, football was played, and at the end of the day, there was dancing and playing cards.

Shrove Tuesday was another well-established winter holiday and the tradition of frying pancakes is still observed in England.

According to Malcolmson (1973), as we moved into the nineteenth century, increasing urbanisation saw a decline of the importance of custom and tradition as factors that regulated leisure activities, and with the greater freedom of choice, the state took a much closer interest and direct involvement in leisure activities that damaged the productive capability of the nation. In particular, the state was active in generating a set of habits in the poor that would see them become more fully active in the labour market. Many local authorities took action to ban street football as it became seen as a serious threat to public order. In the case of the United Kingdom, after the 1835 Cruelty to Animals Act, bull and bear bating were largely eliminated by the 1840s. In addition, a range of anti-blood sports organisations successfully argued that such sports were inhuman and uncivilised, notably the Society for the Prevention of Cruelty to Animals and the RSPCA who also made sure that the Act was observed. However, dog fighting, badger baiting and cock fighting were more difficult to eliminate. The 1835 Act excluded any protection to 'wildlife' so fox hunting, shooting and fishing continued to be legal activities. Sport and leisure became politicised in the urban environment and the institutional framework emerged as such activities changed to accommodate the new industrial social system.

The Evangelical Movement

According to Malcolmson (1973), the Evangelical Movement had a central role to play in the civilising of popular recreation. Not only did the Evangelical Movement maintain a strict observance of any leisure activity on the Sabbath, the evangelical sentiment was 'morally reformist' in nature and stressed the need for social and self-discipline because popular recreation was often seen to fuel the 'evil passions of human nature' and relax our moral defences. As Malcolmson explains, from the evangelical perspective, entertainment should be morally constructive and uplifting, refreshing the people's spirits and making them better prepared for more demanding higher tasks. This evangelical sentiment became one of respectability and was increasingly expressed in parliamentary debates and newspaper editorials. Wesleyan Methodism had a similar perspective on popular recreation.

For Malcolmson, the history of leisure is also a series of sequences of realignment of forces, group dissatisfaction, mobilisation and conflict, with resolution and the establishment of a new balance based upon a framework which is described as 'social–structural' and 'social–psychological' in nature, and which emphasises functional adaptation and conflict and takes into account the role of class and status groups. Dissatisfied individuals who find their leisure activities unsatisfactory in some way generate forces to change the institutional framework for leisure. An alternative account of social change in relation to sport and leisure is presented by Norbert Elias (1939/1978, 1939/1982) whose ideas have had a significant influence in the field. His account explains how violent folk games (such as street football) that were viewed as a serious threat to public order were transformed into organised rule-governed team sports. This transition was achieved by a process of passification of the population that was closely related to the processes of state formation. In the section that follows, we evaluate Elias' argument in relation to the work of the Leicester School of Football Hooliganism. This school is widely recognised as the most avid supporter of Elias' figurational approach.

Figurational Sociology: The Leicester School of Football Hooliganism

The concept of governance is central to the institutional framework that emerged in the nineteenth century, although some researchers, such as Giulianotti (1999), have suggested that Elias' approach is little more than a collection of 'untestable' and 'descriptive' generalisations. Bairner (2006) explains that the school has made a valuable contribution to the analysis of English hooligan behaviour. Moreover, King (2002) goes further and argues that the Leicester School's research is 'exemplary' because of its grasp of sociological theory and procedure. As Bairner suggests, the work of Norbert Elias is central to the study of sport and leisure because his figurational approach clearly explains how modern day sports emerged out of disorganised and violent folk games.

The civilising process is central to an understanding of the emergence of governance in sport. Elias explains why people choose to give up violence and accept rigid sets of rules and polite ways of behaving. For Elias, society is becoming more civilised and individuals more passified. In this section, an outline and evaluation of figurational sociology is presented that explains what Norbert Elias had to say and explains the influence that his ideas have had on one of the most influential groups of sociologists working in the field of Figurational Sociology: the Leicester School of Football Hooliganism. However, you may ask whether football hooliganism is a thing of the past.

The changing nature of *fandom*: the terminal decline of the football hooligan?

There is a widely accepted opinion that in England, football hooliganism is now a 'thing of the past' and that for reasons such as increasing ticket prices, much of the traditional fan base such as poor working-class young men, are unable to attend matches.

For over 20 years, Eric Dunning and the other members of the Leicester School have shaped the theories and research on crowd disturbances at football grounds. In contrast to the 'catharsis theory', the Leicester School argues that it draws upon the work of Norbert Elias to: 'effect a synthesis of sociological, historical and psychological approaches' (Dunning et al., 1988: 217), in order to understand crowd behaviour at football grounds. For Dunning and his colleagues, the social world can be understood independently of its location in time and space and is a product of the situated activities of human agents.

In this 2006 paper, Maguire traces the history of crowd disorder at the Den, the home of Millwall FC. For Maguire, spectator disorderliness at Millwall was directly related to the rough features of the social composition of the crowd and the structure of the community – hooligan behaviour is a hangover from nineteenth-century cock-fighting and bear-baiting. The 'rough' working-class Millwall fans and their communities have resisted colonisation by the 'civilising' actions of the state and groups such as the rational recreationalists.

Activity: Cat burning on Midsummer Day

In Paris during the sixteenth century it was one of the festive pleasures of Midsummer Day to burn alive one or two dozen cats. This ceremony was very famous. The populace assembled. Solemn music was played. Under a kind of scaffold an enormous pyre was erected. Then a sack or basket containing the cats was hung from the scaffold. The sack or basket began to smoulder. The cats fell into the fire and were burned to death, while the crowd revelled in their caterwauling … The cat-burning on Midsummer Day was a social institution, like boxing or horse racing in present day society. (Elias, 1939/1978: 203–4)

Question: Why do you think that people would be appalled by this activity in the twenty-first century?

The Civilising Process

For Elias, social change is a normal characteristic of all societies. Social change is conceived by Elias as a long-term social process brought about by structural changes in the figurations brought about by large numbers of interdependent people thinking and acting differently. Within the consciousness of people, there developed a distinction between the public and private spheres of life that transformed our personality structure. Individuals experienced much greater embarrassment and discomfort at the sight of people exercising their bodily functions openly in a public place.

What is a figuration?

The network of interdependencies among human beings is what binds them together. Such interdependencies are the nexus of what is here called the figuration, a structure of mutually oriented and dependent people. Since people are more or less dependent on each other first by nature and through social learning, through education, socialization, and socially generated reciprocal needs, they exist, one might venture to say, only as pluralities, only in figurations. (Elias, 1939/1978: 261)

Question: Figuration is a central concept in Elias' work. In your own words, give a short account of what you understand by the term figuration.

For Elias, the process of state formation included the centralisation of society under an absolutist form of rule that was central to the spread of processes of civilisation. In addition, a network of interdependencies intersects the lives of increasing numbers of people as they become dependent on maintaining the network of integration, differentiation and social function for their livelihood. The changing nature of the figuration in the late Middle Ages is not a product of individual design, nor is it a product of nature or the 'regularities of the mind', argues Elias. The processes of social change are evolutionary in nature, over and above the intentions and actions of individual human beings.

Sportisation

A sub-process of the wider civilising process is the process of sportisation – this is the transition of traditional games into modern sports, a process that involved a strict separation of the role of participant from the role of spectator and the gradual removal of violence and the imposition of codes of rules that maintained excitement and tension, but within a framework of restraint and regulation. In particular, there was a great deal of pressure brought to bear on activities that involved any form of cruelty to animals. A number of activities such as angling and fox hunting appeared to slip through the net and were still legal activities into the twenty-first century. However, fox hunting was always a restrained activity with well-established ritualised codes of behaviour used to control the activities of the participants.

Elias takes his starting point for the analysis of the state from Weber, who argued that the state has a monopoly of physical violence. The state emerges because it has more violent resources than any other group in the population. From this position of strength, the state attempts to impose internal passification on the population. Quilley (2004) argues that central to Elias' theory of the civilising process is the idea of a progressive internalisation of more restrained codes of conduct and more automatic patterns of self-control.

Wouters (2004) explains that the regime of manners is a form of regulated sociability that functions as a system of inclusion and exclusion from social circles, to maintain manners by excluding undesirable people who break the rules. Manners became the central marker for the identification of social rank and prestige. But such classifications were in relation to race, class and gender, argues Elias, rather than in terms of individual personal failing – however, repression and shame were experienced at a personal level. Shame was a central agent in the processes of social control for Elias and appropriate training into the *Kultur* of the society could develop both character and self-esteem.

Turner (2004) argues that religion had a central role to play in the processes of civilisation, in that religion always had a regulatory role to play in any society. However, Elias largely ignored this regulatory role and concentrated on the use of violence and the state.

Dunning and colleagues draw upon Elias' conception of state formation and passification to explain that the working class became increasingly 'incorporated' over the course of the nineteenth century and became increasingly uncomfortable and appalled at acts of violence in public places. On the basis of their research from within this Eliasian framework, the Leicester School argues that:

- crowd disturbances at football grounds is not a solely British or English phenomena, but is found in a range of sports across the world
- football hooliganism has a long history stretching back into the nineteenth century.

However, the Leicester School's account of hooligan behaviour is explained in terms that have little direct relevance to the Elias civilisation thesis. The emphasis is upon the rough working class forming an 'ordered segmentation', a separate cultural grouping within a wider working-class community that remains structurally disconnected from the broad sweep of civilising tendencies. Dunning and colleagues argue that the people who live within rough working-class areas develop their own set of 'moral standards' that emerge from the experience of living within a given locality and these 'moral standards' underpin *rough* behaviour.

This notion of figuration is not central to the Leicester School's conception of incorporation. According to Collins (2005), the problem at the centre of the Leicester School's application of the theory of the 'civilising process' is the assumption that the 'civilising process' always flows from the upper classes, whilst 'de-civilising' behaviours necessarily emerge from working-class culture and other groups at the bottom of the social order. It could also be suggested that the Leicester School takes a moral stance towards the behaviour of many working-class people who attend football matches, in particular by labelling such behaviour as 'hooligan'.

Incorporation

From the Middle Ages to the present day, across all levels of society, there has been a movement towards higher levels of civilised behaviour. According to Dunning et al. (1988), this movement is the outcome of the intentions of people interweaving their intentional actions and becoming more sensitive to acts of violence. Dunning describes the acceptance of such forms of civilised conduct as 'incorporation': 'the constellation of developments which have served over the past century to integrate increasing sections of the working class into the mainstream of British society' (Dunning et al., 1988: 227).

However, there is a group within the working class who have remained less incorporated – what Dunning refers to as the 'rough' working class minority. These 'roughs' face economic insecurity and their lives are regularly disrupted by violence. The 'roughs' also have less opportunity to exercise power than all other income groups in the population and this has significant consequences for the development of their personality. Their life chances, life experiences and intellectual attributes are all restricted. This is partly caused by their parents' 'inimical' attitude to formal education and partly by their attitude of 'present-centred fatalism'. Elias did point out that the civilising process was not following a straight line; instances of 'de-civilising spurts' and 'regressions' were possible. However, the data from the Leicester School does not present crowd disorder as a 'de-civilising spurt' or 'regression' but rather as a long-term historical trend identified as the 'perpetuation of a "rough" subculture' (Dunning, 1993: 68).

In the last analysis, Dunning is pointing to educational failure, limited employment opportunities and high rates of unemployment as central to a process of underclass or 'rough' working-class formation and it is this process of class formation, rather than the 'immanent dynamics of figurations', that underpins the continuing levels of crowd disorder at football matches.

Dunning and colleagues give a central place to the rough working class but largely ignore the processes that bring about the formation of this underclass. Giulianotti and Armstrong (2002) outline a number of criticisms of the Leicester School's use of the concept of 'ordered segmentation'.

- First, they challenge the idea of football fans as 'segmented rivals'. Teams often draw their fans from a wide range of locales and are not one homogenous hooligan group.
- Hooligans accept the dominant cultural ideal and beliefs and are 'incorporated' to the point that they share the disapproval of other teams' reported hooligan 'outrages'.
- Leicester is not the ideal site for the study of 'ordered segmentation', because Leicester is a one-club city, and as such lacks the complex hooligan identification that exists in two or multi-club cities.

- The Leicester School's account of how the processes of 'ordered segmentation' operate and its causal dynamics are unclear.
- 'Ordered segmentation' does not accommodate the temporal and cultural variations in hooliganism, related to changing friendships and animosities between groups of fans.

Most importantly, ordered segmentation is both static and controlling and does not sit well with the dynamic relationship between agency and structure in Elias' conception of figuration.

There are two issues that need to be addressed within the Leicester School conception of incorporation. Firstly, given the nature of the Elias argument, Dunning and colleagues need to explain how and why one of the least powerful groups of people in the population avoided becoming incorporated within the civilising process. This is especially as this group is involved in acts of violence and other ways of behaving that were, according to Elias, commonplace amongst all classes in previous generations. The important point for any analysis of how a group of relatively poor and powerless people in the population could escape the broad civilising thrust of history is left unaccounted for. 'Free-floating moral choices' (Dunning et al., 1988: 221) are not possible in the original Elias account of the civilising process. Elias has a tendency to undervalue the role of the human agent. The restriction and total control of a choice to behave in an uncivilised manner, by the use of state-sponsored violence if necessary, is one of the central planks of Elias' work.

Secondly, if we accept the Leicester School account of incorporation, what data do they present in support of this analysis?

A Short Methodological Detour

According to Dunning, the figurational approach is historical and developmental in nature – it also involves an exploration of the meanings of hooligan behaviour on the basis of the hooligan's own accounts of their actions. There are two principal methods of data collection that the Leicester School uses in its analyses. In *Hooligans Abroad* (Dunning et al., 1984), the School employs an ethnographic approach in which one of the team carried out a series of observations, participant observation and informal interviewing that took the form of informal conversations with football supporters. This data was collected by John Williams who has since parted company with the other members of the School, without the knowledge or consent of the 32 people under investigation. This ethnographic account tends to be individual-oriented, uncontrolled and takes the form of vivid reportage about the lives of individuals involved in acts of violence at football grounds. In terms of ethnographic research, the minimum requirement for a valid and reliable approach is to give an account of the process of data collection and data analysis and in particular how the inference was drawn from the observations made. This is simply not provided in the Leicester accounts; the readers are simply not provided with the opportunity to draw their own inference from the data collected and presented.

We usually face a surplus of explanations in our research and the goal of data analysis is to produce information that will allow us to make decisions about hypotheses. Inference is the process of arriving at a conclusion and this is integral to the production of information. However, without a full description and explanation of how and why one particular inference is drawn, rather than one of the many alternatives, we should be unwilling to accept the conclusions reached. The Leicester research is unclear in terms of its unit of analysis and the focus is on a sole researcher attempting to collect descriptions of behaviours and snippets of conversation that have an Eliasian feel to them.

The other method of data collection that the Leicester School uses is a form of documentary analysis. Again, Maguire's (2006) paper can provide a useful focus. In the Leicester tradition, Maguire's primary method of data collection is an unsystematic documentary analysis of mainly local newspapers, not the 'qualitative discourse analysis' (Maguire and Poulton, 1999) that Maguire had used earlier in his analysis of the newspaper reports of England games in Euro '96. Maguire's Millwall analysis involved looking at reports of crowd disturbances at the Den that contained words or phrases that could be related to 'rough' working-class people's involvement in such disturbance, with no explanation or account of whether these reports are typical or representative of the majority of local newspaper reports. This unsystematic documentary approach is simply a case of finding examples of what the researcher wants to find. A more systematic approach, including such forms of documentary analyses as a simple content analysis, would give a more valid and reliable picture. For example, if all reports of Millwall FC matches over a given period were analysed, it would be possible to judge how much of the reporting was in relation to crowd behaviour and assign a numerical value, demonstrate how much of that crowd behaviour reporting was related to disturbance and how much of that disturbance reporting made reference to causes of behaviour and what those causes were.

There is no description of the documentary analysis in the Leicester research but it is not a formal content analysis, rather it appears to be a form of thematic analysis whereby Dunning and colleagues examine copies of a local newspaper, the *Leicester Mercury*, from the middle of the nineteenth century until the early 1980s and attempt to find examples that again have an Eliasian feel to them. Both methods are largely anecdotal in nature and are seriously lacking in validity and reliability. Without any systematic plan or procedure of data collection that the reader can follow, Dunning and colleagues appear to have simply gone out and actively attempted to find instances of behaviour that support what they want to say in their books.

The Leicester School often makes very ambitions claims for the data collected, for example Dunning (2000), somewhat naively, argues that the increase in reporting of crowd disorder at football grounds from the 1960s to the mid-1980s 'reflects both a factual increase in the incidence of football hooliganism during that 30-year period and a correlative increase of press interest in football hooliganism as a "newsworthy" subject' (Dunning, 2000: 144). However, the Leicester School's data collection is often impressionistic, Elias-based figurational concepts are not operationalised, variables are not clearly identified, indicators are not recognised or justified and the findings are forced into a figurational analysis that may or may not be appropriate. And, finally, the Leicester School rejects the *quest for excitement* in favour of an explanation based upon incorporation that has no direct relationship to any of Elias' central concepts.

Activity

Over the course of the Middle Ages, the power of the state as a central authority grew. For Elias, social change is a normal characteristic of all societies. Social change is conceived by Elias as a long-term social process brought about by 'structured changes in the figurations formed by large numbers of interdependent human beings' (Elias, 1939/1978: 248). The processes of social change are evolutionary in nature, over and above the intentions and actions of individual human beings. A sub-process of the wider civilising process is the process of sportisation. Elias takes his starting point for the analysis for the state from Weber, who argued that state has a monopoly of physical violence. Shame was a central agent in the processes of social control for Elias and appropriate training could develop both character and self-esteem.

Question: Does the Leicester School's account of crowd disorder at football grounds draw upon the work of Norbert Elias? Give the reasons for your answer.

Conclusion

In this chapter, we have argued that social change is not an objective historical process that takes place outside of the perception and control of people within societies; social change must be viewed in relation to the social significance that people place on issues and events within a social context.

Rapid urbanisation reduced the opportunities for working-class people to engage in regular exercise. In addition, the State had serious concerns about limited opportunities for working-class people to improve intellectually and concerns about the moral content of the leisure pursuits that working-class people chose to engage in, particularly if the activity was accompanied by alcohol or gambling. To put it briefly, working-class leisure raised a number of public order issues. The Rational Recreation Movement was a movement for greater state and private sector intervention to regulate working-class leisure in public places.

Rational recreation was seen as an instrument for educating the working classes in the social values of middle-class orthodoxy. The aim was to stimulate working-class self-help and create self-regulating and balanced working-class communities. The legacy of rational recreation, including the belief that unregulated leisure is potentially dangerous for individuals and the wider society, is still with us today.

References

Bailey, P. (1978) *Leisure and Class in Victorian England: Rational Recreation and the Contest for Control, 1830–1885*. London: Routledge.

Bairner, A. (2006) 'The Leicester School and the study of football hooliganism', *Sport in Society*, 9 (4): 583–98.

Beck, U. (1992) *Risk Society: Towards a New Modernity*. London: Sage.

Bloch, H.A. (1951) 'The sociology of gambling', *American Journal of Sociology*, 57 (3): 215–21.

Casey, E. (2003) 'Gambling and consumption: working class women and UK National Lottery play', *Journal of Consumer Culture*, 3 (1): 109–27.

Casey, E. (2004) 'Metaphorical and physical leisure spaces: women, pleasure and the UK National Lottery', in C. Aitchison and H. Pussard (eds), *Space, Leisure and Visual Culture*. Eastbourne: LSA.

Casey, E. (2006) 'Domesticating gambling: gender, caring and the UK National Lottery', *Leisure Studies*, 25 (1): 3–16.

Cherry, S. and Munting, R. (2005) '"Exercise is the thing"? Sport and the asylum c.1850–1950', *The International Journal of the History of Sport*, 22 (1): 42–58.

Clapson, M. (1992) *A Bit of a Flutter: Gambling and English Society 1823–1961*. Manchester: Manchester University Press.

Collins, T. (2005) 'History, theory and the "Civilizing Process"', *Sport in History*, 25 (2): 289–306.

Cornish, D.B. (1977) *Gambling: A Review of the Literature and its Implications for Policy and Research*. London: HMSO.

Csikszentmihalyi, M. (1990) *Flow: The Psychology of Optimal Experience*. New York: Harper and Row.

Devereux, E.C. (1949) *Gambling and Social Structure*. Cambridge: Harvard University Press.

Devereux, E.C. (1968) 'Gambling in psychological and sociological perspective', in D.L. Sills (ed.), *International Encyclopedia of the Social Sciences*, 6: 53–62 (Free Press, New York).

Doggett, R. and Mahoney, R. (1999) *The Leisure Environment*. London: Nelson Thornes.

Dunning, E. (1993) 'Sport in the civilizing process: aspects of the development of modern sport', in E. Dunning, J.A. Maguire and E.R. Pearton (eds), *The Sports Process: A Comparative and Developmental Approach*. Champaign, IL: Human Kinetics.

Dunning, E. (2000) 'Towards a sociological understanding of football hooliganism as a world phenomenon', *European Journal on Criminal Policy and Research*, 8: 141–62.

Dunning, E., Murphy, P. and Williams, J. (1984) *Hooligans Abroad: Behaviour and Control of English Fans in Continental Europe*. London: Routledge.

Dunning, E., Murphy, P. and Williams, J. (1988) *The Roots of Football Hooliganism*. London: Routledge.

Elias, N. (1939/1978) *The Civilizing Process: The History of Manners*. Trans. E. Jephcott. Oxford: Basil Blackwell.

Elias, N. (1939/1982) *The Civilizing Process: State Formation and Civilization*. Trans. E. Jephcott. Oxford: Basil Blackwell.

Flavin, M. (2003) *Gambling in the Nineteenth Century English Novel: 'A Leprosy Is O'er the Land'*. Brighton and Portland: Sussex Academic Press.

Giulianotti, R. (1999) *Football: A Sociology of the Global Game*. Cambridge: Polity Press.

Giulianotti, R. and Armstrong, G. (2002) 'Avenues of contestation: football hooligans running and ruling urban spaces', *Social Anthropology*, 10 (2): 211–38.

Goffman, E. (1967) 'Where the action is', in E. Goffman (ed.), *Interaction Ritual*. New York: Doubleday. pp. 149–270.

Gordon, J. and McArthur, J. (1988) 'Interior decorating advice as popular culture: women's views concerning wall and window treatments', in M. Motz and P. Brown (eds), *Making the American Home: Middle-class Women and Domestic Material Culture, 1840–1940*. Bowling Green, OH: Bowling Green State University Popular Press. pp. 105–20.

Greenaway, J.R. (1998) 'The "improved" public house, 1870–1950: the key to civilized drinking or the primrose path to drunkenness?', *Addiction*, 93 (2): 173–81.

Henry, I. (1990) *Management and Planning in the Leisure Industries*. Basingstoke: Macmillan.

Huizinga, J. (1949) *Homo Ludens: A Study of the Play Element in Culture*. London: Routledge and Kegan Paul.

King, A. (2002) *The End of the Terraces: The Transformation of English Football in the 1990s*, revised edn. London: Leicester University Press.

Kingma, S. and Boersma, K. (2004) 'No Time to Spare? Time and Technology (Review)', *Time & Society*, 11 (2–3): 351–5.

Kirk, D. (2003) 'Sport, physical education and schools', in B. Hoolihan (ed.), *Contemporary Issues in Sport and Society*. London: Sage. pp. 143–44

Lowerson, J. and Myerscough, J. (1977) *Time to Spare in Victorian England*. London: Harvester Press.

Lyng, S. (1990) 'Edgework: a social psychological analysis of voluntary risk taking', *American Journal of Sociology*, 95 (4): 851–86.

Lyng, S. (2005) *Edgework*. New York: Routledge.

Maguire, J. (2006) 'Millwall and the making of football's folk devils: revisiting the Leicester period', *Sport in Society*, 9 (4): 599–615.

Maguire, J. and Poulton, E. (1999) 'European identity politics in Euro '96: invented traditions and national habitus codes', *International Review for the Sociology of Sport*, 34 (1): 17–29.

Malcolmson, R.W. (1973) *Popular Recreations in English Society 1700–1850*. Cambridge: Cambridge University Press.

Munting, R. (1996) *An Economic and Social History of Gambling in Britain and the USA*. Manchester: Manchester University Press.

Neal, M. (1999) 'The ongoing effects of deregulation on betting shop customer profile and behaviour', *Managing Leisure*, 4: 168–84.

Parratt, C.M. (2001) *More Than Mere Amusement: Working-Class Women's Leisure in England, 1750–1914*. Boston, MA: Northeastern University Press.

Paton, D., Siegel, D. and Vaughan Williams, L. (2002) 'A policy response to the E-commerce revolution: the case of betting taxation in the UK', *The Economic Journal*, 112 (June): F296–314.

Perkins, H.W. (1991) 'Religious commitment, yuppie values, and well-being in post-collegiate life', *Review of Religious Research*, 32: 244–51.

Quilley, S. (2004) 'Ecology, "human nature" and civilising processes: biology and sociology in the work of Norbert Elias', in S. Loyal and S. Quilley (eds), *The Sociology of Norbert Elias*. Cambridge: Cambridge University Press.

Rajah, V. (2007) 'Resistance as edgework in violent intimate relationships of drug-involved women', *British Journal of Criminology*, 47 (2): 196–213.

Redfern, A. (1988) 'Crewe: Leisure in a railway town', in J.K. Walton and J. Walvin (eds), *Leisure in Britain 1780–1939*. Manchester: Manchester University Press.

Reid, D.G. (1995) *Work and Leisure in the 21st Century: From Production to Citizenship*. Toronto: Wall and Emerson.

Rendell, J. (1999) 'Introduction: Gender, space', in B. Penner and I. Borden (eds), *Gender, Space, Architecture: An Interdisciplinary Introduction*. London: Routledge.

Rendell, J. (2002) 'Almack's assembly rooms – A site of sexual pleasure', *Journal of Architectural Education*, 55(3): 136–49.

Rosett, R.N. (1965) 'Gambling and rationality', *Journal of Political Economy*, 73: 595–607.

Shpayer-Makov, H. (2002) *The Making of a Policeman: A Social History of a Labour Force in Metropolitan London, 1829–1914*. Burlington, VT: Ashgate.

Skeggs, B. (1997) *Formations of Class and Gender: Becoming Respectable*. London: Sage.

Slater, D. (1997) *Consumer Culture and Modernity*. Cambridge: Polity Press.

Smith, B., Wingard, D.L., Smith, T.C., Kritz-Silverstein, D. and Barrett-Connor, E. (2006) 'Does coffee consumption reduce the risk of type 2 diabetes in individuals with impaired glucose?', *Diabetes Care*, 29 (11): 2385–90.

Smith, J. (2000) 'Gambling taxation: Public equity in the gambling business', *Australian Economic Review*, 33: 120–44.

Turner, B. (2004) 'Weber and Elias on religion and violence: warrior charisma and the civilising process', in S. Loyal and S. Quilley (eds), *The Sociology of Norbert Elias*. Cambridge: Cambridge University Press.

Urry, J. (1990) *The Tourist Gaze*. London: Sage.

Weitzman, M. (1965) 'Utility analysis and group behaviour: an empirical study', *Journal of Political Economy*, 73: 18–26.

Witkowski, T. (2004) 'Re-gendering consumer agency in mid-nineteenth-century America: a visual understanding', *Consumption, Markets & Culture*, 7 (3): 261–83.

Wouters, C. (2004) 'Changing regimes of manners and emotions: from disciplining to informalizing', in S. Loyal and S. Quilley (eds), *The Sociology of Norbert Elias*. Cambridge: Cambridge University Press.

6

THE UK'S CONTEMPORARY
INSTITUTIONAL FRAMEWORK
FOR LEISURE

Building upon the discussion of rational recreation in the previous chapter, some of the themes developed here include:

- the emergence of a heritage industry and the socio-political significance of museums in developing a colonial and post-colonial narrative
- the role of the National Endowment for the Arts in the United States and the Arts Council
- the arguments surrounding the introduction of the National Lottery
- the state sponsorship of leisure and sports participation via Sport for All, the Sports Council, Sport England and UK Sport
- the development and significance of public service broadcasting within an international context: with reference to the Glasgow Media Research Group
- an evaluation of the commonly held opinion that leisure was a nineteenth-century invention and a direct consequence of the process of industrialisation.

Introduction

With the success of the Labour Party in the 1945 British General Election, a new episode of rational recreation was unveiled that involved the enthusiastic physical and cultural protection of citizens. These new institutions were similar to the Forestry Commission and the BBC in that they were regulatory bodies with statutory responsibilities for recreation. The British government introduced a number of new paternalistic public organisations that attempted to defend people from potentially harmful leisure activities, whilst at the same time attempting to regulate and encourage forms of leisure participation that were thought to be good for the public, notably access to the arts, sport and open spaces such as national parks and forests. Until the twentieth century, the

British government had little direct involvement in the shaping of the cultural experiences of working-class people.

Art, Empire and Industry

Art, including painting, sculpture, music, literature and poetry, is believed to have a special significance in the culture of any society, and in the nineteenth century, artistic human creative activity was believed to be morally uplifting for the human spirit and soul of the working classes. Art appreciation is the sign of a cultivated and civilised society. Hence, galleries and museums were central to the rational recreation movement. Public funding for the arts has continued up to and including the present day.

In the nineteenth century, it was commonly assumed that one of the most effective ways of civilising the population was to give the public access to 'high culture', notably the arts. The first involvement by the British government in the area of heritage was in 1753 with the purchase of Sir Hans Sloane's (1666–1753) private collection of paintings, sculpture, coins, books, manuscripts and natural history specimens. The collection became the foundation of the British Museum, the first national, public, non-religious museum in the world. The collection was added to if an exhibit was believed to add to national prestige, so for example in 1816, the Elgin Marbles were acquired. The British Museum building itself however was paid for out of the profits from a private lottery. In 1824, the government purchased the Angerstein collection of paintings that was to form the basis of the National Gallery. The Great Exhibition of 1851 demonstrated that many British manufacturers were commercially less successful than their foreign competitors because of the inferior design of many British products. In response, the government established the Department of Art and Science and its head, Henry Cole, was asked to investigate art and design training in Britain. One of Cole's central ideas was the creation of the South Kensington Museum, which became the Victoria and Albert Museum in 1899. Cole envisaged the V and A specifically as a museum that would demonstrate well-designed products to the public. The profits of the Great Exhibition also financed:

- the Imperial College of Science and Technology
- the Royal College of Music
- the Science Museum
- the Geological Museum
- the Natural History Museum
- the Albert Hall.

Outside of London, the Libraries, Museums and Gymnasiums Act (1845) made it possible for local authorities to establish museums with money from local taxes. According to 'figurational' sociologists, such as Eric Dunning (1999), this local authority provision of museums and galleries was primarily concerned with providing working-class people with access to objects that were beautiful and morally uplifting – together with open space and public baths, the arts were believed to be central in maintaining public order by *civilising* the working class. By the time of the Great Exhibition, there were 50 museums in Britain and as the century moved on, museums and galleries became symbols of civic wealth and pride.

The National Portrait Gallery was established in 1856. However, because this form of art did not contribute directly to commercial design, over 40 years passed before sufficient money could be raised for suitable accommodation for the collection. Similarly, the modern art collection contained within the Tate Gallery did not open to the public until 1897. The Imperial War Museum and the National Maritime Museum were opened after the First World War.

Also in the nineteenth century, there was a concern amongst many middle-class people about the destructive impact of unregulated urban expansion and the rapid industrialisation of the countryside. William Morris helped to form the Society for the Protection of Ancient Buildings in 1877, one of the first movements to put pressure on the government for greater preservation and restoration of the built environment, especially historic buildings and ancient monuments. This movement successfully campaigned for the Ancient Monuments Act (1882). The Victorians' taste for gothic together with preservation and restoration led to the restoration of many medieval churches. The National Trust was formed in 1895 and was followed by:

- the Ancient Monuments Society (1921)
- the Council for the Care of Churches (1922)
- the Council for the Protection of Rural England (1926)
- the National Trust for Scotland (1931)
- the Georgian Group (1937)
- the Vernacular Architecture Group (1952)
- the Civic Trust (1957)
- the Victorian Society (1958)
- the Landmark Trust (1963)
- SAVE Britain's Heritage (1975).

The Town and Country Planning Act of 1947 gave the British government responsibility for 'scheduling' ancient monuments and 'listing' historic buildings. The purpose of these continuing categories is to provide a guide to local authorities when carrying out their planning powers.

Activity: Heritage and government

Heritage is commonly understood to cover a range of institutions and activities including:

- museums
- galleries
- archaeology
- architecture, townscape, great country houses and ancient buildings
- landscape
- industrial heritage sites
- coastline
- treasures
- libraries and very old books and manuscripts
- wildlife
- old crafts and ways of life
- the natural environment.

Questions

Should the government provide funding for museums and galleries?
Should admission to museums and galleries be free?
Should the government provide library facilities?
Outline the reasons for your answers.

The Heritage Industry

The idea of *heritage* became a significant element in the search for a credible British national identity from the 1970s onwards. For Robert Hewison (1995), from the mid-1970s, Britain has experienced a range of economic anxieties in relation to social exclusion, unemployment, inflation, social unrest, industrial disputes, rising crime and moral panics in relation to such social division as race. These anxieties generated a crisis of national identity. Thatcherism was the authoritarian response to this crisis and *heritage* acquired a special meaning that attempted to generate both value and reassurance. Hewison (1995) quotes from Mrs Thatcher's first conference speech in 1975 as leader of the Conservative Party, in which she criticised the loss of old values, standards and ancient traditions: 'the deliberate attack on our heritage and our great past' (Hewison, 1995: 190). Thatcherism was never a coherent set of beliefs, argues Hewison (1995) but was rooted in what Mrs Thatcher described as 'Victorian Values': patriotism, private charity, self-help, hard work and thrift. However, Thatcher selectively drew upon history to construct a conception of 'heritage' that supported her political agenda – as Hewison explains, the castle and the country house and the patterns of deference that accompanied them had an attractiveness directly related to the authoritarian side of Thatcherism. The Thatcherite conception of 'heritage' was presented a 'common' to the people, but it excluded many migrants and their British-born children.

   Hewison (1989) argues that in the Thatcher years, museums were made to change as a result of political decisions in relation to deregulation and privatisation. As museums were forced into the market place, the notion of *heritage* emerged. Even if the museum were to remain in the public sector and remain free at the point of entry, the facility will be judged in terms of the number of visitors per year and its ability to exploit its commercial opportunities, such as sales of souvenirs and refreshments. The conception of heritage is 'an entirely contemporary creation' (Hewison, 1989: 16) and a 'product of conflicting interests in our culture' (p. 17). The danger to our heritage, argues Hewison, is *the heritage industry,* the transformation of 'the past' into an entertaining cultural commodity. Hewison quotes Sir Roy Strong who at a press conference to relaunch the Victoria and Albert Museum gave a speech with the title 'Towards a more consumer-oriented V and A', in which Sir Roy argued that the V and A should become the Laura Ashley of the 1990s.

For Hewison (1990), our obsession with the past is a symptom of a much deeper cultural crisis – the dissipation of modernism. This is reflected not simply in terms of 'style' but was a consequence of an emerging post-industrial society. Art at the beginning of the 1990s reflected a new manufactured and commodified public culture that was accessible, undemanding and above all else did not draw upon the public purse but rather made money. What Hewison describes is a commodified version of authorised history that reflected a comfortable and false impression of the past and locked British culture into a form of nostalgia. This form of heritage was used by Thatcherism to conceal conflicts and resistance in the 1980s.

We experience this struggle as 'personal' but its causes are found within 'the social'. Those forms of culture that are not commodified are viewed as 'decentred, schizophrenic and extreme'. Success and certainty are to be found in the market place – if it sells, if it makes money, then it must be good. Even the Notting Hill Carnival was commodified under the guidance of accountants Coopers and Lybrand to give it a closer fit with the enterprise culture of the 1990s. Hewison (1990) gives an account of how on Wednesday 5 July 1989, at the opening of the Design Museum on the south bank of the Thames, Mrs Thatcher rejected the concept of a museum as 'something that is really rather dead' – she preferred to call this new design museum an 'exhibition centre'. In particular, Mrs Thatcher liked the fact that the Design Museum had a number of commercial sponsors: Perrier, Sony, Kodak, Apple, Fiat, Black and Decker, Coco-Cola, Olivetti, Courtaulds and Addis.

In the last analysis, this leads to a new form of museum – the museum with no collection, the Heritage Centre. The original purpose of the museum may have been to maintain and interpret the past in a scholarly fashion; the role of the heritage centre was to provide a 'pleasurable experience' to the customer. Hewison gives the example of the Jorvik Centre in York where the significant finds from the archaeological dig could be displayed on the top of a single table. Interestingly, many of the most significant artefacts found at the site are not on display at the Jorvik Centre.

Museum policy is now more concerned with manufacturing social and cultural meaning in an effort to help generate employment within the local economy. In order to understand the heritage industry, Hewison draws upon three central concepts:

- Spectacle – a concept derived from the work of Guy Debord (1967) in which society becomes a spectacle that as individuals we have little control over.

- Hyperreality – a concept concerned with the loss of the real; the criteria for understanding the 'completely authentic' are unable to differentiate this from what is 'completely imitation' – image and reality implode reflecting the commodified and mediated nature of everyday life.
- Historicism – in which the past is refashioned and reinvented on the basis of a set of ideas rooted solely in the present.

There has been an invasion of our private life and personal experiencing – private memory has become subjected to a process of commodification, where heritage centres attempt to reproduce a sanitised reconstructed image of the 'way we were'. This reconstructed experience is a direct and deliberate replacement for the often harsh and unpleasant reality of individuals' life experiences of the past. History is refashioned into *heritage*, a form of nostalgia in which a simulacra, a congenial construction of the past that never existed, replaces *real* history. This sanitised vision of the past refuses to acknowledge the existence of exploitation, oppression and struggle as key factors in the formation of the present. The purpose of the heritage centre was to celebrate some element of history and identity in a distorted fashion 'to compensate for the poverty of the present' (Hewison, 1995: 191).

Activity

Lowenthal (1998) argues that when heritage becomes history, entertainment becomes the overriding factor in our interpretation of the past:

> Lack of hard evidence seldom distresses the public at large, who are mostly credulous, undemanding, accustomed to heritage mystique, and often laud the distortions, omissions, and fabrications central to heritage reconstruction. (Lowenthal, 1998: 249)

> The rewriting of history into Heritage is calculated not only to deny the pluralisms of the past, by converting the conflicts, contradictions and false turnings of events into a single narrative that leads remorselessly up to the powers that be of the present day: it is a means towards denying change in the present, where the only destiny is that already constructed from the past. Pluralism is a danger to any power structure, because to accept pluralism is to acknowledge "the other". To acknowledge the other is to accept that you yourself are an other, and that possibility exists that your truth might be false. (Hewison, 1990: 86)

Question: Think about a museum that you have visited recently – does the museum support or contradict what Hewison has to say about 'heritage'?

Museums and Post-colonialism

Colonialism is the global expansion of capitalism by direct political and economic domination or control of other people's land through invasion. Post-colonialism literally means 'writing after empire' and is concerned with the problems and issues that former colonies have faced. As Bennett (1999) explains, museums functioned as 'laboratories' that provided the context in which people could critically reflect upon the past. Exhibition practices within museums were used to introduce new forms of cultural governance into late nineteenth-century public culture. The understanding of what constituted a museum in the United States was based upon the idea of a distinct memory machine, which promoted an opportunity for white Americans to reflect upon their central role in history.

In the case of the United Kingdom, Barringer (1999) views the Victoria and Albert Museum as an 'imperial archive' that contained a distinctly modern world view shaped by Victorian imperialism. From the 1870s onwards, exhibitions became 'increasingly populist' and imperial in nature. A rich variety of cultural objects from across the Empire were brought to London, and the transportation changed the way in which they were interpreted. When objects were moved from the *periphery* to the *centre,* this symbolically gave London an identity as the heart of the Empire. The peoples of the periphery were presented as defeated, and racially and culturally inferior in nature. For example, the Colonial and Indian exhibition (1886) was held to celebrate Queen Victoria's role as Empress of India, and Barringer argues that the exhibition publicised the Victorian ideal of empire and national self-aggrandisement.

A museum: what is it? What purpose does it serve?

For Simpson (2001), the concept of 'the museum' is a distinctly Western concept based upon Western ideology. Museum culture involves the removal of objects from a place where they have real cultural significance and attempting to preserve them for passive display. On the surface, the aim of the museum is simply to disseminate information to the public. However, the interpretative process within museums is never objective and 'value free', but always a highly politicised process. All displays of exhibits and collections contain a political stance. What museums say or do not say will be political in nature. When the Tropenmuseum in Amsterdam decided to hold an exhibition to explore the racist imagery and metaphors in popular mediums such as comics and advertising, many visitors objected to the content on the grounds that it was racist. Drawing upon material from fieldwork in Europe, North America, Australia and New Zealand, Simpson (2001) suggests that the origin of museum culture is rooted in a celebration of the colonial achievements of European cultures. The traditional conventions of museum display were invented in the colonial era when many of the larger collections were established, and continue to influence present-day museum practice. Even today, many Aboriginal Australian writers argue that the representation of Aboriginal arts and culture is within a colonial framework of understanding. As such, museums have often become the focus for criticism because of their colonial Eurocentric approach. During the American civil rights demonstrations of the

1960s, the Black Emergency Cultural Coalition campaigned against the representation of black Americans in the Whitney Museum and the Museum of Modern Art. People who work within museums tend to be 'white' and educated within a Western conception of *the other*. Museum culture was said to ignore key aspects of the history of black people within the United States, notably the slave trade and racism, and to not be accessible and representative of the lives of the black urban poor. In Britain, the Wilberforce House Museum in Hull is said to have celebrated the role of white abolitionists but to view black people as dependent victims. Hence, museum culture does not provide black people with a space for personal and historical reflection. Where the history of black people is represented, such representations tend to be of traditional or 'tribal' societies but never of living cultures.

Such objections resulted in the development of the neighbourhood museum and 'the eco-museum' concept, first invented by George Henri Riviere and Hugues de Varine, in which communities develop museums of their own and where the interpretative process is taken out of the hands of museum curators and placed in the hands of the community itself. Such centres often become the focus of the cultural life within an area. Within this context, Tchen (2001) discusses the emergence of the 'dialogue-driven museum' that provides 'a learning environment in which memory ... inform[s] and [is] informed by historical context and scholarship' (Tchen, 2001: 291). The exhibitions in such institutions tend to focus on the lives of people who have traditionally been ignored by mainstream museums. The Koorie Heritage Trust in Australia, for example, produced a 'Massacre Map' identifying known sites of killings of Aboriginal peoples by European settlers in the nineteenth century. For Simpson (2001), this form of exhibition medium confronts visitors with truths which are frequently censored or removed completely from white histories, exposing facts of which many Westerners may have little awareness.

Activity

Consider the following questions:
   Should museums take risks in taking a potentially controversial stance to issues?
   Can museums be a valuable educational resource for urban people?
   Do museums have any advantage over classroom-based history lessons as an educational resource?

Wittlin (1946) described the purpose of *the museum* in the mid-twentieth century as educational in nature. The objects and artefacts exhibited can be of any character and are simply made available to members of the public who wish to see and enjoy them. The contents of museums can include such diverse things as: art objects, animals, skeletons of animals, machines, relics, geology and crafts from home and overseas. The nature of the collections contained within museums may be difficult to define and, over the course of previous centuries, *the museum* has had a range of different meanings, however what has remained constant, argues Wittlin, has been the underpinning conception of the museum as a 'public service'.

Wittlin argues that the main functions of the museum are to provide enjoyment, and to preserve important objects for future generations. Although, as Wittlin herself points out, this raises the important point of 'instruction in what and for whom?'.

The origin of the modern public museum is found in a range of preceding collections in the hands of states, individuals and religious groups – Wittlin classifies these as:

- economic hoard collections
- social prestige collections
- magic collections
- collections as an expression of group loyalty
- collections stimulating curiosity and inquiry
- collections of art stimulating emotional experience.

In the *Iliad,* Homer (1998) describes the treasure chamber of the King of Troy – such collections had an important economic purpose before the emergence of a banking system and a money economy. The hoard of treasure did not perish, as food would, but could be stored as a surplus to satisfy future needs in times of economic decline or crisis. On a lesser scale, Sombart (1923) argues that the hoarding of metals, especially in the form of ingots, was common until the end of the thirteenth century when it was replaced by the hoarding of gold coins. Such forms of hoarding also had the benefit of enhancing the prestige of the owner. Magic collections, such as unicorn horn and Egyptian mummies, were believed to have supernatural powers or mysterious forces that offer the owner some protection. This was very important in the pre-modern world where humans have very limited ability to control the environment. Religious relics such as the jaw bone of John the Baptist, or a tear from Jesus when he learned about the death of Lazarun, held at the Benedictine monastery at Vendome in France, were also believed to offer protection. Even in the nineteenth century, people still went on pilgrimage to worship relics, such as the skeletal remains of saints, within Europe. From the sixteenth century, Wittlin argues, collections of inventions and discoveries were also established. This reflected a shift in the European mind, from valuing an object because of its supposed magical property to valuing the human skill that went into creating an object. The concept of the museum as a research institute had its origins in the work of key thinkers of the period such as Kepler, Descartes, Bacon, Newton and Leibniz. The first Society of Antiquaries was established in London in 1572 to separate truth from falsehood and to evaluate the evidence present in tradition.

In addition to pushing forward the frontiers of knowledge, such collections were also regarded as a form of entertainment by the general public, those informed people who wished to view them. One of the most well known of such collections was that of Sir Hans Slone which, as we saw above, went on to form the basis of the British Museum. Finally, Wittlin discusses collections of art. Art gave people the opportunity to experience emotion by association with a visual image. Wittlin cites G. Gutierrez de los Rios who in 1600 argued that royal collections of paintings and tapestries should stimulate people to bravery. This established a tradition of royal households commissioning famous battle scenes. Mythological scenes were also popular in the sixteenth and seventeenth centuries as they allowed Europeans to establish links with ancient Mediterranean culture and provided a legitimate opportunity for artists to depict nudes.

Collections were assembled in a variety of violent and peaceful ways. When the French invaded Italy in 1797, Napoleon took artefacts from individuals, churches, monasteries and public galleries. After Napoleon fell from power, much of this collection was distributed across Europe and not always to its previous owners. Many of the Egyptian antiquities acquired by Napoleon found their way to England. Revolutions, including religious revolutions, also had consequences for the transfer of artefacts. In 1653, the English Parliament ordered the sale of Charles I's collection.

Wittlin described the period from the middle of the nineteenth century up until 1914 as the 'foundation era' of museums. It was during this period of museum expansion that we saw the emergence of the specialisation of the subject matter within museums:

- The National Museum – specialisms were often developed here with the aim of stimulating group loyalty and patriotism.
- The Ethnological Museum – Sir Hercules Read in his forward to the *Handbook to the Ethnographical Collections of the British Museum* (1910) suggested that such collections gave the museum visitor an insight into the manners and customs of overseas peoples that would assist in the administration of colonies and assist in the export of British goods.
- The Museum of Science – the aim here was to satisfy the growing interest in science and technology and to play a *civic* role in the education of children.
- The Museum of Arts and Crafts – this again had a *civic* role to play in the education of children.

T. Greenwood's book *Museums and Art Galleries* (1888) raises the important question: Why should every town have a museum? The answer that Greenwood gives has a distinct rational recreation element to it.

The museum and, with it, a free public library should be treated as significant for the mental and moral health of the citizens as good sanitary arrangements, water supply and street lighting are for people's physical health. In the mid-twentieth century, Wittlin argues that the function of the museum was also to aid people in their understanding of social change, to provide the visitor with a 'relation set' that links past to present. The 'relation set' is a coherent narrative within a collection of exhibits as in the difference between a 'scrap book' and a 'book'. One of the key factors in social change is the increase in global communication and world trade – the museum can help us adapt to this by transforming our view of the world from one that is 'parochial' to one that stresses 'world citizenship'.

Before you read on, ask yourself two questions: What is the role and purpose of a museum today? And why should every town have a museum?

Activity: English Heritage

English Heritage is a national body which was created by Parliament in 1984 to be the British government's official adviser on all matters concerning heritage conservation. English Heritage is also responsible for the protection of the historic environment, for promoting public understanding and enjoyment of the historic environment and for managing 400 historic properties. English Heritage also helps to provide funding for archaeology, conservation areas and the repair of historic buildings.
English Heritage's principal aims are:

- to secure the conservation of England's historic sites, monuments, buildings and areas
- to raise the understanding and awareness of heritage and thereby increase commitment
- to promote people's access to, and enjoyment of, this shared heritage.

Question:

Does commodification always lead to a loss of historical or artistic integrity?

Activity: Conceptual art

Writing in *The Times* about the notion of 'conceptual art', Edward Docx (2001) said that such art needed 'to ask questions and breach popular boundaries'. In contrast, a report in the *Sun* claimed: 'An art gallery cleaner binned a £5000 work by Damien Hirst because he mistook it for rubbish. Emmanuel Asare spotted the pile of full ashtrays, beer bottles, cola tins, coffee cups and sweet wrappings – and thought it was leftovers from a party. Hirst, 35, who shot to fame after pickling a sheep in formaldehyde, claimed the heap of rubbish represented his messy studio' (Crosbie et al., 19 October 2001).

The Turner Prize has become an annual showpiece event for conceptual art, and short-listed works have included:

- Tracey Emin's actual bedroom complete with unmade bed, stains, cigarette ends, knickers, a used condom and an empty bottle of vodka
- Tracey Emin's 'Everyone I've Ever Slept With, 1963–1992' that was a tent with names embroidered on it
- 'light coming on, light going off' – a light that turned on and then off in an empty room
- a written description of a pornographic film
- a film of Canary Wharf in London filmed from a moving crane.

Questions:

Does 'conceptual art' 'ask questions and breach popular boundaries'?
Should public money be used to buy conceptual art for public view?

The National Endowment for the Arts

In the United States, the National Endowment for the Arts is the public body responsible for providing Americans with greater access to the arts. The NEA uses public money to support excellence in the arts and the NEA views itself as providing leadership in arts education. The NEA was established in 1965 as an independent federal agency. It is commonly assumed that the NEA is the official arts organisation of the United States government. It is assumed that access to visual arts, theatre, opera, ballet, symphony orchestras and museums will make the United States a better place to live.

The NEA awards grants to 'not for profit' organisations under three headings:

- Access to Artistic Excellence
- Learning in the Arts
- Challenge America.

Activity: The National Endowment for the Arts

The NEA has close links to arts agencies at state level and there are six regional arts organisations that it supports financially. However, the NEA has a number of critics. Consider the passages below and answer the questions that follow.

In a society that constitutionally limits the powers of government and maximizes individual liberty, there is no justification for the forcible transfer of money from taxpayers to artists, scholars, and broadcasters. If the proper role of government is to safeguard the security of the nation's residents, by what rationale are they made to support exhibits of paintings, symphony

(Continued)

(Continued)

orchestras, documentaries, scholarly research, and radio and television programs they might never freely choose to support?...

Among its more famous and controversial grant recipients were artist Andres Serrano, whose exhibit featured a photograph of a plastic crucifix in a jar of his own urine, and the Institute of Contemporary Art in Philadelphia, which sponsored a travelling exhibition of the late Robert Mapplethorpe's homoerotic photographs. (Thanks to an NEA grantee, the American taxpayers once paid $1500 for a poem, "lighght." That wasn't the title or a typo. That was the entire poem.) ...

Taxpayer subsidy of the arts, scholarship, and broadcasting is inappropriate because it is outside the range of the proper functions of government and it needlessly politicises, and therefore corrupts, an area of life that should be left untainted by politics' (Source: www.cato.org/pubs/handbook/hb105-14.html).

The economics of the arts has attracted a great deal of attention from academics. Henderson (2003) explains that the arts can generate lucrative business opportunities (Myerscough, 1988), notably through tourism (Gilbert and Lizotte, 1998) and generate both jobs and urban regeneration programmes. Using the case of Singapore, Joan Henderson presents a model of the evolution of government arts policy in newly independent states, incorporating a series of stages and determinants. Henderson's model proposes that, after relative neglect in the early years of independence, there is a period of involvement in which the arts acquire importance as a means of binding together a possibly disparate population and reinforcing a sense of nationhood. Development then takes place and the arts, as part of the creative industries sector, may be employed as both an economic and political tool. In particular, Henderson (2003) argues that the state sponsorship of the arts can be used to fulfil 'hegemonic goals'.

Questions

Is the 'proper role' of the government no more than to 'safeguard the security of the nation's residents'?

Could you identify any similarity between the work of the NEA and the movement for rational recreation in the nineteenth century in the United Kingdom?

Does state support necessarily politicise and corrupt the arts?

The Arts Council

In the case of public funding for the arts in the United Kingdom, the central body is the Arts Council which was established in 1946 by Royal Charter. The objectives of the Council are:

- to develop and improve the knowledge, understanding and practice of the arts
- to increase accessibility of the arts to the public in England
- to advise and cooperate with government departments, local authorities and the Arts Councils for Scotland, Wales and Northern Ireland.

In March 1994, the Arts Council was reconstituted by Supplemental Charter and became 'The Arts Council of England'. The new structure had much greater regionalisation of its organisation and activities with regional councils made up of 15 members with the power to:

- decide spending plans
- manage and spend any delegated budgets from the Council
- decide the regional strategy and priorities
- establish an appropriate staffing structure, and make staff appointments
- seek out sources of funding such as donations, gifts and legacies
- acquire property for its work.

One of the central roles of the Arts Council of England is to distribute the money raised through the National Lottery (see below) to the arts in England and it does this through:

- **The Arts Capital Programme** – this programme is designed to support arts capital projects, including buying equipment and commissioning public art (grants from this programme are for sums over £100,000). One of the best-known examples of this type of Arts Council funding is in the case of the Royal Opera House, Covent Garden which received £78 million.
- **Grants for the arts – individuals, organisations and national touring** – these grants are designed to support activities that benefit people in England or that help artists and arts organisations from England to carry out their work. Applications can be made at any time between 1 April and 31 December the following year.
- **Grants for the arts – stabilisation and recovery** – these grants are aimed at larger-scale organisations that are believed to be essential to arts provision and have a financial turnover of over £250,000 and attract audiences of 25,000 people per year.

These grants give organisations a degree of financial security to allow them to re-focus their central objectives, and to rethink their strategic position in relation to the market and other arts organisations.

UK government guidelines for distributing Capital Lottery grants to the arts

There are strict guidelines for the distribution of lottery money in relation to the arts. Capital Lottery grants are mainly for arts buildings and equipment – examples of capital arts building projects would include:

- constructing new buildings
- refurbishing existing buildings
- improving existing buildings.

Capital Lottery grants are also available for public art including feasibility studies and development work. Capital Lottery grants are available to a range of organisations planning a capital arts project, for example:

- a community group, club or society
- a registered charity
- a non-profit-distributing group or trust
- a local authority
- an education institution
- a public-sector agency.

The organisation has to have been running for more than 12 months, it must have a formal constitution and it must have at least one year's accounts. Finally, individual people are not allowed to apply for a Capital Lottery grant.

Capital grants are intended to cover the cost of buying, improving or restoring a building that must be used continuously. The organisation must not intend to put the building on the market. In some circumstances, the Arts Council can provide a limited amount of funding to deal with any related start-up costs.

However, capital grants cannot be used to cover any retrospective costs, or costs that the organisation has already agreed to pay. Similarly, running and administration costs for the project cannot be covered. The project has to meet the Arts Council's strategic aims and benefit the widest possible number of people across all regional, cultural and economic sectors.

An example of money spent by the Arts Council is Antony Gormley, who in 1994 won the prestigious Turner Prize, and was reportedly paid £800,000 for his sculpture 'the Angel of the North'. This is the largest sculpture in Britain and is believed to be the largest angel sculpture in the world. One possible reason why the Arts Council was so willing to fund this project was because the Angel of the North is one of the most viewed pieces of art in the world, as the structure is visible from the A1 and the A167, both of which are busy roads. This means that the structure is estimated to be seen by more than one person every second, which is equivalent to 90,000 people every day or 33 million people every year.

Activity

What rationale can you provide for the state to use taxpayers' money to support the arts?

Sport England and UK Sport

Sport England and UK Sport are two of the main vehicles for implementing sport policy in the United Kingdom.

Sport England emerged from the Sports Council, which itself emerged from the Central Council of Physical Recreation (CCPR) that was established in 1935. CCPR commissioned the Wolfenden Report (1960) that identified the need for a national sports development council – as a consequence of this, the Sports Council was established in 1965. The assets and staff of the CCPR were transferred to the Sports Council in 1972 when the Sports Council was given its Royal Charter.

The main aims of the Sports Council were:

- to promote a general understanding of the social importance and value of sport and physical recreation
- to increase the provision of new sports facilities and stimulate fuller use of existing facilities
- to encourage wider participation in sport and physical recreation as a means to enjoying leisure
- to raise standards of performance.

There were three national councils:

- the Scottish Sports Council (1972)
- the Sports Council for Wales (1972)
- the Sports Council for Northern Ireland (1974).

The Sports Council also had nine regional offices, each with responsibility for implementing Sports Council policies within a given region. In addition, these regional bodies also provided technical and advisory services to local authorities, voluntary sports bodies and other organisations.

The Sports Council also administered five national residential sports centres to provide support for elite sports people:

- Crystal Palace – athletics, swimming, boxing
- Holme Pierrepont – water sports, table tennis
- Lilleshall – football, gymnastics, cricket
- Bisham Abbey – tennis, hockey, rugby
- Plas y Brenin – mountaineering.

Sport for All

In 1972, the Sports Council launched the Sport for All campaign to increase participation, to raise public consciousness of the value of sport and physical recreation in society and to improve facilities across the United Kingdom. The concept of 'Sport for All' was first defined at a Council of Europe meeting in Bruges in 1968, where it was argued that 'Sport for All' should provide the: 'conditions to enable the widest possible range of the population to practise regularly either sport proper or various physical activities calling for an effort adapted to individual capacities' (cited in Marchand, 1990: 15).

A Sport for All Charter was launched in 1976 and revised in 1993.

In 1995, the British government published 'Sport: Raising the Game' in which it outlined its plans to replace the Sports Council with two institutions:

UK Sport was established by Royal Charter in January 1997. The central focus of UK Sport is international and coordinating activities. UK Sport was to focus on achieving sporting excellence for the United Kingdom on the world stage, developing a system of coaching and other support capable of producing a constant flow of elite performers.

UK Sport's other responsibilities include:

- development of the United Kingdom's global profile and influence in sport
- encouragement of ethical standards of behaviour
- management of the United Kingdom's anti-doping programme in sport
- attraction of the world's major sporting events to the United Kingdom.

In a similar fashion to the Sports Council, the role of Sport England is to act as the adviser to the United Kingdom government on all sporting matters. In addition, Sport England is responsible for running publicity campaigns to encourage participation. However, there is an important distinction between the old Sports Council and the new Sport England. The Sports Council had a central role in distributing government grants to local authorities, schools and community groups, directly managed the national sporting centres and funded sports development. Sport England has an 'enabling' role – in other words, it provides the overall strategic framework for these things to happen rather than directly providing the service itself. For example, Sport England is responsible for contracting out the tenders for private companies and other bodies interested in running the national sporting centres.

One of Sport England's central roles is as the distributor of National Lottery funding to sporting good causes. There has been a distinct shift from 'direct grant' to 'lottery funding'. This role also allows Sport England to shape the strategic plans of national governing bodies, promote best practice in the management of sporting facilities and influence the location and design of sports facilities.

Ravenscroft (1996) argues that since the first election victory of the Thatcher administration in 1979, the United Kingdom has witnessed a cultural transformation from the municipal socialism enshrined in the post-Second World War development of the Welfare State to a form of post-industrial entrepreneurialism based largely on market rationality. This has had a profound effect on all aspects of civil society, not least the redefinition of the role of active leisure. Since the late 1950s, the dominant policy for active leisure has been 'Sport for All' – this campaign represented a set of important social rights or values. Sport England, Compulsory Competitive Tendering and later Best Value mark a transformation from government support for active leisure as an element of citizen rights to the use of leisure to promote the government's interest in legitimating a new social order based not on rights but on means. As a consequence, access to active living is no longer a societal goal for all, but rather a discretionary consumer good, the consumption of which signifies 'active' citizenship. It furthermore signifies differentiation from the growing mass of 'deviants' who are unwilling or unable to embrace this new construction of citizenship. Such deviants are, increasingly, denied access to active living and, hence, active citizenship.

The National Lottery

In order to understand the funding of sport and arts in the United Kingdom, the reader must have an understanding of the National Lottery and how it distributes money for 'good causes'.

The Department for Culture, Media and Sport is responsible for the lottery in the United Kingdom, but it does not run the lottery. Interested parties have to bid for a licence to run the National Lottery. The first licence was granted in 1994 to Camelot Group plc, a commercial company that runs the lottery for profit. Camelot successfully retained its licence since 1994. Initially, the National Lottery was regulated by OfLOT (the Office of the Regulator of the National Lottery), however in April 1999, the British government decided to abolish OfLOT and its functions were transferred to the newly formed National Lottery Commission.

The Commissioners are appointed by the Secretary of State for Culture, Media and Sport and are responsible for:

- agreeing on who shall be the lottery operator
- making sure that the lottery is run in an appropriate manner
- conducting an appropriate examination of all the individuals and organisations involved with the lottery
- looking after the interests of players
- making sure that the operator raises money for 'good causes'.

At the time of writing, the operator of the National Lottery is Camelot, and as the operator, Camelot is responsible for:

- conceiving new and innovative lottery games and operating them
- promoting the lottery through marketing
- choosing the retail outlets that will sell lottery games
- managing the prize fund.

The income from lottery sales is divided in the following manner:

- Camelot   –   5%
- retailers   –   5%
- the Treasury   –   12%
- prizes   –   50%
- good causes   –   28%

Initially, there were five 'good causes':

(Continued)

(Continued)

- the arts
- sport
- heritage
- charities
- the Millennium Fund.

In 1998, the New Opportunities Fund was added – this body distributes lottery grants to innovative projects in health, education and the environment. The National Lottery Distribution Fund distributes money to organisations which decide on the merits of each application for a lottery grant, and these include:

- Arts Councils
- Sports Councils
- Sport England
- the Heritage Lottery Fund
- the National Lottery Charities Board
- the New Opportunities Fund
- the National Endowment for Science, Technology and the Arts
- the Millennium Commission (this organisation was disbanded on 31 December 2000).

The division amongst the good causes is as follows:

- the arts   –   16.6%
- sport   –   16.6%
- heritage   –   16.6%
- charities   –   16.6%
- the Millennium Commission   –   20.0% (until 31 December 2000)
- the New Opportunities Fund   –   13.3%

In 1994, the Department of National Heritage and the Sports Council established 12 cornerstones for the distribution of lottery grants for sport:

1. For a sport to be eligible to receive a lottery grant, that sport must be recognised by the Sports Council as a sport. This means that activities such as skateboarding were not eligible to receive a lottery grant.
2. Priority was to be given to projects that cater for the widest cross-section of the community.
3. Priority was to be given to projects that improved opportunities for participation.
4. Any capital projects where the total eligible costs amounted to less than £5000 would not be considered for a lottery grant.
5. Projects had to secure additional funding to money from the lottery in order to be eligible to receive a lottery grant. This is known as 'matched funding' – the applicant is expected to raise a minimum of 35% of the total project costs from other sources, with a target of 50% for projects costing less than £5 million.
6. Revenue costs would only be eligible to receive a lottery grant in exceptional circumstances.

7. Applicants were encouraged to affiliate to the appropriate governing body.
8. School facilities would only be considered for a lottery grant if the applicant could demonstrate 'significant levels of managed use for the local community outside of school use'.
9. Applications from professional sports clubs would be unlikely to be accepted for a lottery grant unless 'significant levels of public good and community benefit [could] be demonstrated'.
10. Sports equipment would not be considered unless it was a substantial capital development on a fixed site.
11. Applications would only be considered from bona fide organisations with a written constitution, articles of association or statutory powers.
12. Applications for a grant for children's play activities would not be considered for funding.

Activity

What rationale can you provide for the state to use taxpayers' money to support sport?

The Development of Public Service Broadcasting

During the First World War, radio was used for military purposes and, after the war, the British government, unlike governments in the United States and across Europe, was very unenthusiastic about allowing radio technology to be used for public entertainment. John Reith was the founder of the BBC and public service broadcasting, and he firmly believed that the BBC should provide a range of high-quality programmes that would:

- educate the public
- inform the public
- entertain the public.

The Baldwin government accepted the validity of Reith's paternalistic approach to broadcasting and when the British government took the British Broadcasting Company into public ownership as a public corporation, Reith was retained and appointed as the new British Broadcasting Corporation's first Director General. The government did not want the BBC to be seen as part of the machinery of government propaganda.

  The BBC's independence from government was central to Reith's vision and the reputation for 'impartiality' has contributed to the respect that the BBC has throughout the world. However, the independence from government has been tested at times, for example during the 1926 General Strike when Reith argued that because the BBC was the people's service and the government was the people's choice, so it should be that the BBC should support the government. In addition, public service broadcasting in general and the BBC in particular have a reputation for cultural paternalism.

The BBC monopoly of television broadcasting ended in 1954 when the Conservative Party established the Independent Television Authority (ITA), a government agency established to award commercial broadcasting licences. The commercial companies had to comply with the public service remit to provide good quality television that would educate, inform and entertain.

The structure of broadcasting did change over the years in the United Kingdom: the Pilkington Committee (1962) recommended a second BBC channel, BBC2 (launched in 1964) and the Annan Committee (1977) recommended the launch of Channel 4 in 1983 as a 'publisher broadcaster'. Channel 4 was given a public service remit that involves commissioning programming for diversity and the tastes of minorities. In addition, both the BBC and ITV introduced early morning news and current affairs programming in the early 1980s, commonly known as 'breakfast television'. However, it was only with the election of the Thatcher government that privatisation and a greater role for free enterprise became central to government policy. In addition the position of the BBC as a public service provider was also challenged. Saatchi and Saatchi (1984), then the Conservative Party's advertising agency, published a very radical document: 'Funding the BBC: The Case for Advertising' that cast doubt on the future of the licence fee (a flat rate fee paid by all households who own a television set; the fee continues to be used to fund the BBC).

The Davies Review of the BBC (1999) argued that whilst the BBC is a public sector broadcaster, this should not mean that everything it does should be within its public service remit, opening up the possibility that it could develop some of its services on a 'for profit' basis.

Secondly, the Davies Review argued that a public service broadcaster must provide some element of service that is beyond what a commercial broadcaster could provide. For Davis, rectifying market failure must be central to any concept of public service broadcasting.

However, there was disagreement within the government over the retention of the public service element. On the one hand, commercialism and less regulation, together with market forces, would allow television companies to respond to popular choice. However, Thatcherism always had a paternalistic element, especially in relation to children, and the public service remit would ensure standards of taste and decency.

Public service broadcasting is not unique to the United Kingdom. Australia also has a strong belief in public service broadcasting within the European tradition with two national free-to-air broadcasters: the Australian Broadcasting Corporation (ABC), a non-commercial station, funded through government grant-in-aid and some indirect non-commercial sources, and the Special Broadcasting Service (SBS), a government-owned national, multicultural and multilingual broadcaster that accepts some degree of sponsorship and a limited amount of advertising. In Canada, the main public broadcaster is the national CBC. In addition, several provinces operate public broadcasters, for example TV Ontario operates two networks – one English language and one French language. The French-language TeleQuebec is also a public service provider. PSB is funded by the Canadian Television Fund (CTF), whilst private broadcasting is funded mainly by advertising revenue.

In 1980, the New Zealand public service broadcasting network was broken up in an effort to deregulate the airwaves and encourage greater competition. Up until 1980, New Zealand operated a mixed funding system – the two public service channels run by the Broadcasting Corporation of New Zealand (BCNZ) were funded by both advertising and a licence fee, before the licence fee was abolished in 1999. BCNZ was restructured into a state-owned enterprise – Television New Zealand Ltd (TVNZ) and is run on a commercial basis. The public service tradition still continues and can be found in organisations such as Te Mangai Paho (TMP) that is responsible for Maori programming.

Unlike the European model that stressed that broadcasting should have an important political and civic role within the wider society, in the United States, broadcasting has always been a commercial venture and public service broadcasting has always been regarded as marginal. The Radio Act (1927) and later the Communications Act (1934) established the American broadcasting framework that ensured that money from advertisers would be the central source of funding for both radio and television.

In 1945, the Federal Communications Commission granted a license for 'non-commercial educational' radio stations, and later in 1952, National Educational Television (NET) was established with a grant from the Ford Foundation. The NET was initially a limited service for exchanging and distributing educational programmes but in 1954 it expanded its goals, and started broadcasting hard-hitting documentaries and current affairs programmes about civil right issues in relation to gender and race, with some serious entertainment programmes. A number of the educational programmes were commercially successful, notably Sesame Street. However, because of NET's stance on civil rights in 1966, the Ford Foundation decided to withdraw funding for the network. The government intervened by passing the Public Broadcasting Act (1967) that established the Corporation for Public Broadcasting, a private not-for-profit organisation, to support NET in the short term. The CPB had a central source of funding and some limited authority over affiliated independent local stations. The Public Broadcasting Service (PBS) was created by CPB in 1969. In 1970, NET merged with New Jersey based WNDT-TV Channel 13. In 1973, President Nixon believed that it was necessary for the CPB to give up its control over PBS and local stations had control over their programming. The institutional framework has remained more or less the same since the early 1970s, although there have been significant changes to the funding of the service, reflecting the economic policies of the administration in power at the time.

Public service broadcasting involves a general regulatory framework and a comparatively high degree of public intervention. According to Hargreaves-Heap (2005), all European Union countries have introduced some form of quota system to limit the number of imported, mainly American programming, and to promote their national culture via television.

Hargreaves-Heap (2005) argues that market failure in television broadcasting continues to provide the prima facie grounds for PSB interventions – such interventions can take one of two broad forms:

- the general regulation of all broadcasters
- selective intervention through the targeted subsidy of some broadcasters.

The Prague Resolution (1994) defined public service broadcasting across the European Union within the context of four objectives:

- to support citizenship through providing an impartial and independent news service
- to facilitate public debate and respect for democratic values and human rights of all groups within the European Union
- to offer a broad range of high quality programmes across all genres
- to support national cultures.

Because US programme-makers have much higher budgets than their European counterparts, this gives them a significant competitive advantage. Moreover, if 'home' production quotas were removed, there could be a significant increase in audiences for US programmes in Europe. This would be worrying, argues Hargreaves-Heap (2005), as it would reduce the opportunity for European societies to reflect upon themselves.

What is the nature of public service broadcasting in the twenty-first century? What is the BBC for today?

The Broadcasting Research Unit definition of public service broadcasting stresses:

- geographic universality – all people in the country should be able to access the service
- that the service should cater for all interests and tastes within the population
- that the service should cater for minorities
- that the service should be detached from vested economic and political interests and from government
- that the service should be seen as one broadcasting system that is directly funded by the main body of viewers and listeners

- that the service should compete in terms of providing good programming rather than for audience share
- that the service should have guidelines that help to liberate programme-makers and not restrict them.

Graham Murdock (1997) argues that there have been four central elements of public service broadcasting:

1. That it should be central to the development of a democratic culture.
2. That it should provide space for free expression and open debate, including a forum for the politics of difference.
3. That there should be accessibility without additional charges for services.
4. That audiences should be addressed as citizens, not as consumers.

In 1998, Chris Smith, the then Secretary of State for Culture, Media and Sport gave a speech to the Royal Television Society, in which he outlined the British government's stance on the role of the BBC as a public service broadcaster:

- the BBC should act as a benchmark for quality and good standards
- the BBC should provide something for the whole television audience by 'making the good popular and the popular good'
- the BBC should inform, educate and entertain, and expand horizons with innovative programming
- the BBC should provide value for money by operating efficiently and effectively
- the BBC should act as the cultural voice of the nation, reflecting the cultural activity within the country.

Thomas (1999) described the British government's principal cultural and economic objectives for broadcasting as:

- increasing access to the arts, promoting independent film production
- the protection of vulnerable programming, such as news, children's programmes, high-cost drama
- news services rooted in accuracy and impartiality, giving information to the public as a contribution to the national political debate, and the promotion of good taste and decency, especially in protecting children from viewing harmful material
- international competitiveness, promoting growth within markets.

The then head of ITV, Richard Eyre, gave the 1999 MacTaggart lecture to the Guardian International Television Festival. The subject of the lecture was 'Is there a post-Reithian model of public service broadcasting that can thrive in the communicopia of the future?'. His answer to the question was simple, that public service broadcasting will soon be dead. According to Eyre, public service broadcasting is facing oblivion because:

- it relies on the notion of an active broadcaster and a passive viewer
- it relies on regulators who will be unable to do a comprehensive job
- an enduring definition of public service broadcasting will be impossible to formulate.

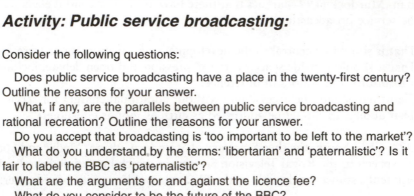

Activity: Public service broadcasting:

Consider the following questions:

Does public service broadcasting have a place in the twenty-first century? Outline the reasons for your answer.

What, if any, are the parallels between public service broadcasting and rational recreation? Outline the reasons for your answer.

Do you accept that broadcasting is 'too important to be left to the market'?

What do you understand by the terms: 'libertarian' and 'paternalistic'? Is it fair to label the BBC as 'paternalistic'?

What are the arguments for and against the licence fee?

What do you consider to be the future of the BBC?

One of the central problems with PSB is the absence of performance indicators in relation to market failure. The problem for policy makers is that without using audience share as the main performance indicator, how can policy makers know if intervention has been effective? Hargreaves-Heap (2005) suggests the following PSB performance indicators:

- information provision
- standards of 'public decency'
- 'horizon stretching'
- innovation.

As Neary (2005) suggests, the under-provision of national news and current affairs programming has a detrimental impact upon our ability to function as active citizens. Well-informed news and current affairs programming provides a voice for dissenting individuals and groups and this is good for the health of a democracy.

Activity

Carol Propper (2005) summarises a number of reasons for policy intervention in the form of PSB. These arguments are presented as the following list:

Because information is a public good, the broadcasting market would produce too little information if left to itself.

Externalities in watching TV mean that unregulated TV would lead to bad behaviour.

Horizon-stretching programmes are merit goods and so will be underprovided.

Poorly defined property rights mean too little innovation.

In monopolistic competition where the price is fixed across customers, goods that are expensive to produce will not be produced even if valued highly by some groups.

Costs are endogenous, so as competition increases, product differentiation will not necessarily occur.

Question: Consider each of the points in the above list and state one argument for and one argument against the point listed.

Activity: Advertising on the BBC

In the United States, there are no restrictions on the amount of advertising that can be broadcast. The only exception is in relation to children's programming, where 10.5 minutes per hour at weekends and 12 minutes per hour on weekdays are the permitted maximums. Within Europe, there are regulations on the amount of time that can be used for broadcasting advertisements. In the United Kingdom, the satellite broadcaster Sky is allowed up to a maximum of 9 minutes per hour, even though BSkyB has no public service remit. ITV and Channel 4 are allowed up to 7.5 minutes per hour.

Questions

Outline what you consider to be the arguments for and against funding a public service provider such as the BBC by the sale of advertising?
Do the same arguments apply to the BBC allowing advertising on its radio stations, television channels and internet sites and in its publications?

As we saw above, the Prague Resolution (1994) stated that a central element of public service broadcasting is to support citizenship through providing an impartial and independent news service. Since the mid-1970s, the Glasgow Media Research Group has argued that in the United Kingdom, both of the two main free-to-air network news services (BBC News and ITN) have fallen short of their legal obligation to present political and industrial news in a balanced, neutral and objective fashion. The Group argues that television news:

- does not reflect the full range of views
- is undemocratic in its choice of who is allowed to speak
- broadcasters defy notions of accuracy and impartiality.

The Group argued that: 'the dominant ideology works in the production of television news' (GUMG, 1980: 497). The Group's early work made a clear distinction between the distorted false consciousnesses generated by the media and the independent reality of events found in true consciousness. They argue that routine news practices led to a misleading portrayal of political and industrial issues and events when measured against the independent reality of events.

Leisure: A Nineteenth-century invention?

Chapman (1940) argues that the Ten Hours Act was one of the most important pieces of social legislation in the nineteenth century. By restricting the number of working hours, the Act created a distinct leisure time – a time free from work. The definition of leisure as a period of time in which people were free from work provided the foundation for many academic definitions of leisure up to the present day.

Activity: Was 'leisure' a direct consequence of the process of industrialisation?

Read the passage below and then answer the question in the title above:

'It is simply inadequate to suggest that industrialisation created leisure, which has subsequently grown to today's level. In fact, industrialisation in Britain began by destroying leisure. When leisure re-emerged, it was given very particular social forms, which need to be understood as the outcome of a continuous struggle between dominant and subordinate groups . . . If leisure was an achievement, it was not achieved by some abstract process called industrialisation, but by the struggles, conflicts and alliances of social groups. Both the right to leisure and the ability to pursue forms of leisure – are products of this history of conflict. (Clarke and Critcher, 1985: 48–9)

Conclusion

The leisure experience significantly changed with the emergence of modernity. The leisure experience became distinct from the work experience in terms of time and place. Popular non-work activities were undermined by industrialisation and urbanisation and a number of leisure activities were suppressed by the State. The state took a great interest in the leisure activities of working-class people on the grounds that many of the activities were a potential threat to the social order. The state and other interested bodies sponsored a range of leisure activities and institutions to rival gambling, drinking and other regrettable indulgencies.

Rational recreation was a paternalistic regimen that attempted, through the management of citizens, to make leisure activities 'morally uplifting' and provide opportunities for working-class people to exercise self-discipline, self-control, public-spiritedness and prevent national disorder.

References

Barringer, T. (1999) 'The South Kensington Museum and the colonial project', in T. Barringer and T. Flynn, *Colonialism and the Object: Empire, Material Culture and the Museum*. London: Routledge.

Bennett, T. (1999) *Past Beyond Memory: Evolution, Museums, Colonialism*. London: Routledge.

Chapman, G. (1940) *Culture and Survival*. London: Cape.

Clarke, J. and Critcher, C. (1985) *The Devil Makes Work*. Basingstoke: Macmillan.

Crosbie, P., Clench, J. and Nathan, S. (2001) 'Cleaner dumps £5k art' *The Sun*, 19 October. Accessed via http://www.thesun.co.uk/sol/homepage/news/article142000.ece

Davies, G. (1999) *The Future Funding of the BBC*. London: DCMS.

Debord, G. (1967) *The Society of the Spectacle*. Paris: Buchet/Chastel.

Docx, E. (2001) 'Take Note', *The Times*, 1 November. Accessed via http://www.timesonline.co.uk/tol/life_and_style/article819758.ece

Dunning, E. (1999) *Sport Matters: Sociological Studies of Sport, Violence and Civilization*. London: Routledge.

Gilbert, D. and Lizotte, M. (1998) 'Tourism and the performing arts', *Travel and Tourism Analyst*, 1: 82–96.

Glasgow University Media Group (GUMG) (1980) *More Bad News*. London: Routledge.

Greenwood, T. (1888) *Museums and Art Galleries*. London: Simpkin, Marshall and Company.

Hargreaves-Heap, S. (2005) 'Public service broadcasting', *Economic Policy*, 20 (41): 111–57.

Henderson, J.C. (2003) 'Government and the arts: a framework for analysis', *Managing Leisure*, 8: 121–32.

Hewison, R. (1989) 'Heritage: an interpretation', in D.L. Uzzell (ed.), *Heritage Interpretation, Volume 1: The Natural and Built Environment*. London and New York: Belhave Press.

Hewison, R. (1990) *Future Tense: A New Art for the Nineties*. London: Methuen.

Hewison, R. (1995) *Culture and Consensus: England, Art and Politics Since 1940*. London: Methuen.

Homer (1998) *The Iliad,* B. Knox (Editor, Introduction), R. Fagles (Translator). London: Penguin Classics.

Lowenthal, D. (1998) *The Heritage Crusades and the Spoils of History.* London: Cambridge University Press.

Marchand, J. (1990) *Sport for All in Europe.* London: HMSO.

Murdock, G. (1997) 'Rights and representations: Public discourse and cultural citizenship', in J. Gripsrud (ed.), *Television and Common Knowledge.* London and New York: Routledge. pp. 7–17.

Myerscough, J. (1988) *The Economic Importance of the Arts.* London: PSI.

Myerscough, J., Bruce, A., Manton, K., Towse, R. and Vaughan, D. R. (1998) *The Economic Importance of the Arts in Ipswich.* London: Policy Studies Institute.

Neary, C. (2005) 'Advertising, public relations and marketing: The hard sell', in H. Shaw, *The Irish Media Directory and Guide 2006.* Dublin, Ireland: Gill & Macmillan. Chapter 10.

Propper, C. (2005) 'Outsourcing of public service provision: When is it more efficient?', European Policy Research Unit (EPRU) Working Papers, accessed via http://www.socialsciences. manchester.ac.uk/disciplines/politics/publications/workingpapers/documents/epru_working_papers.pdf

Ravenscroft, N. (1996) 'Leisure, consumerism and active citizenship in the UK', *Managing Leisure,* 1 (30): 163–74.

Read, C.H. (1910) *Handbook to the Ethnographical Collections of the British Museum.* London: British Museum.

Saatchi and Saatchi (1984) 'Funding the BBC: The case for advertising', accessed via http://www.saatchi.co.uk

Simpson, M.G. (2001) *Making Representations: Museums in the Post-colonial Era.* London: Routledge.

Sombart, W. (1923) *Der Bourgeois.* Munich.

Tchen, J.K.W. (2001) 'Creating a dialogic museum: the Chinatown History Museum Project', in M.G. Simpson, *Making Representations: Museums in the Post-colonial Era.* London: Routledge.

Thomas, A. (1999) *Regulation of Broadcasting in the Digital Age.* London: DCMS.

Wittlin, A. (1946) *The Museum: Its History and Its Tasks in Education.* London: Routledge and Kegan Paul.

7

THE LOCAL STATE AND LEISURE PROVISION IN THE UNITED KINGDOM

This chapter is included for readers who are interested in local authority leisure provision in England and Wales – if you are a reader from outside of the United Kingdom, you may still find the discussion of the local state and the discussion of how the Thatcher, Major and Blair governments viewed local authority leisure provision of interest.

The chapter provides the following:

- an overview of local authority leisure provision within the context of debates about the local state in England and Wales and the changes that have taken place to local authority structures and organisations
- an outline and evaluation of Compulsory Competitive Tendering, together with an outline and evaluation of Best Value
- a discussion of the expectations of leisure service provision for wider social concerns, notably social inclusion
- a detailed case study of local authority leisure provision in Burnley, a small town in the north of England. Burnley had racially motivated 'disturbances' in the early years of the twenty-first century and leisure services were seen as one mechanism for bringing about greater inclusion.

The Local State

Within a specific locality, there will be a range of organisations and institutions that constitute 'the local state'. In the 1990s, many inner-city areas became sites for housing developers and many cities in the United Kingdom experienced an 'urban renaissance', with redevelopment based upon culture, tourism and heritage, and an influx of new residents, notably young professionals, moving initially into fashionable conversions of former industrial premises (Cameron, 2003). In the United Kingdom, under the Conservative governments of Thatcher and Major (1979–1997), there was a shift from local government to local governance, associated with the rise of unelected institutions such as Training and Enterprise Councils (TECs) and Urban Development Corporations (UDCs); in addition, central government encouraged a 'beauty contest' style of competitive bidding for funds such as the Single Regeneration Budget (SRB), an amount of money available to local authorities to help the process of urban regeneration and greater economic competitiveness. The Conservative government argued that competitive bidding for funding would: '…galvanize towns and cities into bringing forward imaginative proposals for regeneration' (Conservative Party, 1992: 39). However, in their case study of Newcastle, González and Vigar (2008) identify what have become 'fuzzy boundaries' between the state, the market and civil society, including the formal and informal organisations, the alliances and partnerships they form, and the confrontation and resistance they encounter in an effort to bring about change. Brenner and Theodore (2005) argue that urban governance often involves contradictory processes, strategies and policies between a range of social groupings. This is particularly true in the United Kingdom where, because of public–private partnerships and the greater use of local and regional networks and inter-agency practice, the local state has become much more dependent on private sector capital to fund its projects.

What is the local state?

The local state is a general term for a governing authority such as a local authority or municipality – the authority has the power to raise taxes from the population within its given geographically bounded area. The local state also has a role to play in local modes of regulation – in the case of the United Kingdom, for example, in the awarding of licenses for the sale of alcoholic drinks. The local state is accountable to central government, is often dependent on central government for resources, and may seek permissions or guidance from central government. The local state will often have to act according to instructions from central government and has to operate within a regulatory framework imposed by central government, such as 'Best Value'.

Aims of the Single Regeneration Budget

The aims are to:

- enhance the employment prospects, education and skills of local people, particularly the young and those at a disadvantage, and promote equality of opportunity
- encourage sustainable economic growth and wealth creation by improving the competitiveness of the local economy, including support for new and existing businesses
- protect and improve the environment and infrastructure and promote good design

- improve housing and housing conditions for local people through physical improvement, better maintenance, improved management and greater choice and diversity
- promote initiatives of benefit to ethnic minorities
- tackle crime and improve community safety
- enhance the quality of life of local people, including their health and cultural and sports opportunities.

Source: Department of the Environment (1995: 2)

In the United Kingdom and the United States, the local state has undergone fundamental restructuring since the 1970s. The ideological shift towards the greater use of markets to decide how local resources are allocated has led to greater convergence in patterns governance within the local state in the UK and the USA. Many Marxists in the 1970s regarded the local state as a branch of the central state and believed that the focus of the local state was the reproduction of labour power. Today, most commentators assume that the local state is more pluralistic in nature and not simply a passive reflection of class divisions. The local state can be an important agent of social change and regulation, and its strategies and structures can bring about conflict as well as forging new social, political and economic agreements within an area. In the United Kingdom, for example, the local authority is responsible for a range of publicly funded forms of collective consumption in areas such as education, social services, policing, fire, and leisure and recreation. In some countries, some services are provided by the local state on behalf of central government and in other areas there is a high degree of autonomy in terms of the provision of municipal service provision. The local state has to balance the many competing and conflicting demands for resources and service provision. As we shall see below in the case of Burnley, a town that did not experience the UK's 'urban renaissance' in the 1990s, this can lead to violent confrontation.

Many British cities have attempted to re-brand themselves along the lines described by Edensor's (2000) phrase 'tourist enclave', stressing their cultural and sporting attractions, tourist entertainment, gentrified shopping, hotels, restaurants and café-bars, within a highly regulated space. Degen (2003) and Harvey (1989a, 1989b) argue that this 'new urban governance' has diminished the public service ethos of local authorities and excluded the poorest members of the community from enjoying the benefits of increasing affluence. Increasing gentrification is usually policed by means of a 'broken windows' strategy of maintaining law and order. In this case, 'order' refers to middle-class culturally prescribed goals and values in relation to civility and respectability. According to Wilson and Kelling (1982), the 'broken windows' style of policing in urban areas is based on the assumption that minor infractions, such as litter, graffiti and broken windows, are often associated in the minds of 'respectable' citizens with theft, prostitution and drug trafficking. Goldberger (1996) argues that this re-branding produces an image of the urban environment that is 'without hard edges, without a past, and without a respect for the pain and complexity of authentic urban experience. It is suburban in its values, and middle class to its core' (cited in Atkinson, 2003: 1841). The 'real' city is something that tourists and other mobile urban visitors are well protected from.

In a series of papers, Roy Coleman (2003, 2004, 2005) draws upon a neo-Marxist explanation, to account for the introduction of CCTV within inner-city Liverpool and Manchester. For Coleman, the motivation behind CCTV is to police existing unequal socio-economic divisions within the city and exclude economically marginalised groups from enjoying the retail and leisure space.

Coleman has argued that the emergence of what he terms the *entrepreneurial city* has brought about 'changes in the surveillance and control of urban space through a myriad of technologies and legal–moral ordering practices' (Coleman, 2005: 131). These changes have come about in the process of cities attempting to re-brand themselves in an effort to attract greater capital investment. Coleman argues that partnerships between powerful local agencies, notably local councils and businesses, are central to the development of what Coleman terms 'entrepreneurial urbanism'. Partnership is not a neutral term, but a central element of neo-liberal governance. Coleman (2004) quotes Atkinson (1999) to explain that the discourse of 'partnership' is not neutral, but used to: 'construct problems, solutions and actions in particular ways that are congruent with existing relations of power, domination and distribution of resources' (Atkinson, 1999: 70).

Re-branding inner-city space involves the careful 'imagineering' or 'rescripting' of inner-city space as 'carnivalesque' in nature, with a greater emphasis on play, spontaneity and cosmopolitanism within a festival market place that draws upon discourses of 'excitement' and 'ordered non-risky risk' as selling points. Changing the 'visual in the politics of the street' to create visually pleasing leisure and retail space in the inner city has led to more effective forms of surveillance that target petty street-level crime, 'nuisance' and 'unconventional' behaviour that affluent people are assumed to find unacceptable and disruptive to their retail and leisure experiences, mainly through the greater use of CCTV, private security, public street warden schemes and new legal sanctions. In other words, argues Coleman, the inner city had to be free from 'yobs', high-spirited gangs of youths, buskers, homeless people, rough sleepers, petty thieves, drunks, beggars and illicit traders. Central to this process has been the 2003 Anti-Social Behaviour Act – under Section 30 of the Act, all 16-year-olds can be photographed and banned from selected urban areas; Anti Social Behaviour Orders (ASBOs) have been used to good effect in the process of criminalising people who are unwilling or unable to perform as effective consumers.

In July 2002, Liverpool City Council banned skateboarders from the inner city, with a fine of between £250 and £1000 for people caught skateboarding. In 2004, Leeds City Council ran a campaign entitled 'Shape up or Ship Out' that attempted to ban sellers of the Big Issue from the inner city. Moreover, it is common for young people to be banned from wearing hooded tops and/or baseball caps in a number of inner-city areas.

Moreover, because surveillance is centrally focused on the street and 'street people', as Coleman (2004) argues, this reinforces the view that 'crime', 'risk', and 'harm' are a product of the presence of powerless and 'disaffected' people. Coleman (2004) explains: 'In Liverpool … undercover policing and targeted surveillance [resulted] in the arrest, caution or charging of over 800 people in 2002 in relation to begging offences. All beggars are now routinely finger-printed and placed on the Police National Computer' (Coleman, 2004: 303).

Activity

Cameras in the cities of the UK are a tool in the politics of vision – helping enforce what can and cannot be observed on the streets, thus aiding the strategic balance between aesthetics and function. For example, any notion of the city as a place of spontaneous fun for young people is being curtained. (Coleman, 2003: 32)

The Crime and Disorder Act (CDA) 1998 was the cornerstone of the first Blair government's approach to crime. Central to the 1998 Act was the Crime Reduction Strategy (CRS). All statutory agencies had an obligation to reduce crime and reduce the fear of crime, from forming 'Community Safety Partnerships' to devising local crime reduction strategies, sharing 'best practice' and tackling low-level anti-social disorder.

The removal of the signs of inequality has been extended to a tradition found in most English cities during October and November. This is Guy Fawkes Night, where children have for over two centuries legitimately asked members of the public for a 'penny for the guy': in an attempt to combat children 'who are a nuisance' and who remind shoppers of images of the street urchins of the nineteenth century, Liverpool City Council denied the continuation of this activity under the Vagrancy Act (1824) and the Children's and Young Persons Act (1933), making it an offence for anyone who is responsible for a child under the age of 16 to allow that child to be in any street for the purposes of begging (Coleman, 2003: 34).

Question: How are the leisure and retail spaces policed in the inner-city areas that you are familiar with? Make a list of what you consider to be the advantages and disadvantages of the 'broken windows' approach to policing.

Municipal Parks

It would be wrong to think that public–private partnership developed solely in the late twentieth century – for example, there has been support for municipal parks in England since the late 1820s and the development of municipal parks has often come from partnerships between the public and private sectors. A Parliamentary Select Committee on Public Walks was appointed in 1833 to investigate securing green open spaces in urban areas for the public to use for walking and exercise.

For Gold (1973), the 'park' is 'any public area of land set aside for aesthetic, educational, recreational or cultural use' (Gold, 1973: 20) in an urban environment. The large urban parks were conceptualised, designed and managed by local elites as areas for public use. In the nineteenth century, under the influence of a philosophy of rational recreation, particularly the need to improve the physical health of working-class people, local elites managed to convince local municipal authorities to construct parks at public expense. There are also some notable cases of private philanthropy that have been used to develop large areas of urban space into parks, such as Peel Park in Manchester. However the role and purpose of the park changes over time, and the aims and objectives of the park differ from country to country. In addition, there are always struggles and conflicts over how these urban spaces should be used and who should have access to the space and on what terms. A case in point is Atlanta's Centennial Olympic Park which was developed as a park for 'passive' leisure as part of the city's successful Olympic bid. Many groups within the city wanted to see the park development move towards a greater use of space for active sports and leisure use, such as football and other team sports, rather than to open space for people to use as they saw fit.

Young (2004) looks at the role of the park in the relationship between nature and American society. From the 1850s to the 1920s, supporters of parks stressed that parks were a public good and pointed to the role of the park in social reform, such as public health. Young identifies periods of park development – he describes the period from the 1850s to the early 1880s as the 'romantic period', where park supporters stressed the pastoral role of the park: the need to provide people in cities with the opportunity to enjoy the tamed wilderness of a rural landscape for contemplation. Young describes the period from the late 1880s to the 1920s as the rationalistic period, where the focus was on more active forms of leisure and social activities within 'programmed' parks.

Property that is located close to inner-city parks frequently sells at a premium. This enhanced 'capitalisation' has been termed 'the proximate principle'. This principle was first identified in relation to London's Regent's Park and John Nash's design provided the financial rationale for many later inner-city park developments. Regent's Park provided 'picturesque country scenery in the Capability Brown/Repton tradition, to the urban context to be enjoyed by detached villas in the center and by great terraces of houses round the periphery' (Davis, 1973: 64). There was also a significant increase in property prices in the areas surrounding Atlanta's Centennial Olympic Park following the games.

Crompton (2007) explains that in 1841, the United Kingdom Parliament offered local authorities up to £10,000 to help fund the development of inner parks, provided that the local authority matched the amount loaned from central government with a similar sum. The loan was to be repaid from the sale of building plots bordering the park.

Frederick Law Olmsted was later to use the 'proximate principle' as a central argument in his rationale for the development of New York City's Central Park. Olmsted had an international reputation following his design of Central

Park – the first large inner-city park in the United States – and influenced more than one generation of urban planners, notably British planners Thomas Adams, Thomas Mawson, Patrick Geddes and Ebenezer Howard (note the latter's garden city movement). American urban planners such as Daniel Burnham and Edward Bennett and others within the American Society of Landscape Architects and the American City Planning Institute took their inspiration from Olmsted. Olmsted's vision was that the park should provide a coming together of the beautiful and sublime to help 'civilise' the urban people – what Olmsted referred to as the 'genius of civilisation'.

The question of who has access to the park, on what terms and for what purpose is a question that has in one case questioned the legitimacy of the local state. In the 1970s, Burnley Borough Council decided to ban the exercising of dogs in public parks – this caused a long-running dispute between the 'dog lovers' and the council that resulted in the formation of the Dog Lovers Party – members fought in the local elections and used direct action for which people went to jail by ignoring the council's ban on dogs in parks.

The Structure of Local Government in England and Wales

The structure of local government is complex and varies across England and Wales. To put it briefly, there are five different types of local authorities and these are divided into single-tier and two-tier authorities. The 1972 Local Government Act established a division between Metropolitan and Non-Metropolitan areas. From 1974 onwards, there were 47 Non-Metropolitan County Councils, 238 Non-Metropolitan District Councils in England and Wales, the Greater London Council (GLC), six Metropolitan County Councils and 36 Metropolitan District Councils.

The six Metropolitan County Councils were:

1. Greater Manchester, which included the following Metropolitan District Councils: Manchester, Salford, Bolton, Bury, Oldham, Rochdale, Stockport, Tameside, Trafford, Wigan.
2. Merseyside, which included Liverpool, Knowsley, Sefton, St Helens, Wirral.
3. South Yorkshire, which included Sheffield, Barnsley, Doncaster, Rotherham.
4. Tyne and Wear, which included Newcastle upon Tyne, Sunderland, Gateshead, South Tyneside, North Tyneside.
5. West Midlands, which included Birmingham, Coventry, Wolverhampton, Dudley, Sandwell, Solihull, Walsall.
6. West Yorkshire, which included Leeds, Bradford, Wakefield, Calderdale, Kirklees.

From 1979 until 1997, there was a Conservative government in the United Kingdom and although the Labour Party had very limited success in general elections, they did have some success in local government, particularly in the Metropolitan District and County Councils, and a new brand of municipal socialism was developed by a new generation of Labour councillors such as Ken Livingstone.

In 1985, the Thatcher government introduced a new Local Government Act to abolish the GLC and the six Metropolitan County Councils. The councils were all under Labour control at the time of their abolition.

Although the Metropolitan County Councils were abolished, their functions remained but were transferred to special joint arrangements – joint boards made up of co-opted councillors from Metropolitan District Councils and Quasi Autonomous Non-Governmental Organisations (Quangos). Key features are that:

- special joint arrangements covered grants to voluntary bodies, roads and traffic management, waste disposal and airports
- joint boards were responsible for fire, police and public transport
- quangos were responsible for some arts and sport, pensions and debt
- district councils remained responsible for leisure, arts, civil defence, planning, trading standards, parks, tourism, archives, industrial assistance and highways.

The rest of England and Wales was covered by the Non-Metropolitan County Councils (often referred to as Shire Counties) which are responsible for:

- education
- social services
- trading standards
- waste disposal
- highways and transport
- strategic land use planning.

Non-Metropolitan District Councils are responsible for:

- housing
- leisure parks, sports, arts
- land use planning permission
- environment health
- waste collection and recycling
- street cleaning.

In 1992, there was a further local government act that introduced more local authority reorganisation to create 46 new unitary authorities in England – these are accountable for all local authority services in the area: leisure, parks, open spaces and countryside education, social services, planning, waste disposal, recycling and collection, trading standards, emergency planning, roads, highways and transportation, housing, environmental health, markets and fairs.

The Local Government Act 2000 introduced changes to the political structures within local authorities, such as the introduction of an elected mayor if the people in the area wanted one – the intention was to streamline and modernise local authority political structures in an effort to make local authorities more accountable. Since 2000, central government has given local authorities additional powers that have impacted on local leisure provision – for example, the Licensing Act (2003) gave local authorities in England and Wales responsibility to issue premises licences and personal licences for licensable activities such as regulated entertainments. In 2007, local authorities became responsible for issuing licences to premises for gambling. Also, in 2007, local authorities became responsible for stray dogs, although the police remain responsible for policing dangerous dogs.

Privatising sport and leisure

What is *privatisation*?

The reduction of state provision, a service once provided by the public sector, is now provided by the private sector.

The reduction of state subsidy, goods or services that were believed to be desirable for the public to consume were partly paid for by the government in the form of a subsidy to reduce the price. With privatisation, this form of subsidy is either reduced or abolished.

With the reduction of state regulation, the government was concerned that the free market may not function to provide everyone with access to leisure services, so the state would intervene to regulate the market place; with privatisation, this is not the case. In local government, three forms of privatisation have come to prominence:

- the sale of local authority assets
- 'market discipline' in service delivery – contracting out
- private sector investment – deregulation.

The Thatcher government adopted a New Right or Anti-Collectivist approach to governance. The central values of this group were:

- liberty and freedom – seen in negative terms as the absence of coercion
- individualism – where individuals are seen as irrational, fallible beings
- inequality – this is seen as a good thing in that it provides people with an incentive to better themselves but also attempts to reduce inequality that can only be achieved by force, such as making people pay taxes they do not want to pay.

The New Right also believes that:

Government intervention is socially disruptive, wasteful of resources, promotes economic inefficiency and obliterates individual freedom – the Welfare State particularly promotes disruption of the social fabric and is dangerous. The critique of resource waste is based on two assumptions:

(Continued)

(Continued)

- 'at nil price demand is infinite' – if a product or service is provided free by the government, people will consume as much as they can irrespective of their needs
- State-funded services engender 'a continual deafening chorus of complaint' – whatever people are provided with by the government, they will always demand more.

Government monopoly leads to unnecessary expenditure, plus lack of concern about costs and efficiency.

Government monopoly leads to tyranny and dictatorship because it inevitably takes away individual freedom.

For the New Right, the role of the government should be to:

- act as 'rule maker and umpire'
- stop market imperfection
- intervene only on 'paternalistic' grounds – to help people who are 'not responsible'.

In September 1987, the British government published *Competition in the Management of Local Authority Sport and Leisure Facilities* – this outlined their plans to add local authority sport and leisure facilities to the Compulsory Competitive Tendering (CCT) process. CCT came into effect in 1989 and allowed private companies from outside, as well as the council's own leisure department or Direct Labour Organisation (DLO), to compete for contracts.

Robinson (1999, 2002) makes a strong case that the introduction of quality management techniques into local authority leisure service provision was strongly influenced by government policy in relation to the introduction of market discipline into public service.

For Robinson (2002), with the election of the Thatcher government in 1979, there was a period of inherent commercialism within local authority provision. The Thatcher administrations were intent on a policy of privatisation of state assets wherever possible. In areas where there was no political will to privatise, the Thatcher government opted for attempting to introduce some other form of market mechanism into the system, for example with an internal market for healthcare. It is commonly assumed that quality management is an appropriate strategy for the management of local authority leisure facilities. The introduction of CCT strongly encouraged the use of quality management techniques within public leisure services. In addition, many local authorities made it a condition of the tendering process that companies must have achieved a recognised quality standard. However, Robinson (2002) argues that the appropriateness of quality management for public services is assumed rather than proved:

The use of quality management techniques in UK public leisure facilities raises two concerns. Firstly, there is evidence to suggest that the inherent commercialism of quality management and its associated techniques has led to an undermining of the social objectives of public leisure facilities. Secondly, in order to deliver high quality services, public leisure facility managers have focused on the expectations of paying customers, to the exclusion of other customer groups. (Robinson, 2002: 33)

In an earlier paper, Robinson (1999) argues that the increasing focus on quality and quality management within the UK public leisure industry resulted in the introduction of quality programmes to facilitate leisure management. However, what has not been debated is why public leisure managers chose to adopt quality programmes in the management of their facilities.

Robinson (1999) carried out research in six local authorities to find the reasons why quality management is used in the UK public sector and found that: 'Compulsory Competitive Tendering had led directly to the use of quality programmes within all of the local authority leisure facilities' (Robinson, 1999: 212).

Robinson (1999) found that quality management programmes were being used in local authority leisure facilities for three reasons:

- First, as a consequence of a greater customer focus
- Secondly, as a response to Compulsory Competitive Tendering (CCT)
- Thirdly, as part of an increasingly commercial and professional approach.

The Thatcher government significantly changed the environment in which public leisure services operated, with greater competition, greater consumerism and legislative changes to reduce the cost to the taxpayer of running public services. Even if a local authority's own direct labour organisation were to successfully bid for a contract, the tendering process itself would make the in-house bid competitive and result in a downward pressure to reduce cost. It was also assumed by the Thatcher government that the private sector could be used to solve social problems because the better commercial quality management techniques are always efficient, irrespective of the problem or issue that needs to be managed. Robinson (1999) argues that public sector managers have had to change their managerial approach strategies to respond to the rapid changes in competition and customer demand.

The result was the introduction of quality programmes to facilitate leisure management, but with a 'public service orientation' (PSO). PSO was based on four principles:

- Local authorities are judged by the quality of service they provide with the resources they have available.
- Local authority services can only be said to provide real value if those services are used by the customers for whom those services are provided.
- Local authority service users need to be seen as *customers* demanding high quality services.
- Local authority service users need to be seen as *citizens* entitled to receive the service.

The Thatcher government believed that the private sector was more efficient and offered a lower cost and higher quality service than the public sector. The concept of quality that the Thatcher government adopted was imported directly from the private sector. In addition, it was hoped that a 'commercial' management culture would emerge because of the tendering process. Service users were seen as consumers and it was assumed that this customer focus should be managed by forms of quality management inspired by notions of 'excellence': 'The government's model of an enabling authority will promote more effective and business-like management which pays more attention to customer requirements and value for money' (HM Treasury, 1991: 1–2).

The Audit Commission (1989), in its report *Sport for Whom*, suggested that CCT would allow local authorities to target minority users and disadvantaged groups more particularly whilst at the same time doing away with blanket subsidies and thereby reducing cost. However, taking up the theme of 'attention to customer requirements', Aitchison (1997) reflected upon the impact of CCT on local authority sport and leisure from a feminist perspective. Aitchison argues that these claims were never investigated by feminists and, in addition, the notion of Total Quality Management was used to marginalise women by attempting to make political arrangements and power gender neutral:

> Feminist critique is not only lacking in service sector research related to sport and leisure provision but is also lacking in research into local government and public policy more generally. If the gender implications of CCT are to be fully understood then there must be a greater awareness of gender issues in local government research ... The emphasis upon Total Quality Management (TQM) within sport and leisure services as a contemporary gender-neutral mechanism for improved service provision is but one example of a strategy which has frequently served to marginalize feminist debate by focusing on the functional and operational aspects of policy implementation rather than the more structural or cultural determinants of policy, employment or organizational culture. (Aitchison, 1997: 102)

In contrast, Best Value requires local authorities to be more inclusive in their service provision and as such focuses on people who have not traditionally used the service.

Best Value

Best Value replaced CCT in 1999 when the British government introduced the local government act. Best Value performance indicators place an expectation on local authorities to achieve continuous improvement in terms of the efficiency, effectiveness and economy of their service delivery. The Department of the Environment, Transport and the Regions outlined Best Value: 'Best Value authorities (should) make arrangements to secure continuous improvement in the way in which they exercise their functions, having regard to a combination of economy, efficiency and effectiveness' (DETR, 1999: 4).

If local authorities fail to meet their Best Value obligations, the government can intervene. The key demands of Best Value are that local authorities must:

- develop a *community strategy*
- determine *strategic objectives and corporate priorities*
- develop a *performance management framework*
- develop a *local cultural strategy.*

Senior managers must achieve the four Cs:

- *challenge* purpose
- *compare* performance
- *consult* community
- *compete* with others (DETR, 1999: 4).

Best Value introduced a number of specific indicators to measures of performance of local authorities in a range of areas by establishing benchmark standards of provision on a national basis. The Best Value indicators are established by the departments in central government, and central government encourages local authorities to develop programmes which are often multi-agency, cross-sectoral, and in partnership with other bodies, within a 'best value environment'. The notion of achieving an improvement in service delivery by the use of performance indicators is not new to local authorities in England and Wales – well before the introduction of Best Value, the Audit Commission had set similar measures of local authority performance. However, the Blair government believed that sport, for example, could contribute to wider social and economic objectives, such as achieving greater social inclusion and urban regeneration, if local authorities and other agencies pursue policies for sustainability and combat social exclusion.

For the Blair government, total quality management became central to its conception of governance – by bringing people and organisations together through partnership working and creating excellent organisations with a commitment to continuous improvement by progressive practice, effectiveness and efficiency, the government's objectives could be achieved.

Best Value

To judge if local authorities in the UK are achieving best value, the British government set measures of performance against key service delivery areas:

- the number of GCSEs achieved
- the level of waste recycling
- the amount of council tax collected.

Best Value performance indicators cover many but not all aspects of services provided by local councils:

(Continued)

(Continued)

- health
- education
- social services
- housing
- housing benefit and council tax
- waste
- transport
- planning
- environmental health and trading standards
- culture services/libraries and museums
- community safety
- community legal services
- fire services

Each department of central government in the UK established national policies, many of which placed an obligation upon local authorities. The Department of Culture, Media and Sport's key strategy issues include: sustaining and developing quality, innovation and good design; creating an efficient and competitive market for culture, media and sport by removing obstacles; and promoting UK culture, media and sport within the UK and overseas. This includes specific initiatives such as:

- Sport in education – one of the Department of Culture, Media and Sport's key strategy issues is to increase the level of sport participation by young people. To do this, the department expects that school sports facilities will be of high quality; that Physical Education will also be of high quality; that after-school activities will be of high quality; and that there will be inter-school sports competitions and access to coaching and support.
- Sport in the community – the Department of Culture, Media and Sport wants to see lifelong participation amongst the UK adult population. Therefore, the department wants to see continual improvement in playing fields and other local authority sports facilities. Local authorities have to provide sports development and policies to enhance social inclusion and the development of sports clubs.
- Sporting excellence – the Department of Culture, Media and Sport puts an obligation on local authorities to identify potential sporting talent within the local community and to develop that talent. Governing bodies of sports organisations are also part of the 'best value environment' and should be central to development and performance plans as well as coaching development.
- Modernisation – the Department of Culture, Media and Sport has the objective of developing closer partnerships within sport. A central element of the 'best value environment' is the emergence of a common set of clear targets and objectives for all governing bodies, again with attention to the

social inclusion of groups who in the past were traditionally excluded, plus greater investment in 'grassroots' sports development, with a stronger emphasis on quality management planning and monitoring rewarded with increased responsibility.

- Access and fairness in sport – the Department of Culture, Media and Sport has the objective of providing sporting opportunities for all people at all levels – agencies within the best value environment should be judged in terms of their ability to provide structures, facilities and resources to fulfil their sporting potential.

Sport England's primary goals are clearly related to the Department of Culture, Media and Sport's objectives.

Sport England's primary goals:

- more people
- more places
- more medals.

Activity

'Best Value requires local authorities to produce a cultural strategy, a 'clear rationale for why the local authority funds, manages, supports, encourages or regulates certain activities (including sport and leisure)' (DCMS, 2001: 8).

For Robinson (2002), the local authority cultural strategy should be based on the needs of the people within the local area and should guarantee adequate access for all cultural services in relation to their needs. The cultural strategy must also meet central government's cultural objectives, notably social inclusion.

Question: The local cultural strategy is drawn up in consultation with local people and organisations. Choose any local authority in the UK, look at its website and find the cultural strategy. Identify what methods of consultation were used to construct the strategy. Were non-users of local authority cultural provision included in the consultation exercise?

New Leisure Trusts

Although CCT was successful in terms of reducing the cost of local authority leisure services research, Nichols and Taylor (1995) reinforced the commonly held belief that the CCT process enhanced market-led objectives but undermined the social objectives of leisure services. Moreover, as Ives (2003) explains, even though Best Value has replaced CCT, the financial pressures on local authority leisure services remain. With the introduction of CCT in 1989, a wider range of organisations became involved in the delivery of leisure services. Under 'Best Value', local authorities continue to review their form of service delivery. 'New Leisure Trusts' is an approach to local authority leisure service provision that allows the service to be competitive and managerialist in nature, in that trust management is largely independent of the local authority, but maintains a public service ethos.

In 1993, Greenwich Council established a form of service delivery for its council leisure provision that was to be later adopted by other local authorities under the name of 'new leisure trusts'. These are non-profit distributing organisations (NPDOs) and many of them have charitable status:

> The setting up of a leisure trust involves the local authority transferring the service to a newly established NPDO (or an existing trust). The council retains ownership of the facilities which are leased to the trust which also receives an annual grant from the council to make up the difference between its income from user charges and the cost of operating the service. (Centre for Public Services, 1998: 5)

The trusts are legally independent of the local authority and operate as not-for-profit organisations managed by a board of trustees drawn from the local community. Most leisure trusts operate a '20% rule' that means that less than 20 per cent of trust board members eligible to vote can be elected representatives or council employees. For Simmons (2001), new leisure trusts occupy 'a middle ground between the public and private sectors' (p. 101) and, according to Pringle (2001: 44), the trusts can 'escape from the dead hand of the council's central departments which have often pursued their own agenda rather than that of the service they nominally support'.

The Centre for Public Services lists a number of financial advantages of trusts: 'a non-profit organization with charitable status can obtain business rate relief and VAT savings which is an attractive option for local authorities faced with hard choices on budget cuts, closures, reduced services and redundancies' (CPS, 1998: 5).

Simmons (2004) lists some of the possible disadvantages of leisure trusts:

- the loss to the council of control over services
- the loss to the council of their ability to plan strategically for the needs of the whole area
- concerns over the future availability of financial advantages
- concerns over trusts' ability to raise capital finance
- an erosion of the 'public service orientation'
- concerns with regard to probity and accountability.

(*Source*: Simmons, 2004: 164–5).

Case Study: The Role of Leisure Services in Burnley

Burnley is a Lancashire mill town in the Pennines. In June 2001, there were riots in Burnley and in the nearby town of Oldham and in the city of Bradford. All three areas have experienced long-term economic decline. Unemployment is high and industry has deserted the area. In Burnley, in 2000–2001, there was a successful bid for money from the single regeneration budget which has been used to redevelop areas of the town that were in greatest need, such as Daneshouses and Burnley Wood. However because housing in the town is divided along racial lines, racists saw the allocation of money as favouring the Asian community. Research by the Burnley Action Partnership (2006) found that the disturbances were in part caused by the failure of local councillors to explain why they spent the money in the way they did – this caused bitterness over what was seen to be unequal council spending on racial grounds.

The task force that investigated the reasons behind the riots concluded that the events were sparked by a confrontation between two criminal gangs of drug dealers in the Burnley Wood area of the town: one white, one Asian. Together with a separate incident involving a serious assault on an Asian taxi driver, such events were used by racists as an excuse to engage in wider violent conflict, notably the petrol bombing of a local pub that BNP activists were believed to frequent.

King and Waddington (2004) explain that the academic accounts have emphasised such factors as:

- social segregation brought about by racism and harassment
- the decline of the textile industry, causing high unemployment and deprivation
- 'Islamophobia'
- police indifference to the problems facing Asian communities
- limited political representation of Asian youth
- the emergence of a more assertive Asian male youth identity
- the 'demonisation' of Asian youth by police and the media.

The political response of the British government to the riots was to establish the Community Cohesion Unit and to issue guidance to local authorities on how to enhance community cohesion. The role of the Community Cohesion Unit was to review government policy and implement the Community Cohesion Pathfinder Programme, to encourage good practice on community cohesion at a local level. The guidance on community cohesion contains a four-part definition of a 'cohesive society':

- a common vision and a sense of belonging for all communities
- the appreciation and positive value of people's diversity
- an equality of opportunity and life chances
- strong and positive relationships in the workplace, in schools and neighbourhoods.

Robinson (2005) questions the government's community cohesion agenda on the grounds that it may be counterproductive. The Independent Review Team (2001) argued that the communities needed to encourage the development of common goals and a shared vision in an effort to challenge the 'us and them' attitude that increased the fragmentation and polarisation of communities, increased social division and damaged community cohesion (Home Office, 2001). The Independent Review Team on community cohesion drew directly on Forrest and Kearns (2001) in their understanding of the central elements of community cohesion:

- common values and civic culture
- social order and social control
- social solidarity and reductions in wealth disparities.

However, as Amin (2002) points out, habitual contact is in itself no guarantor of cultural exchange and may even entrench bitterness. In addition, for Amin, the segregation discourse was focused on Asians being segregated from whites, rather than whites segregating themselves from other racial groups.

Amin (2003) takes a different view, that the disturbances should be seen as a claim of full citizenship by Asian youth, the product of limited economic opportunity in the town that the far right had framed in racial terms and that the police and community leaders were unable to combat. The far right do not believe that Asians in Burnley are fully fledged citizens of a multi-ethnic and multicultural society. Asian participation in the disturbances should be seen as a protest against the long-term marginalisation and discrimination of working-class Asians. There is a need for greater economic opportunity in the town and this is not simply a 'race' issue.

Activity

This activity is about helping you to identify what you understand to be the role of leisure within contemporary society.

Read the passage below about the Thompson Centre in Burnley and answer the questions that follow, giving reasons for your responses.

The William Thompson Recreation Centre owes its existence to the generosity of Mr William Thompson whose benefaction provided an amount in excess of £500,000 towards the provision of the facilities.

The first phase of the project was brought into use on 20 April 1974 but Mr Thompson died on 18 August 1974, ten days before the Centre was officially opened by his sister Miss Sarah W. Thompson and the Mayor of Burnley (Councillor E. Hanson J.P.).

Work continued on the construction of the diving pool and sauna suite, which came into use on 23 July 1975 and 3 November 1975 respectively. The Sports Council provided a grant of £50,000 towards the sub-regional diving facility.

Other facilities included:

- swimming pools
- a future fitness gymnasium
- a weights gymnasium
- sports halls
- squash courts
- a sauna–steam and sun studio
- an aerobic studio
- sunbeds
- a créche.

Source: www.burnley.gov.uk/leisurenburnley/ThompsonCentre.htm

Questions:

How would you define the mission of the Thompson Centre as a leisure facility?
What do you see as the 'core business' of the Thompson Centre?
What objectives would you establish for the Thompson Centre?
Would it surprise you to learn that the Thompson Centre was demolished in 2007?
   After you have read the chapters about management of the leisure sector, you might consider returning to this activity to answer this question: how useful do you believe Drucker's account of the practice of management is in answering the above questions?
The leisure centre management has to take into account national and local political initiatives – in terms of Burnley, this must include the sport and physical activity strategy for the borough devised by the local council.
   The Burnley Sport and Physical Activity Strategy needs to support and make a significant contribution to the strategic vision of the Council by:

- supporting and encouraging individuals in their personal development
- promoting a good environment and more sustainable lifestyles
- making a contribution to the local economy
- striving to involve everyone
- contributing to the development of healthy communities
- enhancing the quality of life for the residents of Burnley

Burnley Community Plan – 'Burnley's Future'

Burnley's community plan, developed and produced by Burnley Action Partnership, was publicly launched in September 2003. 'Burnley's Future' focuses on the period between now and 2021 and identifies four key priorities:

- to celebrate a diverse community and foster pride in the borough
- to develop a prosperous Burnley with a high quality of life and opportunities
- to develop a sustainable Burnley: that is healthy, safe, clean, green and well housed
- to provide high quality integrated services for the people of Burnley.

(Continued)

(Continued)

Sport and physical activity play a key role in supporting several of these priorities in bringing about community cohesion and assisting in sustaining a healthier community.

Burnley Cultural Strategy

The Sport and Physical Activity Strategy will support the aims of Burnley's Cultural Strategy. Some of the aims of the Cultural Strategy that closely link with this strategy are:

- using sport and cultural activity to achieve community cohesion
- developing partnership working between agencies, sectors and communities
- addressing social exclusion
- enabling wider access to physical and cultural activity and opportunities
- recognising and provide for the needs, ambitions and potential of young people.

Source: The Sport and Physical Activity Strategy for the Borough of Burnley, 2003: 8.

Sports associations and music clubs draw on a wide cross-section of the population, they are spaces of intense and passionate interaction, with success often dependent upon collaboration and group effort, their rhythms are different from those of daily habits, and they can disrupt racial and ethnic stereotypes as excellence often draws upon talents and skills that are not racially or ethnically confined. But, here too, the transformational element of interaction needs to be made explicit and worked at in efforts to make them intercultural spaces, through experiments that fit with local circumstances. They need to be made different from the many sports clubs and music clubs that are segregated on ethnic lines precisely as a means of preserving White and non-White communal traditions, often against a background of majority rejection of minority members. (Amin, 2003: 970)

Amin (2003) quotes with approval the Theatre-Forum in Marseilles, the forum stage plays based on the experiences of residents from difficult mixed neighbourhoods, written with the help of the same local residents. The plays attempt to dramatise the daily problems people face and promote 'role exchanges' and audience participation during the play, encouraging inter-ethnic understanding.

In South Yorkshire, there is a similar project called 'Race to Train', which deals with issues of race and diversity in the workplace: 'volunteers from the organisations work with writers and directors talk about their experiences, which are then presented to an audience of employees in a play entitled Crossing the Line' (Housing Today, 22 November 2001: 19). The audience is divided into workshop groups and issues brought up in the play are examined further through drama and discussion. Drama can be used to address community problems in a direct and emotional way, making people question long-held opinions and attitudes.

Amin suggests that legislative theatre, where people are encouraged to engage in an active relationship with the performed event, can have an important role to pay in urban social policy. 'Legislative theatre' is associated with the Brazilian cultural activist Augusto Boal and his Theatre of the Oppressed, an attempt to use theatre to help the public engage in debates that are often a source of conflict, to help create a political context for democracy to work more effectively.

Questions

Can leisure be used to achieve inter-ethnic understanding, engagement, community cohesion and address social exclusion?

If so, what kind of engagement or outcome can be expected?

Does the existence of such national and local strategies make it impossible for the management of the centre to develop a strategy, set objectives or define the mission of the organisation?

Conclusion

This chapter has looked at the changing nature of local government from the election of the first Thatcher government in 1979 until the Brown government in the early twenty-first century. Local government has seen the imposition of greater market discipline and greater privatisation, initially with the introduction of Compulsory Competitive Tendering and many years later with the introduction of Best Value. Leisure remains a discretionary service offered by local authorities and this means that the service is given a lower priority than education or social services. Many commentators have suggested that privatisation involves a loss of public service orientation in local authority leisure provision. However, with the racially motivated disturbances in Burnley, Oldham and Bradford in 2001, both central and local government looked to leisure services to help bring about greater community cohesion.

References

Aitchison, C. (1997) 'A decade of compulsory competitive tendering in UK sport and leisure services: some feminist reflections', *Leisure Studies*, 16: 85–105.

Amin, A. (2002) 'Ethnicity and the multicultural city: living with diversity', *Environment and Planning*, 34: 959–80.

Amin, A. (2003) 'Unruly strangers? The 2001 urban riots in Britain', *International Journal of Urban and Regional Research*, 27 (2): 460–3.

Atkinson, A.B. (1999) *The Economic Consequences of Rolling Back the Welfare State*, Munich Lectures in Economics. Cambridge, MA: CES and MIT Press.

Atkinson, R. (2003) 'Domestication by cappuccino or a revenge on urban space? Control and empowerment in the management of urban spaces', *Urban Studies*, 40 (9): 1829–43.

Audit Commission (1989) *Sport for Whom? Clarifying the Local Authority Role in Sport and Recreation*. London: HMSO.

Brenner, N. and Theodore, N. (2005) 'Neoliberalism and the urban condition: integrated area development and social innovation in European cities', *City*, 9 (1): 101–7.

Burnley Action Partnership (2006) *PERFORMANCE*. Accessed via http://www.burnley actionpartnership. org/

Cameron, S. (2003) 'Gentrification, housing redifferentiation and urban regeneration: "going for growth" in Newcastle upon Tyne', *Urban Studies*, 40 (12): 2367–82.

Centre for Public Services (1998) *Best Value Implementation Handbook*. Sheffield: Centre for Public Services.

Centre for Public Services (1998) *Leisure and Library Trusts*. London: Unison.

Coleman, R. (2003) 'Images from a neoliberal city: the state, surveillance and social control', *Critical Criminology*, 12: 21–42.

Coleman, R. (2004) 'Reclaiming the streets: closed circuit television, neoliberalism and the mystification of social divisions in Liverpool, UK', *Surveillance & Society*, 2 (2/3): 293–309.

Coleman, R. (2005) 'Surveillance in the city: primary definition and urban spatial order', *Crime, Media, Culture*, 1: 131–48.

Conservative Party (1992) *The Best Future for Britain: The Conservative Manifesto*. London: Conservative Central Office.

Crompton, J.L. (2007) 'The impact of parks and open spaces on property taxes', in C.T. F. de Brun (ed.), *The Economic Benefits of Land Conservation*. Wilmington, DE: The Trust for Public Land. pp. 1–12.

Davis, T. (1973) *John Nash: The Prince Regent's Architect*. Newton Abbot: David and Charles.

DCMS (2001) *The Government's Plan for Sport*. London: HMSO.

Degen, M. (2003) 'Fighting for the global catwalk: formalizing public life in Castlefield (Manchester) and diluting public life in al Raval (Barcelona)', *International Journal of Urban and Regional Research*, 27 (4): 867–80.

Department of the Environment (1995) *Partners in Regeneration: The Challenge Fund – Bidding Guidance*. London: Department of the Environment.

Department for the Environment, Transport and the Regions (DETR) (1999) *Implementing Best Value – A Consultation Paper on Draft Guidance*. London: HMSO.

Edensor, T. (2000) 'Staging tourism: tourists as performers', *Annals of Tourism Research*, 27: 322–44.

Forrest, R. and Kearns, A. (2001) 'Social cohesion, social capital and the neighbourhood', *Urban Studies*, 38 (12): 2125–43.

Gold, M. (1973) *Urban Recreation Planning*. Philadelphia: Lea & Febiger.

Goldberger, P. (1996) 'The rise of the private city', in J. Vitullo Martin (ed.), *Breaking Away: The Future of Cities*. New York: The Twentieth Century Fund. pp. 101–38.

González, S. and Vigar, G. (2008) 'Community influence and the contemporary local state', *City*, 12 (1): 64–78.

Harvey, D. (1989a) 'From managerialism to entrepreneurialism: the transformation in urban governance in late capitalism', *Geografiska Annaler*, 71B (1): 3–17.

Harvey, D. (1989b) *The Condition of Postmodernity: An Enquiry into the Origins of Cultural Change*. Oxford: Blackwell.

HM Treasury (1991) *Competing for Quality*. London: HMSO.

Home Office (2001) *Building Cohesive Communities: A Report of the Ministerial Group on Public Order and Community Cohesion*. London: Home Office.

Independent Review Team (2001) *Community Cohesion*. A Report of the Independent Review Team, chaired by Ted Cantle. London: Home Office.

Ives, J. (2003) 'Leisure counting the cost of increased funds: predictions of weary bewilderment as non-statutory services prepare for yet more cuts', *Leisure News*, 27: 3–5.

King, M. and Waddington, D. (2004) 'Coping with disorder?: the changing relationship between police public order strategy and practice – a critical analysis of the Burnley riot', *Policing and Society*, 14 (2): 118–37.

Nichols, G. and Taylor, P. (1995) 'The impact on local authority leisure provision of CCT, financial cuts and changing attitudes', *Local Government Studies*, 21: 607–22.

Pringle, A. (2001) 'Leisure services and local government in Scotland – time for a divorce?', in G. McPherson and G. Reid (eds), *Leisure and Social Inclusion: New Challenges for Policy and Provision*. Brighton: Leisure Studies Association, University of Brighton. pp. 40–51.

Robinson, D. (2005) 'The search for community cohesion: key themes and dominant concepts of the public policy agenda', *Urban Studies*, 42 (8): 1411–27.

Robinson, L. (1999) 'Following the quality strategy: the reasons for the use of quality management in UK public leisure facilities', *Managing Leisure*, 4: 201–17.

Robinson, L. (2002) 'Is quality management appropriate for public leisure services?', *Managing Leisure*, 7: 33–40.

Simmons, R. (2001) 'Mutuality and public services: lessons from the "new leisure trusts"', in D. Birchall (ed.), *The New Mutualism in Public Policy*. London: Routledge. pp. 95–118.

Simmons, R. (2004) 'A trend to trust? The rise of new leisure trusts in the UK', *Managing Leisure, 9*: 159–77.

Sport and Physical Activity Strategy for the Borough of Burnley (2003) Accessed via www.burnley.gov.uk/downloads/Executive_Report_Councillor_Roger_Frost_3_.pdf

Wilson, J. and Kelling, G. (1982) 'Broken windows: the police and neighborhood safety', *Atlantic Monthly* (March): 29–38.

Young, T. (2004) *Building San Francisco's Parks, 1880–1920.* Baltimore: Johns Hopkins University Press.

8

WORK AND LEISURE – POST-FORDISM AND THE CHANGING NATURE OF WORK

This chapter is concerned with the literature on work, organisations and leisure, and the changing relationship between work and other aspects of a person's life in relation to consumption and identity. After completing this chapter, you should:

- have an understanding of the nature of work, organisations and leisure
- have an understanding of the arguments surrounding the transition from Fordism to Post-Fordism
- be able to evaluate the impact of the transition to Post-Fordism on consumption of holidays, football and branded goods
- be able to identify what a range of social researchers have said in the debates about the following topics:

  o ownership and control
  o theories of management, with reference to the differing conceptions of management in the work of Frederick Taylor and Elton Mayo
  o work satisfaction and the differing conceptions of alienation in the work of Blauner and others

- have a critical understanding of the relevant theories and research in the area.

Introduction

Social science research has traditionally identified a clear distinction between work and leisure. For many people, work is dull, boring and monotonous, and people have an instrumental attitude towards it. Work is a means to an end: go to work to earn the money to do the things that you really enjoy. Leisure time becomes defined as non-work time in which people are free to do what they wish and express their real selves. The common assumption has been that the type of work a person did helped to determine the types of leisure they enjoyed. Income is identified as a significant factor in the shaping of our leisure patterns. This could be related to class or engagement in different modes of cultural practice related to education. After the First World War, Taylorism, and later Fordism, became the dominant regime of production. It was during this Taylorist–Fordist period that many of the large corporations that we are familiar with were formed. However, since the late 1970s, there have been major changes in the nature of employment – there has been a 'decentring of the worker' – many skills have become redundant and replaced by new computer-assisted technology, there are new forms of management and supervision, many people's contracts of employment enhance greater 'flexibility' and this has affected people of all classes, income groups and levels of education. As a consequence, the ways in which leisure activities relate to the world of work are also changing. Fordism, with its emphasis on the mass production of consumer goods, mass consumer credit system, marketing and distribution redefined non-work time as time for consumption. Leisure became indistinguishable from consumption. Stanley Aronowitz and William DiFazio (1994) explain that the consumer society has more than one meaning – what we choose to buy and what we are seen to consume has to some extent replaced work as a fundamental measure of our personal identity, and the shift of emphasis from work to consumption, and to the cultural, has become an element of what Giddens (1992) terms 'life politics' – a politics of individual self-realisation, largely defined in terms of forms of consumption.

Juliet Schor (1993) has investigated changing leisure trends over the last 20 years, claiming that Americans' working hours have increased by an average of 163 hours per year from 1970 to 1990; this is the equivalent of one month per year. This increase has affected both men and women, and professionals and low-paid workers.

The causes of this significant increase in working hours include:

- The decline of the power of trade unions that has resulted in employers downsizing, but at the same time increasing the workloads of the remaining workers.
- The need that people have to be fully integrated in consumerism, which encourages them to take on overtime to pay for a consumer lifestyle.

However, Schor's definition of work is very broad and includes a range of non-work 'obligations', such as home improvement, gardening, playing with children and helping children with their homework. In addition, a number of other studies show that average hours of work have not increased dramatically. Robinson and Godbey (1997) argue that working hours for men and women in the United States fell by six hours per week between 1965 and 1985.

Jonathan Gershuny (2000) argues that there has been a transition from a society based upon *low-value-added work* to a society based upon *high-value-added work* in which a significant part of consumption and, therefore, labour, is focused on satisfying our high-value leisure needs. Gershuny examines the trends in paid work, unpaid work and leisure time, by gender, period, employment, family structure and educational level, from the 1960s to the early 1990s. In all nations he examined, paid work time has declined for men and risen for women. At the same time, unpaid work time has risen for men but declined for women.

Men now spend more time engaged in household tasks, notably cooking, whilst for women, time spent on household tasks has declined. However, time spent on childcare has risen for both men and women. Time spent on out-of-home leisure was greater at the end of the 1990s than before; more time was used up on active sports, eating out and going to events, whilst less time was spent going on visits to see friends and family. In the past, the educated tended to work fewer hours than the less educated, however in recent years this trend has reversed and educated men and women have been working longer hours. In addition, better-educated men are also doing more unpaid work, notably more household tasks such as cooking and cleaning. Both men and women are doing more childcare, but again the increase in the number of hours spent on childcare amongst the better-educated shows the highest rise.

A central theme of this chapter is the changing nature of work and the transition from ways of working which were said to be *Fordist* in nature to ways of working which are said to be *Post-Fordist* in nature. For many writers, such as Crook (1992), this transition is part of a greater process of postmodernisation, in which the world is becoming a much more uncertain place. Henry Ford (1863–1947) was one of the first capitalists to make use of the assembly line to mass-produce a standardised product. Ford made extensive use of the principles of scientific management developed by Frederick Taylor (1856–1915) to make the most efficient use of the resources he had available to him in order to maximise profits. Fordism was said to describe a form of society and ways of working within advanced industrial societies for most of the twentieth century. According to Robin Murray (1989), Fordism was based upon four principles:

- standardisation – each task was performed in the same fashion and at the same pace as specified by management
- mechanisation – machines were used where possible to replace the work of people
- scientific management – forms of management were based upon the work of Taylor (1911)
- flowline production – products were on a line which flowed past the worker.

Moreover, under the influence of economist John Maynard Keynes, the influence of Fordist ideals spread beyond places of work to other areas of social life. Increases in wages were used to buy the expanding production of 'massified' products such as cars, TVs and other consumer durables. This would strengthen the power of capital in society, as workers were dependent upon employers to provide employment and wages needed to buy into the consumer lifestyle. However, Fordism had its limits.

Gender and Fordism

Fordism was based upon the assumption that each family had a male breadwinner. Hence the employment practices that are contained within Fordism never fully applied to women's work. Several reviews of women's employment patterns and inter- and intra-generational mobility patterns explicitly identify the overtly patriarchal nature of employment contracts embedded in Fordism. Robust male-breadwinner, gender-based contracts increased the likelihood of women being in low-paid jobs. However as Heidi Gottfried (2000) explains, as Fordism comes undone, this has a significant impact on the gendered nature of contracts in the labour market. Engagement with paid but flexible employment strategies means that employment has become much more important throughout a woman's life, although many women do rotate between full- and part-time work depending on other commitments.

For male and female workers alike, work on the production line was often monotonous. In addition, workers would attempt to assert some control over their work environment by taking industrial action or by forms of industrial vandalism or cutting corners. Moreover, the inflexibility of the bureaucratic work organisations and the work practices that went on within them were slow to respond to changes in consumer taste and fashion. By the early 1980s, the Fordist cycle of increasing wages, consumer demand and production was broken. As Michael Piore and Charles Sabel (1984) explain, capitalist societies expressed a 'second industrial divide'. Taking the lead from the 'just in time' systems first used in Japan, by the early 1980s, new forms of flexible work practices with fewer, full-time, permanent workers and more part-time, temporary or subcontracted workers, were thought to be more profitable as they were much more responsive to changes in consumer taste and consumer demand. In order to enhance profits, there was a need for workers to be multi-skilled, versatile and to work in teams. Post-Fordism, according to Lash and Urry (1987), signalled the end of 'organised capitalism', where employment is both less secure and more fragmented. Post-Fordism brought 'flexible firms' which have 'flexible production' for 'niche' markets.

Activity

Read the following passage and attempt the questions that follow:

Fordist firms retained a permanent staff of salaried, full-benefited personnel and maintained a relatively permanent workforce of production workers who 'clocked in' on a daily basis. By contrast, flexible firms rely on a spatially dispersed network of workers, many of whom maintain very weak ties with the parent firm. Benetton, the Italian fashion-wear company, for instance, does not even own its own stores. The full cost of setting up shop must be borne by the operator although s/he must operate within the rules of Benetton's shop organisation, that is, no backroom stockholding, a particular interior design and the selling only of Benetton products. Benetton's production facilities employ only about 1500 workers, whose efforts are complemented by 200 subcontractors, each employing 30 to 50 workers. Commenting on such trends, the *Economist* (11 June 1994) had remarked on the difficulty of trying to decide whether forms such as Benetton or Nike are 'big' or 'small'. Judged in terms of their core workers, both firms are small local operations; judged in terms of contract workers, however, they are sprawling multinationals. Indeed, organisations such as this are not so much single entities as fluid networks, adding value by coordinating activities across geographical and corporate boundaries. In other words, the best firms are both 'big' and 'small', depending on what they are doing.

Source: adapted from Ashley, 1997: 108–9.

1. Outline what you think are the advantages for Benetton of having a network of subcontractors rather than employing a large workforce directly.
2. Outline what you think are the disadvantages for the consumer of Benetton having a network of subcontractors rather than employing a large workforce directly.
3. Outline what you think are the advantages for the *subcontracted* workers of Benetton having a network of subcontractors rather than employing a large workforce directly.

The effects of these changes for young people have been outlined by Gary Pollock (1997); drawing upon longitudinal data from the BHPS study of 10,000 people every year since 1991, Pollock shows that for people aged between 20 and 24, the labour market trend is for lower levels of work for men, but with an increasing number staying on in education. For women, there had been an increase in labour market participation but this trend had levelled off by 1997. However, the increase was associated with part-time work and short-term contract work. There are many sectors of the labour market that are becoming unavailable to young people, and young people find it difficult to predict which jobs they will do in the future as the supply of labour is greater than the demand for it. Pollock describes the employment market for young people as 'a risk fraught system of flexible, pluralised, decentralised underemployment' (Pollock, 1997: 616).

Ownership and Control

According to Sanders et al. (1998), since the nineteenth century, the capitalist class has fragmented – most notably, there has been a division between the ownership of the means of production and the control of the means of production. Many millions of people place their money in pension funds, endowment mortgages, etc. which provides a source for investment in capitalist enterprises, yet the mortgage payers do not control the means of production that they have indirectly bought.

This fits into a New Right view of the world – the fragmentation of the capitalist class has brought about a property-owning democracy with the mass ownership of houses and share ownership, encouraged by privatisation. Control of these assets is in the hands of managers, who do not own the means of production. A number of commentators have referred to this as a managerial revolution.

In contrast, making use of Marxist, elitist and Weberian concepts, John Scott (1997) argues that a coherent capitalist class still remains as a powerful economic and political bloc. Scott makes a distinction between property for use and property for power. Individuals who pay mortgages and pay into pension funds do so in order to improve their lifestyle, however they do not control how the money they have paid is used, even though they, the individuals who make contributions, would suffer if the investments made on behalf of their pension funds were to crash. Investment decisions are in the hands of finance capitalists or fund managers. Managers and directors are salariat employees: in 75 per cent of the top 250 British companies, they own less than 5 per cent of the shares. However, even if the fund manager is an employee, the decisions they make must be in the interests of the capitalist class, otherwise they may lose their jobs.

Within capitalist society, Scott argues that the power bloc is a tightly integrated group with numerous overlapping business activities – many of these people went to the same public schools and universities and are also linked as friends. In other words, there is what Anthony Giddens has called a high degree of 'closure' at the top of the class structure. People not only attempt to gain advantages for their children by buying them places at private schools etc. but also family and friends prevent individuals from dropping out of the top classes and do not allow individuals from lower positions into the top class.

Theories of Management

In a later chapter, we shall look in some detail at the emergence of different styles of management over the course of the twentieth century. However, we need to mention a few points about management in terms of its influence on the relationship between work and leisure.

According to Frederick Taylor in his book, *The Principles of Scientific Management* (1911), in the nineteenth century, management had little or no understanding of the techniques or skills needed, or the time it took, to produce a product. Managers were generally unpleasant to people who looked as if they were not busy. Taylor termed this form of management 'ordinary management' and workers attempted to undermine ordinary management by:

- natural soldiering – Taylor assumed that people are naturally lazy and, as such, that all individuals have a tendency to do as little as possible
- systematic soldiering – work groups put pressure on individual members to conform and work to an agreed speed. Workers work together at a speed they find acceptable, while individuals who want to work faster are discouraged from doing so

Scientific management empowered the manager, by giving the manager a full understanding of all aspects of the production process. This allowed management to select who were the right people for the job. Production could be broken down into the simplest of tasks, which a worker could learn in a very short period of time. Management would measure how much time was needed to perform each task and individual workers would be given financial incentives to work as quickly as they could. This management style was most vigorously adopted by Henry Ford in his production of the model T car, and formed the basis of 'Fordism'.

Culture Industry

Despite the criticism that Taylorism was dehumanising, it was widely adopted as an effective system of management control. Henry Ford not only adopted Taylorism, but also attempted to control the leisure activities of his workers, so that nothing in their private life would adversely affect their performance at work. Marcuse (1964), together with other members of the Frankfurt School, developed the notion of 'culture industry' to explain how capitalists attempted to organise and direct the non-work time of workers in capitalist societies. 'Culture industry' is a group of entertainment industries devoted to entertaining the masses in their non-work time – this includes film, music, magazines, television and radio; these industries homogenised and commodified people's leisure time.

According to Marcuse (1964), culture industry had a significant impact upon the processes of identity formation. As Held (1980) points out, the development of culture industry:

- falsely brought together public and private interests
- reinforced privatisation and the desire to consume standardised products
- disseminated a view of the world built upon an advertising imagination
- watered down locally created working-class culture
- increased the control of instrumental reason
- manipulated sexuality – leading to the general pursuit of false and limited wants and needs, a form of 'repressive desublimation'.

When our leisure time became both homogenised and commodified, then according to Marcuse, culture industry transformed individuals into a mass, and the process of massification made people 'one dimensional' in that they were manipulated. People, who were critical of the products of culture industry, were branded as loners or unorthodox individuals who had poor taste.

Critiques of 'culture industry'

- Culture industry undervalues the ability of people to reject the products of culture industry.
- Culture industry undervalues the ability of people to use the products of culture industry for their own – personally defined – ends.

(Continued)

(Continued)

- Culture industry overstates the degree to which cultural products have been homogenised and commodified.
- The link between class and culture is unclear, and the degree to which culture is determined by class factors is unstated.
- Culture industry understates the role of fun, pleasure and desire.

Human Relations

In the 1920s and 1930s, during the economic slump, Elton Mayo (1933) and his team carried out a series of investigations at the Hawthorne plant of the Western Electric Company, very much influenced by both Durkheim and Parsons, with their ideas of solidarity and anomie. Mayo and his team feared that during the slump, workers were more likely to experience the sense of normlessness which Durkheim had termed anomie. Mayo observed that this anomic uncertainty led workers to form informal organisations (compact social groups) at work to give their lives a degree of certainty.

In contrast to Taylor, people could not simply be motivated by money. Management had to take into account the deeper psychological motives of workers, and had to gain an understanding of these motives in order to manage efficiently. It is important to note that human relations is still Fordist in nature, as its aim was to enhance management control and increase productivity.

Human relations assumes that:

- a work organisation is a social system, which has norms and defined roles
- worker's behaviour is influenced by feelings and sentiments
- the informal work group affects the individual performance of workers
- management should be democratic
- satisfied workers have higher productivity
- organisations should have opportunities for participation by workers and open channels of communication
- the manager needs competent social skills.

However, according to Rose (1975), by the 1940s, Mayo's Human Relations School of Management had been criticised on a number of grounds:

- Mayo and his team neglected the role of trade unions in empowering workers.
- The managerial bias of the human relations approach is unstated. In the last analysis, human relations is, like Taylorism before it, about making management more effective and making workers more productive.
- Within the human relations approach, there is an acceptance that the manipulation of workers' ideas is an acceptable managerial tool.

- The causes of industrial conflict are not fully or clearly stated.
- There is a failure to relate the social relations factory to the wider social structure. Industrial conflict may be a product of class conflict in the wider society.
- Mayo and his team had a fear of anomie, and its possible consequences in bringing about social change. In the last analysis, the human relations approach is about preventing change and maintaining the social relations within capitalism.

In some areas of industry, by 1970, the ideas of Mayo did provide the basis for schemes of 'job enrichment' or 'job enlargement'. Often, this involved greater decision making within teams at work, for example team-working at Volvo was designed to enhance the workers' motivation and give them a greater sense of identity.

Post-Fordism

In the 1990s, however, many researchers, for example Lash and Urry (1987), have described capitalism as having a 'disorganised' feel to it. Employers demand greater flexibility from their workers, often employing only a small core group of permanent staff, with the rest on short, fixed-term, highly flexible contracts. This type of management practice can be described as Post-Fordist and it gave employment an increasingly insecure feel. Heery and Salmon (2000) outline the key assumptions that underpin the argument that the nature of employment is changing and that the workforce has become increasingly insecure. Firstly, the insecurity thesis assumes that continued employment and remuneration have become less predictable and dependent upon factors that are outside of the individual employee's control. Secondly, there has been a deregulation of the labour markets in the developed economies that have generated feelings of insecurity amongst the workforce. Thirdly, the process of globalisation has reduced the government's ability to regulate the national economy and has led to increased intense economic competition.

Summary: Post-Fordism has led to:

- a shift to new 'information technologies'
- an emergence of a more flexible, specialised and decentralised labour force, together with a decline of the old manufacturing base and of sunrise, computer-based, hi-tech industries
- a contracting-out of functions and services hitherto provided 'in-house' on a corporate basis

(Continued)

(Continued)

- a leading role of consumption and a greater emphasis on choice and product differentiation, on marketing, packaging and design, and on the 'targeting' of consumers by lifestyle, taste and culture
- a decline in the proportion of the skilled, male, manual working class and a corresponding rise in the service and working class and in the service and white collar class
- more flexi-time and part-time working, coupled with the feminisation and ethnicisation of the workforce
- a new international division of labour and an economy dominated by multinationals
- a globalisation of the new financial markets
- an emergence of new patterns of social division – especially those between 'public' and 'private' sectors and between the 'new poor' and under-classes of the one third that is left behind.

Source: adapted from Ashley, 1997: 95–6.

Three transition models

Post-Fordism then can be understood in terms of broad social and cultural change, a move from one dominant form of capitalist development to another. It is possible to identify three transition models for understanding these changes.

Starting with the work of Michel Aglietta, the Regulation School identified three key concepts: the regime of accumulation, mode of growth and mode of regulation. Aglietta (1987) argues that accumulation reproduces the relations of production via a *regime of accumulation,* a systematic and long-term allocation of the product in such a way as to ensure a certain adequation between transformation of conditions of production and transformation of conditions of consumption.

One of the central assumptions of the New Right is that entrepreneurship is central to an effective, healthy and dynamic society – the entrepreneur is the energetic force behind the creation of wealth. Entrepreneurship is the ability to deal with uncertainty. The profitable exchange of goods for money involves identifying those who value a product or service more than the people who value them less. This skill allows the entrepreneur to create an opportunity to make money. Removing barriers to entrepreneurship will have not only a net benefit to society but will also generate the 'social creation of wealth'. Any social distribution of wealth is via the tax and benefits system, identified by the New Right as the major barrier to effective entrepreneurship.

Activity: Impact on the economy

Self-ownership and freedom of contract are necessary prerequisites of a completely entrepreneurial economy because entrepreneurship is an individual phenomenon and can only be expressed socially, by individuals, in the less-than-fully predictable process of earning profit and avoiding loss. (Herbener, 2001: 89)

According to the Public Forum Institute (2003) in the United States, entrepreneurship is a job-creation engine that has a positive impact on local, regional and national economies. After reviewing data from a variety of sources, it appears that the youngest and smallest firms are the biggest job producers.

- Firms of fewer than 20 employees generate the majority of net new jobs in the USA.
- New jobs from start-ups are an immediate and significant boost to the economy.
- Gazelles – defined by business researcher David Birch as 'firms with revenue of at least $100,000 (initial year) that sustained at least 20 per cent growth in revenue over four consecutive years' – contribute approximately 1 out of every 7 gross new jobs added to the economy each year.
- 70 per cent of gazelles are comprised of firms with fewer than 20 employees at the end of four years of rapid growth.
- New dynamic theories of the economy suggest that the prevalence of small firms provide a constant tide of new ideas and experimentation vital to the health of the economy as a whole.

Source: www.publicforuminstitute.org/nde/under/index.htm

Questions

There is another side to this argument. Search the internet and provide answers for the questions below:

1. Identify the number of small businesses that go bankrupt within the first year of trading.
2. Describe the impact that small business failure has on employment.
3. Write a short evaluation of the points made by the US Public Forum Institute (2003).

The flexible specialisation approach and mass consumption

From the 1920s, mass production of manufactured goods and the increasing use of Keynesian demand management techniques encouraged high levels of mass consumption. Economic stagnation in the late 1970s opened up the possibility of more flexible manufacturing technologies and flexible work practices. This allowed producers of non-standard products to service the needs of individuals within new and highly profitable niche markets.

In contrast to Braverman's analysis of deskilling, Michael J. Piore and Charles F. Sabel (1984) argue that by the 1980s, the large Fordist corporations had stagnated and were unable to deliver either profits or desirable products. Flexible specialisation with its decentralised, continually reorganised and innovative production processes was enhancing the skills that the workers had lost in the Fordist era. Workers now had a much greater reliance upon mental abilities than physical effort.

Aronowitz and DiFazio (1994) argue that flexible specialisation has four major components:

- the ability to repeatedly reshape the productive process through the reorganization of its basic component parts
- the use of computer technology to design innovative products for a diverse global market
- local production with a high level of control by the workforce
- recognition of the role of competition in the process of product innovation.

Aronowitz and DiFazio (1994) argue that the concept of 'skill' has given way to knowledge. Knowledge is not simply another form of skill. There has been a break between skill and knowledge. Skill has been decentred; it is no longer central to the labour process. Although Braverman may have had a romantic notion of the skilled craft worker, he forgets that skilled occupations were never open to all and the skill label was always used to exclude women and ethnic minorities from higher paid occupations. However, Aronowitz and DiFazio (1994) argue that it is important not to romanticise technological progress. The Regan–Bush era in the United States and the Thatcher era in the United Kingdom generated a great many low-paid and low-skilled occupations. In addition, computer-aided technological innovations have replaced many skilled occupations, and in this sense deskilling has taken place.

David Harvey (1989a, 1991) argues that one of the consequences of flexible specialisation is the production of 'symbolic capital' in which various income groups are enticed into accumulating status-enhancing luxury goods. Such goods reinforce the good taste of the owner. Postmodern cities are highly image- and culturally charged by urban professionals who react against the modernism of the 1960s that they were brought up with by demanding highly differentiated goods and services upon which they can create a lifestyle. Shopping in this urban space is not about being a rational utility maximiser, getting the greatest value from the lowest cost, but about a constructed leisure experience to be enjoyed as an end in itself. Secondly, flexible specialisation brings with it the 'mobilisation of spectacle' (Harvey, 1989b) – the promotion by both the state and companies of shopping and other leisure experiences within specifically designed complexes such as malls, museums, galleries and theme parks, or in themed areas of cities: Chinatown, Gay Village, etc. – as Harvey explains, it was by making the city space a spectacle for the visitor that the urban postmodern culture was shaped.

However, at the same time, there was a rise in poverty that accompanied flexible accumulation and the numbers of people living on the margins, many of whom engage in the informal economy, again in largely leisure-based activities, such as drug dealing and prostitution.

Globalisation and its impact on employment

Lansbury et al. (2003) argue that although there is broad agreement that the processes of globalisation have affected the international economy, there is little agreement on the impact that globalisation has had on the nature of employment relations. Lansbury et al. (2003) identify three possible different perspectives in this area.

The Globalisation Approach suggests that the competitive nature of globalisation brings about an increasing convergence of employment practices and, in particular, a 'race to the bottom', in which companies give in to global pressure to reduce prices by pushing down labour costs. In addition, national governments also give in to global pressure by introducing forms of deregulation into the labour market and reducing the regulatory constraints on business. Womack et al. (1990) argue that global capitalists converge on best practice in relation to production, irrespective of issues in relation to culture or national identity. They give the example of Toyota's system of lean production that has become widely accepted within the global industry as *the* way to mass-produce cars.

The second perspective is what Lansbury et al. (2003) term the Institutional Approach. This perspective suggests that the globalisation approach has overstated the impact of global social processes and that national governments and other national institutions still have a significant role to play in the mediation of global social forces. Lean production may be common across the globe but it is not of a single character. We live in a world of 'converging divergences' (Katz and Darbishire, 2000).

The third perspective that Lansbury et al. (2003) favour is known as the Interaction Approach – this approach 'explores the interplay of global and lower level factors' (Lansbury et al., 2003: 62). The focus is on the interaction between economic factors that are nationally external and institutional forms at a national level, on the grounds that neither are independent of each other, but coexist in a complex set of relationships. Their conceptual framework involves looking at institutional similarities between countries that are believed to be radically different. In this case, Lansbury et al. (2003) examine the similarities and differences between the car industry and the banking sector in Australia and Korea.

The Australian car industry was exposed to the competitive market place when the Australian government reduced the tariff protection for cars from 57 per cent in 1985 to 15 per cent in 2005. This led to some significant changes in the way that employees were managed within the industry: a reduction in rigid job distinction and demarcation and a greater level of multi-skilling. In contrast, Korea experienced a severe economic and foreign exchange crisis between 1997 and 1998 that resulted in a series of mergers and foreign takeovers: Kia merged with Hyundai and Samsung was taken over by Renault. The end result was widespread redundancy, early retirement and short-term working. With job security significantly diminished, industrial relations changed significantly as a consequence. Lansbury et al. (2003) conclude by saying that regardless of the importance of globalisation to the economies of both Korea and Australia, employment relations outcomes are shaped by complex inter-actions between a wide range of variables which include economic, political and institutional factors.

In contrast, many women in the Third World have experienced significant changes in their working lives because of the processes of globalisation. Barbara Ehrenreich and Arlie Russell Hochschild (2002) explain that more Third World women are on the move than at any other period of history, to do 'women's work' in the First World. Female migration reflects the grow-ing number of First World women who have entered the labour market and advanced in terms of pay, conditions of employment and level of responsi-bility. Women from the Third World are employed to fill the care deficit. However, an alarming number are sold into bondage and are illegally smug-gled to work as sex workers. As a consequence of such migration, Ehrenreich and Hochschild (2002) estimate that some 34–54 per cent of the Filipino population is sustained by money sent by females from the First World. Care is now the Philippines' biggest export. Many children in the Philippines, however, do not have direct contact with their mothers for many years at a time.

Work satisfaction

According to Marx, people have an in-built need and desire to be creative; this is part of what Marx termed our 'species being'. However, within capitalism, work can often be dull, boring and monotonous. For Marx, the overthrow of alienation needs the termination of capitalist relations of production.

In *Alienation and Freedom* (1964), Robert Blauner outlines a non-Marxian but technological determined view of alienation – he explains that the: 'most impor-tant factor that gives an industry a distinguishing character is its technology' (p. 62). Blauner goes on to explain that alienation is both a subjective feeling state and a set of objective conditions that are imposed upon individuals from within the work environment. The work situation, argues Blauner, can bring about four kinds of deprivation which are found within the alienated condition:

- powerlessness – this can be measured by looking at the extent to which workers can manipulate their conditions of employment, for example by regulating the speed at which they work
- meaninglessness – some products which workers make clearly have a meaning for workers; shoes are clearly meaningful for the people who make them, while parts for jet engines may not be

- isolation – this is concerned with the 'absence of a sense of membership in an industrial community', or the absence of a supportive work group
- self-estrangement – this is where work plays only a limited role in a person's self-identity, usually because they treat work as a means to an end; they have, in other words, an instrumental attitude toward work.

Similar studies to Blauner's were conducted by Michael Fullan (1970) in his study of printing, car production and the oil industry in Canada, and Trist and Bamford (1951) in their study of the British coal industry, which both came to similar conclusions.

Blauner's analysis is, however, rather limited – alienation is simply deprivation at work. His analysis does not address wider socio-economic issues outside the work place, most notably class relations. Also, the transition from Fordism to Post-Fordism has brought about significant changes in the nature of work and this has significantly impacted on the nature of the leisure experience.

Post-Fordism, Leisure and Consumption

Consumption is central to the construction of many adolescent identities. For many young people, there is a clear link between what they are seen to consume, their style of living and the construction of an identity that they feel comfortable with. What you are seen to consume has become a token of membership to a neo-tribelike identity that helps to sustain and define group boundaries, especially with the use of cultural artefacts such as music, dress, mobile phones, computer games and electronic media (Du Gay, 1997; Fiske, 1989; Friedman, 1994; Warde, 1996).

Scott Lash and John Urry in their influential book *The End of Organised Capitalism* (1987) trace the transition from Fordism to Post-Fordism with an emphasis on the leisure sector. Branded products such as footwear are not simply to be understood in functional terms, such as 'footwear keeps my feet dry'. A brand is a cluster of functional and emotional values. The Marxist will look at products in terms of their use-value and exchange-value, however this is not enough to understand the complex symbolic – cultural, social, personal – character of the meaning systems that young people attach to branded products. Appadurai (1986) investigates the meaning of things as emerging from *tournaments of value* – social processes in which the economic, symbolic and social value of things is developed.

Bauman (2000) assumes that consumption and the seduction that accompanies consumption are enjoyable *liquid modern* experiences. For many young people, they are not; the other side of subjectivication by seduction is the experience of being a brand failure. Croghan et al. (2006) argue that there are economic costs for teenagers attempting to construct an identity via consumption, but also significant social costs associated with failing to successfully maintain such an identity. Croghan et al. (2006) examine the consequences of such 'style failure' for young people in relation to issues of social exclusion and status loss. Most of the 12- and 13-year-olds interviewed by Croghan et al. made reference to the pressure of wearing the right things to school and said they had been picked on for standing out in some way.

Style groups were also markers of friendship, and style markers were used to construct positive and negative perceptions of self and others in which style became fused with an individual's moral identity. Young people policed each other, looking for style errors. Authenticity was a central style marker, and products had to be genuine, not fake. To be seen to be wearing fake designer goods was a sign of style error. Buying cheap products from the market, or from charity shops, was viewed as a shameful activity. Maintaining such consumption-based identities was difficult for families on low incomes. However, young people constructed style 'failures' as a personal rather than economic failure. The young people believed that style failure was rooted in a lack of skill – it was something that people were seen to 'bring on themselves' through the inability to look 'cool' and was therefore a blameworthy activity. This form of surveillance allowed commodification to blur the boundaries between a person's material and personal resources. In short, young people's efforts to construct and maintain acceptable style identities reduced individual difference and tended to produce conformity.

Post-Fordism and the changing nature of fandom

In February 2008, Premier League clubs agreed to look into the possibility of playing an extra round of matches every season – abroad. Currently, Premier League games are broadcast to over 600 million homes in 202 countries worldwide. An estimated audience of one billion watched Manchester United's match with Arsenal in November 2007.

The Premier League was formed in 1992 and, for the first time, the broadcasting rights were assigned to subscription television. The first agreement between the Premier League and Sky was worth £191m. The last deal for domestic rights is due to run from 2007 to 2010 for £1.7bn between Sky and Setanta. Promotion alone to the Premier League from the Championship was last season valued to be worth about £60m. Overseas rights had leapt to £625m – the biggest overseas deal for sport in the world. Of that, £100m was spent by NowTV to secure the rights for Hong Kong, Showtime Arabia spent £60m for the Middle East and North African market, and WinTV spent £50m to show games in China. In addition, there have been significant changes to the ownership of Premier League clubs – Russian billionaire Roman Abramovich bought Chelsea in July 2003 and, since then, Manchester United, Liverpool, Manchester City, Aston Villa, West Ham, Portsmouth, Sunderland, Fulham and Derby have become either wholly or partly controlled by rich individuals from outside the United Kingdom.

Premier League clubs are increasingly turning to the overseas market in order to boost their fan base and increase their revenue streams. Following a Premier League team in Thailand or Hong Kong allows you to see a live three o'clock (English time) kick off on a Saturday; in contrast, a UK-based fan could not unless he or she was attending the game due to the nature of the rights package.

On 12 May 2005, it was announced that Malcolm Glazer had a controlling stake in Manchester United PLC. Over the next few months, Glazer passed the 75 per cent stake needed to remove the company from the Stock Market. When a 90 per cent stakeholding was achieved, the remaining shares were compulsorily purchased. This change in ownership was achieved by the reported use of £500m of debt. The change in ownership of Manchester United was against the expressed wishes of the majority of supporters. The anti-Glazer opposition was centred on a number of organisations – the readership of three well-established fanzines (*Red Issue, United We Stand* and *Red News*), the Independent Manchester United Supporters Association (IMUSA) and Shareholders United (SU), a small shareholders' organisation. However, because Manchester United fans were unable to buy a sufficient number of shares to prevent the Glazer takeover, they turned instead to direct action such as public demonstrations.

In July 2005, an alienated minority formed a new club, FC United of Manchester. Taking inspiration from FC Wimbledon and Stockport County FC, FC United is a mutually owned Industrial and Provident Society – a not-for-profit organisation. The new club negotiated a ground-sharing agreement with League Two team Bury FC and were accepted to play in the North West Counties League Division Two.

The formation of FC United is interpreted by Adam Brown (2007) as a reassertion of locality amongst Manchester United's Mancunian fan base, a product of the emerging of a politicised local fan culture and opposition to the impact of globalisation on Manchester United. FC United supporters make a distinction between themselves as 'authentic' supporters and Manchester United fans as 'inauthentic' consumers.

According to Brown (2007), FC United's agenda is multi-faceted: to give fans who left Manchester United 'somewhere to go', to 'maintain or re-establish the community' amongst the former Manchester United supporters and to bring football back to ordinary people.

FC United of Manchester is based on the following principles:

- The Board is democratically elected by its members.
- Decisions taken by the membership are on a one member, one vote basis.
- These are strong links with the local community.
- These are affordable admission prices.
- These is an encouragement of young, local participation – both in playing and supporting.
- There is an avoidance of outright commercialism.

John Williams (2007) argues that 'modernist' perspectives on fandom were based on the assumption that one supported the local team which demanded regular match attendance and that the fan had a working-class background. However, there are now new ways of doing fandom, involving many different ways of engaging with the accelerated commodification of European soccer economies. These 'customer' sports fan identities involve subscription to satellite television sports channels and the use of the internet. Such fans are said to lack deep-rootedness and the personal commitment of fans in the past (Boyle and Haynes, 2004; Falcous and Maguire, 2005; Giullianotti, 2002; Nash, 2001; Robson, 2000).

Premier League clubs are increasingly motivated more by the globalised search for profit and the expansion of their customer base than by sporting ambition, hence clubs have pre-season tours of the Far East, United States and China, rather than the traditional pre-season friendly. This new sports market-place is a reflection of the changing nature of the key structural features of late-modern life described by Castells (1996) – transnational corporations are at the heart of global flows of technology, money, people and images.

There has been an aestheticisation of consumer culture, and this culture is distributed via global communication systems. This provides the consumer with new opportunities for forms of identity construction in relation to football and other sports as cultural products.

As we saw in Chapter 1, Gary Crawford (2004) rejects what he claims to be the false opposition between 'authentic' supporters and 'inauthentic' fan consumers. As the more 'traditional' sources of community identity – family, work, the church, neighbourhood networks – decline in relative importance in the late-modern era, the sense of community and 'primary group' belonging offered by contemporary sport becomes increasingly important and is increasingly commodified.

Activity

Is being a football fan today first and foremost a consumer act? Is it possible to be a football fan without physically going to a football ground to watch a match?

Football has become a branded commodity and is part of a wider international division of labour. An economy dominated by multinationals has emerged by encouraging these forms of consumption that are central to the processes of identity formation, and as we have seen with the takeover of Manchester United, production and service delivery are strongly associated with the globalisation of the new financial markets. Globalisation has created the feeling that the world is becoming a single place, with the emergence of new patterns of social division – especially those between the 'public' and 'private' sectors and between the 'new poor' and underclasses.

For Lash and Urry (1987), organised capitalism sank into crisis in the 1970s for several reasons:

- the increasing globalisation of capital
- the fact that employers adopted new attitudes which induced workers to identify with them rather than with their class-based organisations
- the fact that social and cultural life was also no longer organised around social class, but around more fluid social divisions
- the rise of popular culture.

Lash and Urry argue that these developments have provided the basis both for the free-market New Right and for a new brand of politics with a small 'p' – loosely organised new social movements and lifestyle politics. The old structures of organised capitalism have melted away and have been replaced by a pluralist, disorganised brand of capitalism. With the emergence of new social movements and the perceived effectiveness of direct action, the labour movement and the reformist strategy of capturing governmental power to make changes in society are no longer the only forms of opposition to capitalism, as both have been weakened by globalisation. Fordism established the mass consumption of leisure, and Post-Fordism signals a shift to greater diversity in which people can shape their leisure activities to their own wants and desires. One example that reflects Lash and Urry's argument is the decline of the Fordist package holiday where a company would provide a complete holiday experience within a standard 'package' that included the destination, travel, accommodation, catering and entertainment – a high-volume product sold to a mass audience to keep prices low.

One company that has been thoroughly investigated in relation to its place in the increasingly globalised and Post-Fordist economy is Nike.

Nike

From its humble origins as Blue Ribbon Sports, a company founded by Phil Knight in 1964 that imported running shoes from Japan and sold them to serious runners, Nike has become one of the most successful sports footwear companies in the world. The company has become successful by constructing its advertising campaigns around consumers' desire for greater self-empowerment. Robert Goldman and Stephen Papson (1998) argue that we live in an era of 'anomic cultural politics', in which both our personal and public relations are subordinated to the logic of the market. Goldman and Papson argue that Nike's economic success is based upon:

- outsourcing manufacturing activities to low-wage economies overseas
- a *commodity sign* – producing a wide range of branded goods for niche markets that allow people to form new commodified relationships.

Nike's advertising is built upon a 'metacommunicative aesthetic' and 'motivational ethos', in which modern and postmodern motifs are used to present themes that people can feel happy with when they incorporate them into their sense of self: individual will power, self-empowerment, personal transcendence, and a sense of achievement through hard work and discipline, reflected in slogans such as 'Just do it'. In 1995, for example, Nike introduced the 'If you let me play' campaign in the United States aimed at girls aged between 10 and 15 years of age and their parents. The multi-racial cast of girls featured in the advertisements invited the viewer to imagine the long-term benefits of playing sports, through a range of 'if–then' statements that addressed such issues as teenage pregnancy, obesity and leaving abusive partners. However, in the last analysis, the girls are asking '*If* you let me play', so the dependency upon males is still present. Advertising is a very important form of business communication because it is controlled by the company for the purpose of impression management, including brand identity. Lucas (2000) argues that Nike's representation of these girls in the 'If you let me play' campaign is such that it denies them their own agency – the ability to change the situation they find themselves in without the help of Nike products.

Michelle T. Helstein (2003) evaluates Nike's popular 'Just do it' campaign by drawing upon Foucault's conception of discourse. The campaign was targeted at women and on the surface was a vehicle for emancipatory feminist images. However in the last analysis, the Nike campaign merely helped to reproduce and reify the existing gendered order. For Helstein (2003), Nike is embraced by consumers because its products are believed to physically do something for the customer. In addition, the advertisements play upon the consumer's desire and, claims Helstein (2003), Nike reconstructs female desire through the manipulation of political, cultural and economic conditions.

Through 'a careful psychoanalytic reading' of Nike's ideal of excellence for serious female athletes, Helstein (2003) attempts to uncover the Nike discourse. Discourse restricts what can be said by whom and how that utterance can be understood by others. Helstein (2003) quotes Jane Flax, to suggest that Nike advertising constitutes a discourse with 'its own set of rules or procedures that govern what is to count as a meaningful or truthful statement' (Flax, 1992: 452). For Helstein, if we examine any discourse that is widely accepted, only certain statements can be made from within that discourse. According to Foucault: 'it is always possible that one could speak the truth in a void; one could only be "within the true", however, if one obeyed the rules of some discursive "policy"' (Foucault, 1969/1972: 224). Drawing upon Frank (1999), Helstein argues that the authenticity of the advertisements is achieved through a low-budget look that features 'timeless black- and-white imagery, the heroic slow motion at crucial points [and] the unpolished voice-overs' (Frank, 1999: 79). By consuming Nike products, women can maintain their bodies to the standard of the self-emancipated women in the advertisements.

However, it is Nike, rather than the women themselves, that provides the image and the measure of normalcy and excellence that the women use to define their progress.

Discourse

For Foucault, a 'discourse' is a body of statements that is both organised and systematic, and is in the form of a set of rules. The 'rules of discourse' form 'discursive practices' that are used to present knowledge as 'true' and or 'valid'. Foucault's analysis of discourse is in the first instance historical. Foucault referred to this historical analysis of discourse as an 'archaeology' of knowledge, which he used to show the history of truth claims. Archaeology involves describing and analysing statements as they occur within the 'archive', and the 'archive', is 'the general system of the formation and transformation of statements' (Foucault, [1969] 1972: 130).

In other words, for Foucault, there was no objective viewpoint from which one could analyse discourse or society.

Activity

Read the slogans from Nike advertisements over the years and answer the question that follows:

'There is no finish line.'
'Because the competition never stops.'
'We just can't stop playing.'
'You can't explain it.'
'What it touches it changes.'
'It never ends.'
'You can't keep a lid on it.'
'It's all in the imagination.'
'We all want to change the world (*Revolution*).'
'We all shine on (*Instant Karma*).'
'They're not for everyone.'
'In the right place at the right time.'
'When you can't stand standing still.'
'Basketball by Nike.'
'Tennis by Nike.'
'Just do it.'
Source: Levin and Benrens, 2003: 59–60.

What do you consider to be the central themes contained within the slogans above?

Over the course of the 1980s and 1990s, women's sports footwear became central to Nike's commercial success, with slogans such as 'Just do it' and 'Pursue pleasure'. Nike adopted many of the ideological positions of the feminist movement, although this could also be seen as manipulating women's anxieties in an effort to maximise profitability. However, in the 1990s, academics continued to raise issues about how sincere these advertising messages were and whether Nike was drawing upon processes of globalisation, postmodern trends and semiotic symbolism to exploit consumers.

Anti-consumer movements, such as anti-Nike activists, openly challenge consumerist ideologies by asking consumers to question the moral and environmental aspects of how the products they consume are produced. Carty (1997), for example, pointed to the contradiction between the way in which Nike produced its sports footwear and the imagery used in its advertising campaigns. Nike has shifted its production from the Third World to China, Indonesia and Vietnam. This decentring of production was in an effort to find new sources of production with lower labour costs, often with repressive working conditions.

Also, a range of internal Nike documents, such as 'One Factory's Progress' (1998) outlines Nike's commitment to improving working practices, and states their mission for corporate responsibility: 'To lead in corporate citizenship through proactive programs that reflect caring for the world family of Nike, our teammates, our consumers, and those who provide services to Nike' (cited in Levin and Benrens, 2003: 56).

However, as Levin and Benrens (2003) point out, by drawing upon the Nike website, 'Nike reports that it "plans to create almost no waste"' (www.nikebiz.com/storv/pressin.shtml), announcing plans rather than action, the company seeks to convince the reader that steps will be taken when they actually may not. Another summary uses a similar technique: "Nike encourages monitoring of factories and has disclosed factory locations; Nike is fully committed to minimizing the company's impact on the environment" (www.nikebiz.com/storv/pressin.shtml). By "encouraging monitoring" and "minimizing impact", 'Nike can again lead its audience to believe that action will be taken when, in fact, the company has not specified any action' (Levin and Benrens, 2003: 58).

Jessica Rothenberg-Aalami (2004) explains that because of the active campaigning of anti-Nike groups, in 1998, Nike introduced the SHAPE (Safety, Health, Attitude, People and Environment) programme and the MESH (Management of Environmental Safety and Health) programme, and instructed its subcontractors to improve the pay and conditions of service of the workers they employ. However, for many, Nike still has an image associated with 'sweatshop' conditions, such as slave wages, poor conditions of service and abuse of young female migrant workers from poor families. However, Nike does not own any factories, but rather subcontracts production within Asia, especially in Vietnam. These subcontractors are subjected to very little legal regulation in terms of how they treat their workers. In addition, because these workers have no experience of sports shoe manufacture, workers are labelled as 'trainees' and are paid at a lower rate for an initial period of about three months. As Rothenberg-Aalami (2004) explains, Nike expects the subcontractors they employ to follow a number of standardised programmes, notably the SHAPE and MESH evaluations. Subcontractors are required to buy materials from subassembly and component manufacturers that Nike have pre-approved because they conform to Nike's codes of conduct. Subcontractors must pay their workers at minimum wage or above, provide workers with educational opportunities, restrict overtime and give workers one day off in seven. In terms of the environmental impact of the manufacturing process, subcontractors are obligated to replace toxic adhesives with water-based solvents wherever possible to glue shoes, and to ensure adequate ventilation in the factory.

Activity: 'Nikewriting'

According to Boje (1998, 1999), Nike presents itself as an agent of economic development and ecology.

'Nikewriting' is a form of writing either sponsored or contracted by Nike that has the purpose of influencing the way in which people studying on business courses perceive the company – it is, in other words, a form of: 'rhetoric designed to affect economic development' (Boje, 2001: 510). In addition, academic sponsorship, contracts and endowments with universities, and if all else fails, threats of legal action against publishers and journal editors, allow what is essentially *corporate writing* to be treated as independent academic research.

'Many writing opportunities are corporately financed, staged, and otherwise controlled. For example, Nike (2000a, 2000b, 2000c, 2000d) sponsored 16 students from St. John's University to study the code of conduct compliance auditing practices of Price Waterhouse Coopers and to visit *some* Nike factories' (Boje, 2001: 510). 'Some' in the quote was a sample of 32 of 600 global factory locations.

'As an example of this corporate pressure to limit academic freedom, some (but not all) contracts include a clause such as the following between the University of Wisconsin and Reebok: "The university will not issue any official statement that disparages Reebok [and] will promptly take all reasonable steps to address any remark by any university employee, including a coach, that disparages Reebok"'(Boje, 2001: 512).

However, it is not only Nike that engages in such practices, according to Boje (2001) – Disney, McDonald's, Monsanto, RJ Reynolds and Wal-Mart are also engaged in such activities.

Question: What do you consider to be the advantages and disadvantages of 'Nikewriting' for the company and for the individual academic or university?

Conclusion

Social science research has traditionally identified a clear distinction between work and leisure. A central theme of this chapter has been the changing nature of work and the transition from ways of working which were said to be *Fordist* in nature to ways of working which are said to be *Post-Fordist* in nature. For many people, work is dull, boring and monotonous, and people have an instrumental attitude towards it. Fordism, with its emphasis on the mass production of consumer goods, mass consumer credit system, marketing and distribution redefined non-work time as time for consumption, and this has given way to a form of leisure time that is indistinguishable from consumption. This change has affected both men and women, and professionals and low-paid workers. Post-Fordism has also changed our relationship to organised team sports, so that being a football fan is now seen as a *commodity sign,* built upon the consumption of a wide range of branded goods for niche markets that allow people to form new commodified relationships.

References

Aglietta, M. (1987) *A Theory of Capitalist Regulation: The US Experience.* London: Verso.

Appadurai, A. (1986) *The Social Life of Things: Commodities in Cultural Perspective.* Cambridge: Cambridge University Press. pp. 3–63.

Aronowitz, S. and DiFazio, W. (1994) *The Jobless Future: Sci-Tech and the Dogma of Work.* Minneapolis: University of Minnesota Press.

Ashley, D. (1997) *History Without a Subject.* Boulder, CO: Westview Press.

Bauman, Z. (2000) *Liquid Modernity.* Cambridge: Polity.

Blauner, R. (1964) *Alienation and Freedom.* Chicago: University of Chicago Press.

Boje, D.M. (ed.) (1998) 'A wicked introduction to the unbroken circle conference: international business and ecology', in *International Business and Ecology Research Yearbook.* New York: IABD. pp. v–xiii.

Boje, D.M. (1999) 'Is Nike roadrunner or Wile E. Coyote? A postmodern organization analysis of double logic', *Journal of Business and Entrepreneurship,* 2: 77–109.

Boje, D.M. (2001) 'Corporate writing in the web of postmodern culture and postindustrial capitalism', *Management Communication Quarterly,* 14 (3): 507–16.

Boyle, R. and Haynes, R. (2004) *Football in the Middle Ages.* London: Routledge.

Brown, A. (2007) '"Not for sale"? The destruction and reformation of football communities in the Glazer takeover of Manchester United', *Soccer and Society,* 8 (4): 614–35.

Carty, V. (1997) 'Ideologies and forms of domination in the organization of the global production and consumption of goods in the emerging postmodern era: a case study of the Nike corporation and the implications for gender', *Gender, Work and Organisation,* 4 (4): 189–201.

Castells, M. (1996) *The Rise of the Network Society.* Oxford: Blackwell.

Crawford, G. (2004) *Consuming Sport: Fans, Sport and Culture.* London: Routledge.

Croghan, R., Griffin, C., Hunter, H. and Phoenix, A. (2006) 'Style failure: consumption, identity and social exclusion', *Journal of Youth Studies,* 9 (4): 463–78.

Crook, S. (1992) *Postmodernisation*. London: Sage.

Du Gay, P. (1997) *Production of Culture/Cultures of Production*. London: Sage.

Ehrenreich, B. and Hochschild, A. (2002) *Global Women: Nannies, Maids, and Sex Workers in the New Economy*. New York: Holt.

Falcous, M. and Maguire, J. (2005) 'Imagining "America": the NBA and local–global mediascapes', *International Review for the Sociology of Sport*, 41 (1): 59–78.

Fiske, J. (1989) *Understanding Popular Culture*. London: Unwin Hyman.

Flax, J. (1992) 'The end of innocence', in J. Butler and J. Scott, *Feminists Theorise the Political*. London and New York: Routledge.

Foucault, M. ([1969] 1972) *The Archaeology of Knowledge*, translated by A.M. Sheridan Smith. London: Tavistock.

Frank, R. (1999) *Luxury Fever: Money and Happiness in an Era of Excess*. New York: The Free Press.

Friedman, J. (1994) *Cultural Identity & Global Process*. London: Sage.

Fullan, M. (1970) 'Industrial technology and worker integration in the organisation', *American Sociological Review*, Dec: 1028–39.

Gershuny, J. (2000) *Changing Times: Work and Leisure in Postindustrial Society*. New York: Oxford University Press.

Giddens, A. (1992) *The Transformation of Intimacy: Sexuality, Love and Eroticism in Modern Societies*. Cambridge: Polity Press.

Giullianotti, R. (2002) 'Supporters, followers, fans and flaneurs: a taxonomy of spectator identities in football', *Journal of Sport and Social Issues*, 26: 25–46.

Goldman, R. and Papson, S. (1998) *Nike Culture: The Sign of the Swoosh*. London: Sage.

Gottfried, H. (2000) 'Compromising positions: emergent neo-Fordisms and embedded gender contracts', *British Journal of Sociology*, 51 (2): 235–59.

Harvey, D. (1989a) 'Popular capitalism and popular culture', in D. Harvey *The Condition of Postmodernity. An Enquiry into the Origins of Change*. Oxford: Basil Blackwell. pp. 327–59.

Harvey, D. (1989b) 'From managerialism to entrepreneurialism: the transformation in urban governance in late capitalism', *Geografiska Annaler*, 71B: 3–17.

Harvey, D. (1991) *The Condition of Postmodernity: An Enquiry into the Origins of Cultural Change*. London: Blackwell.

Heery, E. and Salmon, J. (eds) (2000) *The Insecure Workforce*. London: Routledge.

Held, D. (1980) *Introduction to Critical Theory*. London: Hutchinson.

Helstein, M.T. (2003) 'That's who I want to be: the politics and production of desire within Nike advertising to women', *Journal of Sport and Social Issues*, 27 (3): 276–92.

Herbener, J.M. (2001) 'The role of entrepreneurship in desocialization', *The Review of Austrian Economics*, 6 (1): 79–93.

Katz, H. and Darbishire, O. (2000) *Converging Divergences*. Ithaca, NY: Cornell University Press.

Lansbury, R.D., Kitay, J. and Wailes, N. (2003) 'The impact of globalisation on employment relations: some research propositions', *Asia-Pacific Journal of Human Resources*, 41 (1): 62–74.

Lash, S. and Urry, J. (1987) *The End of Organised Capitalism*. Cambridge: Polity Press.

Levin, L.A. and Benrens, S.J. (2003) 'From swoosh to swoon: linguistic analysis of Nike's changing image', *Business Communication Quarterly*, 66 (3): 52–65.

Lucas, S. (2000) 'Nike's commercial solution: girls, sneakers, and salvation', *International Review for the Sociology of Sport*, 35 (2): 149–64.

Marcuse, H. (1964) *One Dimensional Man*. London: Routledge.

Mayo, E. (1933) *The Human Problems of an Industrial Civilization*. New York: Macmillan.

Murray, R. (1989) 'Fordism and Post-Fordism', in S. Hall and M. Jacques, *New Times: The Changing Face of Politics in the 1990s*. London: Lawrence and Wishart.

Nash, R. (2001) 'Globalized football fans: Liverpool FC in Scandinavia', *Football Studies*, 2 (2): 5–24.

Nike (1998) 'One Factory's Progress', accessed via http://nikebiz.com/lmedia/n_espn.shtml

Nike (2000a) Fact sheets on learning: taking it to the schools [Online]. Available at: http://nikebiz.com/environ/learn.shtml (retrieved 30 August 2006).

Nike (2000b) Nike response to student monitor report [Online]. Available at: http://nikebiz.com/labor/reports/nr_1.shtml (retrieved 30 August 2006).

Nike (2000c) Nike student monitoring trips conference call [Online]. Available at: http://nikebiz.com/labor/trancipt1.shtml (retrieved 30 August 2006).

Nike (2000d) Statement by Nike regarding ESPN's 'Made in Vietnam: The American sneaker controversy' [Online]. Available at: http://nikebiz.com/media/n_espn.shtml (retrieved 30 August 2006).

Piore, M.J. and Sabel, C. (1984) *The Second Industrial Divide*. New York: Basic Books.

Pollock, G. (1997) 'Uncertain futures: young people in and out of employment since 1940', *Work, Employment and Society*, 11: 615–38.

Public Forum Institute (2003) *National Dialogue on Entrepreneurship*. Washington.

Robinson, J.P. and Godbey, G. (1997) *Time for Life: The Surprising Ways Americans Use Their Time*. University Park: Pennsylvania State University Press.

Robson, G. (2000) *'No One Likes Us, We Don't Care': The Myth and Reality of Millwall Fandom*. Oxford: Berg.

Rose, M. (1975) *Industrial Behaviour: Theoretical Development Since Taylor*. London: Allen Lane.

Rothenberg-Aalami, J. (2004) 'Coming full circle? Forging missing links along Nike's integrated production networks', *Global Networks: A Journal of Transnational Affairs*, 4 (4): 335–54.

Sanders, P., Blackstone, T. and Parekh, B. (1998) *Race Relations in Britain: A Developing Agenda*. London: Routledge.

Schor, J.B. (1993) *The Overworked American: The Unexpected Decline of Leisure*. New York: Basic Books.

Scott, J. (1997) *Corporate Business and Capitalist Class*. Oxford: Oxford University Press.

Taylor, F. (1911) *The Principles of Scientific Management*. New York: Harper Bros.

Trist, E.L. and Bamford, K.W. (1951) 'Some social and psychological consequences of the longwall method of coal-getting', *Human Relations*, 4 (1): 6–24.

Warde, A. (1996) *Consumption, Food and Taste: Culinary Antinomies and Commodity Culture*. London: Sage.

Williams, J. (2007) 'Rethinking sports fandom: the case of European soccer leisure studies', *Leisure Studies* 26 (2): 127–46.

Womack, J.P., Jones, D. and Roos, D. (1990) *The Machine that Changed the World*. New York: Rawson Associates.

9

WORK AND LEISURE – THE LEISURE SOCIETY, UNEMPLOYMENT AND POST-WORK

In this chapter, we will look at the different approaches to the relationship between work and leisure. We will examine:

- the assumption that work is the central activity in a person's life and that leisure is seen as a form of recovery from the stresses of our working lives
- Post-Taylorism work which has become increasingly bureaucratic, McDonaldised and often involves forms of emotional labour, involving a high degree of 'deep acting'
- the *post-work thesis*, including the argument that the labour market is moving towards greater cybernation of labour which would significantly reduce the working week and redefine the notion of a *work* career
- the campaign for a universal basic income
- the link between life politics and the idea of 'the leisure society'.

According to Keith Grint (1993), there is 'no unambiguous or objective definition of work' – he goes on to explain that work is a 'socially constructed activity that transforms something'. The simple definition of work as 'paid employment' does not do justice to the complexity of the labour market or to the meaning of work for individuals. As Grint explains, work becomes part of our identity, giving status, economic reward and the prospect of accomplishing our possibilities. As Ulrich Beck (1992) explains, when we are asked 'what do you do?', we are expected to explain our occupation.

Gershuny and Pahl (1980) make the distinction between the formal economy, which is recognised employment that contributes to a nation's Gross National Product, and the informal economy which they divide into three parts:

- the black economy – any form of 'undisclosed income', work which is done for 'cash in hand'. This can include such diverse types of employment as 'baby sitting', to individuals working while claiming benefit
- the household economy – which includes such things as housework

- the communal economy – which might include activities such as volunteering to work on hospital radio or working for St John's Ambulance. Many of these activities would not be described as fun, even though they may be done in our 'leisure time'.

Rosemary Deem (1995) has further subdivided the 'black economy' into:

- crime – which involves both time and effort, and for which people are motivated by financial gain. This could involve activities such as prostitution and drug dealing
- moonlighting – by the 'unemployed', i.e. not declaring income gained
- stealing from employers.

Deem also divides the informal sector into domestic work and communal work.

Taking his point of departure from Harold Wilensky's (1960) concepts of 'spillover' (where leisure-time activities are a continuation of work-related activities) and 'compensation' (where leisure is used to make up for the dissatisfaction experienced during work time), Stanley Parker developed a functionalist account of the link between work and leisure that is critical of earlier functionalist accounts such as that of Edward Gross (1961). For Gross, work is instrumental and compulsory whereas leisure is expressive and voluntary. However, both work and leisure have a role to play in the maintenance of culture and socialisation into cultural traditions where work is defined in terms of 'free' time; moreover, work gives a person the *right* to leisure.

Activity

This activity will help you draw upon your own personal experience when answering questions about leisure.

Drawing on your own experience, can you define the time spent on the following activities as work or leisure?

1. sleeping
2. washing and feeding yourself
3. washing and feeding your baby
4. feeding and walking the dog
5. walking to work
6. cutting the lawn
7. reading a trade magazine about your own area of paid work, at home

Which of the above activities fit into the following categories?

- time spent on our own physiological (bodily) needs
- work obligations
- non-work obligations, childcare and home maintenance
- a chosen use of discretionary or free time, time which is left over for our use as leisure.

The post-work thesis suggests that in the advanced industrial economies of Europe and North America, technology has become so advanced that commodities can be produced with very little labour power directly employed in the production process. These societies are becoming 'post-scarcity' societies, in which the only forms of poverty are relative, where a small minority of people have a lifestyle that is below what the rest of us consider to be normal. This is a society that no longer requires people to be in paid employment.

Clarke and Critcher (1985) are highly critical of the post-work thesis. For Clarke and Critcher, private ownership of the means of production remains the central characteristic of capitalism. The essential feature of the working class is not manual or blue collar employment – rather, the essential criteria for working class membership is exclusion from the ownership of capital.

Technological Change: Good or Bad?

In attempting to understand the possible effects of technological change on the labour market, it is possible to identify two contradictory views: a pessimistic view and an optimistic view.

Harry Braverman (1974) argues that in the twentieth century, large-scale industrial organisation led to monopoly capitalism and increased the degradation people experienced at work. Braverman argues that the introduction of new technology is an aspect of class relations; it is a tool which can be used by management to exercise greater control over the workforce. For Braverman, a key element of monopoly capitalism was the processes of proletarianisation, processes that changed the market and work situation of many white collar and professional employees to such a degree that they became white collar proletariats. Central to the process of proletarianisation was the application of Tayloristic scientific management to the office.

Graeme Salaman (1987), however, suggests that this view is empirically and theoretically inaccurate. There is no long-term universal tendency towards deskilling and the relationship between capital, technology and work design is shaped by the need for capitalists to maintain competitive levels of profitability. The assumption that millions of people will lose their jobs, because of new technology, is challenged by Salaman. In contrast, Jenkins and Sherman (1979) had claimed that by the end of the 1990s, unemployment caused by the introduction of new technology would be 5.2 million people. However, Salaman suggests that:

- new technology creates as well as destroys jobs
- profitability and employment can be maintained by improvements in quality
- companies reduce staff by 'natural wastage' rather than by mass redundancy.

Goldthorpe and Payne (1986), making use of the data from the British Election Survey, found that individuals in the middle of the class structure, notably routine white collar workers, claimed that they had not experienced either deskilling from new technology or a loss of independence at work. It was people at the bottom of the class structure who were most likely to say that they had experienced deskilling.

The Leisure Society and the Challenges of Mass Unemployment

In more recent years, a number of researchers have attempted to revive the notion of a 'leisure society'. Freeman and Soete (1994) have suggested that the effects of the further introduction of computerisation could lead to a severe decline not only in the numbers of people employed in manufacturing, but also in professional and white collar areas such as banking. Mass unemployment, they claim, can only be avoided by cutting the hours worked by people in these sectors and by making work more flexible. In many respects, Freeman and Soete are echoing Jenkins and Sherman.

Critics might respond to this by pointing out that we have seen before dire predictions about the effects on employment of new technology. We should not accept uncritically that information technology leads to mass unemployment. Employers often do not replace people when they leave the company. Similarly, employers do not recruit young people in significant numbers. It is for these two reasons that significant numbers of workers have not lost their jobs because of the application of information technology.

Robert A. Stebbins (1998) argues that as society becomes more reliant on technology, not only do employment opportunities decline but the role of leisure changes, as people seek the satisfaction from their leisure activities that they previously found in their work.

The notion of 'the leisure society' was a product of the 'post-industrial society' theories of the 1960s and 1970s. Daniel Bell (1973) is one of the best-known theorists of the 'post-industrial society'. Bell's work is underpinned by Weberian conceptions of evolutionary social change moving towards greater *rationalisation* and technological determinism. In Bell's information society, 'theoretical knowledge' became the key source of value as information technology became applied to all aspects of society. In Bell's analysis, 'social frameworks' are conceptual schemata that are built upon a central principle and central structure which provide an *organisational* frame. The changes that Bell identifies have a significant impact on class and class analysis. In contrast to Marx, who argued that the working class were the key agents in social change, Bell argues that it is science and technology that are the key agents in change. The major class within the post-industrial society is a professional class, who have knowledge rather than property.

Giddens (1989) has outlined several criticisms of Bell's analysis. First, Bell assumes that the service sector is a heterogeneous group in the population. Giddens also argues that Bell's analysis tends to over-emphasise changes in the economic sector as factors in bringing about social change.

Frank Webster and Kevin Robins (1986) are also highly critical of Bell's post-industrial society thesis. They suggest that Bell offers no justification for his conception of the social structure.

Clarke and Critcher (1985) argue that post-industrial theorists point to two trends in economic organisation:

- the declining significance of the manufacturing industry
- the expansion of the service sector.

The expansion of the service sector and the relative decline of industrial manufacturing do not change this central organising principle of society, of the social divisions that it generates. Such social changes as the decline of industrial manufacturing and the expansion of the service sector should be seen as the normal working of capitalism's essential dynamic.

In contrast to the liberating assumptions of the post-work thesis, Touraine (1971) and Gorz (1982, 1983) both assume that individuals have an instrumental attitude towards work, that people work only to gain a wage; money is the most important requirement for a full and active access to the leisure economy. The desire to work is really the desire for leisure. They argue that if people find themselves without work, this is certain to cause social unrest unless the state can provide a socially guaranteed wage. Individuals will still be involved in economically and socially necessary tasks, however the obligation to work or face the threat of social exclusion will be gone. This will allow people to work in areas of their choosing, for periods of time of their choosing, without alienation, expressing their 'species being' or creativity.

Andre Gorz (1999) argues that within a Post-Fordist market place, competitiveness is no longer dependent upon achieving massive economies of scale by mass production. For Gorz, within capitalism, work was always a 'social construction', always had a number of clearly defined functions and met a number of socially defined needs. However, in the Post-Fordist era, capitalism has experienced a massive abolition of work, in the sense of paid employment. Capitalist states continue to define paid employment as the basis of social inclusion and social belonging, the basis of self-esteem and the basis of full citizenship rights. The labour force is divided into two clear categories: a small core of full-time, permanent employees and a much larger group of peripheral employees with little job security. These latter workers are what Gorz terms 'post-job' workers who are on fixed-term contracts that only last as long as the project to hand.

Gorz argues that the 'labour theory of value' has little or no explanatory merit within Post-Fordist production arrangements. Post-Fordism is also Post-Taylorism in that it is no longer possible to view 'employment' as 'abstract labour', units of labour time quantifiable and detached from individual workers. This is because in a Post-Fordist society, the 'general intellect', our intelligence and imagination become the central productive force within society. When we are unable to measure working time because we have no units of measurement that can measure creativity, labour power ceases to be measurable. Use-value is still produced but it may bear no relation to the time taken to produce it. What provides a commodity with *value* in Post-Fordism is not the amount of socially necessary labour time that went into its production, but rather the ability of the commodity to meet the desires of the consumer. As Gorz explains: ' ... the liberatory potential of post-Taylorism could only be realized by moving beyond capitalist social relations' (Gorz, 1999: 36). Yet, argues Gorz, employment is still valued: ' ... not mainly for the satisfaction which *work* brings, but for the rights and entitlements attached to the "employment" form and to that alone' (Gorz, 1999: 64).

People have a need for a regular income, but not for paid employment. Gorz argues that there is not a shortage of work, but a refusal to distribute the wealth produced by capital to the significant number of people who have labour power for sale, and a belief that labour power is no longer needed. Gorz's solution is not to 'create work', but to distribute all the socially produced wealth to the people who are doing socially necessary work.

At the start of the twenty-first century, there was a major dilemma about the nature of work and our relationship to the activity – although we live in an economy that has less need for labour than at any other time, the work ethic has not disappeared. As such, people will come to understand that 'work' will play a less significant role in our lives than it did for previous generations. At the moment, we do not have such an understanding – we have a situation in which many people are unemployed and their skills are redundant. Jeremy Seabrook (1988) and Zygmunt Bauman (1998, 2001, 2004) both argue that the work ethic has been reshaped by the rich for their own purposes. The rich have used the work ethic to present a re-moralised image of themselves as the only people who have a 'functional and indispensable role in society' (Seabrook, 1988: 11). Seabrook, in particular, is critical about the prospects of the emergence of a 'leisure society' and what the nature of such a society would be like.

Jeremy Seabrook

In common with the optimistic post-industrial theorists, Seabrook (1988) argues that over the course of the 1970s and 1980s, the industrial base of the West has eroded, with many of the dirty and dangerous jobs going overseas. This is a process that is comparable in magnitude to the transformation of the agricultural labourers into an industrial working class. However, the experience of being unemployed and welfare-dependent cannot be described as leisure because, Seabrook claims, unemployment is an 'unwelcome activity' and 'charged with anxiety'.

If leisure societies do exist, claims Seabrook, then they are bleak places because at their base is a dependency on the poorest people in the world to satisfy our needs. Colonial exploitation has a very long history, but Seabrook argues that by the late 1980s, the economy had become more dependent upon the increased abuse of the environment to satisfy growing consumer demands. The leisure society is then dependent upon continual capitalist expansion, both at home and overseas. In a discussion about working in the fast-food industry,

Seabrook argues that one person's leisure means another person's oppression or enslavement. The unemployed are seen as a burden upon the wider society because their income is provided by the state benefits system. The transition to a leisure society would involve a painful redistribution of work, and income, in which people would have to give up part of their income and spend less time doing their jobs, whilst spending more of their time in more satisfying activities for less money. No political party in Europe or North America has the political will to present such a political programme to the electorate.

Contemporary work, argues Bauman, has a 'liquid modern' feel to it, unlike the rigid and slowly changing modern industrial world. Within liquid modernity, the class system has two key players: the affluent 'globals' and the poor 'locals'. The 'globals' are people who choose to distance themselves from any form of a 'network of connections', prefer the mobile phone to face-to-face contact, have no commitment to loved ones, prefer impersonal sex with strangers rather than intimacy and have a 'facility for disengagement and termination-on-demand' (Bauman, 2004: 31). Identity has become a central element in the imposition of exclusion and is the central form of stratification within liquid modernity (Bauman, 1998: 97).

This 'human waste' has identities imposed upon it; 'resented identities' and 'enforced identities' made up of 'stereotypes, stigmas and labels' (Bauman, 2004: 39). Such people have these identities, and the poverty, humiliation and misery that go with them, because they no longer have a productive role to play within capitalism. Solid modernity had a fixation about purity. The concept of purity was used to define social undesirables who should be excluded from the 'warm circle' of modernity. These 'flawed consumers' or 'wasted humans' are subjected to a range of stigmas and imposed cultural identities.

Drawing upon the work of Levinas, Bauman (1998) argued that we should change our perception of the poor. The aim of Emmanuel Levinas' philosophy, that Bauman fully endorsed, was to go beyond the ethically neutral tradition of ontology. Levinas first outlined his conception of intersubjectivity that he further elaborated in *Otherwise Than Being or Beyond Essence* (1974) – his works are built upon a coming together of modern philosophy and Jewish thought. He draws upon the Jewish concept of *mitzvah* (command) and the Torah's concern with the welfare of the 'widow, the orphan, the stranger'. Understanding 'the Other', understanding their suffering and powerlessness even when the other is a stranger, is central to his conception of intersubjectivity. This is in contrast to what Levinas terms the 'philosophy of subjectivity' – the strong emphasis on self – which underpins most modern philosophy. In contrast to Descartes' (1960) *cogito ergo sum* (I think, therefore I am), Levinas offers the Hebrew phrase *Hineni* (Here I am).

For Bauman, we should regard the Other not as a type or a category but as a unique person. This involves:

- rejecting indifference towards the poor
- rejecting stereotyped certainty towards the poor, the view that 'they always behave that way'
- viewing the poor in a manner that is free from sentiment.

To take a moral stance means to assume some responsibility for the poor. In addition, it means to act on the assumption that the well-being of poor people is a precious thing calling for our effort to both preserve and enhance that well-being.

The Post-work Thesis

In the Reagan–Thatcher years, with its emphasis on deregulation and globalisation, a number of commentators identified the origin of a post-work society. Stanley Aronowitz and William DiFazio (1994) were amongst the first people to explore the *post-work thesis* – they were concerned with how the labour market is moving towards greater cybernation of labour which aims to significantly reduce the working week and redefine the notion of a *work* career.

Rifkin (1995) argues that civilisation was founded upon the organising concept of 'work'. The global economy can produce an increasing level of production with significantly fewer workers. Workers come together in multi-skilled teams, supported by high-quality capital equipment – mainly computer-based information technology. Teams work and plan together and are motivated by the need to secure *continual improvements* in the production process and in product development. Lean production, argues Rifkin, brings together the benefits of craft and mass production, but at the same time avoids the high cost of craft production and the inflexibility of Tayloristic mass production. Rifkin argues that an increasing number of companies are 'deconstructing' their managerial structures by compressing a range of jobs into one single process. Such changes to the nature of work are having a significant impact upon the nature of social solidarity and class structure. Within the Post-Fordist economy, work practices generate a bigger workload, a stepping up of the pace of production and new forms of compulsion and pressure to maintain the obedience of the workforce. Work teams draw upon peer review and similar techniques to introduce a form of 'management by stress', in which team members identify weak points in the production process and take appropriate action.

To counter the effects of these changes, Rifkin argues in favour of an expansion of the voluntary sector, because there is more to work than simply gaining an income. The introduction of 'an adequate social wage' was funded in the United States by the introduction of Value Added Tax, as an alternative to welfare payments – without this guarantee of an income, there may be insufficient purchasing power in the economy to generate employment. The nation state is unable to fund an extensive welfare state because the processes of globalisation are increasingly diminishing the scope and sources of finance. As Rifkin concludes, we are encountering an important historical transformation into a nearly workerless world, a Third Industrial Revolution in which hardware and software already exist to move us towards a new silicon-based civilisation.

In contrast, Chris Rojek (2001) argues that work is still treated as the central activity in a person's life and that leisure is seen as a form of recovery from the stresses of our working lives. However, as Rojek points out, this view always had its critics. Veblen (1899) identified the close links between class and leisure;

the economically powerless imitated the leisure activities of the economically powerful. In a similar fashion, the early Frankfurt School claimed that the 'culture industries' manipulate the ideas of working-class people. Leisure, therefore, had an important ideological role to play within capitalist society. For Rojek, the debate on the transformation of society has been dominated by two theses.

First, Stanley Aronowitz and William DiFazio's (1994) *post-work thesis*, as was suggested above, is concerned with how the labour market is moving into a condition of greater cybernation of labour that significantly reduces the working week and redefines the notion of a *work* career. As Aronowitz and DiFazio (1994) explain, for the first time in human history, paid employment does not have to occupy a central place in our lives. This release from paid employment is not presented by Aronowitz and DiFazio in negative terms, but as an expansion of freedom and citizenship rights. Rojek (2002) explains that the cybernation of work has diminished the demand for paid employment. A new social division has emerged in the labour market between a small number of skilled professional and technical staffs that form an economically active minority of full-time employees and a much larger economically active majority who do not have regular full-time employment contracts but are engaged in intermittent fixed-term contract work. The full-time employees enjoy high financial rewards but they have to bear what Rojek calls a 'time-famine' that significantly disrupts their leisure experience and family life.

The 'post-work' thesis has had a significant impact upon our understanding of leisure. The traditional work–leisure relationship needs to be revised because both theories generate tensions within traditional ideas of leisure and raise important issues about leisure policy and its relationship to citizenship rights.

Joffre Dumazedier (1974) argued that there were two preconditions that must be met if people are to gain leisure: the decrease of ritual obligations prearranged by the community and the strict separation of paid work from other activities. One might imagine that because a politics of individual self-realisation encourages people to question all prearranged community obligations, this should lead to the emergence of a leisure society. However, Rojek argues that life politics stands in opposition to the notion of the leisure society. He draws upon Beck (2000) who argues that the central characteristic of leisure is that it is composed of a range of activities that people engage in for their own sake. Beck uses two arguments to reject the concept of the leisure society.

The social order and reproduction require socially necessary labour time, which he terms *techne*. Socially necessary labour time provides the foundation of system maintenance, as it includes such things as:

- the replacement of depleted natural resources
- the creation of surplus wealth
- the distribution of wealth
- the maintenance of a system of allocative, redistributive justice
- the management of innovation in technology, science and medicine
- the management of cultural production and exchange.

Giddens (1984) and Beck (1992) do not foresee either the end of work or leisure. However, they do expect to see the emergence of a form of 'civil labour' that involves a 'communitarian' redefinition of the relationship between the individual, work and society, in which individuals voluntarily choose to engage in 'socially necessary labour'. This form of work helps to sustain the community and reiterate the individual's responsibilities and obligations to society.

Emancipatory Politics, Life Politics, Risk and Individualisation

Giddens suggests that within late modernity, our political relationships take on many of the characteristics of the 'pure' relationship. Life politics emerges from emancipatory politics and is a politics of self-actualisation. Life politics is not a traditional type of politics concerned with enhancing life chances by the redistribution of income, but a politics of lifestyle in which people can live their lives as they choose.

Beck's analyses are based upon a three-stage historical periodisation of pre-industrial, industrial and risk societies. In modern industrial societies, there are industrially produced hazards. Beck and Beck-Gernsheim (2002) argue that individualisation is a historical process that increasingly questions the traditional rhythm of life. The nationally fixed social categories of industrial society are culturally dissolved or transformed.

According to Rojek (1995), one of the main consequences of life politics is the politicisation of leisure. Life politics also makes the idea of 'the leisure society' outdated. The traditional definitions of leisure were based upon the assumption that there was a period of time or a phase of life which was different from work because it was characterised by greater freedom, choice and self-determination (Dumazedier, 1967; Kaplan, 1975; Parker, 1981). In late modernity, these characteristics underpin all aspects of our daily lives. There is no sharp distinction between 'work' and 'leisure', as both are central to our self-actualisation projects. In the last analysis, argue proponents of the post-work thesis, risk, individualisation and life politics are all significant to the understanding of leisure and leisure policy. If the well-established relationship between paid employment and civil rights is breaking down, we can no longer accept the assumption that our leisure experience is shaped by our experience of paid employment. However, engaging in satisfying leisure experiences will still require money, and the post-work thesis suggests that the establishment of the socially guaranteed wage must now be taken seriously.

Contributors to the post-work thesis, who look at the politics of universal basic income, include Frithjof Bergmann (1977) and Philippe van Parijs (1993, 2000) and it is their arguments that the chapter now addresses.

Frithjof Bergmann

Paternalistic schemes of social engineering to bring about greater equality by social programmes funded through taxation, and the New Right libertarian conception of freedom through tax cuts that return as much of the people's money to them as possible, do not address the fact that people are born into circumstances that are unequal. Wealth allows people to buy advantages for themselves and for their children and thereby maintain a system of inequality.

Frithjof Bergmann (1977) takes his starting point from Nietzsche's ([1906] 1997) notion of the 'will to power' and makes a distinction between *freedom* and *coercion*: an act is free if the individual person exercises their agency and identifies with the motivation from which the action flows; in contrast, a person can be said to have been coerced if the motivation was imposed and the person did not exercise their agency in carrying out the action. If a shop assistant is threatened by a gunman to hand over the contents of the till, that person has not freely chosen to hand over the money, because the shop assistant does not identify with *the elements from which* the act of giving *flows*, namely the threat of being shot. However, if the shop assistant knows that the gun is not real and chooses to hand over the money for compassionate reasons, then the motivation to act flows from within and it is a free act.

Action has to originate from within the true self. Freedom to act is seen as a chosen motivation from within the human agent. When people are made to act in a way that they would not choose, we think of them as being coerced.

In his analysis of work, Bergmann (1977) argues that we need to rethink the work–leisure relationship. The impact of new technology has been generally underestimated by workers and employers alike – potentially, many workers could be made redundant, however there is also the possibility that our working lives can become the site of greater freedom. Bergmann developed the concept of 'new work' as a response to the layoff of large numbers of workers by GM at their plant in Michigan. The new work concept is about the introduction of new technology and flexible working practices in an effort to allow employers to cut cost and increase productivity and competitiveness – in return, employers give their workers more flexibility in their working lives, allowing them to work fewer hours and spend more time on meaningful activities of their own choosing. Instead of employers making workers redundant, the workload is spread amongst the existing workers, who become more skilled at working with new technology. New work means a new consciousness and new values – it can strengthen people and give them greater freedom from having to do work that is dull, dirty and dangerous.

Bergmann makes a number of assumptions about people:

- By nature, people are not greedy and intent only on securing their own advantage.
- People are easily intimidated into doing work tasks that they would not otherwise freely choose to do.
- Most people have little idea of what they want from life.

Philippe van Parijs

For Philippe van Parijs and colleagues (2003), discussions of social policy across Europe are dominated about arguments concerning social inclusion and the reduction of inequality. Van Parijs argues that possible solutions to forms of exclusion are mainly concerned with technical issues that obscure underlying ethical choices. Questions that can be asked include:

- What claims can citizens justly make on society?
- What is the scope of the social solidarity we wish to realise?
- What room should be left for individual responsibility?

For van Parijs, a *demogrant* or universal guaranteed minimum income could be a central strategy against social exclusion caused by both poverty and unemployment.

A demogrant or universal basic income is an amount of money paid by a political community to all individuals who are recognised as members of that community, without a means test or work requirement. Such a lifelong unconditional income would provide everyone with the necessary material resources to pursue their aims, eradicate poverty, end alienation and provide real social justice and freedom for all. Above all, for van Parijs, freedom means having respect for the choices that people make, whether that choice is to take up paid employment, to stay at home and work or not to take up paid employment. Van Parijs' normative standpoint is based upon four convictions:

1. The unit of analysis for a theory of justice should be the individual person over the whole life course.
2. Taking his starting point from John Rawls' (1971) theory of justice, van Parijs argues that priority should be given to the members of a society who are worst off.
3. Distributive justice should take the form of the distribution of 'positive' or 'real' freedom measured in terms of opportunities rather than outcomes, in which individuals are compensated for the inequalities they face embedded in their endowments, either social or personal.
4. Ethical principles must help shape public opinion, rather than simply reflect it.

If the universal basic income (UBI) were above subsistence level, this would provide a guaranteed income whether a person is in or out of work, and the poverty trap would disappear. The UBI is not drawn from transfer payments, because that would have the effect of stigmatising the people who 'live off benefits', rather the UBI is a *universal grant* that should be provided unconditionally to every citizen. Citizens would start earning additional net income as soon as they do any meaningful work, however little and however poorly paid that work may be. Such work could include childcare or looking after elderly relatives.

The UBI would be funded by transferring the benefit of productive growth from an ever-increasing demand for mass produced goods and services into a reduction of the length and irksomeness of work. The UBI is founded on a libertarian conception of justice. Drawing upon John Rawls' conception of *worth of liberty*, Parijs argues that only the UBI can truly support personal liberty, because only the UBI provides people with the resources to make effective use of their liberty. The UBI allows people to only take jobs that they find attractive, and to reduce their working week if and when they want to, for example if they wish to spend more time on household issues or caring for others, in order to look after their children or elderly relatives. Individuals can also choose to become self-employed, to invest in their own skills and abilities through more training, or to join a cooperative. In other words, the UBI allows us greater freedom and control over our own lives. As the economy is currently constituted, there is an immoral imbalance in the distribution of resources, in which the structurally or involuntary unemployed are unfairly excluded from the benefits of a productive economy.

In a similar fashion, Atkinson and Micklewright (1994) proposed a 'participation income' in which the government would give people a minimum income on the basis of the 'social contribution' that the person made to the wider society. The 'social contribution' could include full- or part-time paid employment, self-employment, regular voluntary work, involvement in education or training, active job searching, and providing home care for young children or elderly people. The more broadly the 'social contribution' condition is to be understood, the closer we move to a universal basic income.

Activity

By *universal basic income* I mean an income paid by a government, at a uniform level and at regular intervals, to each adult member of society. The grant is paid, and its level is fixed, irrespective of whether the person is rich or poor, lives alone or with others, is willing to work or not. In most versions – certainly in mine – it is granted not only to citizens, but to all permanent residents. (van Parijs, 2000: 5)

I am convinced that any cogent case for basic income as a first best must adopt some notion of 'real freedom' (not only the right but also the means to do what one may wish) as the *distribuendum* of social justice and combine it with some strongly egalitarian criterion of distribution. The particular 'real-libertarian' conception I offered gives a key role to the view that the substratum of our real freedom essentially consists in very unequal combinations of gifts we have received throughout our existences, among them the opportunities that enable us to hold our jobs. (Van Parijs, 2004: 18)

Above all, for van Parijs, freedom means having respect for the choices that people make, whether that choice is to take up paid employment, to stay at home and work or not to take up paid employment.

Questions:

Do you accept or reject van Parijs' arguments for a universal basic income (UBI)? Does society have a duty to provide income to people who choose not to work?

Activity

There are a number of objections to the introduction of a universal basic income. Consider the three listed below, and state whether you accept or reject each point listed:

- A UBI would cost too much.
- A UBI would have a damaging effect upon the labour supply as many people would choose not to work.
- There is a moral objection to a UBI because the undeserving poor would be given something for nothing.

Question: What counter-argument can you suggest to the three points listed?

For Ackerman and Alstott (2004), modern liberalism is based upon two assumptions. Firstly, modern liberalism upholds equality by maintaining that each citizen has a fundamental right to a fair share of resources at the start of their life. Secondly, modern liberalism upholds freedom and accepts that because people are different, they will use their initial resources differently.

Ackerman and Alstott's stakeholder theory argues that at the age of 21, each citizen should receive a stake of $80,000 from the government to spend as they wish. Ackerman and Alstott argue that the money is a vehicle for the exercise of real freedom. To claim the money, the citizen has to demonstrate their capacity to make meaningful choices. Ackerman and Alstott suggest a number of tests: firstly, the person must graduate with a high school diploma, and secondly the person should not have a criminal record. The scheme would eventually be paid for by having a 'payback requirement' in which stakeholders who have done well in the labour market must repay their $80,000 stake, with interest, upon their death. The stakeholder model means that young people do not have to borrow large sums of money for paying for tuition, training, buying houses or having children.

Both van Parijs' proposal for a universal basic income and Ackerman and Alstott's conception of stakeholding accept that a grant of private property should be accepted as the birthright of every citizen in a modern liberal democracy.

The Labour government under Tony Blair introduced the Child Trust Fund (commonly known as 'baby bonds') – this initiative shares many of the common features of stakeholding in the Ackerman and Alstott model. Under the initiative, each child receives a 'baby bond' at birth that accumulates compound interest throughout the child's life until the age of 18 when the bond matures. An additional amount of money is added to the account on the child's seventh birthday; by the age of 18, the young person can expect to receive a lump sum.

In contrast, from Juan Luis Vives' book *De Subventione Pauperum* ([1526] 1943) onwards, the state has expected to give people assistance with their income on the condition that they perform some work-related task. In the UK, this belief has taken on a variety of forms from nineteenth century workhouses to contemporary private and public welfare to work or workfare programmes, such as the New Deal and Working Families Tax Credit. In the USA, in-work benefits include the Earned Income Tax Credit. Governments in Europe and North America have traditionally regarded paid employment as the only morally right way of funding a lifestyle and, as such, people who do not engage in paid work are regarded as causing a problem to the wider society.

Patterns of Unemployment

Unemployment is not evenly distributed amongst the population. The International Labour Organisation (ILO) definition of unemployment has become the most widely used definition of unemployment. According to the ILO, a person is classed as *unemployed* if she or he has not worked in terms of paid employment for more than one hour during a given reference period but who is available for work and is actively seeking work. Large-scale unemployment is caused by insufficient flexibility of the labour market. The capitalist system in itself cannot always generate sufficient demand to generate full employment. Employment structures the day, provides regular activity and generates social contact between individuals.

Activity

According to the US Bureau of Labour Statistics, in the United States, in September 2004, there were 8 million persons unemployed. This figure constitutes 5.4% of all American workers. The figure can be further broken down into: 5% of adult men; 4.7% of adult women; 16.6% of teenagers; 4.7% of the white population; 10.3% of the black American or African-American population; 7.1% of the American Hispanic or Latino population and 4.3% of the Asian-American population.
Source: adapted from: jobsearch.about.com/gi/dynamic/offsite.htm?
site=http://www.bls.gov/news.release/empsit.nr0.htm

Question: Why do you think some groups of people are more likely to be unemployed than others?

In terms of the UK labour market, the unemployment figures break down in the following fashion:

Source: www.statistics.gov.uk/cci/nugget.asp?id=462

Unemployment amongst Women and Ethnic Minorities

In the case of the United Kingdom, as far back as 1994, the Department of Employment claimed that there were 2,101,300 men unemployed and 633,100 women. However, most married women are not eligible for a wide range of benefits and therefore do not appear on the unemployment register, even though they may be out of work and actively seeking employment.

In 1984, Martin and Roberts claimed that 50 per cent of women who were actively looking for a job were not classed as unemployed.

There is also clear data which shows that ethnic minorities are more likely to be unemployed. One possible reason for this is open racism. Richard Jenkins (1986) carried out a study of the procedures used by managers when selecting people for employment. He identified two selection criteria:

- suitability criteria – which is concerned with the applicant's qualifications and experience
- acceptability criteria – which is concerned with whether the applicant will 'fit in' with the other employees.

The latter criteria are often racist in nature, and prevent many people from entering employment.

Young People

In both the United States and Europe, young people are also much more likely to be out of work. One possible reason for this is that the education system may not provide an education or training which prepares young people for the labour market. In the United Kingdom, in an effort to make young people more employable, the Manpower Services Commission (MSC) was created in 1973 to provide training. The MSC was responsible for a range of Job Creation and Work Experience programmes. In 1978, the MSC launched the Youth Opportunities Programme (YOPs). The YOP was initially a one-year voluntary programme for unemployed school leavers. YOP trainees were given on-the-job training and one day per week of training out of the work environment, usually in a local Further Education college. YOP trainees were given a training allowance which was marginally above what they could claim in benefits, however employers could 'top up' the allowance if they wished. In 1983, the Youth Training Scheme was introduced, and in 1986 it became a two-year programme. In addition, because of changes to the social security system, the YTS had more of a compulsory feel to it, as young unemployed people were no longer allowed to claim benefits. On leaving school, a young person had essentially three choices: get a job, go into full-time, post-16 education or training, or join the YTS.

Dan Finn (1987) conducted a study of the Youth Training Scheme in Coventry and Rugby, and found that contrary to the beliefs of the Manpower Services Commission, who administer YT, most young people had at least one part-time job and hoped to transform this part-time work into full-time employment when they left school. However, it was cheaper for employers to take on YT trainees than full-time staff, and this suggests that YT may have helped to create more youth unemployment rather than make people more employable. However, according to the Department of Employment (1994), 47 per cent of YT trainees got jobs when they had completed their training.

In the United Kingdom, unemployment is also related to geographical region. People in Scotland, Wales and the north of England are more likely to be out of work; this is mainly because in the past, northern regions were more dependent upon heavy industry, which has shown the steepest decline in the last 20 years. However, we must not overlook the fact that in the south-east, particularly in Greater London, there was a significant decline in the number of manufacturing jobs.

New Right theorists are, however, more likely to point to the Welfare State as a cause of increased unemployment amongst the above groups, as benefits are too high and people have no incentive to find work. The Welfare State has created a dependency culture amongst some sections of the population.

The effects of unemployment

In Western society, a person's occupation is a key factor in that person's identity; it also gives people a sense of worth and self-esteem. As Brendan Burchell (1994) explains, it is not surprising then that unemployment can have damaging psychological effects upon people, for example isolation.

As Glyptis (1989) points out from a case study of 60 unemployed people in Nottingham, many unemployed young men aged between 16 and 24 become 'home bound', spending between 17 and 33 hours per week indoors and mainly alone.

Physical health can also suffer during periods of unemployment. Harvey Brenner (1979) suggests that if a country has one million people unemployed for over five years, there are likely to be 50,000 more deaths from general illness.

In 1981, Fagin and Little carried out a series of in-depth interviews with 20 families where the chief male wage earner had been out of work for 16 weeks or more. They concluded that:

- wives who had previously had ill health suffered from relapses – this was often associated with feelings of insecurity, brought about by the unemployment of their husbands
- men who had suffered from ill health at work showed some improvement in their health when initially unemployed
- unemployment can bring about psychological changes in men, including clinical depression, insomnia and suicidal thoughts
- physical symptoms also show themselves: asthma, psoriasis and headaches
- unemployment can also affect children's health, accidents, sleeping difficulties and behaviour problems.

Richard Lampard (1994) has shown that unemployment can have an effect upon marriages – often the lowering of living standards which comes with unemployment can be a major cause of marriages breaking up.

Finally, some researchers have suggested that there is a link between unemployment and crime. David Dickinson (1994) has suggested that as the level of unemployment increases, the number of young unemployed men convicted of crime increases. There is also a possible link between rioting and unemployment which was identified by Gaallie et al. (1994).

One of the most explicit examples of the state linking citizenship rights to paid employment, in the way that Gorz (1999) described, was introduced by the Blair government in 1997 under the title *New Deal*.

The 'New Deal'

The New Deal is a form of work for the benefits system or workfare, introduced by the British Labour government in 1997 – the scheme is said to be based upon Third Way philosophy and its communitarian assumptions. The New Deal was one of Labour's election pledges; its intention was to reduce 'youth unemployment' through a programme of 'welfare-to-work'. The principle aim was to assist the transition from benefit to work for 18–24-year-olds who have been in receipt of benefit for over six months.

It is commonly assumed by people on the right that the benefits system created a dependency culture; in addition, reform of the benefits system had not broken the cycle of dependency. The New Deal involves investing in individual people through training and increasing employment skills. As a consequence, employment opportunities are gained by the individual who in turn creates economic prosperity and competitiveness in the global market. The communitarian edge to this policy is that for a person to take from the community, they must give something back in return. Hence, citizenship rights are earned via work. As Raymond Plant (1998) explained, central to the New Labour concept of citizenship was the idea of reciprocity and making a contribution to the wider community. Individuals cannot have a right to the resources of society unless they contribute to the development of that society through work or other socially valued activities. As British Prime Minister Tony Blair explained in a party political broadcast: 'everybody who has a contribution to make can make a contribution' (BBC1, 24 September 1998, 9.00 pm).

The Labour government claimed that they were committed to eradicating social exclusion. As David Mulligan, director of Demos, a Third Way think tank, has explained, the unemployed: 'are more properly defined as excluded because they live outside the worlds of work, of education, of sociability itself' (quoted in Lloyd, 1997: 14).

However, the question remains: why do we still need the work ethic when the number of full-time jobs is seen to be declining? As we have seen above, the work ethic is used by the non-poor to define the poor as people who lack wits, will and effort.

Organisations

Most of the paid work that we do takes place within some form of organisation. All organisations are assumed to be bureaucratic in nature. However, as we suggested, in a Post-Fordist world, which has an uncertain or postmodern feel to it, new forms of pluralistic or non-hierarchical organisation are possible. People can work within 'quality circles', in which workers are not constrained and powerless, as they would be under some form of Tayloristic scientific management. They are not 'de-skilled' as Braverman (1974) would suggest, but work within structures which empower individuals by allowing democratic participation in decision making.

According to Max Weber (1864–1920), bureaucracy is both the most rational and the most efficient of all forms of administration (Weber, 1922/1978). All forms of bureaucracy need rules. Present-day organisations make use of quality assurance programmes or systems which are rational in exactly the way that Weber described them. Examples include: BS 5750, ISO 9000, and Investors in People, which all involve the establishment of systems which attempt to guarantee that procedures are carried out. Quality is understood as making sure that the formal rules are followed.

Max Weber's Ideal Type of Bureaucracy

For Weber (1922/1978), the ideal type is a useful model by which to measure other forms of administration. This model contains the following characteristics:

- The organisation is in the form of a hierarchy.
- Its operations are governed by a system of abstract rules.
- The ideal official conducts their tasks without friendship or favour to any clients.
- All bureaucrats have a fixed number of recorded duties.
- Employment in the bureaucracy is based upon qualifications.
- From a purely technical point of view, this form of administration has the highest degree of efficiency.

For Weber, the bureaucracy was precise, soul-less and machine-like, a technical instrument for achieving preconceived goals. However, bureaucracy has an inherent tendency to exceed its function, and to become a separate force within society. The source of power for the bureaucracy is based upon knowledge, and by this, Weber understood technical expertise which is protected by secrecy.

The goals of organisations are difficult to measure; long-term goals may have to change while short-term goals may compete with each other. In this sense, it might be better to have an organisational structure which is less durable but which can change to meet the needs of its stakeholders in new circumstances. This idea formed the basis of what came to be known as contingency theory.

Contingency theory is an approach to organisations which has none of the abstraction of general systems theories; it is a pragmatic approach to management, in which the manager has to be both flexible and to have an intuitive sense of the situation.

Henry Mintzberg (1983), in contrast to Weber, argued for what he called the *adhocracy*, which literally means that managers make it up as they go along, without universal principles which are thought to be appropriate to all situations. This is a fluid and flexible administration based upon teams who from their own rules like the informal organisation, rather than attempting to standardise the activities of its members. The adhocracy gains the advantages of the informal organisation, its flexible search for better ways of working in the face of new contingencies or circumstances and its innovative teamwork. These may take the form of quality circles which give individuals opportunities to develop their skills in a number of different areas.

However, as was suggested in the introduction, for many researchers, we have shifted from these Fordist notions of organisation to industrial systems which are Post-Fordist in nature.

Activity

Is bureaucracy necessarily the most efficient form of large-scale organisation?
  Give at least three reasons for your answer.
  Can postmodern organisations:

- encourage initiative, autonomy, flexibility, multiskilling, decentralisation, flatter hierarchies?
- retain a core of detailed rules and procedures, with a centralised overall structure of control and a careful monitoring of performance?

Again, give the reasons for your answers.

McDonaldisation: Accounting for Taste

According to George Ritzer, the process of McDonaldisation is about the application of scientific management to the fast food industry and other consumer services. It is a process, claims Ritzer, by which 'the unique is replaced by the generic' (Ritzer, 2004: 24) on the grounds that it is easier to sell the generic to the largest number of people. All aspects of the process are centrally managed and controlled, not simply in terms of production, promotion and distribution, but also the size, content and appearance of each product is subject to strict regulation as is how products are to be served to customers. Ritzer argues that customer reactions are standardised too, demonstrating the pervasiveness of the capitalist ideology.

Ritzer draws upon a number of themes first introduced by Theodore Levitt in the mid 1970s, but places a negative spin on what Levitt has to say. For Levitt, the 'managerial rationality' that is so effective in the management of industrial processes can and should be applied to service sectors. As Levitt (1976) explains:

> Fast-food restaurants, like McDonald's, Burger Chef, Pizza Hut, Dunkin' Donuts, or Kentucky Fried Chicken. At each the same rational system of division of labour and specialization is rigorously followed to produce speed, quality control, cleanliness, and low prices. (Levitt, 1976: 66)

Management and emotional work

The processes of McDonaldisation take Tayloristic scientific management to a new level by redefining what it means to make workers perform at their 'optimum'. This includes control over the emotions of the worker whilst performing within the labour process.

Emotional labour

Employers are attempting to lay claim to the emotional life of their employees, to such a degree that the worker can become estranged or alienated from their own sense of self. Hochschild (1983) developed the notion of *emotional labour* in which employees are expected to suppress their feelings and sustain an 'outward counternance':

'. . . the management of feeling to create a publicly observable facial and bodily display: emotional labor is sold for a wage and therefore has an exchange value . . . the same acts done in a private context . . . have use value' (Hochschild, 1983: 7). Hochschild's argument draws upon symbolic interactionist assumptions found in Goffman's dramatological approach to the relationship between self and other, or in the case of work organisations, the relationship between employer and employee.

Hochschild (1983) argues that dealing with emotions is an important component of work, particularly in the leisure sector. She takes her starting point from Goffman's distinction between 'front region' and 'back region' within organisations, where what the public see is the product of impression management, a form of work that draws upon the emotional resources of the individual in social situations to give people a perception of what an organisation is like. Leisure employees must learn how to manage their feelings and emotions. Hochschild (1983) described this as *emotional labour* where employees make every effort to 'create and maintain a relationship, a mood, or a feeling' (Hochschild, 1983: 440). Drawing on theories of theatre-acting techniques, Hochschild argues that emotions can be controlled, self-induced or suppressed as part of the labour process. She identifies two forms of emotional labour:

- 'Surface acting' is pretending 'to feel what we do not . . . we deceive others about what we really feel, but we do not deceive ourselves' (Hochschild, 1983: 33). 'Surface acting' is used when workers change how they appear to others by adapting their body language. Employees hide their negative emotions and display positive emotions even if they feel the opposite. With surface acting, the employees know that their behaviour lacks sincerity.
- 'Deep acting' means 'deceiving oneself as much as deceiving others' (Hochschild, 1983: 33). Employees attempt to induce feelings in themselves by using the same techniques as method actors in researching a role. Or, by drawing on emotive memories, the workplace emotions are felt by the employee to be real. Over a sustained period of deep acting, the manufactured feelings become internalised by the employee to the point that they can become separated from their 'real feelings'.

As Townsend (2004) makes clear, emotional labour is part of the service that companies are offering to customers – especially in markets where there is little to differentiate the product or service, the smiles of the employee become part of the brand. Hochschild (1983) argues that emotional labour is a product of the 'commercialisation' of emotions at work and is performed at a personal cost to the employee.

Since the publication of Hochschild's research, people have given much more attention to the role of emotions at work. Much of this research focuses on voice-to-voice or face-to-face services, often with a leisure focus: flight attendants (Hochschild, 1983; Taylor, 1998), debt collectors (Rafaeli and Sutton, 1991; Sutton, 1991), doctors (Smith and Kleinman, 1989), nurses (Bolton, 2000; Henderson, 2001; Scott, 2000; Smith, 1992; Smith and Gray, 2001), midwives (Curtise, 1991; Hunter, 2001; Robinson and Wharrad, 2001), counsellors (Yanay and Shahar, 1998), telephone sales agents (Taylor and Bain, 1999, 2004; Taylor and Tyler, 2000), cashiers (Rafaeli, 1989; Rafaeli and Sutton, 1990), supermarket clerks (Tolrich, 1993), criminal interrogators (Rafaeli and Sutton, 1991), police officers (Pogrebin and Poole, 1995), sex workers (Sanders, 2005), detectives (Stenross and Kleinman, 1989) and university workers (including both academics and administrators) (Pugliesi, 1999). Pugliesi (1999), for example, found that self-focused emotion management had negative effects on employees as it increased personal distress and was a major cause of job-related stress and loss of job satisfaction.

The emphasis of much of this research has concentrated on the 'dark side' of workplace emotions, notably stress and associated physical, personality, behavioural and medical problems. The pressure to continually express and/or suppress emotions at work has long-term implications for the employee, notably that such behaviours can cause stress.

A central dimension of emotional labour is 'emotional dissonance', defined by Hochschild as the sense of 'strain' that results from feigning emotions that are not felt over a long period (Hochschild, 1983: 90). Morris and Feldman (1996, 1997), Rafaeli and Sutton (1991) and Kruml and Geddes (2000) all found that emotional dissonance was a consequence of emotional labour – any employee who is in a job that involves 'emotion work' will suffer from a degree of emotional dissonance. Maslach and Jackson (1986) found that emotional dissonance was a cause of:

- emotional exhaustion
- depersonalisation
- diminished personal accomplishment.

Erickson and Ritter (2001) argue that managing feelings of agitation is the form of emotional labour that is most predictive of feelings of burnout and inauthenticity.

In contrast, Wouters (1989) suggests that Hochschild's preoccupation with the 'costs' of emotion work . . . hampers understanding of the joy the job may bring. Similarly, Ashforth and Humphrey (1993) suggest that emotional labour can enhance feelings of personal and emotional security at work by making difficult and demanding tasks more predictable. Individuals could detach themselves from the high emotional content of potentially stressful situations by adopting the role and the script devised by management, allowing the individual to feel that there was a division between self and performance.

Hochschild's findings have also been challenged by research that points to the pleasurable aspects of emotional labour. In a study of 911 dispatchers Shuler and Davenport-Sypher (2000) found that emotional labour could be enjoyable as it was often a source of amusement in a demanding service. Similarly, Tolrich (1993) found in a study of supermarket employees that 'dealing with the public' was one of the aspects of their work that they 'liked best', in that customers could introduce variety into the routine. Employees took pride in their ability to cultivate customers' loyalty, and in their ability to have fun with the customer.

A number of researchers point to the complex links between emotional labour and the conception of self (Ashforth and Humphrey, 1993; Gordon, 1989; Turner, 1976; Wharton, 1993) – some employees feel a great sense of achievement when they meet 'institutionalised standards', whereas other people feel their sense of self is restricted by any bureaucratic or institutional standards that are imposed upon them.

Hochschild (2003) discusses how the cultural system of capitalism has a hidden social logic, based as it is, claims Hochschild, on Tayloristic principles of scientific management – it has infiltrated the relationship between a mother and child. Mothers in the United States have become obsessed with running their families with the speed and efficiency of the Tayloristic place of work.

Although Hochschild's arguments do have a number of critics, control over the emotions and identity of the workers has become widely adopted on the assumption that the manipulation of the employee's identity and the use of audit can be used to enhance the performance of an organisation.

The Ritzer thesis draws upon the work of both Marx and Weber. From Weber, Ritzer takes the notion of 'rationalisation', which he redefines in terms of increasing *Americanisation* as the dominant evolutionary cultural trend across the globe: ' … an inexorable process, sweeping through seemingly imperious institutions and regions of the world' (Ritzer, 2002: 7).

From Marx, Ritzer draws upon the labour theory of value, alienation and ideology. The central assumptions of the labour theory of value have been seriously challenged over the last few decades. Ritzer attempts to rescue this theory by stating that customers have surplus value extracted from them in an effort to maintain the profitability of the capitalist enterprise.

Ritzer brings together these ideas to form the four dimensions of McDonaldisation:

- Efficiency, which involves ' … choosing the optimum means to a given end' (Ritzer, 1993: 36) – this efficiency is defined by the organisation rather than the individual and is in effect imposed upon the individual.
- Calculability, in which there is ' … an emphasis on the quantitative aspect of products sold (portion size, cost) and service offered (the time it takes to get the product)' (Ritzer, 1993: 9).

- Predictability, in which there is an emphasis on ' ... discipline, order, systemization, formalization, routine, consistency and methodical operation. In such a society, people prefer to know what to expect in most settings and at most times' (Ritzer, 1993: 79). The experience is the same in every shop for the consumer and work becomes routine for the workers.
- Control – management has a need to control both the workers and the customers in an effort to reduce the level of uncertainty within the organisation.

These processes have their own irrational outcomes, which Ritzer describes as follows: 'Rational systems inevitably spawn a series of irrationalities that limit, eventually compromise, and perhaps even undermine their rationality' (Ritzer, 1993: 121).

The inefficiencies generated by these rational processes include:

- longer waiting times and more work for the customer – having to make your own salad in the salad bar, or fill up your own drink in the fast-food restaurant
- dehumanisation of the worker and of the customer
- the emergence of unforeseen anomalies – things that go wrong without being planned for.

However, what Ritzer needed to explain is why it is that: 'apples, yogurt, and milk may go straight into the trash can, but hamburgers, fries, and shakes are devoured' (Ritzer, 2002: 14).

Ritzer's philosophy of life contains the moral critique that reality is becoming increasingly dull and lifeless – as a direct result of the ongoing rationalisation process.

In 'McJobs and the labor process' (2002), Ritzer explains that McJobs are directly related to class, as working-class people are more likely to have such jobs. In addition, Ritzer explains that:

Rationalization is a process that serves the interest of capitalists. They push it forward (largely unconsciously) because it heightens the level of exploitation of workers, allows new agents (e.g. customers) to be exploited and brings with it greater surplus value and higher profits. (Ritzer, 2002: 145) and

Surplus value is now not only to be derived from the labor time of the employee but also from the leisure time of the customer. McDonaldization is helping to open a whole new world of exploitation and growth to the contemporary capitalist. (Ritzer, 2002: 147)

What is most interesting about Ritzer's redefinition of the labour theory of value is that he has recognised that if non-human technology replaces labour power, which in the case of McDonalds it does to a high degree, then the rate of surplus value extracted will fall and the company will have serious problems maintaining its profitability. By drawing the customers into the production process, serving themselves etc., the company can extract a supply of surplus value from a source other than its employees. Interesting though this may be, Ritzer still maintains the Marxian assumptions of exploitation and in particular the arbitrary distinction between 'use value' and 'exchange value'. Use value is based upon genuine need in the Marxian analysis, and is ignored by Marx and later Marxian theorists, whilst exchange value is based upon the capitalist distorting the consciousness of the customer. In the socialist society, all of our use values would be satisfied, however 'genuine need' is impossible to define outside of the context of desire. Ritzer displaces the role of desire in the decision to purchase at McDonalds.

For Ritzer, this ideological manipulation also includes the manipulation of our tastes and preferences for food:

> This brings up another important aspect of McDonaldization, which is that the really major force in the expansion of McDonaldization is the way what McDonald's has, through intense marketing, used children in order to increase its profits, drawing children to it not initially because of the food but because of the toys... The child gets a burst of taste, which makes other foods seem bland in comparison. In time, the child gets hooked on a lifetime of this kind of consumption, this kind of food, which for most Americans is ultimately the last kind of food they need. (Ritzer, 2002: 27)

Ritzer's argument is that McDonald's manipulates our desires and controls our consciousness to such a degree that our personal tastes become rationalised and commodified – we know what to expect before the experience begins, because customer reactions have become standardised too. This is an ambitious claim, especially given that Ritzer does not have any process of data collection other than his own personal observations.

Ritzer's theory of McDonaldisation undervalues the role of the person in controlling their own lives. The McDonald's management are assumed to be capable of taking any object or idea and giving it a new representation or meaning in the minds of their customers – such as the ability to take food that is not wholesome, is high in fat and sugar content and convince the unsuspecting customer that it is 'good' food; the problem here is that Ritzer does not explain how this happens.

Ritzer's theory assumes that McDonald's customers are not knowledgeable about what they do or why they do it. However, McDonald's is a successful company solely because of the purchasing and consumption activities of its customers – without their active decision to enter the restaurant and consume, the company would cease to trade. Why people decide to go to McDonald's and the pleasure that they derive from the experience of their visit have many and varied reasons and cannot be reduced to a capitalistic ideological manipulation of intentions and motivations.

Ritzer has no adequate theory or explanation of why people choose to go to McDonald's or why they enjoy the experience. He suggests a notion of enforced consumption but does not develop it:

' ... the forces in modern capitalism have shifted the control and exploitation of production to the control and exploitation of consumption' (Ritzer, 2002: 147).

In the last analysis, Ritzer is simply propagating the myth of the passive consumer.

Conclusion

In this chapter, we have looked at the different approaches to the relationship between work and leisure. Work is commonly assumed to be the central activity in a person's life while leisure is seen as a form of recovery from the stresses of our working lives, especially when the work we do is emotional labour involving a high degree of 'deep acting'. Within Leisure Studies, there is a widely shared idea that the nature of employment people have may directly affect what people choose to do in their non-work or leisure time; therefore, if people find themselves without work, this can cause social unrest. The post-work thesis suggests that the desire to work is really the desire for leisure. The prospect of mass unemployment because of the cybernation of work has led to calls for the state to cut the hours worked by people and to make work more flexible, or to provide a socially guaranteed wage. For Bergmann (1977), we need to rethink the work–leisure relationship.

Stanley Aronowitz and William DiFazio (1994) were amongst the first people to explore the *post-work thesis* – they were concerned with how the labour market is moving towards a greater cybernation of labour that significantly reduces the working week and redefines the notion of a *work* career. Clarke and Critcher (1985) are highly critical of the post-work thesis. However, does society have a duty to provide income to people who choose not to work? In addition, there is the suggestion that a universal basic income would have a damaging effect upon the labour supply as many people would choose not to work. Giddens and Beck do not foresee either the end of work or leisure. Society will always need a form of work which helps to sustain the community and reiterate the individual's responsibilities and obligations to society. Life politics suggests that the idea of 'the leisure society' is outdated. In the last analysis, it argues that the post-work thesis, risk, individualisation and life politics are all significant to the understanding of leisure and leisure policy.

References

Ackerman, B. and Alstott, A. (2004) 'Why stakeholding?', *Politics and Society*, 32 (1): 41–60.

Aronowitz, S. and DiFazio, W. (1994) *The Jobless Future: Sci-tech and the Dogma of Work*. Minneapolis, MN: University of Minnesota Press.

Ashforth, B. and Humphrey, R. (1993) 'Emotional labor in service roles: the influence of identity', *Academy of Management Review*, 18: 88–115.

Atkinson, A.B. and Micklewright, J. (1994) *Economic Transformation in Eastern Europe and the Distribution of Income*. New York: Cambridge University Press.

Bauman, Z. (1998) *Work, Consumerism and the New Poor*. Milton Keynes: Open University Press.

Bauman, Z. (2001) *The Individualized Society*. Cambridge: Polity Press.

Bauman, Z. (2004) *Identity: Conversations with Benedetto Vecchi*. Cambridge: Polity Press.

Beck, U. (1992) *The Risk Society*. Cambridge: Polity Press.

Beck, U. (2000) *What is Globalisation?* Cambridge: Polity Press.

Beck, U. and Beck-Gernsheim, E. (2002) *Individualization: Institutionalized Individualism and its Social and Political Consequences*. London: Sage.

Bell, D. (1973) *The Coming of Post-Industrial Society: A Venture in Social Forecasting*. New York: Harper Colophon Books.

Bergmann, F. (1977) *On Being Free*. London: University of Notre Dame Press.

Bolton, S. (2000) 'Who cares? Offering emotion work as a "gift" in the nursing labour process', *Journal of Advanced Nursing*, 32 (3): 580–6.

Braverman, H. (1974) *Labor and Monopoly Capital*. New York: Monthly Review Press.

Brenner, H. (1979) 'Mortality and the national economy', *Lancet*, 2(15): 568–73.

Burchell, B. (1994) 'The effects of labour market position, job insecurity, and unemployment on psychological health', in D. Gallie, C. Marsh and C. Vogler, *Social Change and the Experience of Unemployment*. Oxford: Oxford University Press.

Clarke, J. and Critcher, C. (1985) *The Devil Makes Work*. Basingstoke: Macmillan Houndmills.

Curtise, P.A. (1991) 'Midwives in hospital: work, emotion and the labour process', unpublished PhD thesis, University of Manchester.

Deem, R. (1995) 'State policy and ideology in the education of women 1944–1980', in L. Dawtrey, J. Holland, M. Hammer and S. Sheldon (eds), *Equality and Inequality in Education Policy*. Buckingham: Open University Press. pp. 31–45.

Department of Employment (1994) *Labour Force Survey*. London: HMSO.

Descartes, R. (1960) *Discourse on Method and Meditations*, translated by L.J. Lafleur. New York: The Liberal Arts Press.

Dickinson, D. (1994) 'Criminal benefits', *New Statesman and Society*, 14 (Jan): 14–15.

Dumazedier, J. (1967) *Toward a Society of Leisure*. New York: The Free Press.

Dumazedier, J. (1974) 'Leisure and the social system', in J.F. Murphy (ed.), *Concepts of Leisure*. Englewood Cliffs, NJ: Prentice-Hall.

Erickson, R. and Ritter, C. (2001) 'Emotional labor, burnout and inauthenticity: does gender matter?', *Social Psychology Quarterly*, 64 (2): 146–63.

Fagin, L.H. and Little, M. (1981) *Unemployment and Health in Families*. London: DHSS.

Finn, D. (1987) *Training Without Jobs*. London: Macmillan.

Freeman, C. and Soete, L. (1994) *Work for All or Mass Unemployment*. London: Pinter.

Gallie, D., Marsh, C. and Vogler, C. (1994) *Social Change and the Experience of Unemployment*. Oxford: Oxford University Press.

Gershuny, J. and Pahl, R. (1980) 'Work outside employment: some preliminary speculation', *New Universities Quarterly*, 34: 120–35.

Giddens, A. (1984) *The Consititution of Society*. Cambridge: Polity Press.

Giddens, A. (1989) *Sociology*. Cambridge: Polity Press.

Glyptis, S. (1989) *Leisure and Unemployment*. Milton Keynes: Open University Press.

Goldthorpe, J. and Payne, G. (1986) 'Trends in intergenerational mobility in England and Wales', *Sociology*, 20: 1–24.

Gordon, S. (1989) 'Institutional and impulsive orientations in selectively appropriating emotions to self', in D.D. Franks and E.D. McCarthy (eds), *The Sociology of Emotions: Original Essays and Research Papers*. Greenwich, CT: JAI Press.

Gorz, A. (1982) *Farwell to the Working Class. An Essay on Post-industrial Socialism*. Trans. M. Sonenscher. London: Pluto.

Gorz, A. (1983) *Ecology as Politics*. London: Verso.

Gorz, A. (1999) *Reclaiming Work: Beyond the Wage-Based Society*. Trans. Chris Turner. Cambridge: Polity Press.

Grint, K. (1993) *The Sociology of Work*. Cambridge: Polity Press.

Gross, E. (1961) 'A functional approach to leisure analysis', *Social Problems*, 9 (1): 2–8.

Henderson, A. (2001) 'Emotional labor and nursing: an underappreciated aspect of caring work', *Nursing Inquiry*, 8 (2): 130–8.

Hochschild, A.R. (1983) *The Managed Heart*. Berkeley and Los Angeles, CA: University of California Press.

Hunter, B. (2001) 'Emotion work in midwifery: a review of current knowledge', *Journal of Advanced Nursing*, 34 (4): 436–44.

Jenkins, R. (1986) *Racism and Recruitment: Managers, Organisations and Equal Opportunity*. Cambridge: Cambridge University Press.

Jenkins, R. and Sherman, B. (1979) *The Collapse of Work*. London: Eyre Methuen.

Kaplan, M. (1975) *Leisure: Theory and Policy*. Springfield, IL: C.C. Thomas.

Kruml, S. and Geddes, D. (2000) 'Exploring the dimensions of emotional labor', *Management Communication Quarterly*, 14 (1): 8–49.

Lampard, R. (1994) 'An examination of the relationship between martial dissolution and unemployment', in D. Gallie, C. Marsh and C. Vogler, *Social Change and the Experience of Unemployment*. Oxford: Oxford University Press.

Levinas, E. (1974) *Otherwise than Being or Beyond Essence*. Boston: Kluwer Academic Publishers.

Levitt, T. (1976) 'The industrialization of service', *Harvard Business Review*, 54 (5): 63–74.

Lloyd, J. (1997) 'New Deal', *New Statesman and Society*, Feb.: 19.

Martin, J. and Roberts, C. (1984) *Women and Employment: A Lifetime Perspective*. London: HMSO.

Maslach, C. and Jackson, S. (1986) *Maslach Burnout Inventory Manual*, 2nd edn. Palo Alto, CA: Consulting Psychologists Press.

Mintzberg, H. (1983) *Power in and Around Organisations*. Upper Saddle River, NJ: Prentice Hall.

Morris, J.A. and Feldman, D.C. (1996) 'The dimensions, antecedents, and consequences of emotional labor', *Academy of Management Review*, 21: 986–1010.

Morris, J.A. and Feldman, D.C. (1997) 'Managing emotions in the workplace', *Journal of Managerial Issues*, 9 (3): 257–74.

Nietzsche, F. ([1906] 1997) *Beyond Good and Evil*. Trans. Helen Zimmern, 1906, reprinted in New York: Courier Dover Publications.

Parker, S. (1981) 'Change, flexibility, spontaneity, and self-determination in leisure', *Social Forces*, 60 (2): 323–31.

Plant, R. (1998) 'Citizenship', *New Statesman and Society*, Feb.: 15.

Pogrebin, M. and Poole, E. (1995) 'Emotion management: a study of police response to tragic events', in M.G. Flaherty and C. Ellis (eds), *Social Perspectives on Emotion*. Stamford, CT: JAI Press.

Pugliesi, K. (1999) 'The consequences of emotional labor: effects of work stress, job satisfaction, and well-being', *Motivation and Emotion*, 23 (2): 125–54.

Rafaeli, A. (1989) 'When cashiers meet customers: an analysis of the role of supermarket cashiers', *Academy of Management Journal*, 32: 245–73.

Rafaeli, A. and Sutton, R. (1990) 'Busy stores and demanding customers: how do they affect the display of positive emotion?', *Academy of Management Journal*, 13: 623–37.

Rafaeli, A. and Sutton, R. (1991) 'Emotional contrast strategies as means of social influence: lessons from criminal interrogators and bill collectors', *Academy of Management Journal*, 34: 749–75.

Rawls, J. (1971) *A Theory of Justice*. Cambridge, MA: Belknap Press of Harvard University Press.

Rifkin, J. (1995) *The End of Work: The Decline of the Global Labour Force and the Dawn of the Post Market Era*. New York: G.P. Putman.

Ritzer, G. (1993) *The McDonaldization of Society*. Thousand Oaks: Pine Forge.

Ritzer, G. (ed.) (2002) *McDonaldization: The Reader*. Thousand Oaks: Pine Forge.

Ritzer, G. (2004) *The Globalization of Nothing*. Thousand Oaks: Pine Forge.

Robinson, J. and Wharrad, H. (2001) 'Emotion work in midwifery: a review of current knowledge', *Journal of Advanced Nursing*, 34 (4): 436–44.

Rojek, C. (1995) *Decentring Leisure*. London: Sage.

Rojek, C. (2001) *Celebrity*. London: Reaktion Books.

Rojek, C. (2002) 'Civil labour, leisure and post work society', *Loisir et Societé*, 25 (1): 21–35.

Salaman, G. (1987) 'Information technology and the debate about work', *Social Studies Review*, May: 24–7.

Sanders, T. (2005) '"Its just acting": sex workers' strategies for capitalizing on sexuality', *Gender, Work and Organization*, 12 (4): 319–42.

Scott, A. (2000) 'Emotion, moral perception, and nursing practice', *Nursing Philosophy*, 1: 123–33.

Seabrook, J. (1988) *The Leisure Society*. London: Blackwell.

Shuler, S. and Davenport-Sypher, B. (2000) 'Seeking emotional labor: when managing the heart enhances the work experience', *Management Communication Quarterly*, 14 (1): 50–89.

Smith, A. and Kleinman, S. (1989) 'Managing emotions in medical school: students' contacts with the living and the dead', *Social Psychology Quarterly*, 52: 56–9.

Smith, P. (1992) *The Emotional Labour of Nursing: How Nurses Care*. Basingstoke: Macmillan.

Smith, P. and Gray, B. (2001) 'Reassessing the concept of emotional labour in student nurse education: the role of link lecturers and mentors in a time of change', *Nurse Education Today*, 21: 230–7.

Stebbins, R. (1998) *After Work: The Search for an Optimal Leisure Lifestyle*. Calgary: Temeron.

Stenross, B. and Kleinman, S. (1989) 'The highs and lows of emotional labour: detectives' encounter with criminals and victims', *Journal of Contemporary Ethnography*, 1 (7): 435–52.

Sutton, R.I. (1991) 'Maintaining norms about expressed emotions: the case of bill collectors', *Administrative Science Quarterly*, 36: 245–68.

Taylor, B. and Bain, P. (1999) 'An assembly line in the head: work and employee relations in the call centre', *Industrial Relations Journal*, 30 (2): 101–17.

Taylor, B. and Bain, P. (2004) 'Call centre offshoring to India: the revenge of history?', *Labour and Industry*, 14 (3): 15–39.

Taylor, S. (1998) 'Emotional labour and the new workplace', in P. Thompson and C. Warhurst (eds), *Workplaces of the Future*. London: Macmillan.

Taylor, S. and Tyler, M. (2000) 'Emotional labour and sexual difference in the airline industry', *Work, Employment and Society*, March: 77–95.

Tolrich, M. (1993) 'Alienating and liberating emotions at work', *Journal of Contemporary Ethnography*, 22 (3): 361–81.

Touraine, A. (1971) *The May Movement*. New York: Random House.

Townsend, K. (2004) 'When the lost found teams: a consideration of teams within the individualised call centre environment', *Labour and Industry*, 14 (3): 111–26.

Turner, R. (1976) 'The real self: from institution to impulse', *American Journal of Sociology*, 81: 989–1016.

Van Parijs, P. (1993) *Marxism Recycled*. Cambridge: Cambridge University Press.

Van Parijs, P. (2000) 'A basic income for all', *Boston Review*, 25: October/November. Available at: http://bostonreview.net/BR25.5/vanparijs.html

Van Parijs, P. (2004) 'Europe's linguistic challenge', *European Journal of Sociology*, 45 (1): 111–52.

Van Parijs, P., Ackerman, B. and Alstott, A. (2003) *Redesigning Distribution: Basic Income and Stakeholder Grants as Alternative Cornerstones for a More Egalitarian Capitalism. The Real Utopias Project*, Volume V. Available at: http://www.ssc.wisc.edu/~wright/Redesigning%20Distribution%20v1.pdf#page=6

Veblen, T. (1899) *The Theory of the Leisure Class: An Economic Study in the Evolution of Institutions*. New York: Macmillan.

Vives, J.L. ([1526] 1943) *De Subventione Pauperum*. Bruxelles: Valero & Fils.

Weber, M. (1922/1978) *Economy and Society*. Trans. G. Roth and C. Wittich. Berkeley, CA: University of California Press.

Webster, F. and Robins, K. (1986) *Information Technology: A Luddite Analysis*. Norwood, NJ: Ablex.

Wharton, A. (1993) 'The affective consequences of service work', *Work and Occupations*, 20 (2): 205–32.

Wilensky, H. (1960) 'Work, careers and social integration', *International Social Science Journal*, 4 (4): 543–60.

Wouters, C. (1989) 'Response to Hochschild's reply', *Theory, Culture and Society*, 6: 447–50.

Yanay, N. and Shahar, G. (1998) 'Professional feelings as emotional labor', *Journal of Contemporary Ethnography*, 27 (3): 346–73.

10

GLOBALISATION AND LEISURE – THE CONSUMER SOCIETY

By the end of this chapter, the reader should have a critical understanding of:

- the nature of globalisation as a set of economic, technological and cultural processes that have impacted on the leisure sector, including:
  - ○ Bollywood and Western cultural imperialism
  - ○ the modern Olympic Games and the social, political and cultural impact of 'hallmark' events. There is an opportunity to assess the legacy of London 2012
- the Information Society and its impact on the leisure sector, such as the music, soft drinks and credit card industries
- the fact that credit cards have revolutionised consumption, with a discussion of Naomi Klein's *No Logo: Beating the Brand Bullies* and an assessment of José Bové and the anti-globalisation movement.

What is Globalisation?

The concept of globalisation is based upon the idea that the world is becoming a single place. As Roland Robertson has made clear:

> The fact and the perception of ever increasing inter-dependence at the global level, the rising concern about the fate of the world as a whole and of the human species (particularly because of the threats of ecological degradation, nuclear disaster and AIDS), and the colonisation of the local by global life (not least via the mass media) facilitate massive processes of relativization of cultures, doctrines, ideologies and cognitive frames of reference. (Robertson, 1994: 87)

Activity

Before you read on you should reflect on the meaning of the points that Robertson is making in the above paragraph.

For Robertson, the world is becoming more interconnected and, at the same time, we as individuals are becoming more concerned about the risks and uncertainties facing the human race. In addition, the mass media has become global and is destroying local cultures to such a degree that people across the world even appear to think in similar ways. In his view, the concept of globalisation is about developments that have brought about: 'the concrete structuration of the world as a whole' (Robertson, 1994: 53).

Leslie Sklair (1993) has outlined and evaluated a number of different models of globalisation. Firstly, Wallerstein's world system model that is Marxian in orientation. This model suggests that within the world economy, there is an international division of labour. A nation's economy is linked in a number of ways to the international economy and can either be at its core, its semi-periphery or periphery. Those nations which are at the periphery are much more likely to be in poverty. However, for Sklair, this model is too determined by economic factors and ignores cultural factors in the processes of globalisation.

Secondly, the 'cultural imperialism' or 'global homogenisation' model suggests that Western cultural products which promote Western lifestyles are destroying local or traditional cultures.

Finally, Sklair's own model suggests that the global system is built upon transnational practices formed by transnational corporations that encourage economic, political and cultural or ideological practices, such as consumerism, that encourage people and ideas to travel across the borders of nation states, making it difficult for governments to regulate their own economies.

Cultural globalisation: Arjun Appadurai

Appadurai explains the notion of globalisation by looking at a number of global 'flows':

- ethnoscapes – the flow of people, tourists, immigrants, refugees, exiles and guest workers
- technoscapes – the movement of technology
- finanscapes – the rapid movement of money via money markets and stock exchanges
- mediascapes – information and images generated and distributed by film, television, newspapers and magazines
- ideoscapes – the movement of political ideas and ideologies.

This chapter and the next are primarily concerned with the consumption of leisure within a global context and take their starting point from Arjun Appadurai's conceptualisation of cultural globalisation. We look at tourism, the impact of information society on leisure, film and other media products, P2P networks, and the spread of ideas and concepts via global organisations such as the Olympic Movement and hallmark events.

For Anthony Giddens, modernity is essentially 'globalising' in nature and involves a multiplicity of linkages and interconnections that surpass or exceed nation states. However, globalisation is not a single process but a complex mixture of processes, which often act in contradictory ways, producing conflicts, disjunctions and new forms of stratification. Globalisation, then, involves more '...than a diffusion of Western institutions across the world, in which other cultures are crushed' (Giddens, 1990: 175). It involves '... a process of uneven development that fragments as it coordinates' (Giddens, 1990: 175). The major feature of globalisation for Giddens is the compression of the world; this is the profound re-ordering of time and space in social life – what Giddens terms *time–space distanciation*. In Giddens' opinion, this extraordinary, and still accelerating, connectedness between everyday decisions and global outcomes, together with its reverse – the influence of global orders over individual life – forms the key subject matter of the new agenda.

It would be wrong to suggest that the processes of globalisation are one-way traffic, as many of the cultural and leisure practices from food cultures, such as Indian and Chinese food, to film, jazz, reggae and salsa have their origin on the edge of the global economic system. In addition, globalisation encourages the hybridisation or creolisation of cultural practices. Chinese cuisine is one of the most popular in the world and the Chinese restaurant and the Chinese take-away have become a common feature of cities across the world. In all places, these restaurants rely upon clients from outside of the Chinese community in order to survive. The Chinese restaurant owners are cultural entrepreneurs; they have to present their menu as 'authentic' but not so far from the mainstream of food culture that people are unwilling to try it. Towards this end, traditional Chinese menus have had to be adopted to not offend customer tastes in, for example the United States or the United Kingdom, so ingredients such as pig's tongue and duck's feet are taken off the menu and replaced by meats that are more common to the customer. Although the restaurant owners have had to accommodate local taste in their menus, the popularity of Chinese restaurants demonstrates that globalisation is not a one-way process, driven by multinational companies. Chinese, Indian and other ethnic restaurants are usually small family businesses that have to compete in a very competitive market.

Bollywood – Bombay Masala

In a study of the Hindi film *Lagaan: Once upon a Time in India*, for example, Florian Stadtler suggests that Baz Luhrmann's film *Moulin Rouge* (2001) draws upon Bollywood's formulaic themes of spectacular musicality style, extended song-and-dance performances and a confusion of fantasy and reality. This highlights the argument that globalisation is not simply a euphemism for Western cultural imperialism. Bollywood has become part of the global mediascape, as more and more international markets and audiences become attracted to the product.

Florian Stadtler (2005) explains that Indian cinema has an international reputation stretching back to 1913, however since the 1990s, Hindi popular cinema commonly known as 'Bollywood' has positioned itself against the hegemony of Hollywood. Stadtler describes Bollywood film as 'hybrid eclecticism', in that a typical Bollywood film will include a number of different genres to provide several hours of 'escapist entertainment'.

Although film technology was developed in Western capitalist centres and transported to India as part of a process of colonialism, once cinema arrived in India, it soon became an Indian project that represented Indian images and narratives for an Indian audience. Since the 1990s, there has been a shift away from the traditional mixed economy and greater liberalisation within this development. For Kaur (2002), the popular Indian film industry has attempted to renew its popularity by appealing to the newly affluent and mobile globalised Indian middle class, reflecting on their socio-political concerns. In the early years of the industry, the emphasis was on religious and/or nationalist themes, while by the 1950s and 1960s, the emphasis was on rural-to-urban migration, urban slums, feudal oppression and class conflict. The 1970s saw the portrayal of an increasingly dishonest, complex and oppressive social system challenged by a lone crusader.

Although such films as 'Bride and Prejudice' have attempted to recreate the Bollywood formula, creating a new masala formula, and Indian megastar Amitabh Bacchan has used Bollywood to launch films with a 'feminist' narrative such as *Astitva* (2000), according to Sheila J. Nayar (2005), many Bollywood films draw upon Hollywood blockbusters. Nayar lists the following Bollywood films that were adapted or 'inspired' from Hollywood films:

'Kucch To Hai (2003) I Know What You Did Last Summer (1998)
Saaya (2003) Dragonfly (2002)
Qayamat (2003) The Rock (1997)
Samay (2003) Seven (1995)
Sssshhh (2003) Scream (1996)
Jism (2002) Double Indemnity (1944)/Body Heat (1981)
Aapko Pehle Bhi Kahin Dekha Hai (2002) Father of the Bride (1991)/Meet the
   Parents (1999)
Dil Ka Rishta (2002) Magnificent Obsession (1954)
Mere Yaar ki Shaadi Hai (2002) My Best Friend's Wedding (1997)
Raaz (2002) What Lies Beneath (2000)
Kaante (2002) Reservoir Dogs (1992)
Kasoor (2001) Jagged Edge (1985)
Pyaar Tune Kya Kiya (2001) Fatal Attraction (1987)
Mohabbatein (2000) Dead Poets Society (1989)
Ghulam (1998) Rebel without a Cause (1995)/On the Waterfront (1954)
Pyar Tho Hona Hi Tha (1998) French Kiss (1995)
Chachi 420 (1997) Mrs Doubtfire (1993)
Judaii (1997) Indecent Proposal (1993)
Dil To Pagal Hai (1997) Sleepless in Seattle (1993)
Agnisakshi (1996) Sleeping with the Enemy (1991)
Yeh Dillagi (1994) Sabrina (1954)
Khal-Naaikaa (1993) The Hand That Rocks the Cradle (1992)
Darr (1993) Dead Calm (1989)

Baazigar (1993) A Kiss Before Dying (1991)
Hum Hain Rahi Pyar Ke (1993) Houseboat (1958)
Jo Jeeta Wohi Sikander (1992) Breaking Away (1979)
Dil Hai ki Manta Nahin (1991) It Happened One Night (1934)
Main Azad Hoon (1989) Meet John Doe (1941) (Nayar, 2005: 68).

Lakshmi Srinivas (2002) attempted a 'phenomenology of spectatorship' of the audiences for Bollywood films. Indian films have an integrative influence within India and help to shape the national political culture. Srinivas argues that in the 1990s it was estimated that about 10–15 million cinema tickets were sold per day in India. Many of the cinema-goers are described by Srinivas as 'habituees' who are viewed as 'insiders to the culture of commercial cinema, audiences who have developed a relationship with the films based on long acquaintance with them' (Srinivas, 2002: 157). Srinivas goes on to argue that India is the largest producer of feature films in the world, producing over 800 films annually, which is twice the number produced in Hollywood. The Indian film business is not one homogenous body of entrepreneurs and artistes. Cinema in India has to cater for a wide and varied audience with 16 major languages – the states of Bengal, the Karnataka, Andhra Pradesh, Tamil Nadu and Kerala all have their own languages. In addition, there are hundreds of dialects and significant differences of age, class, caste, religion and regional culture.

The most popular films are melodramas that contain both a comedic element and a strong romantic theme. It is unusual for the film to exclude music and dance sequences: 'Even the recently released *Pukar* (2000), which incorporates the subject of terrorism and where the hero is a Major in the Indian army, has three or four dances' (Srinivas, 2002: 157). The film *Border*, which is concerned with the India–Pakistan conflict, includes a number of song sequences. Srinivas suggests that the musical breaks are devices to entertain the audience with spectacle and travelogue. The viewing practices in India are very different from that found in the United States or the European Union. Srinivas observed that people will walk in and out of the cinema during the film if a particular scene is of no interest, allowing audiences to construct and reconstruct a narrative from the film that suits their needs.

Ian Garwood (2006) quotes Tejaswini Ganti, saying:

> Songs are perceived as the quintessential 'commercial' element in a film. Filmmakers working outside the mainstream treat songs as a way of reaching larger audiences, and this gets characterized by the press as either accommodating or pandering to popular tastes. The omission of songs is interpreted as an oppositional stance; a way of making a statement against the dominant form of cinema as well as circumscribing one's audience. (Ganti, 2004: 76, cited in Garwood, 2006: 169)

However, according to Garwood (2006), a number of recent movies have either removed or significantly downplayed the song sequence. The ghost story *Bhoot* (2003) is credited by Garwood as starting this trend, while other examples he cites include *Hawaa* (2003); *3 Deewarein* (2003); *Darna Mana Hai* (2003); *Ek Hasini Thi* (2003); *Ek Din 24 Ghante* (2003); and *My Wife's Murder* (2005).

Garwood examines the explanation as to why the songless Bollywood film emerged in recent years. One central element is related to finance. There is currently a boom in multiplex cinemas in India, especially in large cities, that cater for the new English-speaking, urban middle class who see themselves as part of a global business community. This affluent group form only a tiny section of the cinema audience, but they generate the bulk of the revenue at the box office. This group has tastes in cinema that differ from the traditional Indian cinema-goer and they do not see the traditional song sequence as an integral feature of the film. Also, the new generation of film makers in India is looking to an audience outside of India and has adopted more Western film-making conventions. Secondly, Indi-pop has developed a global audience that does not rely upon an association with film.

Bollywood also hosts its own annual awards ceremony, and like other hallmark events this is a sign of increasing globalisation.

One of the major global hallmark events is the Olympic Games, and it is to this topic that we now turn our attention.

The Modern Olympic Games

Global hallmark events have a long history stretching back to the nineteenth century – such large exhibitions were seen to promote urban development, by improving transport, communications and the provision of open spaces and parks. The 'Great Exhibition of the Works of Industry of All Nations' held in London in 1851 was the first in a number of 'world fairs'. As Chalkley and Essex (1999) explain:

> The Eiffel Tower is a legacy of the Paris Exhibition of 1889 which was held to mark the centenary of the French Revolution and attracted over 30 million visitors. In London, Wembley Stadium is a legacy of the British Empire Exhibition held in 1924–5. In 1931, the Bureau International des Expositions was established, with its headquarters in Paris, to regulate the holding of large exhibitions in order to prevent too many being arranged too frequently in any one part of the world. (Chalkley and Essex, 1999: 370)

Pierre Frédy, later to become Baron de Coubertin, was the founder of the modern Olympic Games. According to Chalkley and Essex (1999), Pierre de Coubertin got the idea of reviving the Olympic Games after observing a series of games organised by a Dr W.P. Brookes at Much Wenlock, Shropshire, in the UK, as an annual event between 1849 and 1889. The Much Wenlock event, also known as the Olympic Games, included track and field sports, cricket matches, tilting at rings while on horseback, and literary and artistic competition. Baron de Coubertin's vision was that the Olympic Movement would bring together all interested parties, including International Federations, athletes, judges and referees who all agreed to be guided by an Olympic Charter that incorporated a spirit of Olympism.

The control and development of the Olympic Movement is in the hands of the International Olympic Committee (IOC), followed by the National Olympic

Committees (NOCs), and the Organising Committees of the Olympic Games (OCOGs). The goal of the Olympic Movement is to further *Olympism* (a state of mind based on equality of sports which are international and democratic) and thereby contribute to building a peaceful and better world by educating youth through sport practised without discrimination of any kind, in a spirit of friendship, solidarity and fair play. However, according to Rick Burton (2003), many cities begin the bidding process to host the Games thinking only about the potential economic impact on the city and little about Olympian values.

'Olympism is not a system, it is a state of mind – it can permeate a wide variety of modes of expression and no single race or era can claim to have the monopoly of it'. (*Source*: Pierre de Coubertin, multimedia.olympic.org/pdf/en_report668.pdf)

Milton-Smith (2002) argues that de Coubertin's Olympian values are a distortion of history and a misrepresentation of contemporary reality. These values are built upon the notion of the 'gentleman amateur' derived from the nineteenth-century, English public school system. Moral development and social harmony through the acceptance of amateurism are no longer at the forefront of how the modern Olympic games are organised. The modern Olympics are now no different from any other commercially organised sporting event.

The IOC was established in June 1894 and it is a not-for-profit organisation incorporated by International Law. The IOC has juridical status within the Olympic Movement and selects new members by a process of cooption that is not made public. The IOC headquarters are in Lausanne, Switzerland.

The IOC selects the host city and selects the games/sports that are included and excluded. The chief aims of the IOC are to:

- 'encourage the organization and development of Sports and Sports Competition'
- 'inspire and lead Sport within the Olympic ideal, thereby promoting and strengthening friendship between the sportsmen of all countries'
- 'ensure the regular celebration of the Olympic Games'
- 'to make the Olympic Games even more worthy of their glorious history, and of the high ideals which inspired their revival by Baron Pierre de Coubertin and his associates'. (*Source*: multimedia.olympic.org/pdf/en_report668.pdf)

The main functions of a National Olympic Committee are to:

- ensure the representation of athletes from its country at the Olympic Games
- help in the development of the Olympic Movement and amateur sports in general

- teach and encourage respect of the fundamental principles of Olympism
- act as a link with National Sports Federations affiliated to the International Federations recognised by the International Olympic Committee
- encourage and assist the government of its country in the enforcement of a sport programme for the youth, with a view to developing its character, health and civic sense
- oppose any political or commercial interference and any religious or racial discrimination in sport
- propagate a programme meant to enlighten the public and the media on Olympic philosophy

(*Source*: multimedia.olympic.org/pdf/en_report668.pdf)

Following financial problems faced by the city of Montreal following the 1976 summer Olympic games, with the presidency of Juan Antonio Samaranch (1980–2001), the Olympic Movement became much more conscious of the commercial benefits of the games. Moreover, when Samaranch declared a games to be 'the best Games ever', he appears to believe that commercial success should be part of that judgement. Brown et al. (2000) quote Samaranch in 1993, saying:

'Marketing has become an increasingly important issue for all of us in the Olympic Movement. The revenue derived from television, sponsorship, and fundraising help to provide the movement with financial independence' (p. 74). However, the IOC still do not allow advertising within Olympic venues except for manufacturers' logos on athletes' clothing.

Samaranch was a staunch supporter of professionalism and was a keen supporter of liberalising the amateur regulations, which the IOC did in 1981. In addition, Samaranch was a fierce opponent of political 'misuse' of the games. The Soviet invasion of Afghanistan led to several non-communist nations staging a boycott of the 1980 Moscow Games. In 1988, North Korea, Cuba and Nicaragua did not participate at the Seoul Games.

According to John Milton-Smith (2002), disillusionment with the processes of globalisation – poverty, third world debt, humanitarian crises, environmental damage – has manifest itself in anti-globalisation protests such as those in Seattle, and have also resulted in growing disenchantment with the Olympics. For Milton-Smith (2002), this includes:

- winning at any price
- commercial exploitation
- corruption – notably of IOC members
- intense national rivalry
- competitive advantage of advanced nations. (Milton-Smith, 2002: 132)

Holger Preuss (2003) traces the economic history of the Games and identifies a number of distinct phases in its history:

- recurring financial problems and the identification of new sources of income (1896–1968)
- the start of publicly funded games (1969–1980)
- increased funding by private finance (1981–1996)
- mixed financing and long-term relationships with sponsors, TV companies and the IOC (1997–2008).

In addition, Preuss (2003) suggests the following reasons as to why a city would want to host the games. Major objectives of the host cities and countries include:

- the promotion of a new image, as in the cases of: Munich 1972, Seoul 1988, Barcelona 1992 and Torino 2006
- the demonstration/promotion of a political system, as in the cases of: Moscow 1980 and Los Angeles 1984
- increasing tourism, as in the cases of: Barcelona 1992 and Sydney 2000
- enhanced city status, as in the cases of: Barcelona 1992, Atlanta 1996 and Nagano 1998
- increasing inward investment, as in the cases of: Lillehammer 1994, Barcelona 1992, Atlanta 1996 and Nagano 1998
- giving out a message – at Beijing 2008, China was keen to demonstrate its growing importance to the world economy.

There a number of active interest groups within the Olympic Movement, from the IOC members who have their own distinct cultural and geo-political interests to nation states who see the games as an opportunity to improve international relations, generate positive psychological aspects for the host population, and improve the performance of the economy by increasing tourism and encouraging the development of the host city.

Preuss (2003) argues that host cities benefit in three ways:

- through improved infrastructure
- through increased employment, income or city image
- through autonomous investment and consumption expenditure.

However, Preuss also argues that upper-income groups benefit disproportionately as poorer groups suffer dislocation.

Waitt (1999) draws upon Harvey's concept of time–space compression to examine the relationship between the Olympic Games as a hallmark event and three characteristics of the postmodern city: government policies informed by entrepreneurial goals rather than welfare goals; the transformation of the city into a product to generate 'cultural capital'; and the importance of marketing places. Time–space compression is an attempt to diminish the notion of distance in an attempt to generate new markets. Waitt (1999) argues that the Sydney Olympic bid was shaped by the needs of global capitalism and built upon a marketing strategy that was no different from the strategies that multinational companies use to sell any product in the marketplace. The Sydney Olympic bid presented the city as an attractive collection of aesthetics and attributes that were commodities waiting to be consumed. Rather than being a modern city that provided people with a place they could call home and which could act as a signifier for identity, Sydney had its historical and cultural roots transformed by a process of decontextualisation, central to promotional culture, and became a centre for postmodern consumption. Anything that was controversial about the city was removed so as to make the city more attractive in terms of its amenities, notably the quality of its natural and built environment and in terms of providing opportunities to work, play and invest; in other words, earning money and acceptance. As Waitt (1999) argues, the social and physical attributes of cities are marketed as commodities to be consumed. Cities are re-imagined into spectacular urban spaces to attract capital and people. Hosting the Olympic Games is important in giving a city the edge in the inter-urban competition and urban entrepreneurialism.

Within Sydney, a number of social movements emerged to challenge the glossy image of the city that the Sydney Olympic bid was attempting to construct; they were built around the concepts of unity, equality, togetherness, progress and achievement. One such group were known as 'Subverting the Sydney Olympic Farce' (PISSOFF) – their main argument was that the public money spent on the Olympics could have gone to more important sectors, such as education, health and the environment. Homebush Bay, for example, was previously owned by Union Carbide as a site for the production of pesticide and was the centre of a row concerning the alleged illegal storage of chemical drums. However, Australian Prime Minister John Howard dismissed such protests as 'unpatriotic' and 'un-Australian'.

Hosting a hallmark event is regarded as central in the rapid transformation of a city. Nauright (2004) argues that over the last 30 years, hallmark events such as the Olympic Games and the FIFA World Cup have had a much more important role to play in the process of globalisation as many societies attempt to develop 'event-driven economies'. Those countries that have the resources to spend on elite programmes can develop a stronger profile through international sporting successes and hosting hallmark events. A central element in the ability to attract such hallmark events is the ability to present a positive image of the host country or city to the outside world. In order to be seen as supporting the broad liberal values of the Olympic Movement, for example, host cities attempt to give the world an outward show of a community united by the celebration of sport, culture and the environment. Therefore, national or city identities have to be reinvented or 'imagineered' and re-packaged to fit an imagined vision of local culture for global consumption, in particular: 'Ethnicity has become significant in event marketing and destination branding, with bid and organising committees increasingly seeking to harness previously excluded groups when promoting events' (Nauright, 2004: 1328).

Paraschak (2000) argues that native Canadian peoples were presented in a 'pre-historical' state in the opening ceremonies for the Canadian Olympic and Commonwealth Games held between 1976 and 1994. Similarly, Coetzee (1995) argues that the history of black South Africans was reconstructed for the Rugby

World Cup: '[in] the South African RWC case, history was not written out, but rather a history was written in ... [with the] promotion of imagined, partial and fictional representations of local identities and histories' (Nauright, 2004: 1328).

The quality of the environment is also important in the construction of a city's image. This form of urban entrepreneurialism was rooted in New Right ideas of self-help, individualism and public–private partnership. Postmodern cities are more about image and the consumption of signs and tokens of esteem than material things. However, this process of postmodernisation is never ideologically neutral as it always involves the transformation of space and the removal of undesirable elements, including people. Some research emphasises the long-term benefits of hosting the Olympics (French and Disher, 1997; Hall, 1987; Kang, 1988; Ritchie and Aitken, 1984; Robin, 1988; Walle, 1996). In contrast, potential negative impacts of hosting the Games are also well investigated (Darcy and Veal, 1994; Hiller, 1990; Leiper, 1997; Mount and Leroux, 1994; Spilling, 1998).

Kasimati (2003) argues that the impact of new money on the local/regional/national economy from hosting a hallmark event such as the Olympic Games can be broken down into three central elements:

1. the direct effect: money spent by outside visitors on things such as accommodation, food and transportation
2. the indirect effect: the subsequent effects of the injected money within the economy
3. the induced effect: the proportion of household income then re-spent in other businesses in the economy. (Kasimati, 2003: 434)

However, the economic benefits are often difficult to measure, especially in the case of Beijing, where as Wei and Yu (2006) explain, the Chinese government has a long-term goal to promote Beijing as a global city, of which the hosting of the Olympics was one of a number of strategies including: an open door policy to encourage foreign investment, the construction of the Central Business District, the development of Zhongguancun Science Park (China's 'Silicon Valley'), as well as the successful bid to host the 2008 Olympic Games. Wei and Yu (2006) argue that foreign trade has become an important source of economic growth, and that this is used by the Chinese government as an indicator of Beijing's assimilation into the global economy. Beijing's gross export value accounted for 27.7 per cent of China's GDP in 1996, and increased to 40 per cent in 2000 and 32.6 per cent in 2002. Exports are central to sustaining China's industrial growth. The city is much more integrated with the global economy by successfully attracting foreign direct investment, regional headquarters and representative offices of multinational companies and foreign political and cultural institutions. In 1992, Beijing introduced its Master Plan, a central element of which was the development of a central business district, a multi-functional business district that would be the centre of China's financial, trade and cultural relationship with the world.

A second element of the plan was the expansion of Beijing's Zhongguancun Science Park:

> By the end of 2002, a group of high-tech firms emerged, such as the Fangzhen Group Inc. (based at Beijing University), Legend Group Inc. (from the Institute of Computation at the Chinese Academy of Sciences), Tsinghua Ziguang Co. (Tsinghua University) [and] Tsinghua Tongfang Co. (Tsinghua University). (Wei and Yu, 2006: 389)

By 2002, Wei and Yu (2006) claim that there were over 8200 registered high-tech enterprises, including 1000 which were the world's high-tech leaders based at Zhongguancun.

London 2012

At the time of writing, London is looking forward to generating a 'sustainable legacy' from hosting the 2012 Olympic Games. Shortly after winning the bid to host the Games, the UK government passed the London Olympic Games and Paralympic Games Act 2006. This piece of legislation aims to protect the commercial interests of the Games by preventing any unauthorised use of association with the 2012 Games, including:

- the Olympic symbol
- the Paralympic symbol
- the London 2012 logo
- the words 'London 2012'
- the words 'Olympic', 'Olympiad', 'Olympian' (and their plurals)
- the words 'Paralympic', 'Paralympiad', 'Paralympian' (and their plurals)
- the Olympic motto: 'Citius Altius Fortius'/'Faster Higher Stronger'
- the Paralympic motto: 'Spirit in Motion'
- the Paralympics GB logo
- the Team GB logo
- the British Olympic Association logo
- the website www.London2012.com (and various derivatives).

One of the reasons why the London 2012 Organising Committee is so keen on strict control over images and words associated with the Olympics is to prevent 'guerrilla marketing', where a non-event sponsor produces adverts that draw upon the event for financial gain. In 1996, the summer Olympics were held in Atlanta, and Reebok was an official sponsor of the games. However Nike ran a series of adverts using the image of sprinter Michael Johnson to associate their products with the event. Atlanta is also the home of Coca Cola and Brown et al. (2000) estimated that Coca Cola spent over $500 million in preventing rival Pepsi from advertising in the same manner. How is London organising the 2012 games? The overseeing of the project and strategic coordination is in the hands of the Olympic Board, a group that initially comprised Ken Livingstone (then

Mayor of London), Chair Sebastian Coe (former athlete and Chair of the London 2012 Organising Committee), Tessa Jowell (government minister) and Colin Moynihan (former Conservative Minister for Sport, former Olympic athlete and BOA chairman). The delivery of new sporting venues such as the newly built Olympic Park and other infrastructure is in the hands of the Olympic Delivery Authority (ODA). The funding of the games is in the hands of the ODA, except for the funding of the transport infrastructure that is in the hands of the UK government. There is £2.375bn of public funding, initially earmarked for infrastructure, other than transport funding, made up of:

- £1.5bn from the National Lottery, including £750m from new Lottery games
- £625m from London Council Tax
- £250m from the London Development Agency. (Source: www.London 2012.com)

The event itself will be run by the London 2012 Organising Committee that expects to have an operational budget of around £2bn drawn from the private sector, a share of the IOC's broadcasting revenue, the IOC's TOP sponsorship programme and ticket sales.

Owen (2005) argues that ex-post studies of the Games have consistently found no evidence of the optimistic, positive economic benefits of hosting the Games. Bid documents often contain seriously flawed economic assumptions that falsely predict huge economic benefits – for example, treating costs as benefits, ignoring opportunity costs, calculating benefits on the basis of gross spending rather than net spending and assuming that the multiplier effect (the economic benefit of spending money that they have earned from the event) is greater than it is.

Kesenne (1999) outlines very clearly the concept of 'opportunity cost'. The argument is that even though a hallmark event may create net economic benefits for a region, the true cost of the event should only be judged in terms of what the event yields in higher net benefits from an alternative project.

As in the case of the London 2012 bid, building a large stadium is central to many hallmark events and the cost of this building work is often seen as an investment in the local economy. However, if the area is already experiencing full employment, the local builders will have to reject other projects to build the stadium. The net impact of the project is then minimal. In the case of Atlanta, the Olympic Stadium became the new home of the Atlanta Braves baseball team. This is little more than public subsidy to a private company and adds little to a legacy of providing future athletes with state-of-the-art track and field facilities. Owen (2005) argues that in the case of Sydney, four years after the Olympic Games: 'the arena that housed the gymnastics and basketball is in receivership' and he goes on to quote the *Sydney Morning Herald*, saying: 'the State government has been propping up other uneconomic venues since the Olympics to the amount of about $46 million a year' (p. 11).

Porter (1999), in his study of the economic impact of hosting the Super Bowl, similarly found 'no measurable impact on spending associated with the event. The projected spending and spillover benefits of regional impact models never materialize' (p. 61).

Porter (1999) explains that the influx of the spectator population is limited to the number of hotel rooms available. In the short term, prices for the available rooms rise, however in cities that already have high occupancy rates for their hotel rooms, hallmark events have little net effect and net spending in the area does not increase. Bid documents and other economic predictions often ignore this impact on other local, non-hallmark event tourism. Owen (2005) argues that hotel occupancy rates in the City of Atlanta fell from 72.9 per cent in 1995 to 68 per cent in 1996 and many hotels and restaurants reported a drop in their normal tourist sales volume. Owen concludes that hallmark events often crowd-out the demand side.

Matheson and Baade (2003) found that the economic impact of the Olympics is temporary and should be viewed as a one-time change rather than a 'steady-state' change. They conducted an ex-post study of the economic impact of the Olympics on the City of Atlanta and found that: 'the City of Atlanta and the State of Georgia spent $1.58 billion to create 24,742 full- or part-time jobs which averages out to $63,860 per job created' (Matheson and Baade, 2003: 28–9). In addition, they also found that: 'only 31 percent of the ACOG expenditures were in areas that could reasonably be expected to provide a measurable legacy' (p. 30). Moreover, Persky et al. (2004) estimate that for every dollar in wages earned by a person in such a newly created job, fifty cents of economic benefit go into the local economy.

Matheson and Baade (2003) argue that the impact of hosting hallmark events is worse for developing countries because there is a much greater cost for providing world-class infrastructure and sporting venues from limited resources.

Brown et al. (2000) calculated that only three Olympic Games have generated a profit:

- Salt Lake City (2002) – $100 million
- Los Angeles (1984) – $225 million
- Lillehammer (1994) – $40–$50 million.

However, it is important to note that nation states, private sector companies and cities are not simply passive recipients of global consequences. Manchester City Council, for example, used the Olympic bidding process to rebuild public services under the Thatcher–Major Conservative governments, at a time when municipal socialism was under great pressure from policies that imposed greater privatisation and marketisation upon local government in the UK.

Cochrane et al. (1996) evaluate the impact of the two Manchester Olympic bids within the context of the city council's attempt to maintain service provision. Cochrane et al. (1996) view the city council strategy as a new form of pragmatism that they call 'competitive localism' – instead of a policy of confrontation with the Conservative government, as adopted by Liverpool City Council and the Greater London Council, Manchester attempted to find new ways of co-existing with the private sector in an effort to use it to seek out new sources of funding for local service provision, including expensive programmes of urban regeneration. The Olympic bids were used as 'a local hegemonic project' to silence critics both inside and outside the Labour Party and were at the centre of the city council's new politics:

> The Olympic bidding process consequently exerts a kind of local hegemonic discipline on urban political actors: it was taken as axiomatic in Manchester that the city's ability to 'deliver' the Games was predicated on the continued strength of its new 'partnership'. (Cochrane et al., 1996: 1328)

The Olympic bid allowed Manchester to construct an image of entrepreneurial activity and private–public partnership that stressed the importance of competitive success – in reality, the public–private partnership successfully campaigned as a grant coalition to direct large sums of public money towards the city. The Manchester strategy was, according to Cochrane et al. (1996), a 'bread through circuses' approach.

Activity: The benefits of London 2012

Read the passage below and write a short paragraph outlining whether you accept or reject the points within the passage:

> There will be a wealth of benefits such as the regeneration of east London, cross-city transport improvements, more training and job opportunities for Londoners and, of course, opportunities for a vast array of London's businesses. The legacy of world-class sporting facilities speaks for itself.
>
> Hosting the Games is already providing a unique and growing opportunity for the city to raise its profile on the global stage and attract inward investment.
>
> The increased profile gives London the chance to showcase its vibrancy, youth and diversity.
>
> It is also an opportunity for businesses large and small to showcase themselves to the world, to find new trading partners and to break into new markets, providing more jobs and prospects for Londoners.
>
> There will be particular benefits for tourism. London is already a popular city to visit, but the Games promise a major boost in terms of both additional holidaymakers and business travellers. (*Source*: www.London2012.com)

The Information Society

The internet has become 'the most important and influential global phenomenon' (Morgan, 2006: 10) and the largest and most successful medium of communication in the world, especially as 'more and more social relationships are meditated by machines' (Lyon, 1988: v). Peter Watts describes the internet as a 'tool among many' (2002: 11) and believes that the internet represents a re-establishment of new ideas of how the world has become one unit, a community, in which people are able to access information about anything they desire. Dick Kaser (2006) suggests that the internet allows individuals to become 'less connected to anything in particular, including the current moment' (Kaser, 2006: 16). In their 'virtual world', people have a tendency to 'normalise abnormal behaviour'. Since the 1990s, the internet has proved to be popular with paedophiles because there was 'little risk of prosecution and lack of law-enforcement scrutiny' (Bryan-Low, 2006: 2), enabling individuals to download images of children. These images were then sold to paedophiles around the world with the help of credit-card companies.

Activity

Question: Do you accept or reject the argument that 'the internet is not transforming society… (but) influencing and changing it' (Watts, 2002: 10)?

According to William J. Martin: 'the information society is an advanced post-industrial society characterised by a high degree of computerisation and large volumes of electronic data transmission, and by an economic profile heavily influenced by the market and employment possibilities of information technology' (Martin, 1988: 37). Martin speculated that an information society would contain:

- increased awareness of the value of information as a resource
- appreciation of the need for widespread computer literacy
- wholesale diffusion of information technologies
- government intervention in support of the key enabling technologies of computing, microelectronics and telecommunications.

Technological developments such as fibre optic cables and microwave and satellite systems allow us to connect the telephone and the television to the home computer and exchange vast amounts of information for business and leisure use.

For Hesmondhalgh (2006a, 2006b), the music industry was the first major sector of cultural production to confront the challenges and opportunities offered by the internet. Jones (2002) argues that the music industry is going through a process of 'disintermediation' in which the barriers between bands and music consumers are breaking down at the expense of recording companies and music shops. Bands can now market directly to their fans without the need for a recording contract. One commentator even suggests that: 'the internet is making people who would never otherwise come across it find music that they like, and then buy it' (McLeod, 2005: 528).

However, various studies, notably that of Condry (2004), found that illegal downloads were often motivated by the perceived greed of recording companies. By 2000, internet users were sharing music files by the use of peer-to-peer

(P2P) networks, the most famous and widely used of which was Napster. P2P networks allow people to exchange or share files that may contain data, such as music, that have been legitimately purchased without breaking copyright. This was of serious concern to the industry because unlike recording vinyl records onto cassettes, digital file sharing provides the consumer with a perfect, high-quality recording. The record companies did manage to close Napster down, although it did re-emerge as a company that operated within the law. However, companies that provided users with the software to exchange files via the internet, such as Grockster, Morpheus and Kaxaa, have proved much more difficult to prosecute.

In contrast to the pessimism that is common in the music press about the impact of the internet, Mann (2000) and Barfe (2003) even go so far as to suggest that the internet may cause the death of the music industry. Hesmondhalgh (2006b) argues that the internet provides the music industry with a range of new opportunities. Digital distribution allows companies to monitor the tastes and preferences of consumers and sell music by subscription for a monthly fee. Yahoo's MusicMatch and Apple's iTunes music store have both achieved significant sales. There is evidence to suggest, claims Hesmondhalgh (2006a), that peer-to-peer networks have become part of the legitimate online music market.

In addition, Hesmondhalgh (2006a) argues that digital sampling (copying from another work to produce a 'derivative' product which generates new meanings not intended in the original recordings) raises a number of issues about the relationship between black musical practice and copyright law.

Digital sampling has changed the debate about musical borrowing and appropriation. Firstly, digital sampling allows the borrowing and appropriation of music to increase because it is significantly easier and of much better quality than it was using old technology such as tape recorders. In addition, it requires very little skill other than a grasp of a few basic programming commands. According to Self (2002), the relationship between digital sampling and copyright law raised new issues about what constitutes creativity. In a print culture, the emphasis is on the ideals of individual autonomy and commodification for profit whilst in a folk culture the emphasis is on communal integration through the sharing of discourse.

However, in his discussion of Moby, Hesmondhalgh (2006b) raises a number of issues about the uneasy relationships between the people who made the original recordings and the creative act of reconstituting these recordings into a new cultural form. The relationship between the sampled and the sampler can be seen as exploitative in that the authors' and performers' creativity of original samples of African-American music and culture are not acknowledged by Moby.

The 'network society's' various cultural and institutional *flows* pass through both rich and poor countries alike in the world. The twentieth-century industrial society was characterised by the social structure of capitalism and statism, organised around relationships of production/consumption and power, with rigidly established personal identities operating within a culture which was itself generally shaped by the industrial society. In contrast, a fundamental feature of social structure in the Information Age is its reliance on networks as the key feature of social organisation.

Castells (1997, 1999) argues that the information society is a network society, characterised by:

- globalisation
- deregulation and privatisation
- the informational paradigm, in which the uses of technology cannot be separated from technology itself
- science and scientific activity, with the possible exception of the development of some military hardware, which is conducted within a shared logic of uncensored networks of interaction and feedback, largely outside of the control of national governments.

No discussion of the internet would be complete without mention of Google.

Google: Larry Page and Sergey Brin

In his history and analysis of Google, David Vise (2005) claims that Google is as important as the invention of the printing press. Whether you agree with this bold statement or not, there is no doubt that Google revolutionised the internet.

What do people search for on the Web?

According to Googlewatch in 2003, 55 billion searches were done on Google. The top three were searching for information on Britney Spears, Harry Potter and the Matrix (David Beckham was at number 5). The top news query was Iraq, followed by Laci Peterson and Kobe Bryant, who were both involved in high-profile celebrity court cases in the USA. Of the top 10 queries, eight were of either sports or entertainment personalities.

On 9 January 1998, Larry Page and Sergey Brin filed a patent for the algorithm PageRank. By 4 September 2001, when the patent was granted, Google was handling over 150 million search queries per day. PageRank allows Google to provide users with more specific search results than any other search engine and in much quicker time. And through the use of sponsored links that are also specifically related to the searches the user is making at the time, Google can make money without having to rely on pop-up adverts that slow down the search and take up a large part of the screen. With sponsored links, companies pay Google an amount of money every time the link is clicked and the sponsored links appear on the right-hand side of the screen triggered by keyword searches, so both the search and the adverts should be relevant to the interests of the user at the time.

PageRank is said by Google to be 'uniquely democratic' in nature by providing each individual page with a value based upon the status of the web page, in a similar manner to the way academic journals are judged in the academic community. Google interprets a link from one page to another in terms of a vote, by page A, for page B. Google is not only concerned with the number of votes or links a web page receives; it also makes a judgement about the page that casts the vote. If a prestigious university has a link to a given site that will count more than an isolated individual, high-quality web pages receive a higher PageRank, which Google takes into account each time a search is conducted. However, as Googlewatch points out: 'a search for Google Watch may show some ads on the right side of the screen for wrist watches. While the technique doesn't work for this example, often it serves its purpose' (*Source*: www.Googlewatch.com).

Also, Googlewatch challenges the claim that the search approach that Google uses is democratic in nature: 'Google's claim that PageRank relies on the uniquely democratic nature of the web' must be seen for what it is, which is pure hype. In a democracy, every person has one vote. In PageRank, rich people get more votes than poor people, or, in web terms, pages with higher PageRank have their votes weighted more than the votes from lower pages' (*Source*: www.Googlewatch.com).

Google is dependent financially on the sponsored links that appear on their web pages. Many of the products that we consume are purchased by the use of a credit card. Credit cards are commonplace today, but they do not have a long history and were only possible because of the application of key elements of the information society to consumerism. Google is a very successful global company that has allowed people to get much greater leisure use from the internet. However, one of the most significant developments within the information society is the credit card. The credit card has revolutionised consumption on a global scale.

Credit Cards

In *The Philosophy of Money* (1900), Simmel investigates the social meaning of money: how money is used as a symbol, the effects of money on individuals and the wider society. Money has become an objectified and impersonal measure of value that generates impersonal and rational connections between people. Person-to-person relationships have become institutionalised and strangers become familiar, because we can read the monetary value of their possessions. Individuals are liberated from traditional ascribed identities imposed by families and close-knit communities, giving greater individual freedom and choice over our style of living. On the other side, however, when we judge all people on the basis of monetary value, we lose the ability to 'trust', leading to feelings of estrangement from others, feelings of fragmentation and uncertainty in our identity construction. Simmel refers to this as a blasé attitude towards 'the other' that develops when we come to see other people as a resource for making money. Hence, greed, extravagance and cynicism come to dominate our relationships with others. Simmel saw the significance of the individual declining as money transactions became an increasingly important part of society.

George Ritzer (1995) is interested in the role of the credit card in shaping the consumption decisions of Americans and draws upon the work of Simmel to explain the impact and significance of the rise of the credit card. For Ritzer, the credit card increases the intensity of the effect of money that Simmel had outlined. The credit card emerged in the decade following 1945 and was a key element in the post-war economic boom. 'The credit card was a kind of "grease" facilitating the development and expansion of many other things' (Ritzer, 1995: 32). Ritzer claims that the credit card:

- is American in origin – only American Express retains the name of its country of origin
- is a symbol of American values
- 'communicates the value Americans place on mastery, especially over others and over their environment' (Ritzer, 1995: 28 on MasterCard)
- has become the preferred mode of payment in suburban malls, service stations, motels and amusement parks.

Ritzer lists the advantages of credit cards – they:

- increase our spending power
- save us money – take advantage of sales
- are convenient – they can be used via phone, mail or the internet
- are global
- allow us to make purchases when our incomes are low
- provide a statement of expenditure
- provide itemised invoices for tax purposes
- provide receipts which help in disputes
- allow payments to be made over time
- are safer than carrying cash.

'The credit card, like the fast food restaurant, is not only a part of this process of rationalization but it is also a significant force in the development and spread of rationalization' (Ritzer, 1995: 134).

Ritzer goes on to argue that the credit card has rationalised the consumer loan business, where:

- it includes car loans and home equity loans
- the same technology is used
- the same scoring system is used in decision making
- telephone banking is similar to the drive-through
- bank work gets deskilled.

Ritzer applies the four dimensions of McDonaldisation to the credit-card industry. Firstly, credit-card companies are highly rational and their products are based upon the notion of calculability, with a clear emphasis on 'quantity': 'Credit card debt allowed tends to lessen people's interest in the quality of things that they can acquire while running up that debt' (Ritzer, 1995: 138). Scoring systems help credit-card companies decide whether to increase credit limits. Credit-card companies not only use scoring systems to make a decision on the customer's ability to pay their bills, but also to decide which customers generate the most profit. Ritzer also claims that credit cards emphasise efficiency and predictability:

- Credit cards are an efficient method of obtaining, granting and expending loans.
- Credits cards enhance the efficiency of shopping.
- Credit cards enhance the speed of the transaction with the time gap reduced.
- Credit cards have made the process of obtaining a loan predictable.
- Human interaction between the customer and staff is reduced.
- Before credit cards, people spent more slowly.

Whereever and whenever possible, credit-card companies would prefer to use 'non-human for human technology', for example in the authorisation of new cards, however, in the same fashion that the fast-food industry has dehumanised places to eat and work, the credit card industry is also highly dehumanised. People generally interact with non-human technologies that produce such things as bills and overdue notices. As in the case of the fast-food industry, credit cards also generate similar forms of 'irrationality of rationality'. Ritzer discusses examples, such as the ways in which credit-card companies:

- tend to discriminate against married women
- tend to discriminate against people who in the past have paid with cash.

However, on the important issue of the position of credit card use within a discussion of agency and structure, Ritzer is not so clear. On the one hand, he argues that some people may overspend on their credit cards because of a medical reason, and here he cites depression, compulsion and addiction (1995: 69). Ritzer also states that: 'individual consumers certainly bear some responsibility for their credit card indebtedness' (1995: 69). On the other hand, he argues that credit-card companies are responsible for: 'fostering rampant consumerism... Credit card firms urge people to go deeply into debt, and make it easy for them to do so' (1995: 69).

Robert Manning: The Development of the Credit-Card Industry

In his study of the role of consumer credit in shaping the consumption decisions of Americans, Robert Manning (2001) found that the credit-card industry's jargon for its customer categories includes:

- 'revolvers' – they roll credit-card balances over month to month, never paying in full
- 'deadbeats' – they pay their balances off in full every month
- 'rate surfers' or 'gamers' – they shift usage between credit cards based upon interest rates.

Unlike almost any other sector of the economy, the credit-card industry is not interested in customers who pay their bill on time. Manning argues that because there is no legal limit on the amount of interest or fees that can be charged to customers, credit cards have become the most profitable sector of the banking industry in the United States. Manning estimates that the credit-card sector made more than $30 billion in profits in 2003, with MBNA's profits being one-and-a-half times that of McDonald's in 2003.

In 1951, Diners Club issued the first credit card (invented by Diners Club founder Frank McNamara) to 200 customers who used it to settle their bills at 27 selected restaurants in New York. The concept became popular with travelling salesmen and, by the end 1951, 20,000 people were using the Diners Club credit card, making the company a profit of $60,000.

However, it was only after what Manning describes as the revolution in consumer financial services in the 1970s, with the deregulation of depression-era banking regulations, that the credit-card industry developed.

The 1933 McFadden Act limited national banks from crossing state boundaries and competing with state-chartered banks. The McFadden Act, together with state usury laws and interstate banking restrictions, limited the growth of the credit-card industry. However, in 1978 came the US Supreme Court decision in Marquette National Bank of Minneapolis *v*. First of Omaha Service Corporation. The Marquette Bank decision allowed a nationally chartered bank to charge the highest interest rate permitted by its 'home' state and export these rates to its out-of-state credit-card clients. Therefore, where the bank is chartered became irrelevant. Therefore, if the state of South Dakota had a 25 per cent ceiling, banks could charge 25 per cent, even to a loan on the other side of the country.

Manning (2001) argues that the credit card brought about a change in the way people think about debt, with a shift from *instalment* to *revolving loans*. From the point of view of the credit-card company, the best customers will never repay their high-interest balances. Unlike the traditional instalment lending system used by banks, whereby an individual applies for a personal loan and pays back the sum in instalments over a fixed period of time, with credit-card debt, the most economically disadvantaged customers are never in a position to pay off their balance in full.

According to Manning (2001), this is essentially an arrangement whereby people with the least amount of money not only generate the greatest amount of profit for the company but also subsidise the low cost of credit to the convenience user who is in a position to pay off their balance every month: 'These largely unprofitable accounts (depending on monthly charge volume and rebate/reward programs) increased substantially in the last decade, from 29 percent in 1991 to 37 percent in 1996 and then peaking at 43 percent in 1999' (Manning, 2001: 26).

According to Manning (2004), in 2003, less than 40 per cent of credit-card users paid off their balances in full and the cost of credit-card debt was disproportionately carried by middle-income and working-class families. In the United States, the average credit-card debt for three out of five 'revolver' credit-card users was $10,000 in 1998 and $12,000 in 2002. This is in addition to the $1 trillion in other outstanding debt such as non-mortgage consumer instalment debts, notably store cards, lease contracts (cars) and loans from financial institutions such as pawnshops and 'payday lenders'.

Karen Rowlingson, in the 19th British Social Attitudes Survey (2003), found that most credit cards are used by people in their 30s and 40s, especially if they have children. While there are some people who overspend, the main reason for default was found to be loss of income, often through small business failure. There are a number of credit-card holders who default simply because they misunderstand the system of payment, or are just disorganised. There is no evidence that credit-card companies were issuing cards to people who could not afford to use them. Customers who default were often surprised by the relatively sympathetic approach adopted by the credit-card company.

Activity

Read the passage below and answer the question that follows:

The trouble with anecdote-driven studies – and what makes them distinct from journalism – is that we get only one side of the tale. The teller is always presented as an upright, honest worker with a heart of gold, victimized by callous and unfair employers and other authority figures who never get to offer a rebuttal. It's not particularly difficult, in some cases, to wonder if some of these individuals aren't at least partly responsible for many of their own problems.

This is especially true of *Credit Card Nation*, which asks for our sympathy, for instance, in the case of a college kid who compounded his debt problems with a spring break trip to London, because begging off the trip would have embarrassed him before his cosmopolitan pals.
(Review, *Washington Post*, 4 March 2001)

Question: What is the central critical point in the review of Manning's book? There can be little doubt that without the credit card, consumption would take a very different form.

Naomi Klein: *No Logo: Beating the Brand Bullies* (2000)

According to Giddens (1998), we live in a post-scarcity society in which the basic physical necessities that maintain life are available to all of us. In these circumstances, nearly everyone spends their surplus money and time on cultural goods. On the one hand, we might expect that the movement towards a post-scarcity society would generate new forms of democratisation in everyday life. However, Jean Baudrillard (1988) explains:

> On the contrary, it appears that the *constraint of a single referent only acts to exacerbate the desire for discrimination*. Within the very framework of this homogeneous system, we can observe the unfolding of an always renewed obsession with hierarchy and distinction. With the barriers of morality, of stereotypes, and of language collapse, new barriers and new exclusions are erected in the field of objects: a new morality of class, or caste, can now invest itself in the most material and most undeniable of things. (p. 20)

Globalisation has also brought with it greater levels of protest about the impact of global processes on the construction of everyday life and the destruction of local cultures. O'Dair (2000) investigates the cultural significance of consumption and argues that: 'inequality is not only a matter of class defined in terms of one's relationship to production but also a matter of status, of prestige, defined largely in terms of one's relationship to consumption, that is, in terms of one's lifestyle or culture' (p. 337).

Consumption provides the space for status differentiation to manifest itself. For the new poor, it is not simply a lack of money that negatively affects their class position, but their inability performatively to make a legitimate claim for status; in other words, they have bad taste.

Until the early 1970s, logos on clothes were generally hidden, while some small designer emblems were found on golf wear and tennis wear. However, by the 1990s, logos had grown in size – essentially, logos transformed the clothing. Clothing has become an empty carrier for brand names. In the 1990s, Nike, Polo and Tommy Hilfiger not only branded their own products but also 'the outside culture as well – by sponsoring cultural events' (Klein, 2000: 28). Much more than traditional corporate sponsorship because of deregulation and privatisation, schools, broadcasters, museums, etc. make up the shortfall in their funding by attracting sponsorship from branded products. For Klein, this change in the nature of sponsorship seriously challenges the independence of an institution. Klein gives the example of American teen drama *Dawson's Creek* which was launched in 1998. All the characters in the programme wore J. Crew clothes and the set looked like a J. Crew catalogue. In addition, the characters had lines such as 'you look as if you have come off a J. Crew catalogue' and, in 1999, the cast appeared on the front cover of the J. Crew catalogue.

Klein's best selling book *No Logo* is divided into four parts:

- Part One – 'No Space' examines the influence of marketing on culture and education.
- Part Two – 'No Choice' looks at the impact of mergers, predatory franchising and corporate censorship on consumer choice.
- Part Three – 'No Jobs' is about the changing nature of employment, the emergence of McJobs and outsourcing.
- Part Four – 'No Logo' is about the emergence of activism against global capitalism.

She argues that global capitalism is undermining the 'three social pillars of employment, civil liberties and civic space' (Klein, 2000: xxi). In addition, she argues that the growth of global capitalism in the 1980s was built upon one idea: 'that successful corporations must primarily produce brands, as opposed to products' (p. 3). Nike, Microsoft, Tommy Hilfiger and Intel do not primarily produce 'things' but 'images' of their brands. Products are mass-produced and are 'virtually indistinguishable from one another', so 'competitive branding became a necessity...within a context of manufactured sameness, image-based differences had to be manufactured along with the product' (p. 6); for example, IBM does not sell computers – it sells 'business solutions'.

For Klein, the global marketplace is a product of 'accelerated deregulation' (p. 114). She cites a paper by Theodore Levitt, 'The globalization of markets', (1983) saying that multinational companies should not 'bow to local habit or taste'. Klein assumes that the notion of Culture Industry is a fact and claims that American corporations are 'homogenising' global culture, by the use of such phrases as: 'American cultural imperialism' and a 'cultural Chernobyl'.

> Savvy ad agencies have all moved away from the idea that they are flogging a product made by someone else, and have come to think of themselves instead as brand factories, hammering out what is of true value: the idea, the lifestyle, the attitude. Brand builders are the new primary producers in our so-called knowledge economy. (Klein, 2000: 195–6)

Klein quotes Phil Knight, the founder of Nike, saying that production is a 'marginal chore' – not the core business (2000: 197).

Cola: A Global Branded Product

According to Groves et al. (2003), during the Second World War, Coca Cola had an exclusive contract to provide cola to servicemen and, as such, Coca Cola was carried around the world. Similarly Cadbury-Schweppes provided drinks such as tonic water during British colonial expansion. Hence, today, cola drinks have the highest level of product loyalty of any type of product and were one of the first products to globalise their appeal. The Coca Cola and Pepsi logos are known around the world. However, cola is not a basic or staple food item and has little nutritional value, so marketing strategies are used to create a need. Groves et al. (2003) argue that the adoption of a product within a culture depends upon how the product is placed and presented in relation to wider cultural values. Coca Cola, in particular, makes use of sport tourism strategies to enhance the image of a destination and promote high-status events. The Winter Olympics, for example, attracted $US 850 million of sponsorship from multinational companies. Pepsi, in contrast, has traditionally opted for personal endorsement from people in the global entertainment industry, such as Michael Jackson, to promote their product. Groves et al. (2003) suggest that Australia and South Africa are amongst the easiest cultures in which products can gain acceptance, whereas France, Germany and Japan are amongst the most difficult to gain acceptance. The difficulty of acceptance for a product is associated with the attitudes of the people within the culture and the political institutions. Trade agreements, such as those established by the European Union and the North American Free Trade Area, help to depoliticise the process of globalisation, standardise tariffs and thereby provide a degree of security. Pricing strategies can encourage undecided consumers to try the product. Also, the image of the product can be manipulated to have a broader appeal to the culture. Sport is a useful vehicle for this because it generates strong feelings in the hearts and minds of supporters and, ideally, from the point of view of the company offering sponsorship, supporters come to associate the product with the feeling state.

Groves et al. (2003) identify the differing strategies for the three main cola companies:

- Coca Cola is described as the most culturally sensitive of the three, and opt for a sports-sponsorship approach.
- Pepsi Cola adopts what Groves et al. (2003) refer to as a political/engineering approach, with high-level advertising and connections with popular entertainment.
- Cadbury-Schweppes has an approach whereby they develop associations with companies already in the market, such as acquiring Dr Pepper, 7 Up and A&W Root Beer.

José Bové and the Anti-globalisation Movement

José Bové (2002) is one of the most widely recognised members of the anti-globalisation protest movement in the world today. In the early years of the twenty-first century, he acted as a spokesperson for the anti-globalisation protest at the meeting of the World Trade Organisation in Seattle and elsewhere. He first came to world attention in 1999, after the Organisation of the Confédération Paysanne (a farmers' confederation) was involved in dismantling a partly built McDonald's in the French town of Millau. This symbolic action against McDonald's was primarily a stance against the centralisation and genetic manipulation of food production, but was widely interpreted as anti-American and protectionist French food snobbery, and simply a response to a tariff placed on French cheese (including Roquefort) by the United States because the French had refused to allow hormone treated beef to be imported from the USA. For Bové, the protest was a form of natural justice to strike back at McDonald's as a symbol of malbouffe (bad food). After the action, McDonalds' filed a complaint and Bové and four others were placed in jail.

Bové saw the protest as being essentially part of an anti-globalisation movement and was at pains to state that attacking McDonald's should not be seen as anti-American. Rather, Bové sees the struggle as being against 'free trade global capitalism'. According to Naomi Klein, José Bové is one of the most courageous, natural, honest voices left in a world where the rest are tarnished by compromise, a global campaigner for the rights of the individual against the corporation, for the small farmer against big business and state coercion.

His ongoing critique of capitalism is based on his life experience of working in a local agricultural community. His approach is to focus on issues of concern to local communities and then to examine these in relation to wider global forces. By taking direct action, he is able to focus on the powers of the ordinary people in challenging the forces of technology and global capitalism. The heart of his approach is to identify popular issues and to expose the contradictions in the relationship between human and technological development.

Bové's key ideas:

- technology as stripping meaning from life
- the primacy of popular protest – in the form of direct action
- alternative institutions for world trading
- a critique of 'Malbouffe'.

Conclusion

This chapter has looked at a number of theories of cultural and economic globalisation and applied them to various areas of leisure participation, including the consumption of major global hallmark events like the Olympic Games. We looked at why publicly funded games fell out of fashion and how cities use a successful and unsuccessful bid to enhance the status of a city and city image, and increase employment and income. However, the suggestion that hosting a hallmark event such as the Olympic Games will always impact favourably on the local, regional and national economy should not be accepted without question. The British government has taken what is considered to be the necessary legal steps to prevent global companies attempting to use the London 2012 Games to unofficially further their commercial ambitions. However, without official commercial partners, the Games would be unable to open. Owen (2005) argues that in the case of Sydney, four years after the Olympic Games, there is still a cost to be paid by local residents and Brown et al. (2000) calculated that only three Olympic Games have generated a profit.

The chapter also looked at the impact of the application of the PC to the telephone that gave rise to the information society and how this allowed the development of the modern credit-card industry that has revolutionised consumption on a global scale. For Ritzer, the credit card increases the intensity of the effect of money that Simmel had outlined. Although Ritzer claims that the credit card has many advantages over using cash, before credit cards, people spent more slowly. Ritzer applies the four dimensions of McDonaldisation to the credit-card industry. Scoring systems help credit-card companies decide whether to increase credit limits. Ritzer also claims that credit cards emphasise efficiency and predictability.

References

Barfe, L. (2003) *Where Have all the Good Times Gone? The Rise and Fall of the Music Industry*. London: Atlantic Books.

Baudrillard, J. (1988) *Selected Writings*, ed. Mark Poster. Stanford: Stanford University Press.

Bové, J. (2002) *The World is Not For Sale – Farmers Against Junk Food* (with François Dufour). London: Verso.

Brown, G., Jago, L., March, R. and Woodside, A. (2000) 'Monitoring the tourism impacts of the Sydney 2000 Olympics', *Event Management*, 6 (4): 231–46.

Bryan-Low, C. (2006) 'Nokia aims to distribute content with deal for digital-music firm', *Wall Street Journal*, 9 August: 2.

Burton, R. (2003) 'Olympic Games host city marketing: an exploration of expectations and outcomes', *Sport Marketing Quarterly*, 12 (1): 37–47.

Castells, M. (1997) *The Power of Identity*. Oxford: Blackwell.

Castells, M. (1999) 'Flows, networks, and identities: a critical theory of the informational society', in P. McLaren, *Critical Education in the New Information Age*. Lanham, MD: Rowman and Littlefield.

Chalkley, B. and Essex, S. (1999) 'Urban development through hosting international events: a history of the Olympic Games', *Planning Perspectives*, 14 (4): 369–94.

Cochrane, A., Peck, J. and Tickell, A. (1996) 'Manchester plays games: exploring the local politics of globalization,' *Urban Studies*, 33 (8): 1319–36.

Coetzee, J. (1995) 'Retrospect: the World Cup of Rugby', *Southern African Review of Books*. Available at www.uni-ulm.de/ ~ rturrell/antho4html/CoetzeeJ.html.

Condry, I. (2004) 'Cultures of music piracy: an ethnographic comparison of the US and Japan', *International Journal of Cultural Studies,* 7: 343–63.

Darcy, S. and Veal, A.J. (1994) 'The Sydney 2000 Olympic Games: the story so far', *Australian Journal of Leisure and Recreation*, 4 (1): 5–14.

French, S.P. and Disher, M.E. (1997) 'Atlanta and the Olympics: a one-year retrospective', *Journal of the American Planning Association*, 63 (3): 379–92.

Ganti, T. (2004) *Bollywood: A Guidebook to Popular Hindi Cinema*. London: Routledge.

Garwood, I. (2006) 'The songless Bollywood film', *South Asian Popular Culture*, 4 (2): 169–83.

Giddens, A. (1990) *The Consequences of Modernity*. Cambridge: Polity/Blackwell.

Giddens, A. (1998) *The Third Way and the Renewal of Social Democracy*. Cambridge: Polity Press.

Groves, D., Obenour, W. and Lengfelder, J. (2003) 'Colas and globalization: models for sports and event management', *Journal of Sport Tourism*, 8 (4): 320–34.

Hall, C.M. (1987) 'The effects of hallmark events on cities', *Journal of Travel Research*, 26 (2): 44–5.

Hesmondhalgh, D. (2006a) 'Digitalisation, copyright and the music industries', in P. Golding and G. Murdock (eds), *Unpacking Digital Dynamics: Participation, Control and Exclusion*. New York: Hampton Press.

Hesmondhalgh, D. (2006b) 'Digital sampling and cultural inequality', *Social and Legal Studies*, 15 (1): 1–15.

Hiller, H.H. (1990) 'The urban transformation of a landmark event: the 1988 Calgary Winter Olympics', *Urban Affairs Quarterly*, 26 (1): 118–37.

Jones, S. (2002) 'Music that moves: popular music distribution and network technologies', *Cultural Studies*, 16 (2): 213–32.

Kang, H.B. (1988) 'Accelerating the future-state: the urban impact of hosting the 1988 Seoul Olympic Games', in *Hosting the Olympics: the Long-term Impact – Conference Report*. Seoul: East Asian Architecture and Planning Program, MIT and Graduate School of Environmental Studies, Seoul National University. pp. 17–32.

Kaser, D. (2006) 'Breaking all the (editorial) rules', *Information Today*, 23 (8): 16.

Kasimati, E. (2003) 'Economic aspects and the Summer Olympics: a review of related research', *International Journal of Tourism Research*, 5: 433–44.

Kaur, R. (2002) 'Viewing the West through Bollywood: a celluloid Occident in the making', *Contemporary South Asia,* 11 (2): 199–209.

Kesenne, S. (1999) 'Miscalculations and misinterpretations in economic impact analysis', in C. Jeanrenaud (ed.), *The Economic Impact of Sports Events*. Neuchâtel, Switzerland: Centre International d'Etude du Sport. pp. 29–39.

Klein, N. (2000) *No Logo: Beating the Brand Bullies*. London: HarperCollins.

Leiper, N. (1997) 'A town like Elis? The Olympics: the impact on tourism in Sydney', in Proceedings of the Australian Tourism and Hospitality Research Conference, Sydney, 13–19 February.

Levitt, T. (1983) 'The globalization of markets', *Harvard Business Review*, May–June: 92–102.

Lyon, D. (1988) *The Information Society*. Cambridge: Polity.

McLeod, K. (2005) 'MP3s are killing home taping: the rise of internet distribution and its challenge to major record label music monopoly', *Popular Music and Society*, 28 (4): 521–31.

Mann, C.C. (2000) 'The heavenly jukebox', *Atlantic Monthly*, 286 (3): 39–73.

Manning, R. (2001) *Credit Card Nation: America's Dangerous Addiction to Consumer Credit*. New York: Basic Books.

Manning, R. (2004) *Give Yourself Credit: The Power of Plastic in the Credit Card Nation*. San Francisco: Alta Mira Press.

Martin, M.J. (1988) *The Information Society*. London: Routledge.

Matheson, V. and Baade, R. (2003) 'Mega-sporting events in developing nations: playing the way to prosperity?', Working Papers 0404, College of the Holy Cross, Department of Economics. Available at: http://ideas.repec.org/p/hcx/wpaper/0404.html

Milton-Smith, J. (2002) 'Ethics, the Olympics and the search for global values', *Journal of Business Ethics*, 35: 131–42.

Morgan, J.M. (2006) 'The Toyota way in services: the case of lean product development', *The Academy of Management Perspectives*, 20 (2): 5–20.

Mount, J. and Leroux, C. (1994) 'Assessing the effects of a mega-event: a retrospective study of the impact of the Olympic Games on the Calgary business', *Festival Management and Event Tourism*, 2 (1): 15–23.

Nauright, J. (2004) 'Global games: culture, political economy and sport in the globalised world of the 21st century', *Third World Quarterly*, 25 (7): 1325–36.

Nayar, S.J. (2005) 'Dis-orientalizing Bollywood: incorporating Indian popular cinema into a survey film course', *New Review of Film and Television Studies*, 3 (1): 59–74.

O'Dair, S. (2000) 'Beyond necessity: the consumption of class, the production of status, and the persistence of inequality', *New Literary History*, 31 (2): 337–54.

Owen, J.G. (2005) 'Estimating the cost and benefit of hosting the Olympic Games: what can Beijing expect from its 2008 Games?', *The Industrial Geographer*, 3 (1): 1–18.

Paraschak, V. (2000) 'Aboriginal inclusiveness in Canadian sporting culture: an image without substance?', in F. van der Merwe (ed.), *Sport as Symbol, Symbol in Sport*. Aachen. pp. 247–56.

Persky, J., Felsentein, D. and Carlson, V. (2004) *What are Jobs Worth?* Kalamazoo, MI: Employment research, Upjohn Institute.

Porter, P. (1999) 'Mega sports events as municipal investments: a critique of impact analysis', in J. Fizel, E. Gustafson and L. Hadley (eds), *Sports Economics: Current Research*. New York: Praeger Press.

Preuss, H. (2003) 'Olympics', in B. Hoolihan (ed.), *Sport and Society*. London: Sage.

Ritchie, J.R.B. and Aitken, E.C. (1984) 'Assessing the impacts of the 1988 Olympic Winter Games: the research program and initial results', *Journal of Travel Research*, 22 (3): 17–25.

Ritzer, G. (1995) *Expressing America: A Critique of the Global Credit Card Society*. Newbury Park, CA: Pine Forge Press.

Robertson, R. (1994) *Globalization*. London: Sage.

Robin, D. (1988) 'Hosting the Olympic Games: longterm benefits to sport and culture', in *Hosting the Olympics: the Long-term Impact* – Conference Report. Seoul: East Asian Architecture and Planning Program, MIT and Graduate School of Environmental Studies, Seoul National University. pp. 245–64.

Rowlingson, K. (2003) 'From cradle to grave: social security over the lifecycle' in J. Millar (ed.), *Understanding Social Security*. Bristol: The Policy Press.

Self, H. (2002) 'Digital sampling: a cultural perspective', *UCLA Entertainment Law Review*, 9: 347–59.

Simmel, G. (1900) *The Philosophy of Money*. London: Routledge.

Sklair, L. (1993) *Sociology of the Global System*. London: Sage.

Spilling, O.R. (1998) 'Beyond intermezzo? On the longterm industrial impacts of mega-events: the case of Lillehammer 1994', *Festival Management and Event Tourism*, 5: 101–22.

Srinivas, L. (2002) 'The active audience: spectatorship, social relations and the experience of cinema in India', *Media, Culture and Society*, 24: 155–73.

Stadtler, F. (2005) 'Cultural connections: *Lagaan* and its audience responses', *Third World Quarterly*, 26 (3): 517–24.

Vise, D. (2005) *Google*. Basingstoke: Macmillan.

Waitt, G. (1999) 'Playing games with Sydney: marketing Sydney for the 2000 Olympics', *Urban Studies*, 36 (7): 1055–77.

Walle, A.H. (1996) 'Festivals and mega-events: varying roles and responsibilities', *Festival Management and Event Tourism*, 3 (3): 115–20.

Watts, P. (2002) 'Cyber schmyber: or how I learned to stop worrying and love the net', in D. Cummings (ed.), *The Internet: Brave New World*. London: Hodder and Stoughton.

Wei, Y. and Yu, D. (2006) 'State policy and the globalization of Beijing: emerging themes', *Habitat International*, 30: 377–95.

11

GLOBALISATION AND LEISURE – MCDISNEYISATION AND POST-TOURISM

This chapter develops a number of the themes introduced in the previous chapter. We look at:

- the Disney leisure experience
- the notion of the Tourism gaze
- Ritzer's argument about the way in which Disney has controlled and mass-produced the tourist experience
- the impact of the War on Terror on the leisure sector – we attempt to unpick the reasons why terrorists appear to be more likely to select leisure venues as targets.

Supercalifragilisticexpialidocious: The Disney Experience

The Walt Disney Corporation is one of the most commercially successful media companies in the world and in 2004 had a turnover of $30.8 billion.

As Dick Hebdige (2003) points out, Disney is a large global company comprising:

- five motion picture studios
- two major publishing houses
- eight theme parks (with three more coming in the near future)
- 466 franchised retail outlets
- a major TV network (ABC)
- 21 radio and 20 TV stations
- a global chain of hotels and family restaurants
- multimedia companies, sports franchises and insurance companies
- two 'edutainment' universities (one affiliated with Disneyland, the other with Disney World)

- Celebration – a town in Florida
- a proposed $2 billion 'creative campus' in Anaheim

(*Source:* adapted from Hebdige, 2003: 151).

The Disney company has had a bad press at the hands of academics. For example, in his book *The Disney Versions*, Richard Schickel (1968) argues that Walt Disney was anti-Semitic, racist, rigidly conservative and chauvinistic. Disney's conceptualisation of women was that they were by nature characterised by emotionalism, domesticity, maternal concerns, beauty and romance. In addition, not only was Walt Disney staunchly anti-communist but in his testimony to the Un-American Activities hearings in 1947, he named people whom he considered to be communists. In terms of his creativity, Schickel argues that the magic, mystery and individuality contained within the stories that Disney adapted for film were consistently destroyed. Not only were stories 'sanitised', by blanketing often complex narratives with layers of fantasy, but original work was put into the Disney machine to produce a distorted version of it.

Later critics have applied similar critiques to the Disney approach to urban planning – Disneyfication of the metropolis as seen in the town of Celebration in Florida, where it is suggested that the social order is controlled by an all-powerful organisation supported by Disney's own police force. Brenda Ayers (2003) describes Disney as an Ideological State Apparatus that contains a 'pure corporate id'. Disney ideology 'is fraught with colonizing messages that continue to advocate white, Anglo-Saxon, middle class, Protestant, heterosexual, patriarchal American superiority' (Ayres, 2003: 195). The film *Aladdin*, for example, vilifies Islamic law and promotes a jingoistic and childish understanding of Islam. *The Little Mermaid* typifies a 'male defined fantasy of female biological perfection' (Ayers, 2003: 55).

Janet Wasko (2001), in her influential book *Understanding Disney: The Manufacture of Fantasy*, argues that there is a *problematisation* of authenticity and reality in the minds of children because of the representations of social divisions within Disney films. Children often make use of popular stories, myths and fairy tales to make sense of themselves and their surroundings: 'these films inspire at least as much cultural authority and legitimacy for teaching specific roles, values and ideals than more traditional sites of learning such as public schools, religious institutions and the family' (Giroux, 1995: 25). Such themes include:

- Gender – investigated in Arcus (1989); Beres (1999); Beveridge (1996); Tseelon (1995); Wiersma (2001)
- Cultural, racial and ethnic analysis – in Gooding-Williams (1995); Martin-Rodriguez (2000); Palmer (2000)
- Representations of mental illness – in Beveridge (1996).

These arguments are reinforced by Mark Pinsky (2004) who argues that Disney products contain a consistent set of moral values based upon Western, Judeo-Christian faith and religious principles, including:

- good triumphing over evil
- faith as the key to success
- hard work as a virtue.

In addition, Dundes' (2001) analysis of *Pocahontas* argues that although the film was an improvement on *Snow White*, who concerned herself solely with domestic duties and later passively waited to be rescued, Pocahontas puts the needs of her community before her own personal desires, notably her desire for a romance with John Smith. In a similar fashion, Ariel in *The Little Mermaid* also ignores paternal disapproval, and shows both determination and perseverance in marrying Eric, the prince. In addition, Ariel demonstrates a strong sense of adventure by embarking on a new life as a human. However, in the last analysis, Dundes (2001) argues that Disney representations of women have not changed but rather have become disguised. However, not all the representations of women are so easy to interpret – in her analysis of *Beauty and the Beast*, Allison Craven (2002) demonstrates that Belle/Beauty is always in control, declining suitors and taming the beast. A notable moment in the film is when Belle/Beauty commands the Beast to 'step into the light'. However, Craven also points out that Belle/Beauty is caught up in discourses of bestiality that place Belle/Beauty's femininity within a 'horror fantasy' genre. Amy M. Davis (2005) presents evidence to show that there are strong female characters, such as Mary Poppins and Winifred Banks who is involved in the suffragette movement.

Belinda Stott's (2004) analysis of Cinderella also raises issues about female assertiveness. On the surface, Cinderella is presented as an appealing, attractive, female victim. However, when her father dies, her stepmother and her 'mean and ugly daughters' stop pretending to like her and 'her only friends are the birds and the mice' (Disney, 1996: 6). However, is Cinderella a passive victim? asks Stott when she has the forethought to conceal the other glass slipper and to produce it at the most opportune moment.

In terms of systematic research findings, Tanner et al. (2003) conducted a thematic analysis of families and couples within 26 Disney films and four themes emerged:

- Family relationships have a strong priority.
- Families are diverse, but diversity is often simplified.
- Fathers are elevated and mothers are marginalised.
- Couple relationships are created by love at first sight, and are easily maintained.

The film *Mary Poppins* raises a number of important issues about Edwardian England. Finance capitalism, gender and imperialism indicate the contradictions of capitalism, such as class and inequality, but not directly the issue of class struggle – these are central themes in the film.

Much of the joy that Mary brings to the Banks' children comes from her disregard for class boundaries. The *jolly holiday with Mary* reveals the potential of a world in which human relations and needs matter more than the accumulation of capital. Similarly, when the children visit Mr Banks in the bank, Mr Dawes explains to Michael Banks how he can make a profit without any effort and turn his two pence into a pound by the use of a song 'While stand the banks of England, England stands':

> If you invest your two pence wisely in the bank, safe and sound,
> Soon that two pence safely invested in the bank will become a pound.
> And you'll achieve that sense of conquest as your affluence expands.
> You'll be part of railways through Africa, dams across the Nile, ...
> majestic self-advertising canals, plantations of ripening tea.

But Michael is more interested in the use-value of his money, in the satisfaction it can bring. Michael Banks wants to give his two pence to an old woman selling pigeon feed on the steps of St Paul's, an image that Mary had revealed in the snow-storm model of St Paul's. In the scenes that follow, customers overhear Mr Dawes refusing to return Michael's two pence which causes a run on the bank and the invasion of the family home by chimney sweeps, followed by Mr Banks' dismissal from the bank.

Activity

The Disney universe is the near universality and global reach of the company, its products and its recognised values which include:

- escape and fantasy
- innocence
- romance and happiness
- sexual stereotypes
- individualism
- the reinvention of folk tales.

Question: do you accept or reject Rojek's (1993) point that Disney culture is a moral order imbued by an image of leisure as 'rational recreation'?

Harvey and Zibell (2000) attempt to make sense of the Disney leisure experience by drawing upon the ideas of Csikszentmihalyi and Baudrillard. For Csikszentmihalyi, for a person to be happy, they must have a consciousness that is ordered and we experience optimal experience or *flow* when there is a balance between the challenges of the environment and our capabilities to deal with that environment. Consciousness is always partly environmentally framed. The Walt Disney resorts are highly controlled 'synthetic sites'. Harvey and Zibell (2000) describe synthetic sites as completely manufactured places that endeavour to generate the optimal experience for the visitor by attempting to regulate their consciousness in a technologically concentrated, thematised and physical environment.

The environment is manufactured in such a way that the guests have no direct contact with the world outside of the resort. This allows people to be guided by the large amount of vivid information and story lines put in place by the Disney imagineers. Such sites draw upon the simulacra and we experience them as being more real than real, better than the real thing, and what Baudrillard referred to as 'hyperreality'. In the last analysis, the experience can make the guest a passive consumer of the experience as the imagineers provide the appropriate emotional response for the experiences provided.

Baudrillard

For Baudrillard, the postmodern self has a confusion of categories. What were once fixed categories such as 'value' can no longer be measured against clear and objective goals. Postmodern *society* is founded upon proliferation. What we have is a situation of great uncertainty. The postmodern self attempts to escape from uncertainty by having a greater degree of dependency on information and communication systems, however with the collapse of codes in the political, sexual and genetic spheres, and the constant exposure on all sides to images and information, this merely exacerbates the feelings of uncertainty.

The Disneyisation of Society

Alan Bryman (1999, 2004) describes Disneyisation as the 'process by which the principles of the Disney theme parks are coming to dominate more and more sectors of American society' (Bryman, 1999: 26). Bryman points out that 'Disneyisation is associated with a global process of cultural homogenisation, the "culture-ideology of consumption"' (Bryman, 2004: 158). Disneyisation takes the form of a *systemscape*: 'the flow of contexts for the production and display of goods and services' (p. 161) and 'what Disneyisation describes is a set of strategies for "manipulating" consumers into parting company with their money' (p. 160).

Bryman (1999, 2004) looks at Disneyisation in terms of four trends: theming; differentiation of consumption and hybrid consumption; merchandising; and emotional and performative labour.

Theming

The theme provides the visitor with a narrative that gives the various rides, attractions and shopping experiences a more coherent feel. Disneyland, for example, was conceived as a celebration of America's past and a challenge to the future. Bryman quotes the Disney prospectus to support his argument:

'Rather than presenting a random collection of roller coasters, merry-go-rounds and Ferris wheels in a carnival atmosphere, these parks are divided into distinct areas called 'lands' in which a selected theme ... is presented through architecture, landscaping ... costume, music, live entertainment, attraction, merchandise and food and beverage. Within a particular land, intrusion and distractions from the theme are minimized so that the visitor becomes immersed in its atmosphere' (Disney prospectus, p. 13). For Bryman, this makes the Disney resort more attractive for adult visitors and increases the likelihood of them purchasing merchandise.

Dedifferentiation of consumption (1999)/Hybrid consumption (2004)

Both of these concepts are concerned with a general trend whereby the forms of consumption associated with different institutional spheres become interlocked with each other and increasingly difficult to distinguish, most importantly: theme park = shopping.

In the 2004 second edition of the book, Bryman explains that hybrid consumption is concerned with forms of consumption connected with different institutional spheres that become interlocked, so that the shopping experience is incorporated into the leisure experience.

One of the central purposes of hybrid consumption is to make people stay longer within the park. This technique has been used by other leisure providers. Bryman gives the example of the Museum of Modern Art which has sales of $1750 per square foot, compared to $250 for most malls and $600 for the Mall of America.

Merchandising

Merchandising is a central element in the 'commodification of culture', stressing the central idea that consumption is a means of seeking pleasure and fulfilling desire. The Disney resorts are designed to maximise opportunities for purchasing. Disney did not invent merchandising, however Bryman argues that they were the first to realise its immense profitability. Cartoon characters in Disney films were designed with cuteness in mind. Mickey Mouse, for example, had no rodent-like features. Bryman explains that: 'The key principle behind merchandising is a simple one of extracting further revenue from an image that has already attracted people' (Bryman, 2004: 80).

Emotional labour (1999)/Performative labour (2004)

Emotional labour, as we have seen in previous chapters, is the control over the behaviour of the theme park employees, notably the Disney language and Disney smile which give the impression to customers that the employee is having fun. Smiling and a helpful demeanour may help to encourage spending. As Bryman goes on to explain, the Disney University was opened in order to train employees in the techniques needed to encourage the visitor to feel at ease and to spend their money. In the 2004 edition of the book, Bryman prefers to use the term 'performative labour', rather than 'emotional labour'. The assumption here is that work at Disney becomes like a theatrical performance and the workplace like a stage. Customer care, within a Total Quality Management approach, is still central to the process. Performative labour is always important when attempting to 'brand' a service because it becomes a distinguishing factor when the service has little else to distinguish it. In addition, the imposition of performative labour is assumed to enhance the employee's organisational commitment.

Bryman (2004) explains that the first guideline for guest service is: make eye contact and smile. However, echoing the critique in previous chapters, Bryman suggests that with performative labour, the Disney employees' sense of an authentic self is undermined and that performative labour can damage the employee psychologically. In addition, Bryman points out that Disney also has notions of aesthetic labour – a strict appearance and grooming policy. The Disney employees do not have control over how they wish to wear their hair or make-up whilst at work.

Control and surveillance are not only imposed upon the employees, but guests at the Disney parks are also subjected to control. Bryman (2004) identifies six levels of control:

- Control over visitors' behaviour – visitors must not be barefoot or 'inappropriately attired', such as not wearing a top. Signs direct visitors around the park, where a camcorder or photography are permissible. There is also surveillance by security guards.
- Control of the theme park experience – interaction between employees and guests is scripted and if possible audio-animated animals and actors will be used rather than employees. Also, audience participation is restricted, because guests are unpredictable and may damage the impression that Disney is attempting to create.
- Control over the imagination – Bryman takes up the argument that Disney presents simplified and pre-digested versions of classic literature.
- Control as a motif – one motif Bryman discusses is the attraction 'Living with the Land' sponsored by Nestle, formerly called 'Listen to the Land' sponsored by Kraft Foods. The attraction is based upon the assumption that nature is something that needs to be controlled by technology.
- Control over the immediate environment – this involves attempts to control approaches to the parks and control over the height of buildings etc., so that they cannot be seen from inside the parks.
- Control over its destiny – the attempt to anticipate potential threats to the company and deal with them at the earliest possible opportunity.

McDisneyisation and Post-tourism

George Ritzer and Allan Lisker (1997) argue that Disney has become the model for the tourist industry. Large sections of the leisure industry embrace the four principles of McDonaldisation that Ritzer developed and apply them to the tourist experience. In 'McDisneyization and post-tourism', they argue, for example, that Disney World is efficient – in that it processes large numbers of people in a rational, predictable and calcubable fashion:

- the pricing structure is clear, with clearly displayed prices for a daily or weekly pass
- signs indicate how long one can expect to wait for a ride or attraction
- the shopping mall is designed to get people to spend more.

Ritzer and Lisker (1997) go on to argue that every theme park is now in the process of becoming McDisneyised as are cruise ships and tourist attractions. McDonaldisation runs counter to the Post-Fordist argument, found in the work of Urry (2002), who argues that we have rejected the Fordist conception of the package holiday and that we have moved into a Post-Fordist era of tourism. For Ritzer and Lisker (1997), people want 'their tourist experiences to be about as McDonalized as their day-to-day lives' (Ritzer and Lisker, 1997: 96–113). This means that people have a taste for:

- highly predictable vacations
- highly efficient vacations
- highly calculable vacations
- highly controlled vacations.

McDonaldisation is undermining the fundamental reason for tourism – to experience something new and different. Tourists understand that there is no 'authentic' tourist experience and, as such, people do not need to leave home because the locales to which we journey are themselves now McDonaldised.

Rojek (1993) argues that the post-tourist has three characteristics:

- they accept the commodification of tourism
- they view tourism as an end in itself – not a means to a loftier goal
- they are drawn to spectacular signs.

For Bryman: 'Disney may well have played a prominent role in stimulating the attitude of the post-tourist' (1995: 177). However, it is important not to overemphasise the importance of signs because tourism still has a material aspect.

Activity: Cultural globalisation – a shark's tale

McWorld is an entertainment shopping experience that brings together malls, multiplex movie theatres, theme parks, spectators, sports arenas, fast-food chains (with endless movie tie-ins), and television (with its burgeoning shopping networks) into a vast enterprise that, on the way to maximising its profits, transforms human beings. (Barber, 1995: 97)

In September 2005, the latest Disney resort opened on Lantau Island, Hong Kong. At the two hotels within the resort, sharks fin soup was available to customers. Sharks fin soup is a traditional Chinese delicacy served at important social occasions such as weddings and is seen as a sign of affluence. However, the process by which the fins are harvested is roundly condemned by environmentalists, including WWF, as cruel and the soup is illegal in many Western countries.

Questions: By offering sharks fin soup to customers, Disney is clearly showing that the company is sensitive to local cultures. However, by choosing to withdraw the soup from the menu, is Disney bowing to the pressure of cultural globalisation? What significance does the dispute about sharks fin soup on Disney menus in Hong Kong suggest about Barber's McWorld thesis?

The Tourist Gaze

Tourism has a long history – The Grand Tour: 1600–1800, for example, provided sons of the aristocracy and the gentry with the opportunity to travel for scholastic reasons and was expected to play a key role in the cognitive and perceptual education of the English upper class.

However, before the nineteenth century, very few working-class people had the opportunity to travel. Travel, especially overseas, was a mark of status. Today, however, argues Urry (2002), the mass tourist market aims to provide groups of gullible consumers with opportunities to get pleasure from highly staged inauthentic events. These 'pseudo-events' disregard the culture of the indigenous populations and the 'real' world outside. Over a period of time, tourist entrepreneurs have to produce evermore extravagant displays for the tourists and the display becomes evermore removed from the local people.

Places to visit are chosen to be gazed upon because there is an anticipation – through daydreaming and fantasy – of intense pleasures.

The tourist gaze is constructed through difference; there is no one tourist gaze, no one true experience of the tourist. The tourist gaze involves the notion of 'departure' – a limited breaking with established routines and the practices of everyday life, allowing our senses to engage with a set of stimuli that contrast with the mundane.

Such anticipation is constructed and sustained through a variety of non-tourist practices. Film, TV, literature, magazines, records and videos help to construct the gaze and reinforce it in the mind of the tourist: Frenchness, typical Italian behaviour, exemplary Oriental scenes, typical American thruways, traditional English pubs.

Tourist professionals attempt to develop ever-new objects for the tourist gaze. All tourists have a quest for authenticity, however they are often faced with what Urry terms 'tourist kitche'. Tourist spaces are organised around 'staged authenticity' in which everywhere shows the tourist his own image of what the place should look like, generated within the tourist's origin culture rather than by the cultural offerings of the destination. The cultural experiences offered by tourism are consumed in terms of prior knowledge, expectations, fantasies and mythologies and the exotic and diverse become uniform. A number of these themes are taken up by Alain de Botton (2002) in his book *The Art of Travel*, one of the most interesting books on tourism in recent years.

Alain de Botton: *The Art of Travel*

This popular book is described as a philosophy of travel: departure, motives, landscape, art and return. De Botton opens his book with an account of the Duc des Esseintes, the hero of J.K. Huysmans' nineteenth-century novel, *A Rebours* (1969). The Duc lives in a large villa that he seldom ventures out of, mainly because he cannot stand being reminded of the ugliness and stupidity of his fellow humans. One day, however, while reading Dickens, he is overcome by a desire to visit London, which is surprising because the Duc had never travelled further than the next village. The Duc books a ticket, purchases an umbrella and a bowler hat. On reaching Paris, he goes to an English café and whilst he is waiting for the train to Dieppe, he eats roast beef and stares with pleasure at the English women present. However, shortly before the train is about to depart, the Duc changes his mind – he asks himself what is the point of going to London when he has already been there in his imagination? Surely the real thing can only be a disappointment? So the Duc goes back to his villa with his umbrella and his bowler hat, and never leaves home again.

The Art of Travel is a series of nine essays based upon his personal experience of travel linked to the thoughts of a great thinker from the past to guide the reader through each of the essays: Edward Hopper, Baudelaire, Wordsworth, Van Gogh, Ruskin and Xavier de Maistre, who wrote two books about travelling around his own room one night, in pink and blue pyjamas. Alain de Botton contrasts the anticipation of travel with its reality: airports, landscapes, museums, holiday romances, photographs, exotic carpets and the contents of hotel mini-bars.

De Botton contrasts the reality of travel with the anticipation of arriving at a place. He explains that few things are as exciting as the idea of travelling somewhere else, somewhere far from home, a place with better weather, more interesting customs and inspiring landscapes. The reality of travel hardly ever lives up to our expectations. In reality, our experience of travel can often be disappointing as we experience disorientation, mid-afternoon despair and lethargy before ancient ruins. De Botton explains that the reasons why we experience such feelings of disappointment are rarely explored. We get a great deal of advice on where to travel to, but the important questions of what the point of travel might be, why we should go and how we could be more fulfilled are never really addressed.

Following the advice of John Ruskin, Alain de Botton argues that to get the most of the travel experience, we need to sketch what we see rather than take photographs. Painters can often tell us more about a place than photographers. Ruskin writes about the value of drawing as a way of seeing places, however primitive your technique, and says that he began to appreciate the identity of oak trees after spending an hour drawing one in the Langdale Valley.

Other advice Alain de Botton gives us includes:

- Wherever you go, pretend to yourself that you have never been there before.
- Start by travelling on familiar ground.
- Don't set out to see what other people see.
- Don't be ashamed to go on a bus tour.

The first chapter explores the idea that travel is a metaphor for life: people are often seduced and deceived by the holiday brochure. The central idea is that many things are easier to experience in art and in anticipation than in reality. Reflecting upon his personal experience of travel, De Botton explains that a person may find themselves sitting in a deck chair, on the beach, on a perfect Caribbean morning, reflecting on issues such as the deepness of the ocean or why the sky is so blue. However, when you go on holiday, you have to picture yourself in the photographs that appear in the brochure and the place will change because of your presence. Some places are better in anticipation and you will enjoy them more if you do not visit. In the last analysis, Alain de Botton argues that the pleasure we get from a journey is dependent upon the mindset we have when we travel rather than on the place we travel to.

Leisure and 'The War on Terror'

One factor that has affected the travel plans of many people is the threat of terrorism. In this section, I want to address the question of why tourist attractions, shopping areas, resorts and transport links within or between tourist destinations are much more likely to be targeted by terrorists than other so-called legitimate targets, such as the agencies of social control, notably the armed forces. Is there something distinctive about the leisure experience that makes it such a prime target for terrorists?

The 7/7 London bombers

The motives underpinning the acts of terrorism or martyrdom of suicide bombers are complex. Moreover, terrorists and suicide bombers-to-be are not available to complete questionnaires or agree to be interviewed. I conducted a narrative analysis of the martyr videos of the 7 July London suicide bombers

Mohammad Sidique Khan and Shehzad Tanweer. Both of the videos were accessed on You Tube, but they are additionally available on the websites of Islamic Jihad (www.qudsway.com), Hamas (www.qassam.net or www.palestine-info.info/arabic) and Al-Aqsa Martyrs Brigade (www.fateh.tv and www.katae balaqsa.net).

Narrative is defined by Lieblich (1998) as: 'a discourse, or an example of it, designed to represent a connected succession of happenings' (Lieblich, 1998: 2). Narrative research is study that draws upon narrative materials such as literary works, diaries, oral histories or, as in this case, martyr videos of suicide bombers. The approach is interpretive and involves *dialogical listening*, in which the researcher becomes sensitive to the narrator's voice and meaning. The assumption is that people are storytellers by nature and that their stories provide coherence for their experiences. The central methodological approach is the life story and the assumption that the narrative provides access not only to a person's identity and personality, but to the wider culture. As Lieblich explains: 'People are meaning generating organisms; they construct their identities and self-narratives from building blocks available in their common culture and beyond their individual experience' (Lieblich, 1998: 9).

In this study, I adopted the holistic content approach. I read the accounts given by both Mohammad Sidique Khan and Shehzad Tanweer several times until a pattern emerged. I then attempted to identify the events that have significance for them, including the episodes or issues that seem to disturb them and motivate them to take the actions they did, follow the theme through the text and identify transitions from one theme to another before drawing an inference.

Both Mohammad Sidique Khan and Shehzad Tanweer's videos address the same themes: they think of themselves as soldiers and in war. Both make a division of the world into Muslims and *others*, together with a definition of self that is not British but Muslim (with reference to Muslim people across the globe as 'my people', a transnational Muslim community or umma). Islam is a marker of an imagined global community. This draws on comments from Bin Laden (2001) that stated that civilians in the West are legitimate targets because they vote and pay taxes to support military action against Muslims across the world. The justification for the actions of both Khan and Tanweer is made by reference to *jihad* and the duty of Muslims everywhere to support the oppressed Muslims in Palestine, Afghanistan, Iraq and Chechnya. In addition, because people in the West democratically elect their governments, Khan and Tanweer assume that Western governments act on behalf of the people who elected them. This assumption is used to question the innocence of people in the West and provide the justification for killing innocent people. The dominant theme in both videos is an appeal to all Muslims to be true to their faith and to take action against Britain, the United States and Israel. Vengeance is a holy duty and Muslims who find the culture of the West appealing are tainted and are turning their back on Islam. Finally, both videos contain warnings of more indiscriminate violence against British people in the future unless the political demands of Al-Qaeda are met. The narrative of blame against civilians assumes that dying justifies killing and as such neither Khan nor Tanweer should be classed as a murderer. As Crenshaw (2002) comments: 'The truth of the cause is established by the individual's willingness to sacrifice everything on its behalf' (Crenshaw, 2002: 28). These findings echo the comments of Mohammed Hafez (2006) that a central theme that emerges from the discourse of suicide bombers is:

> the redemptive act of martyrdom. Suicide bombings are not only an opportunity to punish an enemy and fulfil God's command to fight injustice, it is also a privilege and a reward to those most committed to their faith and their values ... the act of martyrdom is seen as an attempt to redeem society of its failure to act righteously. (Hafez, 2006: 176)

The term *suicide* is not used in either video, moreover there is no reference to personal problems or family issues. Rather, the videos are used to justify their actions as a form of martyrdom that is part of a wider military campaign against the foreign policy of Britain, the United States, Israel and the 'Crusader West'.

As Mohammad Sidique Khan explains:

> Our religion is Islam – obedience to the one true God, Allah, and following the footsteps of the final prophet and messenger Muhammad ... This is how our ethical stances are dictated.

> Your democratically elected governments continuously perpetuate atrocities against my people all over the world.

> And your support of them makes you directly responsible, just as I am directly responsible for protecting and avenging my Muslim brothers and sisters.

> Until we feel security, you will be our targets. And until you stop the bombing, gassing, imprisonment and torture of my people we will not stop this fight.

> We are at war and I am a soldier. Now you too will taste the reality of this situation.

Shehzad Tanweer's opening comments in his video are directed to the non-Muslim population of Britain:

> To the non-Muslims of Britain, you may wonder what you have done to deserve this. You are those who have voted in your government, who in turn, and still to this day, continue to oppress our mothers, children, brothers and sisters, from the east to the west, in Palestine, Afghanistan, Iraq, and Chechnya.

Tanweer goes on to explain that:

> What you have witnessed now is only the beginning of a series of attacks that will continue and pick up strengths till you pull your soldiers from Afghanistan and Iraq and stop your financial and military aid to America and Israel.

However, most of Tanweer's comments are directed at Muslims in Britain:

> Oh Muslims of Britain, you, day in and day out on your TV sets, watch and hear about the oppression of the Muslims, from the east to the west. But yet you turn

a blind eye, and carry on with your lives as if you never heard anything, or as if it does not concern you. What is the matter with you that you turn back not to the religion that Allah has chosen for you? You have preferred the *dunya* [concerns about status in relation to possessions rather than spiritual concerns] to Allah …

Oh Muslims of Britain, stand up and be counted. You are those who Allah has honored with Islam, and know that if you turn back from your religion, Allah has no need for you. As Allah, in *Surat Al-Maida*, says: 'Oh you who believe, whoever from amongst you turns back from his religion, Allah will bring a people whom He will love, and they will love Him. Humble towards the believers, stern towards the disbelievers, fighting in the cause of Allah, never fear the blame of the blamers, that is the grace of Allah, which He bestows upon whom He wills, and Allah is All-sufficient for His creatures' needs.

Fight against the disbelievers, for it is but an obligation made on you by Allah …

Oh Muslims of Britain and the world, the *dunya* is just a fleeting enjoyment, and unto Allah will be your return. Obey Allah and His messenger, if you are indeed believers. Fight against the oppressors, the oppressive British regime.

Tanweer ends his video with the comment:

Oh Allah, grant us martyrdom in Your cause, and accept us among the righteous on the day we shall return to You.

The journalistic accounts of 7/7 have tended to look at the personality profile of the bombers and ignore the social and political conditions that may underpin suicide bombing. Such accounts assume that suicide bombers are chaotic and irrational individuals who have motives that are rooted in psychological trauma, or who are victims of paranoia, depression and internal persecution, and engage in suicide bombing to escape highly personal psychological problems. As such, it is assumed that suicide bombers have a limited perception of the risk associated with their actions. Such journalistic accounts provide little understanding of why the occurrence of such attacks is increasing. More importantly, there is nothing in Khan and Tanweer's videos to support this form of psychological reductionism.

What is terrorism?

Terrorism is difficult to define because it takes a variety of different forms and can be motivated by a variety of different reasons.

The US State Department defines terrorism as: 'premeditated, politically motivated violence perpetuated against civilians and unarmed military personnel by subnational groups … usually intended to influence an audience' (Sonmez et al., 1999: 417).

In a series of books and papers, sociologist Ulrich Beck (1999, 2002a, 2002b) has argued that the social sciences are conceptually inadequate to explain the war on terror or the nature of the global threat. Beck (2002a) argues that we live in a 'world risk society' in which the expanding technological advancement of the information society, notably its financial and communication technologies, make global terrorism possible. Beck (2002a) differentiates between three axes of conflict: ecological conflicts, global financial crises and global terrorism, the latter being a conflict that he claims has the ability to: 'flourish with particular virulence under the weak states that define the periphery' (p. 42). Beck goes on to argue that the 'war on terror' will lead to a much greater emphasis placed on the formation of new global institutions and greater global governance. The purpose of the war on terror for Beck is to 'find a way to civilize world risk society' (p. 50). However, for Beck (2002a), the social sciences are not conceptually equipped to explain the nature of global terror or the 'war on terrorism'. The social sciences are rooted in a form of 'methodological nationalism' that assumes the nation state is a 'socio-ontological given' – to better understand the nature of the world, the social sciences must embrace a more transnational and cosmopolitan conceptual framework of the world. In contrast to Beck's opinion, in the (2002a) paper, there is a brief outline of two approaches that can be used to address events post September 11: one rooted in the recent work of Stanley Cohen (2001) which suggests that the war on terror is about the manipulation of news events to hide the true and unpleasant fact that the Bush–Blair administrations were engaged in an attempt to control the world by violent means and the other in the work of Norbert Elias whose work can be used to suggest that the war on terror is part of a more general global process of civilisation.

The motives behind terrorist-related activities are seldom explored in any detail – usually it is assumed that if the organisation is by nature *political, religious* or *single-issue,* such as animal rights-oriented, then this is sufficient to explain the motivation. In this section, I want to address the question of why tourist attractions, shopping areas, resorts and transport links within or between tourist destinations are much more likely to be targeted by terrorists than other so-called legitimate targets such as the agencies of social control, notably the armed forces. Is there something distinctive about the leisure experience that makes it such a prime target for terrorists? In addition, counter-terrorism has traditionally been in the hands of individual nation states and no one organisation has taken responsibility for the safety of people travelling overseas.

Pizam and Smith (2000) conducted a quantitative analysis of major terrorism events from around the world and concluded that terrorist activity did generate a significant decline in revenue in the leisure sector during the period of 1985–98. The negative impact of September 11 on the tourist industry in the United States is well documented (Blake and Sinclair, 2003; Hall, 2002; Pratt, 2003; Sloboda, 2003). However, counter-terrorism efforts, either by the state or by leisure companies, such as increasing the amount of CCTV surveillance or increasing the number of police in tourist locations, can damage the relative freedom that underpins the leisure experience.

According to Essner (2003), terrorists choose to target tourists for several reasons. Firstly, tourists are easy to attack. Trains and buses are predictable – they have timetables that are published and readily available, making public transport an ideal target. Secondly, terrorists often live within the country where the attacks take place and to attack local people is to run the risk of losing local support. Thirdly, targeting international tourists generates a great deal of publicity.

The island of Bali is part of Indonesia, a country where the vast majority of the population is Muslim; however, the majority of the Bali population is Hindu (Soekirno, 2006). Since 1920, Bali has been seen by people in the West as a land of exoticism that Westerners could use as a place to rest. Its image is constructed as something beautiful, innocent, traditional, oriental and exotic. Since October 2002, there have been a number of Islamic-fundamentalist terrorist attacks: 202 people died in a bomb blast in October 2002; on 9 September 2004, the Australian embassy in Jakarta was bombed and several people were killed; and on 1 October 2005, 23 people were killed by three suicide bombers. Why has Bali become a site for terrorist bombings in the name of Islam? From the perspective of the tourist, Bali is a popular tourist destination and an exotic and beautiful island; however, from the perspective of the terrorists, Bali has become an 'illicit place' where non-Islamic practices, such as drinking alcohol and prostitution, are institutionalised.

Activity:

For Rojek (2005):

> There are several reasons why terrorists target public space. To begin with, it symbolizes civil society's commitment to order, progress and companionship. Parks, tourists sights and shopping areas are also locations in which citizens feel free and invulnerable ... By exposing the vulnerability of citizens in locations like these, terrorists hope to propagate a climate of civil distraction and paranoia that destabilizes government and discourages public support for policies of which the terrorists disapprove. (Rojek, 2005: 14)

Public spaces are locations for mobility and freedom. This raises serious issues for the management of public space. Take a look at the list of terrorist incidents below and answer the following question: as leisure managers, how do we protect customers from terrorist attack but maintain traditional liberties?

- 'Bloody Friday' (1972) – 22 bombs kill nine and seriously injure many more, with the 130 targets including railways, hotels, bridges, buses, banks and other places of work
- Birmingham pub bombings (1974) – bombs in two pubs kill 19 people
- Guildford pub bombings (1974) – bombs kill five people and injure 182
- Tower of London bomb (1974)

(Continued)

(Continued)

- Hyde Park bomb and Regent's Park bomb (1983) – the first blast was a large nail bomb hidden in a parked car, which killed three ceremonially uniformed soldiers on horseback instantly, while one soldier died later from the injuries he sustained. Nails and shrapnel injured the large group of tourists watching the parade and seven horses were also killed. Then a bomb hidden within a bandstand in Regent's Park exploded during a performance by the Royal Green Jackets' band of music from *Oliver!* The band were killed and 120 people watching suffered injuries
- Harrods bomb (1983) – a Harrods department store bomb planted by the IRA during the Christmas shopping season kills six people (three of whom were police officers) and wounds 90
- Ebury Bridge Road, London bomb blast (1981) – the bomb kills two people and injures 39
- Pan Am Flight 103 bomb (1988)
- Warrington Shopping Centre bomb (1993) – two IRA bombs at opposite ends of a shopping street in Warrington explode within minutes of each other, and kill two children, Jonathan Ball and Tim Parry
- Arndale shopping centre, Manchester bomb (1996)
- Cairo bomb (1996)
- Luxor bomb (1997)
- Bali disco bomb (2002)
- Killings in Mombasa (2002)
- Sarin gas attack on the Tokyo subway system (1995)
- Madrid railway bomb (2004)
- London tube bombs and Russell Square bus bomb (2005)
- Shooting of a tourist in Jordan (2006)
- Bombings in Turkish holiday resorts (2006)
- World Trade Centre attacks (2001)

Question: Are we safe to travel around the world?

In the contemporary world, terrorism is difficult to define. It is commonly assumed that the objective of terrorism is to *intentionally* damage the 'active trust' of people in conducting their everyday lives. Post September 11, Al-Qaeda has brought about a wholesale reorganisation of the way of life within the United States and Europe. The Bush Administration has launched two major military engagements as part of the 'war on terror':

- Operation Enduring Freedom – the war in Afghanistan
- 'Operation Iraqi Freedom' – the war in Iraq.

In many respects, these operations have questioned our traditional distinctions between 'war' and 'peace', and attack and self-defence have collapsed. When George Bush launched Operation Enduring Freedom, for example, his justification was one of 'self-defence'. The idea of achieving peace through war is not new. However, from the point of view of some, the 'war on terror' can be seen as an attempt by President Bush to assert American domination over the contemporary world by violent means. Bush's foreign policy allows the United States to impose its economic, military and cultural power on the world, whilst presenting these actions as an alliance of reasonable people against an undemocratic, violent and unaccountable minority. The Taliban regime in Afghanistan and Saddam's regime in Iraq may have been driven from power and Al-Qaeda driven even further underground, but both countries remain violent, occupied and politically unstable. Terrorist suspects have been taken to the Guantanamo Bay naval base in Cuba that the United States leases from the Cuban government. The detainees are held under presidential order but are not considered to be prisoners of war and therefore the Geneva Convention does not apply. The detainees are held without criminal charge or any known release date. In addition, there have been a number of well-documented cases of controversial detention practices including humiliation and physical and mental abuse against the detainees. According to Welch (2003, 2006), excuses for measures such as the violation of civil liberties or civil rights are often done by denial. Welch draws upon Stanley Cohen's (2001) concepts of denial and moral panic in relation to the post September 11 concerns about homeland security and terrorism in the United States. Although there was widespread political support for the Patriot Act (2001) and the Homeland Security Act (2002), one reason behind the widespread support for this legislation is that Al-Qaeda has become a folk devil and, Walsh argues, the government-sponsored moral panic about the fear of terrorism is much greater than the reality of personally being affected by a terrorist action. In addition, Welch argues that there are many legal and civil rights concerns about issues such as the profiling of ethnic minorities, detention and government secrecy that become lost within the panic.

The Patriot Act (2001)

The Patriot Act (2001) was developed as anti-terrorism legislation in response to the September 11, 2001 attacks; the Act expands law enforcement's surveillance and investigative powers. The Act provides new and additional search and surveillance powers to law enforcement and intelligence agencies, including the monitoring of phone calls and access to people's Internet Service Provider records. In addition, it provides a new search warrant that allows security services and the police to enter private property without the occupier's knowledge or consent and without notification that such a search was carried out.

The Homeland Security Act (2002)

The Homeland Security Act (2002) created the Department of Homeland Security which has responsibility for all issues in relation to immigration. In addition, there are new powers for the intelligence services to search for data on individuals and groups, which set limits on the data that can be released under the Freedom of Information Act, and provide a revision of the open meeting laws to allow government advisory committees to discuss anti-terror measures and related issues of national security and new powers for government agencies to declare national health emergencies.

Denial and the War on Terror

Operation Iraqi Freedom saw the emergence of *embedding,* where television reporters are attached to coalition military units for onsite reporting of the action. One might view this as an attempt by broadcasters to give a much more objective account of the action as it happens. Embedding also allows the government to use news reports as a central element in their processes of denial. Reporters have to stay behind United States forces' lines – to venture onto the front line would be to run the risk of being shot. Such broadcasts are always from the physical perspective of the American soldier and are constructed within a context of US military protection. The management of news in relation to the war on terror is about the construction of a narrative of fear that allows governments to take actions against its own citizens and foreign nationals that would otherwise be regarded as lacking in legitimacy.

Stanley Cohen's analysis can be used to explain how 'denial' can perpetuate long-term social problems and contribute to a deeper understanding of growing threats to human rights. Cohen (2001) argues that at the beginning of the twenty-first century, there was a much higher degree of 'denial' concerning global atrocities. Cohen argues that we need to ask questions about the 'content of denial', notably who is doing the denying – an individual person or an official on behalf of the state – or is the denial rooted in the culture? Is the denial contemporary or historical in nature? We also need to ask who the 'agent' of denial is: is it the victim, the person responsible for the event or a potential eyewitness? Statements about events in the world may differ from our own interpretation of them for a number of reasons. First, we may be mistaken and the statement might be accurate. Second, the statement might be a lie. Third, an individual may choose to distort or repress the truth or the person's ideas may be manipulated by wider social or cultural forces.

Such denial is to be found at all levels: state, society and the individual. Cohen attempts to explain this increased state of denial by expanding on his well-known conception of 'moral panic'. For Cohen (2001), the process of *knowing* is never obvious and statements of denial are assertions that take a number of different forms:

- literal denial – the event did not happen, which often involves the meaning of the facts being altered
- interpretive denial – the event may have happened, but its meaning is misunderstood
- implicatory denial – the event happened, but its significance is different from the common understanding.

As Hajjar (2004) argues in relation to the ill treatment of the Guantanamo Bay detainees, the United States government acknowledges that ill-treatment has taken place but blames it on 'rotten apples' who have contravened official policies.

A concept that Cohen uses here is the 'denial paradox'. For Cohen, we can only legitimately use the word 'denial' when a person makes a statement such as: 'I did not know', when we believe that the person did know about what it is that they claim not to know. Cohen discusses the vocabulary for perpetrators' denials. Denial can take the form of a denial of 'responsibility', acknowledging that an event did happen but denying the suggested cause. There is also the notion of 'moral indifference' and 'denial of injury', on the grounds that there is no real injury to the 'victim'. There is also 'denial of the victim', in which people condemn the people who are issuing the condemnation, often by arguing the person responsible for the event is really the true victim.

Activity

The first detainees arrived at Guantanamo Bay on 11 January 2002, and were placed initially in *Camp X-Ray* – a collection of outdoor cages on the base. The United States Department of Defence claimed that the holding conditions for the detainees were humane and did conform to the Geneva Convention. However, there have been many claims of mistreatment including a list of 29 issues of concern raised by an International Red Cross team who were allowed to visit the camp in January 2004. United States Secretary of Defense Donald Rumsfeld described Guantanamo Bay in the following terms: 'I would consider Guantanamo Bay, Cuba as the least worst place we could have selected … Its disadvantages … seem to be modest relative to the alternatives' (*Source*: www.ertatcrg.org/cri6224/guantanamo_denials.htm).

Question: Is it possible to apply Cohen's (2001) points about denial to these comments by Donald Rumsfeld?

Norbert Elias: a global civilising process?

According to Norbert Elias (1939/1978, 1939/1982), in the Middle Ages, with the emergence of words such as the French *civilite*, the English *civility*, the Italian *civilta* and the German *zivilität,* there was a change in the lives of people in the West, and over the course of the Middle Ages, the power of the state as a central authority grew. The state had a monopoly of physical power and placed restrictions upon the use of violence and imposed standards of 'mutual consideration' upon the population. It is possible to apply this work to events surrounding the 'war on terror', and view the actions of the Bush Administration as part of a more general historical or *civilising process*. The difference here is that whereas Elias was concerned with the processes of state formation, we would have to view Elias' ideas within a global context and view the 'war on terror' as part of a global civilisation process. In a similar fashion to Beck's argument, the purpose of the war on terror is to 'find a way to civilize world risk society' (Beck, 2002a: 50). The application of Elias' ideas allows us to understand why the United States is so keen to impose its economic, military and cultural power on the world, and why these actions are presented as an alliance of reasonable people against an undemocratic, violent and unaccountable minority.

From this perspective, the United States, because it has more violent resources than any nation state or terrorist group, is waging the war on terror in an attempt to impose *passification* on large sections of the world's population.

The War in Iraq

Bush's war on terror is not an ill-disguised attempt to assert American domination. It's solely to spread freedom for the sake of all non-evil humans. Most importantly, us, because after all – he swore to uphold and protect the great United States constitution. That includes killing those who want to kill us before they have the chance!!!! Pretty good leadership. (*Source*: answers.google.com/answers/threadview?id=507444)

The strategy underpinning Operation Iraqi Freedom makes it clear that the purpose of fighting the war in Iraq is to: '*Build* stable, pluralistic, and effective national institutions that can protect the interests of all Iraqis, and facilitate Iraq's full integration into the international community' (The Whitehouse, 2005).

Question: Is it possible to view the war on terror as part of a United States-led mission to impose civilisation upon the world?

Theories of Terrorism

A significant number of the most dangerous terrorist groups are motivated by religious concerns (Hoffman, 1993; Kraemer, 2004; Stitt, 2003). According to Juergensmeyer (2001), destruction or self-destruction is a central motivating factor underpinning such terrorism. Religion-based terrorists, such as Islamic fundamentalists, believe that their targets are evil and as such God not only approves of their action, but also demands such action. From this perspective, terrorism is assumed to be pathological in nature and related to mental illness. Terrorists are delusional and have severe personality disorders caused by such factors as negative childhood experiences that damage their sense of self and generate aggressive forms of rebellion. Other causal factors include inadequate parenting and a range of syndromes. David Long (1990), a former assistant director of the US State Department's Office of Counter Terrorism, argues that terrorists are attracted to groups with charismatic leaders and enjoy risk-taking because they suffer from low self-esteem (Margolin, 1977; Merari, 1990; Post, 1984, 1990; Ross, 1996, 1999; Stern, 1999).

An alternative to the explanation that all terrorists are pathological, religiously motivated and insane is provided by rational choice theory. The suggestion is that some groups find terrorism useful. Terrorists are rational utility maximisers who are attempting to generate maximum terror for minimum cost. Nyatepe-Coo (2004) draws upon rational choice theory to view terrorist motivations in terms of *psychic* costs and benefits. Individuals will make use of terror after rationally considering the costs and benefits of such actions against the cost of possible punishment or failure. Crenshaw (1998) builds upon Gurr's (1970) notion of the copycat effect. Groups engage in terror to publicise a cause – this is what Crenshaw (1998) refers to as the *contagion effect*.

For Nassar (2004), terrorism is socially constructed within the processes of globalisation. Globalisation is rooted in an unequal exchange, and the structural constraints that prevent the poorest countries in the world from participating as equal partners in global networks can generate feelings of resentment and anger. Western capitalists own most hotels, airlines and resort complexes and it is they, rather than the local population, who collect most of the profits made. Although international travel has a long history, with nineteenth century industrialism generating the disposable income to create a market for travel and tourism, as we moved forward from the early years of the twentieth century, increasing numbers of people from the advanced industrial societies had sufficient income to engage in greater periods of foreign travel to further away places, in greater luxury. Butcher (2005) suggests that 74 million people are directly employed in tourism and 200 million people in tourism-related activities. However, Go and Jenkins (1997) quote one influential Caribbean politician as saying that 'tourism has turned us into a nation of barkeepers and waitresses' (Go and Jenkins, 1997: 54). Moreover, the pay and conditions of service of many of these people are poor. In addition, tourists consume disproportionate amounts of food and water compared to the local population and engage in activities that have little regard for the environment, culture or social structure of the countries they visit. Jones (2006) suggests that one third of the world's coastline has been damaged or destroyed in order to build accommodation or services for tourists. The impact of globalisation upon the lives of people in the less-developed world is well documented on the internet and for many researchers, the growth of the internet has been central to the growth of global terrorism.

In contrast, for political theorist John Gray, '9/11 spelled the end of globalisation'. Gray argues that the end of the Soviet era was welcomed in the West as an opportunity to create a global society based upon a model of Western modernity. The assumption was that the Soviet Union had collapsed because globalisation was an irresistible historical trend that reflected what we all wanted. However, the events of September 11 clearly demonstrated that there is a dark side to globalisation. We can no longer accept the liberal position of convergence where all societies are moving towards a similar set of Western values, attitudes and beliefs. For Gray, it is the rejection of modernity that lies behind the terrorist attacks in America (Gray, 2007).

Activity

The villagers of Sinquerim (Goa) were denied piped water and have to rely on a well. Water is piped through the village to the nearby Taj Holiday Village and Fort Aguada complex. Golf courses consume vast tracts of land with 350 new golf courses built every year. The golf courses demand large volumes of water for irrigation; the pesticide, fertiliser, and herbicide run-off effects local water courses bringing damage to fisheries, polluting drinking water.

In Thailand the health of many local people has been damaged through eating fish poisoned by pesticide run-off from golf courses.

In Bali local people were forced from their land to make way for a golf course and hotel complex by shutting off the water that irrigated their fields.

Not everywhere are local people compliant. In Vietnam when Daewoo (one of the biggest exploiters in Vietnam) planned a £93 million golf course near Hanoi local villagers set up barricades and refused to budge. They were offered a paltry £125 per family to move.

Sexploitation is a growing sector of the tourist trade, with many tour companies offering special package tours to the best sex spots … Many children are forced to work as prostitutes in brothels. In Sri Lanka a survey showed that 86% of children had their first sexual experience with a foreign tourist, for the majority of the children they were aged between 12 and 13 years old at the time.

(*Source*: 'Globalisation – tourism the new imperialism', at home.clara. net/ heureka/gaia/global03.htm)

Question: Would you accept or reject the argument that terrorism is neither pathological nor an aberration, but a product of global inequality? Give the reasons for your answer.

O'Connor (1994) has developed a neo-functionalist conception of terrorism, in which terrorism is rooted within the action frame of reference. The balance of Parsonian pattern variables, in particular the core values of achievement, competition and individualism, are related to the structural subsystems (economy, polity, religion, law) of any social system. If individuals are unable to perform the role that fulfils their expectations, then one of five possible outcomes are possible. In the last analysis, O'Connor (1994) looks to individual psychological states as the cause of terrorism, and lists these as:

- the frustration–aggression hypothesis
- the relative deprivation hypothesis
- the negative identity hypothesis
- the narcissistic rage hypothesis
- the moral disengagement hypothesis.

World Trade Centre site: a global heritage site

In the months and years following September 11, the World Trade Centre site has been in a continual process of becoming a world heritage site. Greenspan (2005) argues that the people who visit the site have an important role to play in its construction as a world heritage site through the way in which they make use of the space. Visitors become part of an 'imagined community' that is not confined by any national borders. Greenspan (2005) identified a number of 'patterns of memorialision', in which visitors placed flags, poems and teddy bears on the walls and put other home-made memorial objects on the fences surrounding the site that defined ground zero as a heritage site. These areas became the primary viewing and memorial areas later recognised by the city council, UNESCO and the World Heritage Fund.

Conclusion

In this chapter, we have attempted to look at a number of large global leisure providers, notably Disney. Harvey and Zibell (2000) attempt to make sense of the Disney leisure experience by drawing upon the ideas of Csikszentmihalyi and Baudrillard. The Walt Disney resorts are highly controlled 'synthetic sites'. Bryman points out that 'Disneyization is associated with a global process of cultural homogenisation, the "culture-ideology of consumption"' (Bryman, 2004: 158). Control and surveillance are not only imposed upon the employees, but guests at the Disney parks are also subjected to control. The Disney resorts are designed to maximise opportunities for purchasing and they do this by the effective use of emotional/performative labour.

Ritzer and Lisker (1997) argue that people want highly controlled vacations and, because they deliver this, Disney has become the model for the tourist industry. In 'McDisneyization and post-tourism', they argue, for example, that Disney World is efficient – in that it processes large numbers of people in a rational, predictable and calculable fashion. Disney has brought together the shopping mall, designed to get people to spend more, with theme rides to create a leisure/shopping experience.

In this chapter, we also returned to the notion of the tourist gaze. The tourist gaze is constructed through difference; there is no one tourist gaze, no one true experience of the tourist. Tourist professionals attempt to develop ever-new objects for the tourist gaze. However, Rojek (1993) argues that the post-tourist accepts the commodification of tourism and indeed post-tourists are drawn to spectacular signs.

One of the major threats facing the leisure sector is the global threat of terrorism. According to Essner (2003), terrorists choose to target tourists for several reasons. Firstly, tourists are easy to attack. Secondly, terrorists often live within the country where the attacks take place and to attack local people is to run the risk of losing local support. Thirdly, targeting international tourists does generate a great deal of publicity.

The social sciences may not be conceptually equipped to fully explain the nature of global terror or the 'war on terrorism' in the way that Beck (2002a) suggests, however that is not to say that social science provides no opportunities for the discussion of such topical issues. In this section, we have contrasted two very different approaches to making sense of the war on terror: Stan Cohen's work on denial looks at events post 9/11 in terms of moral panic, ideology and/or the management of news, authority and political legitimacy. In contrast, Norbert Elias' ideas can be used to discuss the nature of the war on terror in relation to a number of more broad processes of social change, state formation and control of violence.

References

Arcus, D. (1989) 'Vulnerability and eye color in Disney cartoon characters', in K.J.S. Reznick (ed.), *Perspectives on Behavioral Inhibition*. Chicago, IL: University of Chicago Press. pp. 291–7.

Ayers, B. (ed.) (2003) *The Emperor's Old Groove: Decolonizing Disney's Magic Kingdom*. New York: Peter Lang Publishing.

Barber, B. (1995) *Jihad vs McWorld*. New York: Times Books.

Beck, U. (1999) *World Risk Society*. Cambridge: Polity Press.

Beck, U. (2002a) 'The terrorist threat', *Theory, Culture & Society*, 19 (4): 34–55.

Beck, U. (2002b) 'The cosmopolitan society and its enemies', Special Issue on Cosmopolism, *Theory, Culture & Society*, 19 (1–2): 17–44.

Beres, L. (1999) 'Beauty and the beast: the romanticization of abuse in popular culture', *European Journal of Cultural Studies*, 2: 191–207.

Beveridge, A. (1996) 'Images of madness in the films of Walt Disney', *Psychiatric Bulletin*, 20 (10): 618–20.

Bin Laden, U. (2001) 'Dawn: an interview with Usama bin Laden' (10 November 2001), in B. Rubin and J.C. Rubin (eds) *Anti-American Terrorism and the Middle East*. New York: Oxford University Press.

Blake, A. and Sinclair, M.T. (2003) 'Tourism crisis management: responding to September 11', *Annals of Tourism Research*, 30 (4): 813–32.

Bryman, A. (1995) *Disney and His Worlds*. London: Routledge.

Bryman, A. (1999) *The Disneyization of Society*. London: Sage.

Bryman, A. (2004) *The Disneyization of Society*, 2nd edn. London: Sage.

Butcher, J. (2005) 'Sun, sea and saving the world: travel snobs have turned holidaymaking into a moral dilemma.' Article in Spiked online magazine, Spiked essays section at www.spiked-online.com

Cohen, S. (2001) *States of Denial: Knowing about Atrocities and Suffering of Others*. Cambridge: Polity Press.

Craven, A. (2002) 'Beauty and the Belles: Discourses of feminism and femininity in Disneyland', *The European Journal of Women's Studies*, 9 (2): 123–42.

Crenshaw, M. (1998) 'The logic of terrorism: terrorist behavior as a product of strategic choice', in W. Reich (ed.), *Origins of Terrorism: Psychologies, Ideologies, Theologies, States of Mind*. New York: Woodrow Wilson Center Press.

Crenshaw, M. (2002) 'Suicide terrorism in comparative perspective', in *Countering Suicide Terrorism*, T.I.P.I.F. Counter-Terrorism. Herzliya: Anti-Defamation League.

Davis, A.M. (2005) *Good Girls and Wicked Witches: Women in Disney's Feature Animation*. Eastleigh: John Libbey & Co Ltd.

de Botton, A. (2002) *The Art of Travel*. London: Penguin Books.

Disney (1996) *Cinderella*. Paignton: Ladybird.

Dundes, L. (2001) 'Disney's modern heroine Pocahontas: revealing age-old gender stereotypes and role discontinuity under a façade of liberation', *Social Science Journal*, 38 (3): 353–65.

Elias, N. (1939/1978) *The Civilizing Process: The History of Manners*. Trans. Edmund Jephcott. Oxford: Basil Blackwell.

Elias, N. (1939/1982) *The Civilizing Process: State Formation and Civilization*. Trans. Edmund Jephcott. Oxford: Basil Blackwell.

Essner, J. (2003) 'Terrorism's impact on tourism: what the industry may learn from Egypt's struggle with *al-Gama'a al-Islamiya*.' Available at: sand.miis.edu/research/student_research/Essner_Tourist%20Terrorism.pdf

Giroux, H.A. (1995) 'The politics of insurgent multiculturalism in the era of the Los Angeles uprising', in B. Kanpol and P. McLaren (eds), *Critical Multiculturalism – Uncommon Voices in a Common Struggle*. Westport, CT: Bergin & Garvin.

Go, F.M. and Jenkins, C.L. (1997) *Tourism and Economic Development in Asia and Australasia*. London: Pinter.

Gooding-Williams, R. (1995) 'Comments on Anthony Appiah's *In my Father's House*'. Paper presented at the American Philosophical Association, Central Division Meetings. Chicago, April.

Gray, J. (2007) *Black Mass: Apocalyptic Religion and the Death of Utopia*. London: Allen Lane.

Greenspan, E. (2005) 'A global site of heritage? Constructing spaces of memory at the World Trade Centre site', *International Journal of Heritage Studies*, 11 (5): 371–84.

Gurr, T. (1970) *Why Men Rebel*. Princeton: Princeton University Press.

Hafez, M. (2006) 'Rationality, culture, and structure in the making of suicide bombers: a preliminary theoretical synthesis and illustrative case study', *Studies in Conflict & Terrorism*, 29 (2): 165–85.

Hajjar, L. (2004) 'Torture and the Future', Global and International Studies program, University of California.

Hall, C. (2002) 'Travel safety, terrorism and the media: the significance of the issue-attention cycle', *Current Issues in Tourism*, 5 (5): 458–66.

Harvey, C.W. and Zibell, C. (2000) 'Shrinking selves in synthetic sites: on personhood in a Walt Disney World', *Ethics and Information Technology*, 2: 19–25.

Hebdige, D. (2003) 'Dis-Gnosis: Disney and the re-tooling of knowledge, art, culture, life, etc.', *Cultural Studies*, 17 (2): 150–67.

Hoffman, B. (1993) *Holy Terror*. Santa Monica: RAND.

Huysmans, J.K. (1969) *A Rebours*. New York: Dover.

Jones, C. (2006) 'The Protection of Indigenous Medical Knowledge: Towards the Transformation of Law to Engage Indigenous Spiritual Concerns', PhD thesis, Department of Law, Macquarie University.

Juergensmeyer, M. (2001) *Terror in the Mind of God: The Global Rise of Religious Violence*. Berkeley: University of California Press.

Kraemer, E. (2004) 'A philosopher looks at terrorism', in A. Nyatepe-Coo and D. Zeisler-Vralsted (eds), *Understanding Terrorism: Threats in an Uncertain World*. Upper Saddle River, NJ: Prentice Hall.

Lieblich, A. (1998) *Narrative Research: Reading, Analysis and Interpretation*. Applied Social Research Methods Series, 47. Thousand Oaks, CA: Sage.

Long, D. (1990) *The Anatomy of Terrorism*. New York: Free Press.

Margolin, J. (1977) 'Psychological perspectives in terrorism', in Y. Alexander and S.M. Finger (eds), *Terrorism: Interdisciplinary Perspectives*. New York: John Jay Press.

Martin-Rodriguez, M.M. (2000) 'Hyenas in the pride lands: Latinos/as and immigration in Disney's *The Lion King*', *Aztlan*, 25: 47–66.

Merari, A. (1990) 'The readiness to kill and die: suicidal terrorism in the Middle East', in W. Reich (ed.), *Origins of Terrorism: Psychologies, Ideologies, Theologies and States of Mind*. Cambridge: Cambridge University Press.

Nassar, J. (2004) *Globalization and Terrorism*. Lanham, MD: Rowman and Littlefield.

Nyatepe-Coo, A. (2004) 'Economic implications of terrorism', in A. Nyatepe-Coo and D. Zeisler-Vralsted (eds), *Understanding Terrorism: Threats in an Uncertain World*. Upper Saddle River, NJ: Prentice Hall.

O'Connor, T. (1994) 'A neofunctional model of crime and crime control', in G. Passmore, *Fascism: A Very Short Introduction*. New York: Oxford University Press.

Palmer, P.J. (2000) *Let your Life Speak: Listening for the Voice of Vocation*. San Francisco: Jossey-Bass.

Pinsky, M.I. (2004) *The Gospel According To Disney: Faith, Trust, and Pixie Dust*. Westminster: John Knox Press.

Pizam, A. and Smith, G. (2000) 'Tourism and terrorism: a quantitative analysis of major terrorist acts and their impact on tourism destinations', *Tourism Economics*, 6 (2): 123–38.

Post, J. (1984) 'Notes on a psychodynamic theory of terrorist behavior', *Terrorism*, 7: 241–56.

Post, J. (1990) 'Terrorist psycho-logic: terrorist behavior as a product of psychological forces', in W. Reich (ed.), *Origins of Terrorism: Psychologies, Ideologies, Theologies, States of Mind*. Cambridge: Cambridge University Press.

Pratt, G. (2003) 'Terrorism and tourism: Bahamas and Jamaica fight back', *International Journal of Contemporary Hospitality Management*, 5 (3): 192–4.

Ritzer, G. and Lisker, A. (1997) 'McDisneyization and "Post-Tourism"', in C. Rojek and J. Urry, *Touring Cultures: Transformations of Travel and Teory*. New York: Routledge. pp. 129–33.

Rojek, C. (1993) 'Disney culture', *Leisure Studies*, 12: 121–35.

Rojek, C. (2005) 'An outline of the action approach to leisure studies', *Leisure Studies*, 24 (1): 13–25.

Ross, J.I. (1996) 'A model of the psychological causes of oppositional political terrorism', *Peace and Conflict: Journal of Peace Psychology*: 2–11.

Ross, J.I. (1999) 'Beyond the conceptualization of terrorism: a psychological–structural model', in C. Summers and E. Mardusen (eds), *Collective Violence*. New York: Rowman and Littlefield.

Schickel, R. (1968) *The Disney Version*. New York: Simon & Schuster.

Sloboda, B. (2003) 'Assessing the effects of terrorism on tourism by use of time series methods', *Tourism Economics*, 19 (2): 179–90.

Soekirno, S. (2006) Hati-hati minum di jalan, bisa ditangkap … Kompas, 2 March. Available at http://www.kompas.com/ kompas cetak/0603/02/utama/2478744.htm.

Sonmez, S.F., Apostolopoulos, Y. and Tarlow, P. (1999) 'Tourism in crisis: managing the effects of terrorism', *Journal of Travel Research,* 38: 13–18.

Stern, J. (1999) *The Ultimate Terrorists.* Cambridge: Harvard University Press.

Stitt, B.G. (2003) 'The understanding of evil: a joint quest for criminology and theology', in R. Chairs and B. Chilton (eds), *Star Trek Visions of Law and Justice.* Dallas: Adios Press.

Stott, B. (2004) 'Cinderella the strong and reader empowerment', *New Review of Children's Literature and Librarianship*, 10 (1): 15–26(12) April.

Tanner, L.R., Haddock, S.A., Zimmerman, T.S. and Lund, L.K. (2003) 'Images of couples and families in Disney feature-length animated films', *American Journal of Family Therapy,* 31: 355–74.

The Whitehouse (2005) 'National Strategy for Victory in Iraq'. Available at www.whitehouse. gov/infocus/iraq/iraq_strategy_nov2005.html

Tseelon, E. (1995) 'The Little Mermaid: an icon of woman's condition in patriarchy, and the human condition of castration', *International Journal of Psycho-Analysis*, 76: 1017–30.

Urry, J. (2002) *The Tourist Gaze.* London: Sage.

Wasko, J. (2001) *Understanding Disney: The Manufacture of Fantasy.* Cambridge: Polity Press.

Welch, M. (2003) 'Trampling human rights in the war on terror: implications to the sociology of denial', *Critical Criminology,* 12: 1–20.

Welch, M. (2006) *Scapegoats of September 11th: Hate Crimes and State Crimes in the War on Terror.* Piscataway, NJ: Rutgers University Press.

Wiersma, B.A. (2001) 'The gendered world of Disney: a content analysis of gender themes in full-length animated Disney feature films', *Dissertation Abstracts International, A: The Humanities and Social Sciences,* 61 (12): 4973-A.

CONCLUSION

In this book, we have traced the history of the institutional framework for leisure from the mid-nineteenth century to the present day. The leisure experience is a very pleasurable and desirable aspect of the human condition. However, as we have seen, the motivation behind the leisure experience can involve the individual wanting to engage in forms of edgework, abnormal leisure or deviance in an effort to seek out the optimum experience. Often, such motivations can cause harm to one's self or others. It is for this reason that the state has taken such a keen interest in our leisure experiences and, in the nineteenth century, the state encouraged forms of rational recreation which were morally uplifting for the participants. The state is still engaged in a moral regulation of the leisure sector.

The chapters have explored a range of social and political debates and I have attempted to show how these debates have relevance for the way we spend our leisure time.

In the nineteenth century, leisure was believed to have an essential quality, with restrictions on what was considered to be an appropriate leisure experience for working-class people, women, children, older people, people with disabilities and people with learning disabilities. Over time, such restrictions on leisure have been highly politicised or have largely disappeared for many people.

With the coming of the twentieth century, many of our leisure experiences became global in nature. Companies such as Disney and McDonald's were assumed to be involved in forms of global leisure and were believed to be engaged in a process of cultural globalisation in which American culture, habits and ideologies were spread across the world, making the world a single place. With the emergence of the information society, many leisure experiences are accessed via the internet, and again the processes of cultural homogenisation upon an American model are assumed to be dominant. With events post 9/11, many of the global trends have slowed down as terrorists often target leisure venues, transport links and retail spaces. Many of the cultural forms we enjoy, such as Chinese and Indian food, salsa, jazz and Bollywood have their origin outside of the dominant capitalist multinational corporation. Often, such cultural forms have their origins on the periphery of the global economy and are transferred to the centre by small family companies or even isolated individuals.

Future leisure trends might suggest that people will experience greater freedom, choice and opportunity in their leisure experiences. In addition, our leisure experiences might become more mediated by the more advanced forms of technology becoming applied to our leisure.

Government agencies across the world are expressing serious concerns about the environmental impact of leisure, particularly from tourism. Leisure in the future will have to come to terms with the 'limits to growth' thesis and become more sustainable. The air transport industry, in particular, has become a cause for concern as it continues to experience growth. The income inequality between tourists and people in many parts of the world who service their needs and the environmental damage that tourists cause through their demands for water, the provision of new golf courses, hotel accommodation and the enforced relocation of local populations have all been identified as possible causes of terrorism.

Finally, the state continues to take an active interest in the leisure of the population, and leisure continues to be associated with the dark side of human motivation.

INDEX

Research Methods Books from SAGE

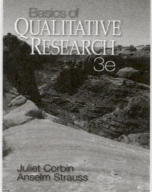